Warrior Nation

Warrior Nation

Images of War in British Popular Culture, 1850–2000

Michael Paris

REAKTION BOOKS

Published by Reaktion Books Ltd
79 Farringdon Road
London EC1M 3JU, UK

www.reaktionbooks.co.uk

First published 2000

Designed and typeset by Libanus Press
Printed and bound in Great Britain by Cromwell Press, Trowbridge, Wiltshire

British Library Cataloguing in Publication Data

Paris, Michael
    Warrior nation : images of war in British popular culture, 1850–2000
    1. War and society – Great Britain 2. Mass media and war
    3. War in literature 4. War – Public opinion – Great Britain
    5. Boys as soldiers – Social aspects – Great Britain
    I. Title
    303.6´ 6´ 0941

    ISBN 1 86189 065 6

Contents

Introduction

Give me a lad with pluck and spirit, and I don't care a snap of the
fingers whether he can construe Euripides or solve a problem in
higher mathematics. What we want for India are men who can ride
and shoot . . . who will scale a hill fort with a handful of men, or with
half a dozen sowars tackle a dacoit and his band. What do the natives
care for our learning? It is our pluck and fighting powers that have
made us their masters.   G. A. Henty, *Through the Sikh War* (1894)

Jaeger crumpled to the ground, blood pumping from his right
shoulder, his gun lying useless on the concrete three yards away where
it had spun as the shot hit him. Graham looked around wildly, then he
swung his gun to point at Henderson, just as the tall Texan kicked up,
knocking the gun out of Graham's hand. Graham turned to scramble
after it, but a punch from Henderson crunched into his face, smashing
the bones in his nose and sending him sprawling to the ground.

Lee James, *The Fantasy Soldiers: Killer in the City* (1995)

Britain's brave Harrier pilots blitzed the Serbs last night as Nato
launched a devastating air bombardment . . . RAF Top Guns joined
waves of awesome attackers after Tony Blair gave the go-ahead to
pound Serb leader Slobodan Milosevic into submission.

The *Sun*, 25 March 1999

War has always been a major factor in the history of Britain, but never more so
than in the 150 years beginning in the mid-nineteenth century. During this
period, an almost endless succession of 'little wars' of empire were succeeded by
the world wars, by the counter-insurgency operations of decolonization and
the peculiarities of the Cold War. As this book was being completed, units of the
British Royal Air Force, now part of a coalition force, were active over Serbia in
yet another 'police action' in the Balkans, as the jingoistic press urged Tony
Blair's government to 'CLOBBER SLOBBA' or jeeringly told Slobodan Milosevic

'SERBS YOU RIGHT'.[1] While the British have always been exceedingly vocal about their dislike of violence, there has always been a general acceptance, even in this enlightened age, that the use of force is sometimes necessary in a just cause. But what constitutes a 'just cause' for the British has invariably been defined while they basked in yet another victory over some technologically inferior foe. In popular culture, Britain's wars were always just and the men who fought them heroic agents of retribution who took up the sword of justice only when peaceful methods of resolution had failed. However, what is argued here is that war has always been an acceptable extension of national policy, and that acceptance of conflict was so commonplace that war and preparation for war became deeply embedded in popular culture, particularly in the cultural artefacts that are created for the youth of the nation – a culture that has transformed war into an entertaining spectacle, and reconstructs battle as an exciting adventure narrative.

By the 1850s many Britons had come to believe in the nation's imperial destiny. The acceptance of a divinely ordained mission, the pervasive influence of a crude Darwinian theory of the survival of the fittest and growing antagonism between the Great Powers which made war increasingly likely, permeated society inducing a mood dominated by what Anne Summers has called 'popular militarism' – the widespread acceptance that the practice of war was a natural and legitimate activity, a new respect for the army and military-style organization and admira-tion for the soldier as a masculine ideal.[2] This mood was reflected in the developing mass culture of the period, and the public's fascination with warriors and warfare was manifested in fiction, poetry and the visual arts: even the images used in advertising succumbed to the perceived excitement and glamour of war to sell their products. Such images reflected public interest in conflict and rein-forced ideas about the legitimacy of war and the romance of battle: there grew up, in fact, a 'pleasure culture of war', to adapt Graham Dawson's expressive phrase,[3] in which war and the heroic but violent deeds of the warrior became a widespread and popular theme in mass entertainment.

By the end of the nineteenth century, much of society had come to believe that as wars of imperial expansion or national defence were inevitable, the nation must be prepared for such conflicts – particularly the young, the impressionable twelve to twenty year olds, the imperial warriors of the future – and this became even more urgent in the 1890s, when many Britons had come to believe that they were facing the most serious threat of all: the challenge of ambitious and aggressive continental empires actively seeking to topple Britain from her premier position in the imperial hierarchy. Preparing the nation's youth to serve and defend the far-flung frontiers of empire or to stand ready to accept the challenge of European rivals was considered to be of paramount importance, for the fate of the empire would soon be in their hands. Preparing the nation's youth for war was achieved through education – the public school ethos was largely constructed around the chivalric ideal, the medieval code of the warrior with its emphasis on the qualities of duty, loyalty, sacrifice and honour[4] – and through the para-military youth organizations that flourished around the turn of the century. However, much more was achieved through the pleasure culture of war which permeated the cultural artefacts aimed at boys and young men – novels, story papers, toys, games and visual images – all teaching that war was moral, legitimate and, above all, exciting and romantic.

The popular novelist George Alfred Henty, perhaps more than any other individual, was instrumental in making war an acceptable literary subject. Henty adopted the warrior as the masculine ideal in his immensely successful and patri-otic boy's stories. He taught his young readers that war was inevitable if the empire, the greatest force for civilization in the world, was to be preserved and extended; but war was far more than just a necessity for imperial survival, it was also an exciting adventure, and through the experience of battle boys became men, made their mark in the world and gained honour and position. Almost single-handedly, Henty created a new sub-genre of juvenile adventure fiction, the war story. And where the master led, others followed, eager both to demon-strate their patriotism by inculcating the values they believed necessary to ensure the survival of the empire and to profit from a popular and expanding market for the war story, until, as Cecil Eby has pointed out, 'for an English youth growing up in the late Victorian period, infatuation with empire, with its inevitable corollaries – the vision and paraphernalia of war – was as natural as breathing.'[5] What is read in childhood can often be remarkably influential. As George Orwell pointed out:

> Most people are influenced far more than they would care to admit by novels [and] serial stories . . . from this point of view the worst books are often the most important because they are usually the ones that we read earliest in life. It is probable that many people who would consider themselves extremely sophisticated and 'advanced' are actually carrying through life an imaginative background which they acquired in childhood . . .[6]

What is true of literature is equally true of the visual images, and of games and toys, for all helped to form attitudes and beliefs that were carried forward into adulthood. The consequences of the pleasure culture of war can be clearly seen in 1914, when literally millions of young, and not so young, Britons flocked to join Kitchener's armies, their heads full of romantic and glamorous images of war that had been absorbed in childhood. Their only fear was that the war would end before they got to France! But even that brutal and bloody conflict failed to destroy the fascination and excitement of war, so deeply was it ingrained in popular culture. While much lip-service was paid to peaceful intent during the inter-war years, most images of past and future wars were still presented for the nation's youth as exciting adventures fought for noble purpose. Even a second great war, all the horrors of modern weaponry and the televised devastation wrought on civilian populations have had little impact on the positive way in which war is still portrayed for our children.

This book, then, explores the way in which war became an important theme in popular culture, and how it was adopted for the entertainment and instruction of British youth during the second half of the nineteenth century; it examines how the nation's later wars were reconstructed or imagined for later generations. The major focus here is popular literature, simply because, for much of the period, the printed word was the main agent for the transmission of such ideas. However, most books were illustrated with stirring and heroic images that visually reinforced the narrative. Story papers and comics provided not only heroic tales but were also a rich source for the visual excitement of war, as were posters, postcards and photographs. From around the time of the First World War, the cinema became a major source for the representation of war and carried such images to an even wider audience; subsequently, computer and interactive video games have offered the young new dimensions of experience for 'playing war'.

In this book I concentrate, firstly, on the work of the most popular and widely read authors such as G. A. Henty and W. E. Johns, in the mass-circulation story papers such as the *Boy's Own Paper* and those published by the Amalgamated Press and D. C. Thomson; secondly, on the posters, photographs, advertisements and toys that would have been commonly available to boys and young men, and, thirdly, on films that were widely seen by young audiences during the period. While I have attempted to show that the pleasure culture of war invaded virtually every area of childhood entertainment, I am keenly aware that, in order to keep this present work within reasonable length, some areas have been accorded less attention than they deserve. But wherever possible, I have attempted to consider the consequences of the pleasure culture of war by reference to the memories of those who grew to manhood under its spell.

Here, perhaps, I should make it clear that I take no moral position on the vexed question of images of violence and children's behaviour. Whether or not exposure to such imagery, on the printed page or the screen, creates a tendency to violent behaviour among the young is a much-debated issue, but one where there seems to be a singular lack of hard evidence. Here, and more appropriately for a historian, I wish simply to chart this neglected but powerful theme in popular culture and draw some general conclusions about the direct effects of the 'war story'. However, what does emerge here is that, far from being the peace-loving and commercially-minded people of liberal historiography, the British, like most of the nations they have decried, have themselves resorted to war on the slightest of pretexts when it was believed that conflict could secure their goals, and have deliberately immersed their children in a culture that promotes the martial spirit, elevates the warrior to heroic status and romanticizes war. In much of the popular entertainment created for the nation's youth, the overriding national image is of an aggressively militant warrior nation.

SOME THRILLING STORIES BY
PERCY F. WESTERMAN

Frontispiece from "The Keepers of the Narrow Seas"

PUBLISHED BY A. & C. BLACK LTD.
(Incorporating S. W. PARTRIDGE & CO.
4, 5 & 6 SOHO SQUARE, LONDON, W.1
AND OBTAINABLE AT ALL BOOKSELLERS

July 1934

1 Discovering the Pleasures of War

> Man has always been seeking after a Utopia where he will enjoy peace and plenty, ease, comfort and perfection in all things, but universal peace is an unattainable ideal which to practical men is a mere will-o-the-wisp . . . the means of improvement must be the same as in the past, namely war, relentless war of extermination of inferior individuals and nations. The process will be slower than in the past, because natural selection is hindered and thwarted by civilised man.
>
> Brigadier-General R. C. Hart, 'A Vindication of War' (1911)

Most historians have portrayed nineteenth-century Britons as an essentially peace-loving, commercially-minded people who shunned warlike activity and had little interest in or respect for their army. Only during the last decade of that century were they led astray by arch-patriots and bellicose imperial propaganda and infected with a malignant jingoism. This aggressive, warlike mentality of the 1890s, it has been argued, was not just a British sickness, but a supra-national disease which afflicted all Europe at that time, and led ultimately to the tragedy of 1914. For most of the period, we have been told, the British avoided war as far as possible, seeing it as a disastrous impediment to trade and human progress.

This idealized portrait reveals only one dimension of the nation's story – that which the British, and particularly the English, told themselves – for throughout the century, and particularly after the 1850s, Britain was also an aggressive warfare state committed to the use of violence to maintain commercial predominance and territorial expansion. Certainly it was during the 1890s that militarism became most evident, but throughout the century the essentially aggressive nature of the British was reflected as a powerful theme within popular culture, a culture which legitimized war, romanticized battle and portrayed the warrior as a masculine ideal. Britain's pacific self-image was possible because of the Victorians oft-repeated denunciation of aggression, and because they deluded themselves that their wars and punitive expeditions were fought only when absolutely necessary, and then for noble humanitarian reasons or to punish the wicked.

Such self-delusion was reinforced by the outwardly visible trappings of a society firmly dominated by 'civilianism':[1] the rejection of any form of military conscription, and denying the army any part in political decision-making.

Far from avoiding war, there was rarely a year when British soldiers were not in action somewhere in the world defending or extending their empire. It is certainly true that, despite the army's continual concern over recruitment, conscription was never introduced, but the voluntary system somehow always managed to produce just enough men for the nation's military requirements. So what need was there for an expensive compulsory system? Better by far to rely on a small but professional force of battle-hardened veterans. And while military leaders were indeed denied a voice in the councils of state, it might well be argued that, as the political and military elites shared the same background, assumptions, attitudes, interests and objectives, the aristo-military elite had little need for its own representatives. The Victorians oft-stated distaste for war and the soldier, and the exclusion of the military from politics, has disguised just how far war was generally accepted by much of society as central to the continued well-being of the nation.

War, as Linda Colley has pointed out, was the midwife of national unity. The hundred years of warfare which ended with Waterloo also witnessed the creation of the modern nation. 'Great Britain' was an invention forged above all by war. Time and time again, war with France brought Britons, whether they hailed from Wales or Scotland or England, into confrontation with an obviously hostile Other and encouraged them to define themselves collectively against it. They defined themselves as Protestants struggling for survival against the world's foremost Catholic power.[2]

Protestantism under threat, then, was the bedrock on which national identity was founded, breaking down sectarian and regional barriers and creating a powerful national unity. And because for over 200 years the 'Island Race' had successfully withstood the challenge of their powerful Catholic enemies, 'there developed a mystic belief among many Britons that in some way they had become the Chosen People; a shared understanding that they had inherited the special relationship with God first experienced by Old Testament Israel.'[3] These convictions were particularly strong within the Evangelical movement – the most active branch of Anglicanism and a major influence on intellectual development during the nineteenth century.

The foundations of the Evangelical movement lay in traditional Puritanism, but, as Harold Perkin has pointed out, the nineteenth-century version was mutated and often remarkably secular, the only form of Christianity compatible with the selfish economic doctrine of competition.[4] Evangelicals certainly wanted a 'moral' revolution at home, but their creed was inextricably linked with the expansion of the empire and intertwined with nationalism and military activity. As John Wolffe has shown, extreme nationalism was a recurring theme in evangelical thought – a belief that while Britons enjoyed a privileged position in the ordered universe, they also had responsibilities to the less fortunate, particularly those thus far denied the word of God.[5] Such ideas led to aggressive missionary activity and, of course, provided a divinely sanctioned underpinning for an imperialistic world view. These ideas were often expressed in popular hymns of the period:

> 'Tis to thy sovereign grace I owe
> That I was born on British ground,
> Where streams of heavenly mercy flow
> and words of sweet salvation sound.

or,

> And shall there not be Christians found
> Who will for Christ appear;
> To make a stand on heathen ground,
> And preach salvation there.[6]

Aggressive nationalism, combined with a powerful belief in a religious and moral duty to the unenlightened, helped to justify war as an essential element in God's plan. The armed forces were the means by which the nation's unique relationship with the Almighty would be protected from Popery and other evils, while also ensuring that missionary activity could safely take place in dangerous heathen lands. This developing relationship between missionary and military was manifested in a number of ways through the nineteenth century, and particularly in the Evangelicals' mission to the army itself; a conscious attempt to create a Christian army by the introduction of scripture reading groups and 'conversion' of the rank and file. Such activity was rewarded by an increasing number of soldiers, both officers and men, who publicly proclaimed themselves to be 'warriors of Christ': John Greene's 1827 memoir of his service in the 68th Regiment, or William Surtees's account of his experiences with the Rifle Brigade (published in 1833), were certainly not the only occasions when soldier-authors declared themselves to be 'true soldiers of Christ'.[7] They may well have been so; equally, they may simply have been expressing the sentiments they believed would please their readers. Either way, what they produced was powerful propaganda for the soldier as Christian warrior. The Church–military relationship can also be seen in the increasingly martial metaphors and imagery used by the religious and widely employed in sermons and popular hymns. It could be claimed that, in an age where church attendance was in decline, particularly among the urban population, little weight should be given to this. However, as John Wolffe has argued, through sermons but above all through the Sunday School movement and City Missions, these nationalist-religious ideas gained a wide currency:

> The real significance of evangelical views of the nation is to be found not in the relatively small number of people who would have espoused them in their entirety, but in the far larger numbers who imbibed portions of the evangelical creed and allowed its presuppositions to shape their subconscious.[8]

It seems likely that an unsophisticated, poorly educated audience missed the finer points of such teaching and its metaphorical meaning, and were left with only the obvious and the literal: that Britons were somehow a 'chosen' people destined to dominate the lesser races, that force was a legitimate activity in the cause of conversion, and the army an agent in the divine plan. These ideas may well have contributed to a somewhat idealized image of the soldier, but they undoubtedly had considerable influence on the country's political and commercial elites, and underpinned British expansion.

That Britain was able to establish a dynamic commercial economy in the late eighteenth century was in no small part due to the use of force, justified by a belief in the manifest destiny of the British race. The military maintained stability at home, which enabled industrial and commercial activity to take place while continually expanding the empire. Almost all of those engaged in trade benefited in some way from 'Britain's ruthless pursuit of colonial markets and from its intermittent struggle with the other main contender for imperial and commercial primacy, France'.[9] British victories in a succession of late eighteenth-century wars brought enormous territorial gains – including Canada, the West Indies, southern Africa and substantial parts of the Indian sub-continent – and unlimited opportunities for commercial exploitation. These 'opportunities', of course, had been gained at the point of a sword, and the future would increasingly dictate that they would have to be held by the sword as well. As Linda Colley has pointed out, before the Seven Years War the empire had 'been small enough and homogeneous enough to seem reasonably compatible with the values that the British . . . believed they uniquely epitomised'.[10] But the dramatic expansion in the period between 1763 and 1815 meant that the empire no longer comprised British emigrants, was no longer predominantly Protestant or even Christian, but now included diverse 'heathen' races most of whom had little liking for their new masters. If the commercial exploitation of this empire was the lifeblood of the British nation (and it was clearly so perceived by contemporaries), then it was essential to hold that empire together, and only military force could ensure its survival. The importance of the developing ideology of imperialism in the early decades of the nineteenth century has too often been ignored or dismissed by historians, but as Martin Green, Patrick Brantlinger and others have revealed, the imperial dynamic was a powerful influence throughout the period.[11]

While war was clearly necessary to maintain the empire and allow God's work to take place, it was also an obvious symbol of the power and prestige of the monarchy. British monarchs have historically been closely involved with their armies, but this was particularly true of the Hanoverians, who took great interest in military matters, redesigning military dress, ordering elaborate displays and appearing in uniform themselves – even Queen Victoria wore a military-style costume at army reviews.[12] Such a close relationship between monarch and military clearly helped to justify the activities of the army. But war also provided a means by which the patrician caste could ensure their survival in an age of revolution and social turmoil. As Linda Colley has noted:

> All aristocracies have a strong military tradition, and for many British patricians the protracted warfare of this period was a godsend. It gave them a job and, more more important, a purpose, an opportunity to carry out what they had been trained to do since childhood: ride horses, fire guns, exercise their undoubted physical courage and tell other people what to do.[13]

The British aristocracy were able to convince themselves and others that they were an elite dedicated to serving the nation and prepared to sacrifice life and limb to achieve national greatness. The wonderful description of the guests at a royal levee in 1818, by the American ambassador, quoted by Colley, captures the awesome quality of aristo-military sacrifice:

> 'That's General Walker', I was told, 'pierced with bayonets, leading on the assault at Badajos'. And he, close by, tall but limping? 'Colonel Ponsonby, he was left for dead at Waterloo . . .' Then came one of like port, but deprived of a leg . . . and the whisper went, 'That's Lord Anglesea'. A fourth had been wounded at Seringapatam; a fifth at Talavera; some had suffered in Egypt; some in America. There were those who had received scars on the deck with Nelson; others who carried them from the days of Howe.[14]

Patrician military function was underlined by the wearing of uniform for both private and public occasions, and even extended into the realm of civil dress, where foppish silks gave way to less flamboyant clothes of quasi-military cut,[15]

1 Nineteenth-century uniforms emphasized the male physique. From a print of *c.* 1839.

while their heroism became the subject of battle paintings, prints, ballads and epic poetry. The sons of the aristocracy, and even the sons of the aspiring rich who could afford to buy a 'gentleman's' education for their offspring, went to public schools and universities where the curriculum was built around the classics – a 'constant diet of stories of war, empire, bravery and sacrifice . . . and exuding a lush appreciation of masculine heroism'.[16] Even uniforms were designed to draw attention to the wearer's masculinity: headgear to exaggerate height, short tight jackets with epaulettes to emphasize the width of the shoulders and tight-fitting trousers to demonstrate slim hips and strong legs (illus. 1). Thus the heroic virtues of war and the soldier were continually reinforced and even more widely disseminated with the rapid growth of the public school system later in the century. War, then, was central to the continued existence of the nation and of the patrician elite, but it was also a subject of considerable interest for the common people.

It has often been suggested that the British public had little interest in war and the soldier until late in the nineteenth century, and that most of the population was indifferent to such activities. However, as Colley and others have shown, even eighteenth-century conflicts were a focus of public interest.[17] The long-drawn-out wars against Revolutionary and Napoleonic France were even more a source of national pride, and victories were celebrated in songs, paintings, prints, poetry, statues and spectacle. This recurring imagery helped to create a more positive view of the army, as Geoffrey Best has noted: 'the common soldier and his trade were a bit better respected, not to mention better publicised, after the war than before it'.[18] Despite isolated incidents (Edward Spiers, for example, cites the cavalier treatment of the 30th Regiment by the citizens of Ramsgate on its return from Waterloo), most soldier memoirs record an enthusiastic welcome on their return from the wars. Sir George Bell was 'feted, feasted, and flattered' in Dublin and many of the rank and file testify to the same treatment.[19]

While most praise was lavished on naval heroes, especially Nelson, attention was also paid to the exploits of the soldier, particularly in the Peninsula campaign and at Waterloo. Waterloo Day was an annual celebration until mid-century, and the Duke of Wellington, Sir John Moore and others were acclaimed as national heroes, joining a succession of popular military icons that reached back to the Duke of Marlborough, Clive of India and Wolfe of Quebec. Memories of the war and of the soldier's role were maintained through a steady stream of veterans' diaries, memoirs and autobiographies, many written by the rank and file, which found a ready market and testify to public interest in the wars. Paintings commemorating the war and the military were, as Joan Hichberger has shown, never as popular in Britain as in France.[20] Nevertheless, there were numerous battle sketches, costume studies and cheap woodblock prints available from printsellers at the lower end of the art market, which indicate the popularity of heroic images glorifying the battle experience. Plays, pageants and spectacles also reflected the public interest. Until about 1812, naval dramas dominated; the Sadlers Wells spectaculars, for example, culminated with huge battles between model ships and played to substantial audiences.[21] However, from that time onwards military themes became extremely popular, clearly demonstrating pride in the exploits of Wellington's army. Even as late as 1824, Astley's Amphitheatre in Birmingham played J. H. Amherst's spectacular production, *The Battle of Waterloo*, boasting a cast of more than 200 and elaborate and 'novel' effects. The century of warfare that ended with Waterloo thus created great interest in war and the exploits of military heroes, and this was encouraged during the post-war period by an increasing use of the theme of war in popular culture.

The twenty years or so after 1815 saw Britain at its most pacific. This was partly due to war weariness after the prolonged struggle with France,[22] and partly, as Cain and Hopkins have argued, because the 'costs of war had escalated the national debt to a point where it was threatening to topple the structure it was

supposed to support'. This led to a move to bring public expenditure under
control and generate extra revenue. Governments became committed to a new
overseas development that mobilized the empire while also moving towards free
trade.[23] Cutting defence costs was one means of saving money, and the military
budget was reduced from £43 million in 1815 to less than £8 million by 1836,
which further enhanced the self-image of a peace-loving nation. Such savings
were possible because Europe was settled, and foreign policy depended upon
the idea of a balance of power developed by Castlereagh and Canning. While the
Royal Navy guarded trade routes, only a small army was necessary to maintain
order at home and deal with rebellion abroad. However, the army was also
engaged in several wars of expansion, for example in Nepal (1814–16), the
Second Maratha War (1817–18) and the Second Burmese War (1824–26), which
added considerable territory to the empire. Even in a period of 'peace', the nation
still engaged in considerable military activity. But from the 1830s, increasing
trade competition from America and Europe made the search for new markets
an urgent priority, and this, combined with depression and discontent at home,
forced governments to develop a more aggressive imperial policy. Palmerston,
like many others, was concerned to find overseas solutions to domestic
problems.[24] In 1860, he reflected that 'trade ought not to be enforced by cannon
balls, but on the other hand trade cannot flourish without security, and that
security may often be unobtainable without the exhibition of physical force'.[25]
During the first half of the century it was not just a question of a 'show of force',
but of using aggression to create trade 'opportunities'. This was clearly shown
by events in the late 1830s and early '40s.

In India in 1838, for example, the Viceroy, Lord Auckland, fearful that upheavals
in Afghanistan would unsettle the frontier regions, attempted to depose the Amir
and install a puppet regime in Kabul backed by British troops. That the attempt
misfired and resulted in the loss of a British army of 4,500 (including 700 Britons)
during the retreat from Kabul in 1842, does not detract from an inherently
aggressive policy designed to secure northern India. Around the same time,
British policy towards China demonstrates even more clearly a willingness to
resort to war to secure national advantage. China offered enormous potential for
trade, but the Chinese had little interest in what the British had to offer – except
opium. Despite edicts from the Chinese government forbidding the trade
in opium, the East India Company persisted. In 1839, relations with China became
so strained that Palmerston ordered a blockade of the Chinese coast and the
seizure of Hong Kong as a base for operations. When even this failed to achieve
the desired result, the British resorted to war, eventually forcing the Chinese
to negotiate.[26] Under the Treaty of Nanking (1842), the Chinese were forced to

open their ports to British trade. While some Victorians expressed moral doubts about British policy in China, majority opinion, with some hypocrisy, saw the war as morally justified, fought not for sordid commercial gain, but to bring enlightenment to the heathen. A report in the *Illustrated London News* clearly expressed this view:

> The Chinese war was not a war of mighty prowess, it was not a war of trophy, vanity, and pride, but it was a great war for mankind. It opened the eyes of millions of human beings who were buried in the dark recesses of idolatry and unfurled the wings of commerce . . . It shed the glorious gleam of Christianity upon an almost pagan world.[27]

While civilians might need to salve a tender conscience with religious cant, soldiers were often less circumspect. In 1843, for example, just before Sind was conquered and added to British India on the pretext of pacifying the region, the commander of the British forces, Sir Charles Napier, said 'we have no right to seize Sind, yet we shall do so, and a very advantageous, humane, and useful piece of rascality it will be'. Napier believed, as did many others of his generation, that the 'great recipe for quieting a country is a good thrashing first and great kindness afterwards: the wildest chaps are thus tamed'.[28] Thrashing the Baluchis was ultimately for their own good, putting them under British rule and exposing them to the civilizing influence of Christian Britons! The Baluchis, incidentally, were very soundly thrashed, since Napier and his troops, in the general's own words, 'butchered' over 6,000 of them. Yet even Napier was unable to rid himself completely of contemporary hypocrisy and was still able to consider his actions 'humane'. Popular illustrations of these wars constantly emphasized the ferocious and 'outlandish' appearance of the enemy, and reinforced ideas of their racial inferiority when compared with their 'civilized' conquerors (illus. 2). This acceptance of aggression and brutality was continually demonstrated by politicians like Palmerston, who could suggest that, 'half-civilized governments [needed] . . . a dressing [down] every eight or ten years to keep them in order', and even with the major powers a show of force was a necessary thing: 'Diplomats and protocols', he once remarked, 'are very good things, but there are no better peace-keepers than well-appointed three-deckers' [ships].[29]

Clearly Victorian governments never really subscribed to their oft-repeated peaceful policies. To believe that they did, as David French has pointed out, is to mistake the rhetoric of a handful of politicans like Richard Cobden and the Manchester School for the reality of government, as most politicians 'were quite capable of pursuing simultaneously both what they conceived to be Britain's national interests and high moral principles'.[30] Thus, for all their much-vaunted

2 'The Other': Afghan warriors, 1880.

humanitarian aims and peaceful commercial objectives, the Victorians inherited, accepted and considerably extended an empire held together by force of arms, and, as we shall see, were prepared to unleash terrifying retribution upon those foolish enough to resist. War, the controlled use of violence, was simply one means by which the British maintained their position in the world.[31]

This tendency to resort so easily to war, to employ organized violence for commercial gain, inevitably created a crisis of conscience for some. How could these self-proclaimed champions of freedom equate their role as imperial warlords with their professed claims of being peaceful traders? This moral dilemma was never wholly resolved, and was reflected in the pacifist movement – a diverse collection of individuals and associations who could unashamedly renounce war and aggression.[32] But these dissenters were always a minority, and subtle propaganda and appeals to patriotism could usually isolate them even further from the mainstream of political life. Most nineteenth-century men and women could quote the Evangelical creed and justify the increasing use of military force as 'necessary for the greater good', and 'Heaven's Command' to spread Christianity and civilization. Bolstered during the later nineteenth century by a developing racist ideology and appeals to the biological necessity of war (see below), it became increasingly easy to morally justify virtually any act of aggression. And the acceptance of war was undoubtedly made easier by the rediscovery of chivalry early in the century.

As Mark Girouard has explained, chivalry, the code of behaviour evolved for medieval warriors, softened the potential barbarity of war by 'putting it into the hands of men committed to high standards of behaviour' and noble ideals: 'The ideal knight was brave, loyal, true to his word, courteous, generous and merciful. He defended the Church and wrongfully oppressed but respected and honoured his enemies in war, as long as they obeyed the same code he did'.[33]

Chivalry, then, removed the most brutal elements of war by creating a strict moral code for the warrior – the generally accepted 'rules of war'. The nineteenth-century interest in chivalry was, in large measure, due to the popular historical novels of Sir Walter Scott, particularly *Ivanhoe* (1820) and *Quentin Durward* (1823), which helped shape the heroic chivalric stereotype. Scott himself was not blind to the less noble aspects of the Middle Ages, for example, the fanaticism and superstition, but while he saw chivalry as something of the past, other writers, in their tales of the Crusades, translations of medieval romances and histories of chivalry saw it as something vital and relevant for contemporary society. Chivalry gave women an honourable place in society (while of course defining them as weak and in need of protection), provided an education for young men calculated to imbue them with physical strength, bravery, grace, courtesy and respect for women, but, above all, it dignified the conduct of war, essential for a 'civilized' society in an 'enlightened' age.[34] The most important of the didactic works on chivalry was Kenholm Digby's *The Broad Stone of Honour*, published in 1823. Digby's book, subtitled 'Rules for the Gentlemen of England', provided guidance, through historical example, for the conduct of gentlemen. As the author states, to be born a gentleman is a 'high privilege', but implicit in such privilege are obligations both to self and society.[35] Here

Digby clearly echoes contemporary ideas about national identity, allegiance to
the state and the teaching of nationalistic evangelicalism.

In the 1820s, interest in chivalry was limited to social elites, but it was soon taken
up by middle-class journalists and novelists and its values were disseminated
throughout society. Indeed, at a time of rapid change and social instability it is
not difficult to see the nostalgic appeal of a more ordered period, when kingship
and the church were unquestioned and when all knew and accepted their place
in the scheme of things. The chivalric code was later adopted by Charles Kingsley
(a self-proclaimed 'joyous Knight-errant of God') and Thomas Hughes and would
provide the underpinning for the cult of 'Muscular Christianity' – the cornerstone
of reformed public school education. Chivalry appealed to a diverse audience,
from Prince Albert to the radical William Morris and the pre-Raphaelite
Brotherhood (whose paintings would disseminate an idealized and romantic
reconstruction of the medieval world); and to churchmen, teachers and the
aspiring middle classes. It was interpreted as the guide for behaviour of a 'true
gentlemen' and appropriate for civilian life. Scott and the other exponents of
chivalry created, as Martin Green has perceptively argued, romantic daydreams
and illusions, an alternative to the 'banks, counting houses and trading companies
most readers saw as contemporary reality'.[36] What is relevant here is that, above
all, chivalry was the way of the warrior – a para-military code of conquest and
inherently aggressive.[37] As the knights of the Middle Ages were idealized as
Christian warriors doing battle for a noble cause, so logic dictated that the
chivalric warrior of the nineteenth century would likewise only take up arms in
a righteous cause. And what could be more just and righteous than the defence
of the realm – God's chosen people – or to defend Protestantism and assist
missionary activity in heathen lands?[38] Digby clearly stresses the connection. In
the section of his book exploring honourable professions for those who wish
to conduct themselves according to the chivalric code, the army, a 'noble calling',
features strongly:

> The great advantage of the profession of arms, is its practical influence,
> the effect which it produces upon the character; and this, you will
> remember, is the criterion by which we should judge of all professions
> and modes of employment. The soldier is religious and brave, humane
> and merciful, open-hearted and just, frank, sincere, faithful and firm . . .
> The lamb and flag were borne by the knight templers, to signify the union
> of these qualities, of gentleness with the martial spirit.[39]

While some soldiers appear to contradict this opinion – Frederick the Great
and Napoleon Bonaparte, for example – these are exceptions to the general rule:

The soldier is often deficient in learning, but is frequently more religious without hypocrisy, and most sound in his judgement . . . his piety will be sincere. Like the centurion of the Acts, like the grand master of the order of St John, the saviour of Rhodes . . . like a Bayard, a Hopton, or a Falkland, he will be devout towards God, and benevolent to man.

Digby ends the section on the profession of arms by reminding his readers that, 'Still there is a holy war, still it is our duty to engage in it . . .'[40] The author thus merges the concept of the chivalric warrior and the evangelical zealot into a new, and ideal image – the new crusader for empire. As Jeffrey Richards has explained, the 'Chivalric ideal was deliberately promoted by key figures of the age in order to produce a ruling elite for the nation and for the expanding empire who would be inspired by noble and selfless values,'[41] including, we might add, the martial spirit. Most Victorian gentlemen, of course, saw little attraction in a military career, but heroic images of chivalric warriors offered a pleasing and exciting fantasy, an antidote to the tedium of everyday life.

This public interest in war was, in large part, made possible because after 1745 the nation's battles were fought on foreign fields; even the upheavals of the Revolutionary and Napoleonic wars were played out on a stage far removed from native shores. The civilian population of Britain was thus spared the horrors visited upon the inhabitants of France, Spain and other warring states and could distance itself from the reality of battle and enjoy the vicarious excitements of war. Real but distant wars were thus little different from the exciting stories reconstructed for the theatre or in the words of storytellers and balladmongers. Thus was born what Graham Dawson has called 'the pleasure culture of war' – the reconstruction of war for entertainment.[42] And, as Myerly notes, the army itself was very much a 'theatrical' institution: uniforms, manoeuvres, flags and stirring music were all part of a spectacle designed to arouse the soldier to courageous acts and intimidate the enemy.[43] At home, reviews and parades enhanced the prestige of the state but were regarded by the people as entertainment and were enormously popular. In 1830, for example, to celebrate the accession of William IV, three grand reviews were held in London. All drew huge crowds, as did military entertainments later in the century (illus. 3). It was a short step from public enjoyment of this kind of military entertainment to enjoying the entertainment provided by war – it was after all, just another military spectacle! The radical Douglas Jerrold was well aware of the dangers of portraying the essential brutality of war as theatre:

When nations . . . cut each others throats . . . we must have red coats and muskets and sabres; but seeing how that the duty of their bearers squares

3 Military occasions provided entertainment for the public: a print of the funeral of the
Duke of Wellington, 1852.

neither with our innate good sense, nor our notions of what ought to
be – we are fain to gild the matter over – to try to conceal, from ourselves,
the butchering nature of the business we are sometimes forced to
undertake, and so spring up military spectacle – military finery – military
music . . . Clothe war therefore in gayer colours than peace . . . let the
steel which cuts glitter like valued gems; the evolutions which destroy,
be graceful as the motions of dancing girls.[44]

The pleasure culture of war reflected national interest in war, but recreating it
as exciting and romantic spectacle distanced the public from the brutality and
provided a forum through which moral uncertainties over the use of violence
could be partially resolved. In the pleasure culture of war, battles were fought far
away; they were never unjust, but fought for high moral purpose by chivalrous
volunteers who performed their killing function according to the well-defined
rules of war, and, of course, the majority of casualties were to be found among
the Other – the uncivilized and outlandish foreigner. The notion of war as entertaining spectacle made conflict even more acceptable and attractive, and from
the 1830s, as a genuinely mass popular culture began to develop, war became
an increasingly popular theme.

In 1838 the *New Monthly* magazine serialized an account of the military exploits of Major Goliah O'Grady Gahagan during the Second Maratha War of 1803. Gahagan, who by his own estimate was 'worth at least a thousand Indian combatants', is the ultimate martial hero: 'I sheared off three hundred and nine heads in the course of a single campaign', he boasts.[45] *The Tremendous Adventures of Major Gahagan*, by William Makepeace Thackeray, is of course, a mock-epic, a satire on the very popular martial adventures written by novelists such as Frederick Chamier, Edward Howard and others; the type of heroic fiction that through the 1830s provided the staple fare for *Metropolitan* magazine and populist publishing houses. The very fact that Thackeray could create a successful satire on the martial story testifies to the widespread popularity of the sub-genre. Thackeray was by no means a pacifist, but realized, as Brantlinger has noted, that the 'theme of "the indomitable majesty of BRITISH VALOUR" could be taken to ridiculous extremes'.[46] Even Charles Dickens commented cynically on this belief in national achievement through martial valour. In *Nicholas Nickleby*, for example, the politician Mr Gregsbury exclaims at one point:

> ... Whether I look merely at home, or, stretching my eye farther, contemplate the boundless prospect of conquest and possession – achieved by British perseverance and British valour – I clasp my hands, and turning my eyes to the broad expanse above my head, exclaim, 'thank Heaven, I am a Briton'.[47]

The vast majority of martial novels of the period never made it into the canon of Victorian literature and have been virtually lost. Like other cultural artefacts, however, they not only reflected public interest in war, but helped to establish positive notions of violence by turning combat into an entertaining moral crusade and creating heroic images of the warrior.

The tone of these military adventures was largely influenced by the very successful novels of Captain Frederick Marryatt, the leading exponent of the naval romance – exciting stories of daring young Britons set during the French wars. What is important in his fiction is the deeply ingrained themes of 'patriotism and martial valour', which provide a 'nostalgic, swashbuckling, but also conservative contrast to the literature of social reform . . .'[48] Marryatt's heroes are full-blooded warriors, fighting the just war. While his early novels dealt with naval themes, he later moved into other territory: his best-remembered novel is probably *Children of the New Forest* (1847), a romance of the Civil War and of heroic and chivalric cavaliers. However, his other novels have relevance here. The 1844 tale of the adventures of an immigrant family, *The Settlers in Canada*, makes clear his admiration for aggressive masculinity. The Sioux Indians, who make life difficult for the settlers, rank highly in the author's hierarchy of race because they are 'savage and warlike' and therefore admirable (they are defeated only by the superior fighting skills of the British!). And Patrick Brantlinger has pointed to other races which received the Marryatt stamp of racial approval precisely because they have outstanding martial characteristics: the Ashanti, the Zulu and the Burman. In his tale of South Africa, *The Mission* (1846), he discusses the 'Caffres' – a fine, warlike race with Hottentot blood in their veins.[49] Clearly, then, for Marryatt and other contemporary writers, real masculinity depended upon the qualities of the warrior. What is interesting here, of course, is that later in the century the acceptance of Social Darwinist thought would legitimize this racial hierarchy as scientific fact.

By the 1840s, then, this idealized masculine image began to influence the popular representation of the soldier, which was disseminated through novels, poems and reports by now forgotten authors. Sir Francis Doyle, for instance, a popular and successful poet and eventually professor of poetry at Oxford, was frequently inspired by war and the nobility of the soldier-hero. In the aftermath of the Sind campaign he published several works based on stories related to him by General Charles Napier. Here heroic deeds are not exclusive to the officer class, and in 'The Red Thread of Honour', for example, he praises the rankers:

> Eleven men of England
> A breastwork charged in vain;
> Eleven men of England
> Lie stripped, and gashed, and slain.
> Slain; but of their foes that guarded
> Their rock-built fortress well,
> Some twenty had been mastered,
> When the last soldier fell.[50]

The poem goes on to explain that it was the custom of the heathens to bind the wrist of a dead hero with red thread, but for these brave men of England, both wrists were bound – a double honour for the valiant, fearless Britons. Doyle's later works are rich in references to the Christian soldier – the private, captured by the foe but who refuses to bow before them in order to save his life, declaring he would only honour God and the Queen in such a fashion:

> . . . So let his name through Europe ring –
> A man of mean estate,
> Who died, as firm as Sparta's king,
> Because his soul was great . . .[51]

The sinking of the troopship *Birkenhead* off the African coast in February 1852 became a frequently cited example in the cult of the soldier-hero. Having put the women and children into the available lifeboats, the soldiers formed up on deck and heroically went down with the ship singing hymns. Their courage was celebrated in a variety of epic poems, and was used as an example of 'Muscular Christianity' in Thomas Hughes's later didactic text, *The Manliness of Christ*. But one of the first poems based on the incident appeared within weeks of the disaster. 'The Birkenhead', by Sir Henry Yule, set the tone for many later accounts. The poet rhetorically asks his audience, 'who were these heroes'? 'Ordinary men', he answers:

> . . . Weavers from the stocking-frame;
> Boys from the plough; cornets with beadless chin
> But steeped in honour and in discipline . . .

So give thanks, the poet tells us for:

> These undegenerate sons who sank
> Aboard the Birkenhead . . .[52]

Clearly, these 'ordinary' men had been reared in the chivalric warrior tradition and knew the sacrifice expected of them. Nor were such noble images exclusive to poets and storytellers, for soldiers themselves played a part in the creation of their heroic image. In late 1842, troops under the command of General Sir William Nott were accused of 'excesses and outrages and looting' during the withdrawal from Afghanistan. The good general mounted a vigorous defence of his men which was published in the British press and, for good measure, he accompanied his correspondence with an epic poem extolling the virtues of his 'Christian' soldiers:

> When the savage came with his traitor's eyes –
> Wild – furious – mad for gore,
> They looked – fought – smiled – and all was done,
> They conquered and forebore.
> No blood of triumph stained the soil
> Where'er my soldiers trod,
> For 'mid the madness of turmoil
> They kept a thought of God . . .
> Yet discipline and mercy joined
> To keep the Christians back;
> They did not let the bloodhound slip,
> They would not swarm his track.

They bade fierce, fiery passion yield
To mercy's gentle rein,
And so our British soldiers raised
Their glory above gain . . .[53]

Such ideas were not only found in literature but were common in other cultural forms. The theatre is a good example. During the Sind campaign, Astley's Amphitheatre was playing 'Crusaders of Jerusalem', an epic production noted for the finale where the Christian warrior Richard the Lion Heart fights a single combat with the Prince of Darkness, Saladin. Even more popular with the middle and respectable working classes from the late 1830s were the elaborate pyrodramas staged at Manchester's Belle Vue or the Surrey Pleasure Gardens. Pyrodramas were open-air evening entertainments, dramatic reconstructions of famous battles, sieges or heroic episodes from British history, which climaxed with bonfires and spectacular firework displays.[54] If we add to these entertainments the reviews, parades, ceremonies and royal occasions in which the army performed, it is clear just how far war had become a powerful theme in popular culture.[55]

Thus in 1848, when Thackeray published *Vanity Fair*, the author made it explicit that it was the qualities of the soldier which earn a man the admiration of society:

What qualities are there for which a man gets so speedy a return for applause, as those of bodily superiority, activity and valour? Time out of mind strength and courage have been the theme of bards and romances; and from the story of Troy down to today, poetry has always chosen a soldier for a hero. I wonder is it because men are cowards in heart that they admire bravery so much, and place military valour so far beyond every other quality for reward and worship?[56]

Much has been written about society's negative attitude towards the army,[57] but, like much of the Victorians' mindset, their attitude to the soldier is paradoxical and ambiguous. Here we must be careful to draw a distinction between officers and the rank and file, because officers were respected, admired and had considerable social status. The army's role as the main agent of social control at home during the early part of the century certainly led to radicals criticizing the ordinary soldier as a brutal agent of repression. Among the rest of the population, we have been told, the reputation of the rank and file was little better; soldiers were often regarded as bullying rascals who terrified honest citizens, and respectable families were shamed when a son 'went for a soldier'.[58] Few working men would willingly enlist, and the army was under strength for much of the century. Even among the well-to-do, the potential officer class, the crudities and dangers of military life and the purchase system, which ensured that only the wealthy or influential gained promotion, meant that most middle-class men had little interest in a military career. This reluctance to serve has often been cited as evidence of society's anti-militarism, yet the reality is more prosaic. While there may well have been a certain political incorrectness about enlisting among the more politicized working classes, the simple truth was that going for a soldier had little to offer; conditions of service were so unattractive and the dangers so great that the army simply had little appeal as a trade. Even as late as the beginning of the twentieth century, the Secretary of State for War, H. O. Arnold-Foster, writing of the continual problem of recruitment, pointed out that '. . . if there be too great a contrast between the amenities and decencies of life which he is compelled to live as a soldier and those of the life to which he is accustomed as a civilian, he will not become a soldier.'[59] And, during the first half of the nineteenth century, the ferocious discipline and appalling conditions inflicted on the rank and file made those contrasts even more dramatic.

However, this reluctance to enlist should not be taken as evidence of the peace-loving nature of the British people, nor of their abhorrence of war and soldiering. It may well be that much of this negative view of the soldier resulted from radical-pacifist propaganda. We need to remember that during the early decades of the century less than one per cent of the male population had direct experience of military life; the army was small and usually far away. Soldiers were used to maintain order during times of civil unrest, but these were usually local affairs. Most people, it would seem, had little real contact with the military, and this distance between soldier and civilian may well have given the soldier an exotic and romantic appeal. There is certainly evidence to suggest considerable public interest in the veterans' tales of military adventure.[60] And as one officer noted in the early 1830s:

> The radical and leveling press . . . has for years directed [its] fiercest attacks against the British army, but has not yet been able to destroy, or even weaken its popularity: the failure may seem strange to some but . . . there is an honest manliness of feeling about the people of Britain that makes them delight in even the contemplation of deeds of hardihood and danger; and makes them proud of the unrivaled achievements of their sons, brothers and countrymen, as well as of the country that produced, and of the institutions that fostered such men . . .'[61]

The soldier, then, may perhaps have been a less reviled figure than we have been led to believe. Nevertheless, while much of society subscribed to an idealized

notion of the 'Christian' warrior and while some soldiers might proclaim
themselves as such, the reality was that the army was still an imperfect tool for
a nation that believed itself motivated by divine inspiration and high moral
purpose. However, the importance of the events of the 1850s, the Crimean War
and the Indian Mutiny was that they provided dynamic examples of the Christian
warrior in action – the idealized image given flesh and blood and fighting the
just war.

Initiatives to turn rank and file into a Christian brotherhood had begun as
early as the 1820s, when the Naval and Military Bible Society forced the authorities
to provide £800 a year for prayer books, Bibles and religious tracts for troops
in an attempt to improve their spiritual life. Missionary activity was undertaken in
garrison towns such as Woolwich and Chatham,[62] and recreation rooms and
libraries for enlisted men were created as an alternative to the doxy and the grog
shop. But it was the war in the Crimea that created enormous public sympathy
for the army, as Olive Anderson has explained:

> It was undoubtedly the Crimean War which began a dramatic change
> in the attitude towards the army of British society in general, and of
> the religious public in particular. For the first time troops were hailed
> as 'the people's army', and idealized notions of what they were fight-
> ing for, together with unparalleled public identification with their
> hardships before Sebastopol, combined to give them an immense
> emotional appeal.[63]

More important than engendering mere sympathy for the suffering of the
rank and file, was the manner in which the war impacted upon the mind of the
nation and created the idea of the army as the instrument of the nation's will.

Throughout the 1840s, Britain's relations with Russia had been marked by
mutual suspicion, and most Britons viewed the Tsar as a tyrannical and despotic
ruler. Thus, in October 1853, when the Turkish government declared war on
Russia in order to preserve its geographical integrity, British public opinion
was firmly on the side of the Turks. The Anglo–French declaration of war in
March 1854 was greeted with enthusiasm in Britain, and even radicals and liberals
could lend their support to what was generally perceived as a moral crusade to
defend a weak, oppressed nation against tyranny. 'The War is popular beyond
belief', noted the Queen, and effigies of Bright, Cobden and other critics were
burnt in the streets of Manchester, as workers who professed to despise Russian
absolutism took to the streets 'shouting slogans and singing patriotic songs'.[64]
But the expeditionary force sent to the Crimean peninsula soon became bogged
down, and more troops began to die from disease than from Russian bullets.

At this point the British public began to identify with its 'suffering heroes' to an unprecedented degree, largely because of the manner in which the popular press reported the war.

After the removal of stamp duty on newspapers in 1836, the press in Britain developed rapidly. Technical improvements meant that by 1851 there were no fewer than 563 newspapers in circulation.[65] The calotype printing process of the 1840s enabled illustrations to be used, and by 1842 the first fully illustrated weekly was on the market (the *Illustrated London News*). So too, the growth of railways and the electric telegraph meant that news could be transmitted more rapidly than ever before. War, of course, had always been a major ingredient for newspapers, but war news had been gathered in a fairly haphazard manner. Traditionally, the British press borrowed from Continental papers or employed junior officers as correspondents to send dispatches from the front. These were neither exciting nor enlightening, and invariably arrived long after the events described. However, in February 1854 *The Times* took the dramatic step of employing William Russell, a freelance correspondent, to accompany the British forces to the Crimea. As Philip Knightley has pointed out, Russell's reports, written as 'letters to the Editor', marked the beginning of an organized method of reporting wars for the civilian population at home,[66] and in the process ended the remoteness of war by giving events an immediacy that made civilians feel a part of the experience.

Russell was soon joined by other correspondents, and their reports, sent home by fast steamship, brought the war news rapidly to the public, excited interest in the doings of the military and created demand for more news. Although Russell and the others were not slow to reveal the appalling suffering of the ill-equipped British soldiers and the inadequacy of medical facilities provided for the sick and wounded, they were equally determined to reveal the soldier's nobility and heroism. 'A thin red streak topped with steel', wrote Russell of the 93rd Highlanders facing the Russian onslaught at Balaclava; and the 'sheer steel and sheer courage' of the Heavy Brigade, 'in all the pride and splendour of war'. His literary image of the heroes in action combined to fire the imagination of the reading public and glorify the experience of war. The suffering of the army drew a sympathetic humanitarian response from the public, while the guts-and-glory reports had an immediacy and excitement which powerfully reinforced ideas about the heroic nature of the rank and file. The reputation of the soldier, a Christian warrior in a righteous war, was further enhanced by an item of hagiographical literature which had 'exceptional impact' on the public imagination.[67]

Catherine Marsh's account of the life and heroic death of a young Christian soldier. *The Memorials of Captain Hedley Vicars* (1856), was clearly intended to inspire other young men to emulate the hero, for, as the author noted in the preface, 'Most grateful to God will the writer be, if the courage of any such be exalted and confirmed, and their manly hearts inspired to emulate the noble example of a CHRISTIAN SOLDIER'.[68] Marsh told the story of a young officer who, after enjoying the gaiety and idleness of garrison life in the West Indies, was converted to true Christianity in 1851. Vicars, however, despite his new role as a Christian zealot, found little to conflict with his duties as a soldier and, indeed, spent much time in spreading the Gospel among his men. In November 1854 his regiment was sent to the Crimea. The following March, Vicars was commanding an outpost in the lines before Sebastopol when his position was attacked by a large Russian force. Bravely, he ordered his men to counter-attack:

> With his first war shout, 'Now 97th. on your pins, and charge!' Himself foremost in the conflict, he led on his gallant men to victory, charging two thousand with a force of barely two hundred. A bayonet wound in the breast only fired his courage the more; and again his voice rose high, 'Men of the 97th, Follow me!' as he leaped the parapet he had so well defended, and charged the enemy down the ravine.[69]

Vicars died from his wounds soon after the engagement, but Lord Raglan's dispatch, published on 6 April, noted the part played by Vicars in the defence of the position, 'I am assured that nothing could be more distinguished than the gallantry and good example which he set to the detachment under his command'.[70] Vicars's story had, as Anderson has pointed out, an enormous contemporary appeal: 70,000 copies were sold in the first year of publication and the volume remained in print until the 1914–18 war.[71] *The Memorials* created an exciting but sympathetic portrait of the Christian soldier and offered documentary proof that a real soldier could live and die as nobly as the chivalric ideal.

The Crimean War was featured widely in stage dramas and spectaculars. At Belle Vue, George Dawson's production, *The Siege of Sebastopol*, was performed in 1855, and the following season the venue offered *The Storming of the Malakoff and the Redan*, which, according to David Mayer, brought cries of alarm from women in the audience as 'an occasional stuffed soldier was hurled over the ramparts'.[72] The events of the war were reconstructed as drama and in epic poetry such as Tennyson's 'Charge of the Light Brigade'. More important in disseminating the noble idea of a 'peoples' army' were visual images of the soldier. Interest in the war was such that the *Illustrated London News* sent a number of artists to the Crimea, including Constantin Guys, Edward Goodall and Joseph Archer Crowe; while the London print-seller Colnaghi took the unprecedented

4 A war correspondent pays tribute to British dead in the Crimea, 1855.

step of sending William Simpson to produce pictures suitable for lithographic reproduction. In 1855, Colnaghi published 80 of his pictures in a double folio, *The Seat of the War in the East*, which included imaginative reconstructions of the charges of the Light and Heavy Brigades.[73] Nor were these war illustrators reluctant to take a neutral stance, since for all their criticism of the military authorities they were anxious to be seen as patriots and participants. Joseph Archer Crowe's sketch for the *Illustrated London News* (3 February 1855) is a useful example. Entitled *Our artist on the Battlefield of Inkerman*, it shows Crowe, head bowed and holding the reins of his horse, gazing in silent tribute at the heroic British dead (illus. 4).

The Crimean campaign was also the first war to be photographed. Agnews of Manchester sent out the well-known photographer Roger Fenton, and eventually published over 300 scenes of trench and camp life and portraits. The limitations of early photographic equipment meant that battle scenes were impossible. Thus Fenton could only reveal posed and sanitized images of the campaign, a relatively 'cosy' view of the war (illus. 5). Nor would editors wish to offend the susceptibilities of their readers with graphic images of the horrors of battle. Nevertheless, the effect of such images on the public should not be underestimated, for they were first photographic record of an army at war. More important was the series of cullodians by Cundall and Howlett, 'Crimean Heroes'. These featured officers and enlisted men who had distinguished themselves in battle: many, in fact, had been awarded the new but highly coveted award for bravery, the Victoria Cross. The importance of these studies, together with artist Louis Desange's series

5 Roger Fenton: a posed photograph of a trench scene in the Crimea, c. 1855.

of portraits of holders of the Victoria Cross, was to demonstrate how ordinary men, often of humble origin, had shown exceptional qualities in action (illus. 6). Nobility under fire was clearly no longer confined to the aristocratic officer class. It was frequently noted that some 90 NCOs had been commissioned during the war. Even *The Times* wrote of Alma and Inkerman as 'soldiers' victories', and remarked upon the 'religious feeling' in the correspondence it had received from enlisted men. As Spiers has noted, the 'patient fatalism of the ranks as they endured the hardships of the camp before Sebastopol had aroused immense emotional feeling, an unprecedented interest in their plight and welfare.'[74]

The revelations of Russell and other correspondents about the incompetence of the military high command drew attention to the scandalous conditions, and stimulated a general demand for army reform as well as extensive public interest in military affairs. Above all, the Crimean War, a triumph over Russian tyranny, reinforced the idea that Britain's wars were legitimate, even righteous, activities. The warlike mood of the nation was reflected in the election of 1857, when Cobden and Bright, the most outspoken critics of the war, both lost their seats, while the role of the army as an essential tool of national policy was made clear by Lord Panmure, Secretary of State for War, in 1855:

> I trust our present experience will prove to our countrymen that our army must be something more than a mere colonial guard or home police; that it must be the means of maintaining our name abroad' and causing it to be respected in peace as well as admired and dreaded in war.[75]

These ideas were dramatically reinforced two years later when native troops mutinied in India.

6 'The Heroes of the Crimea': Colour-Sergeants McGregor and Staunton, 1856.

The revolt of sepoy regiments at Meerut and elsewhere in May 1857, and their subsequent capture of Delhi, was perceived as a major challenge to British rule in India – an heroic struggle in which fewer than 40,000 British soldiers faced the wrath of the Indian population. In reality, the Mutiny was the result of British arrogance, insensitivity and flagrant attempts to ride roughshod over Indian religious practices and traditions. Many Indian regiments remained loyal, and the mutineers represented only a tiny fraction of the population of the sub-continent. Yet, as Olive Anderson has pointed out:

> The dramatic circumstances of that event, and particularly its suddenness and ferocity and the fact that women and children were involved, quickly created a climate of hysterical tension at home. Among many of the pious this was intensified by their conviction that the Mutiny was in reality a challenge to Christianity itself, which had been allowed as a divine punishment for official compromise with false religions.[76]

As we have seen, by the 1850s the popular press was undergoing radical transformation in gathering and disseminating the news. But, as Graham Dawson has suggested, reports from India at this time were still 'irregular, uncritical and unreliable', allowing full play for sensationalist exaggeration and prejudice. A typical example from *The Times*, purported to be a letter to Lord Shaftesbury from Lady Canning, described how English women had had their ears and noses cut off by sepoys and that their children had been:

> Tortured in cold blood with the utmost refinement of imagination before the eyes of their parents, who were made to witness the cruelties and who were made to swallow portions of flesh cut from the limbs of their children, and afterwards burnt over a slow fire.[77]

These horrendous accounts of Indian atrocities caused a widespread demand for revenge, as Thomas Macaulay noted: 'The cruelties of the sepoys have inflamed the nation to a degree unprecedented in my memory. Retribution, when it came was greeted with delight by the people who 'three weeks ago were all against capital punishment'.[78]

The campaign to subdue the rebels was more than a military exercise to regain control and punish the tormentors of women and children, because India, as Brian Stanley has argued, possessed 'unique significance' for Victorian Christians. 'Religious minds had seized upon the informal and often unofficial annexations . . . as proof that India had been entrusted to Britain by God to be reclaimed by missionary activity'.[79] Since the 1830s, India had been the main area for missionary activity and the most challenging. Thus it was common to think of the sub-continent as a battleground in which soldiers of Christ struggled against the forces of darkness. It was an easy transition, then, to see the army's campaign to restore order as an extension of this missionary activity, and the British soldier as the new crusader fighting for the opportunity to renew the struggle for conversion.

These 'warriors of Christ' were feted as heroes, particularly generals such as Lawrence and Campbell, but it was Henry Havelock who was to be elevated to the status of soldier-saint. Virtually unknown before 1857, he became a national hero after his victories at Cawnpore and Alambagh, and then at the relief of Lucknow, where he died a martyr's death. But it was more than military prowess that ensured his elevation to the pantheon of Victorian heroes. As Anderson has noted, his death occurred at a time when Victorian society was rediscovering Puritanism, 'primarily under Carlyle's influence, and Puritans were made to stand, not for specific religious beliefs or practices, but for self-discipline and fearlessness'.[80] Thus Havelock, through religious devotion, courage and military prowess, could be hailed as a true Puritan soldier. He was also of the middle class, an officer who had achieved his rank not through wealth or patronage, but by hard work and ability, proving that military skill and leadership were not the prerogative of the aristocracy. He was, in fact, a perfect role model for middle-class Victorians.

When the Mutiny broke out, Havelock was Adjutant-General in Bombay.

Promoted Brigadier-General, he was given command of a flying column with orders to put down the insurrection in Allahabad and relieve the besieged garrisons at Cawnpore and Lucknow, and between 12 July and his death on 22 November, he won a series of spectacular victories, often against vastly superior numbers. After his first engagement at Fetchpur, he issued the first of his 'spirit stirring' orders to his troops. Having described what had been achieved, he then explained to what the victory was owed:

> To the fire of the British artillery . . . To the power of the Enfield rifle in British hands; to British pluck, that great quality which has survived the vicissitudes of the hour, and gained intensity from the crisis; and to the blessing of Almighty God on a most righteous cause, the cause of justice; humanity, truth, and good government in India.[81]

Presumably it was also God's will, as interpreted by Havelock and the other chivalric Christian warriors, that the rebels should be taught a lesson they would never forget. Graham Dawson recounts a number of brutal acts of revenge by the British, summed up by General Bernard's report that, 'We burnt every village and hanged all the villagers who had treated our fugitives badly until every tree was covered with scoundrels hanging from every branch', and the comments of an ordinary soldier who, having witnessed the Mutineers blown apart by cannon, claimed, 'it was a horrible sight but a very satisfactory one . . . The pieces were blown about in all directions'.[82]

When Havelock reached Lucknow his force was insufficient to lift the siege and joined the beleaguered garrison. It was only the arrival of Colin Campbell's troops some weeks later that relieved the city. When Havelock arrived at Lucknow he was suffering from acute dysentery. His condition worsened, and on 22 November he died. However, it was commonly accepted that 'if [he] did not actually fall under the deathshot of the enemy, he perished from disease aggravated by unsparing exertion', and was thus considered a martyr.[83] His military triumphs and heroic death won him enormous public acclaim in England. This was partly due to the manner in which his progress had been reported in the press. Given the problems of gathering news from India, these reports appeared at intervals and read almost as instalments of an adventure serial – Havelock leaves Bombay! – Havelock at Cawnpore! – Havelock marching to Lucknow! Clearly, such reporting intensified the excitement of his exploits and turned them into a dramatic adventure narrative. The report of his death was the final element in the saga and it was widely believed that Havelock, by his willing sacrifice, had saved India for the British!

Havelock's religious convictions, his military skill and his martyr's death before Lucknow, ensured that the public recognized him as the very epitome of the Christian Soldier. As the *Bombay Times* put it:

> Under God, this heroic captain, with his brave Englanders, has served India. His march has been so triumphant, his success so marvellous, as to impress even the public mind with the conviction that he has received his mission from a higher than earthly rule.[84]

At home, streets, terraces and ironically even public houses were named in his honour (Havelock was a total abstainer). A statue was erected in Trafalgar Square and a flood of articles, pamphlets and biographies celebrating his life and achievements were rushed into print during 1858.[85] The *Illustrated London News* published a wonderfully mawkish verse accompanied by an image of the British lion weeping for his favourite son (illus. 7). In 1860, Havelock's brother-in-law, John Clark Marshman, published what became the definitive biography, *The Memoirs of General Sir Henry Havelock*. The book remained in print until

Havelock.

HE is gone. Heaven's will is best :
Indian turf o'erlies his breast.
Ghoul in black, nor fool in gold
Laid him in yon hallowed mould.
Guarded to a soldier's grave
By the bravest of the brave,
He hath gained a nobler tomb
Than in old Cathedral gloom,
Nobler mourners paid the rite
Than the crowd that craves a sight,
England's banners o'er him waved—
Dead, he keeps the realm he saved.

Strew not on the hero's hearse
Garlands of a herald's verse :
Let us hear no words of Fame
Sounding loud a deathless name :
Tell us of no vauntful Glory
Shouting forth her haughty story.
All life long his homage rose
To far other shrine than those.
" In Hoc Signs," pale nor dim,
Lit the battle-field for him,
And the prize he sought and won,
Was the Crown for Duty done.

7 *Illustrated London News* pays tribute to Indian Mutiny hero Sir Henry Havelock, the Christian warrior, 1858.

1909, and a children's version became a favourite text for Sunday school and class prizes. But Havelock was one of many, albeit the most celebrated, and it was widely believed that Christian soldiers in India had been given the victory because it was God's will. It thus confirmed all the nationalistic tendencies of the Evangelicals. As the *Baptist Magazine* put it:

> The tide of rebellion [has been] turned back by the wisdom and prowess of Christian men, by our Lawrences, Edwardes, Montgomerys, Freres, and Havelocks ... God, as it were, especially selecting them for this purpose.[86]

In the last half of the century, Havelock would be joined by other soldier-martyrs, most notably Charles Gordon 'martyred' at Khartoum in 1885 – Christian warriors prepared to make the ultimate sacrifice for God and empire and provide perfect role models for an imperial race.[87]

The Havelock myth, however, was only one strand in the cultural representation of the Mutiny, which impacted upon the popular mind even more dramatically than the Crimean War. 'The Mutiny', claimed John MacKenzie:

> ... Secured more public attention than any other imperial event and had far-reaching cultural consequences. No event was more alluded to more frequently in painting, sculpture, public monuments in both India and Britain, journalism, popular biography, memoirs, books of heroes, as well as the Anglo-Indian literature of the late nineteenth century.[88]

The events of 1857 were frequently used as the basis for popular fictions which began to be published even before the end of the year and continued to inspire novelists until the late 1970s.[89] One of the earliest, by Charles Dickens and Wilkie Collins, was published in the Christmas edition of *Household Words*. 'The Perils of Certain English Prisoners' is a thinly disguised Mutiny story and demonstrates a far less humanitarian side of the novelist, clearly revealing that his concern for the wretched of the earth stopped with the white race. As Brantlinger tells us, his correspondence and journal at this time were full of anxiety about the Indian crisis, the fate of the Europeans and his concern that the 'race upon whom the stain of the late cruelties rested ... should be exterminated'.[90]

Dickens and Collins were followed into print by a series of novels of which George Lawrence's *Maurice Dering* (1864) was perhaps the best known.[91] But besides prose, the events of the Mutiny and the heroes of the army inspired a number of epic and lesser poems, including Tennyson's 'Havelock' ('Every man in Britain/ Says, "I am of Havelock's blood"'). Curiously, the Mutiny provided inspiration for Tennyson's epic, 'The Defence of Lucknow', over twenty years later.

The bloody events of 1857 also provided material for dramatists anxious to
play to the morbid fascination of the public. *Keereda and Nena* [sic] *Sahib* was
performed at London's Victoria Theatre in November 1857; and was quickly
followed by *India* at the Surrey and *The Fall of Delhi* at the Marylebone. The spectacular *The Storming and Capture of Delhi* was offered at Astley's in Birmingham,
and in 1859 Glasgow offered *The Indian Revolt*. Until well into the 1860s, theatres
all over the country offered a variety of dramas, pageants, spectacles, panoramas
and dioramas reconstructing the violent history of the revolt. These included
The Storming of Delhi (pyrodrama at Belle Vue, 1858), *Sites and Scenes of the
Indian Revolt* (diorama, London, 1858), and the most successful of the Mutiny
dramas, Dion Boucicault's *Jessie Brown or, The Relief of Lucknow*, which opened in
London in 1862 after a highly successful run in New York.[92]

Through technical developments in printing, visual representations of the
soldier in action were accessible to a far greater public than ever before. As we
have seen, war correspondents and special artists, even photographers, were sent
to the Crimea, but India was too far away for newspapers to send their agents,
and engravers at home were forced to create imaginative illustrations with scant
regard for reality. Hichberger has noted that there was only one European artist
in India at the time of the Mutiny – Egron Lundgren, a Swede. However, the
printer Agnew was quick to make contact and eventually bought many of his
sketches as the basis for T. J. Barker's epic, 'The Relief of Lucknow' – a canvas
showing the meeting of Havelock, Outram and Campbell.[93] Later important
paintings of the events were Edward Armitage's 'Retribution' (1858) and George
Jones' 'Lucknow', exhibited at the Royal Academy in 1865. There was little demand
for large-scale oil paintings other than as the basis for engravings, but the real
market for visual material was in the illustrated weeklies, cheap prints and in the
illustrations accompanying the many histories and memoirs of the campaign.[94]
One of the most common themes for illustrators was of barbaric mutineers
slaughtering the innocent; a powerful justification for the British presence in
India and for the savage reprisals taken against the rebels (illus. 8).

The Crimean War and the Indian Mutiny did much to legitimize war. Both
events were portrayed as righteous acts and appeared to justify evangelical
convictions that Britons were indeed the chosen people. British aggression was
hypocritically portrayed as a chivalric defence of the weak or a religious crusade
against the forces of darkness, while conquest brought order to chaos and took
the benefits of civilization to the unenlightened. These events also enhanced the
reputation of the British soldier, which, as we have seen, had been undergoing
transformation since the French Wars. By the 1860s, in the popular imagination,
the soldier had become an honest and heroic figure, and the army an instrument

8 The Indian Mutiny: the massacre of the British at Jhansi, 1857.

of the 'peoples' will'. This perception of war and the soldier created a growing acceptance that the security of the empire and the achievement of national goals depended upon force of arms. By the 1860s, admiration for the soldier, the prevalence of military sentiments and ideals and the willing acceptance of force, had taken root in the cultural life of the nation and marked the final acceptance of the military rationale for the Empire. As Michael Howard has explained:

> . . . [T]he Mutiny transformed what had been basically a trading empire into an explicitly military one, with an army of occupation whose primary duties were to assist the civil power in maintaining British rule. Simultaneously the advance of Russian power towards the Oxus gave Britain what she had not had . . . since the Act of Union . . . a land frontier with another and potentially hostile state. The British Army for the first time had a permanent 'raison d'etre', comparable to those of its great continental rivals . . .[95]

The acceptance of war and military force had dramatic consequences for the British people, not least for the perception of masculinity. Graham Dawson has suggested that, by the 1860s, the soldier had become the 'quintessential figure of masculinity', an idealized figure who represented all that was best in the English character, the epitome of national identity, a chivalric and Christian warrior. Even that most unmilitary of gentlemen, John Ruskin, could tell his officer audience in 1866 that '. . . the great veteran soldiers of England are now men every way so thoughtful, so noble, and so good, that no other teaching than their knightly example, and their few words of grave and tried counsel, should be either necessary for you, or even . . . endured by you'.[96]

It has been suggested that, for the early Victorians, the image of manliness represented a concern with the 'successful transition from Christian immaturity to maturity, demonstrated by an earnestness, selflessness and integrity' [and] only later did it come to stand for a neo-Spartan virility'.[97] But as we have seen, behind the more sensitive imaginings of the early Victorians lay a fundamental admiration for the man of action, the warrior-hero. In 1859, as war and preparation for war became even more widely accepted as essential to national well-being, heroic male fantasies could be acted out as thousands of men volunteered to be part-time soldiers in the Rifle Volunteers. The opportunity to wear uniform and share in the martial image without any of the hardship or danger faced by the regular soldier proved enormously popular, and men flocked to join (illus. 9). The Volunteers were initially created through fear of a French invasion. That crisis soon passed, but the Volunteers themselves, who never mustered less than 200,000 men annually, remained active until 1908, when they were absorbed into the Territorial Force.[98] It seems clear, then, that while few men were willing to serve in the regular army, the idealized image of the soldier was a powerful icon of masculinity which could be indulged through this dimension of the pleasure culture of war.

Ideas about war and masculinity were disseminated through a variety of popular cultural forms which suggested that war was normal, romantic and exciting. As we have seen, the pleasure culture of war, the reconstruction of conflict as entertainment, served a number of important functions within British society. It distanced the public from the realities of war and made conflict acceptable; it helped to resolve moral uncertainties about the use of violence, and may well have contributed to stability and peace at home by

9 A Volunteer Festival at Grimston Park, 1864. Men flocked to join the Volunteer Rifles.

encouraging Britons to direct their hostility, not at their fellow countrymen, but at the Other. Harold Perkin has suggested that:

> Between 1780 and 1850 the English ceased to be one of the most aggressive, brutal, rowdy, outspoken, riotous, cruel and bloodthirsty nations in the world, and became one of the most inhibited, polite, orderly, tender-minded, prudish and hypocritical.[99]

Much of this change was due to the acceptance of the evangelical creed and increasing educational provision; but it seems that much of the inherent aggression, brutality and bloodthirstiness of the English was never really eliminated; it was simply redirected into acceptable channels through the pleasure culture of war, and focused outwards at European rivals or the subject races of Asia or Africa. Thus, while the Other was subjected to that aggression and brutality, society at home became more orderly and peaceful. In 1860, the government issued arms to substantial numbers of the working class in the Rifle Volunteers, safe in the knowledge that those weapons would be directed at the French or other invaders, and not at fellow Britons or the ruling elites.

During the second half of the century, the legitimation of conflict was powerfully reinforced by the emergence of a seemingly 'scientific' justification for war. In 1859, Charles Darwin published *The Origin of Species*, and while few actually read the book, most literate Britons thought they had grasped its meaning. However, it was not long before evolutionary theory was being applied to human societies, and under the heading 'Social Darwinism', it was crudely argued that nations, like animals, were also involved in the struggle for survival. As Bernard Semmell has pointed out, it was widely believed that human progress was the 'result of an evolutionary struggle between groups of men, between tribes or nations or races, the fittest group predominating in the ceaseless warfare which constituted the evolutionary process'.[100]

By the end of the century, Britain's leading exponent of Social Darwinism, Karl Pearson, could suggest that national progress depended on racial fitness to win the battle for survival, and the supreme test of that fitness was war: 'the fiery crucible out of which comes the finest metal'. For Pearson, war was the ultimate challenge for the nation, and he went on to claim: 'when wars cease, mankind will no longer progress for there will be nothing to check the fertility of inferior stock'.[101] War, then, served another vital function for the nation. In Cecil Eby's felicitous phrase, 'it functioned rather like well-managed pruning shears, eliminating the weak and undesirable shoots and allowing the development of luxurious blossoms'.[102] War ensured that only the strong would survive and procreate, and in a climate where fear of racial deterioration was widespread, war not only culled the weak and inferior but stiffened the sinews of society. As Michael Adams has noted, it was widely believed that a 'little bloodletting . . . [was] good for the body politic as well as for the individual'.[103]

As success in war was essential for national well-being, it was sometimes suggested that a military-style model was the most effective means of organizing the nation to take part in the enduring human struggle. Military success was due to discipline, order, an accepted hierarchy and efficiency and, despite occasional setbacks, the British Army was remarkably successful in numerous imperial wars. By the end of the century, many, like Robert Owen and Samuel Smiles

IN "GENERAL" USE.

A Commanding Spirit finds its way to the front. PATTISONS' WHISKY commands success because it has been found by the public to be a genuine, wholesome, palatable beverage, carefully blended and thoroughly matured. It is cream-like in taste, with all the stimulating qualities of the pure Highland spirit. Sold Here, There, and Everywhere.

Sole Proprietors: PATTISONS, Ltd., Highland Distillers, BALLINDALLOCH, LEITH, and LONDON.

Head Offices: CONSTITUTION STREET, LEITH.

10 A true officer enjoys his tot: advertising using the excitement of war to sell products, 1899.

before them, came to believe that the military paradigm offered the best route to individual improvement and national efficiency.[104] A military-style structure was adopted by religious bodies like the Salvation Army (who fought an endless 'war' against moral decay) and by youth organizations, while workers were sometimes encouraged by their employers to join the Volunteers in order to be imbued with a sense of discipline, order and self-respect. After 1870 even school-children were subjected to regular drill in the hope of producing an orderly and disciplined population. On the eve of the Great War, the Secretary of the Navy League, H. F. Wyatt, combined religious and biological ideas about war with the notion of a military-style social structure, in a forceful argument that war was actually part of God's plan for the improvement of humankind: 'Preparation for war is the enemy of sloth . . . Preparation for war is the dissolvent of apathy . . . Briefly, victory is the crown of moral quality, and therefore . . . the "survival of the fittest" means survival of the ethically best'.[105] An extreme view, of course, but such ideas, albeit in less dramatic form, permeated society in the last decades of peace. War had become such an accepted commonplace activity for the British that its images could even be used in the marketing of such domestic items as embrocation, Scotch whisky and tobacco (illus. 10, 11).

By the end of the nineteenth century, the public was fascinated by war; by the romance and glamour of battles in exotic locations where plucky British Tommies made short shrift of the Queen's enemies. In dramatic prose and heroic

11 War added glamour to cigarette advertising, 1902.

illustrations, newspapers pandered to this interest and war correspondents were, as Kipling cynically noted, 'sent out when a war begins, to minister to the blind, brutal, British public's bestial thirst for blood. They have no arenas now, but they must have special correspondents'.[106] Correspondents such as Bennett Burleigh and Archibald Forbes, and artists like Melton Prior and Richard Caton Woodville, reinforced the idea of imperial warfare as chivalric adventure and that Britons had inherent war-like abilities. While sometimes critical of military leadership, they largely identified with the army, played down the unpleasant realities of battle and created negative stereotypes of the 'enemy'. Never for a moment did they question Britain's right to empire. And while military leaders like Wolseley, Roberts and Baden-Powell may well have regarded the presence of correspondents on the battlefield as a 'damned nuisance', they were only too well aware that favourable reports were essential in building their reputation at home.[107] The popular press, then, helped to spread the gospel of righteous war in the cause of empire, and helped perpetuate the myth of the soldier-hero.

By the last decades of the nineteenth century, popular militarism had become a major strand in the cultural fabric of the nation. But, as Anne Summers has pointed out, British militarism was 'utterly different from "Prussianism" . . . more than a ruling class ideology, and far more than an ideological instrument of the professional armed forces'.[108] It was a genuinely popular movement which reflected acceptance of war as a means of achieving national goals, an admiration for and pride in the exploits of the army and its heroes; a belief that military values and attitudes would improve the health of the people, create a more efficient work force and eliminate social ills. Popular militarism appealed as much to Liberals as to Tories, and even to socialists like H. M. Hyndeman and Robert Blatchford; it was embraced by the established Church and Non-Conformists alike, and became a major theme in a rapidly developing popular culture which would guarantee that successive generations of young Britons, the guardians of the future, would be indoctrinated with such ideas and thus ensure the survival of the British Empire.

2 The Little Wars of Empire

'Little Wars' is the game of kings – for players in an inferior social position. It can be played by boys of every age from twelve to one hundred and fifty – and even later if the limbs remain sufficiently supple, by girls of the better sort, and by a few rare and gifted women.

H. G. Wells, *Little Wars* (1913)

The first half of the nineteenth century witnessed a dramatic increase in literacy. By 1830, perhaps as much as two-thirds of the working classes could read and write, and this created a continually expanding market for broadsheets, chapbooks, popular journals, newspapers and books.[1] The serious minded, non-Conformists and most Anglicans believed that reading matter should be religious in nature or aimed at moral improvement, and fiction was dismissed as time-wasting fantasy. Even as late as 1843, a reviewer in the *Northern Star* argued that 'novel reading, at its best, [is] only an indifferent substitute for a worse occupation'.[2] But the new readers were far more interested in fiction than in the dry literature of improvement, since fiction provided an alternative to the dreariness of everyday life. The historical romances of Sir Walter Scott and the socially conscious novels of Charles Dickens and Mrs Gaskell did much to make fiction acceptable, as their work also contained a moral message and taught socially approved lessons. But in their wake came the escapist, the sensational and the scandalous, and by mid-century, as Richard Altick has pointed out, the spread of circulating libraries, popular journals and the publication of fiction in journals such the *Family Herald* (1843) or the *London Journal* (1845), meant that fiction was available to 'suit every taste but the crudest and the most cultivated'.[3] What the moralists initially failed to understand, however, was that fiction was often a far more effective means of transmitting moral messages and social training than dull, over-didactic tracts. By the 1840s, adult fiction was well established; entertaining certainly, but in a form which nevertheless mirrored the concerns of society and reinforced dominant ideas and values. However, the battle over what constituted suitable reading material for children remained hotly contested.

Even at the beginning of the century there was concern among the middle classes that the youth of the industrial cities were beyond the reach of the Church or any other civilizing influence – wild, violent, and at the mercy of any radical orator who could play upon their emotions. This led, as Linda Colley has suggested, to attempts to politicize them with the values and beliefs of the ruling elites through some form of education. Initially, this was provided through the Sunday School Movement. In 1800, some 200,000 children attended Sunday Schools, but by 1830 this figure had increased to over 1.4 million.[4] The regulation of child labour and the growth of day schools meant that more and more children were literate and had at least some leisure time, and reading material for children came to be seen as an important dimension in the socialization process. The development of children's literature has been well documented elsewhere.[5] What concerns us here is that reading was one way in which the young were inculcated with the beliefs that society deemed worth promoting. As Jeffrey Richards has explained:

> The aim of juvenile literature was clearly stated for a century. It was both to entertain and instruct, to inculcate approved value systems, to spread useful knowledge, to provide acceptable role models. This objective derived from the work of the Evangelicals, who as part of their bid to pacify and purify the urban and industrial society of the early decades of the nineteenth century, consciously set out to instruct the young . . .[6]

But, as Bratton notes, by mid-century, the old-style Sunday School tract or the overtly religious text lacked interest for most children.[7] The young were subject to the same influences as adults. They wanted to be entertained in their leisure moments and craved excitement and diversion from everyday routine.

The need for an appealing literary format through which to instruct young people resulted in the development of the adventure mode. The popularity of travel books and adventure stories primarily intended for adults (Defoe, Marryatt and Scott, for example), 'led the Evangelicals to seize on the model as an ideal for juvenile instruction'.[8] From mid-century, adventure fiction began to be written specifically for the nation's youth. The juvenile market, with gender-specific books and magazines, grew through the 1860s. The Education Act of 1870 gave further impetus to the development of juvenile fiction and convinced some publishers to increase their material intended for 10 to 18-year-old readers. By the 1880s, more than 900 juvenile titles were being published annually, and the market was well covered by magazines carrying both fiction and factual articles. At the same time, the growth of 'boy labour' in urban areas ensured that young men had money to spend on leisure activities.[9] The growth of this market encouraged some authors to write almost exclusively for the young. Initially, juvenile fiction was dominated by W. H. G. Kingston and R. M. Ballantyne, with a second generation of writers emerging in the period 1870–80 (G. Manville-Fenn, Gordon Stables and the prolific George Alfred Henty). Publishers, however, did not rely only on sales to juvenile readers and parents. Substantial numbers of books were bought by education authorities and Sunday Schools to be distributed as prizes and rewards. In order to appeal to this market the books had, of course, to promote the dominant values of society and, in the guise of exciting adventures, teach moral lessons. Such fiction, then, clearly provides a valuable insight into the values and attitudes the Victorians wanted to instil in their children.

Mid-century books for boys did not openly glorify the martial spirit. As Dennis Butts has explained, to see literature as a straightforward response to social conditions is too deterministic and reductionist. 'Literary creation is a process in which the writer often struggles with the world he or she sets out to depict, so that while some works undoubtedly do reflect their society . . . others articulate its contradictions, question its values, or even argue against them'.[10] We can see this process at work in the novels of the early writers of juvenile fiction, W. H. G. Kingston and R. M. Ballantyne. Deeply influenced by the evangelical creed, both wholeheartedly believed in the nation's imperial destiny. Kingston, indeed, was convinced that the colonies offered great opportunities for working-class men, and his fiction thus promoted an exciting world of overseas adventure and opportunity. As Bratton points out, Kingston's heroes become involved in episodic adventures in an imperial context as the rite of passage through which the hero emerges as a 'responsible Christian gentleman'. The novels are full of moral lessons, but above all they promote Britain's imperial mission. As a character in *Mark Seaworth* explains:

> I have an idea, that savages exist to employ the energies of Christian men
> in converting them . . . We have to toil to make the earth yield us produce,
> thus to strengthen our physical qualities; and I believe we have many
> moral duties to perform, in order to draw forth and strengthen our moral
> qualities. We have the poor to feed and clothe, the ignorant to educate,
> the turbulent to discipline; why should we not believe that, situated as
> Great Britain is, with more extensive influence than any other nation
> on the earth, she has the duty committed to her of civilising the number-
> less savage tribes with whom her commerce brings her in contact.[11]

Kingston does not glorify war – it can only be justified as self-defence – yet there is no lack of violence in his stories: the 'turbulent' are disciplined, be they pirates or savages, and force is sometimes a necessary first step in civilizing the 'heathen'. The author, then, takes the ambiguous position of the true Evangelical:

a belief in the divinely sanctioned mission of empire, a dislike of force but the grudging acceptance that it is sometimes justified as part of God's plan. Interestingly, in the late 1850s he became an enthusiastic supporter of the Volunteer Movement, a voluntary organization for national defence. Nevertheless, in Kingston's work war and violence are incidental to the main themes – exploring, hunting and trapping and colonizing.[12]

Ballantyne wrote in a more obviously religious style, indeed, his evangelical messages are often intrusive, yet it cannot be denied that his stories are extremely exciting. Using the standard plot of the tenderfoot hero engaging in episodic adventures, the author shows how moral courage and good moral sense will always triumph over adversity.[13] His novels are also set in the colonies, and, as in Kingston, involve trapping, hunting and exploring. His heroes never shrink from a fight and often tackle formidable foes. In the *Young Fur Traders*, for example, the central characters Harry and Charley, together with their guide, are pursued by Sioux Indians led by the warrior Misconna. The Europeans lay an ambush, and:

> As the foremost, a tall, muscular fellow . . . bounded over the bush behind which Jacques was concealed, he was met with a blow from the guide's fist, so powerfully delivered into the pit of his stomach that it sent him violently back into the bush, where he lay insensible. This event, of course, put a check upon the headlong pursuit of the other . . . The hesitation, however, was but for a moment. Misconna . . . suddenly drew his bow again, and let fly an arrow at Jacques, which the latter dexterously avoided; and while his antagonist lowered his eyes for an instant to fit another arrow to the string, the guide, making use of his paddle as a sort of javelin, threw it with such force and precision that it struck Misconna directly between the eyes and felled him to the earth.[14]

Ballantyne had few doubts as to the inherent superiority of the white race; an early illustration for *Martin Rattler* clearly reveals the superiority of European technology, and especially the gun, in overawing native populations (illus. 12). While the 'savage' is subdued by the European, the conqueror also offers the means of salvation, for the native can, and often is, redeemed through the Word of God. Thus was Britain's imperial expansion justified. It has been suggested that both authors retreated from the more aggressive imperial mood after 1870.[15] Yet in later novels, like *The Settler and the Savage: A Tale of Peace and War in South Africa* (1877) and *Blue Lights; or Hot Work in the Soudan* (1888), Ballantyne began to reflect the more bellicose mood of the age without condoning it; pointing out in 1878 that while brave deeds are done in battle, war itself is wrong:

12 The superiority
of the white man's
technology. From
R. M. Ballantyne,
Martin Rattler
(1859).

Such a deed is done when a handful of brave men sacrifice their lives
at the call of duty, and in defence of country . . . And such a deed is
done, still more gloriously, when a soldier, true to his Queen and
country, is true also to his God and preaches while he practices the
principles and gospel of the Prince of Peace, in the presence of those
with whom he acts his part in this world's drama. There is indeed much
that is glorious in the conduct of many warriors, but there is no glory
whatever in war itself. The best that can be said of it is, that sometimes
it is a stern yet sad necessity.[16]

Here we see these authors beginning to grapple with the emerging militarism of
the later nineteenth century. Influenced by the Evangelical notion of Britain's

divine right to empire, they accepted that violence was sometimes necessary
in achieving worthwhile ends, but were hypocritically reluctant to condone the
act of war.[17] But while Kingston and Ballantyne virtually established the adventure mode as the pre-eminently popular reading for juveniles, it was Charles
Kingsley, Queen Victoria's favourite preacher, who contributed the idea of war
as adventure to the form, and established a pattern that would be followed by
many later writers.

In Kingsley's writings, particularly in his popular and successful novel *Westward
Ho!*, an epic tale of the war in Spain, we can clearly see how many of the central
ideas of the nineteenth century came together to form the model of aggressive
masculinity that became so prominent later in the century. Kingsley, deeply
concerned at the plight of the poor and the self-interest of the rich, was a found-
ing member of the Christian Socialist Movement of the late 1840s.[18] He was
active in the attempt to improve the conditions of rural labourers and provide
educational opportunities for working men. Yet, steeped in Scott's romances and
deeply influenced by Carlyle's notions of heroism and Digby's chivalric ideal,
he saw himself as a knight-errant fighting to right the social evils of his day.
From Evangelicalism he drew upon notions of the imperial destiny of the British
race and their manifest right to predominate overseas.

Through his friendship with Thomas Hughes he became interested in physical
toughness and endurance, delighting in strenuous walking tours and swimming
in icy pools. This obsession with physical prowess developed into a fascination
with war as the ultimate test of manliness. His parish at Eversley was close to
Aldershot, and officers would often ride over to hear his sermons. Kingsley had
great respect for these martial figures: 'I like to have men of war about me', he
once said.[19] In 1854, he became intensely excited by the Crimean War which he
saw as an opportunity for the nation to demonstrate its manliness. In awe of
the bravery of the British rank and file, he was inspired to write *Westward Ho!*,
intended for an adult readership but which proved immensely popular with boys.

Dedicated to Rajah Sir James Brooke of Sarawak and Bishop Selwyn of New
Zealand, Kingsley directed his readers to the continuities between the heroic past
and the heroic present, between the new apostles of empire and their Elizabethan
forebears, the adventurers who had broken the Roman Catholic challenge
to Britain's overseas expansion.[20] The novel deals with the adventures of Amyas
Leigh in Ireland and the Caribbean and climaxes in the battle with the Armada –
a battle to determine whether 'Popery and despostism, or Protestantism and
freedom', were to dominate half of Europe and the whole future of America'.
Amyas and his Devon men represent 'brave young England longing to wing its
way out of its island prison', and blazing the trail for future generations who will

realize the destiny of the race. Amyas is typical of 'young England' – well-born but not wealthy, well-versed in the ways of nature but not intellectual – he knows only his Bible and the 'Morte d'Arthur'. True to his God, his race and his comrades, and convinced of his right to rule the world, Amyas is both gentle with his friends and hard on his enemies; 'the most terrible fighter among the Bideford boys'. Yet, because he follows a chivalric code (he had been raised on Malory), his strength is used to defend the weak and oppressed. His comrades are equally terrible in battle. An illustration from the novels reveals Amyas as an agent of both redemption and punishment as, sword in hand and fierce mustaches bristling, he frees the slaves aboard a Spanish galley while at the same time ordering the death of the Spanish crew (illus. 13). In one escapade, the Devon men are attacked by Spaniards on Barbados. John Brimblecombe,

13 Amyas Leigh, agent of redemption and retribution. From Charles Kingsley, *Westward Ho!* (1855).

a parson's son, is reading his Bible when the attack comes. Putting down the Book, he:

> caught up his arquebus, ran like a mad dog right at the Spanish Captain, shot him through the body stark dead, and then, flinging the arquebus at the head of him who stood next, fell on with his sword like a very collbrand . . . and striking right and left such ugly strokes, that the Spaniards . . . gave back pell-mell.

John frenzedly hacks and kills until, chasing the retreating foe, he trips and knocks himself out. When he recovers consciousness, he asks his friends how many he killed, 'nineteen at least', is the reply.[21] Kingsley is suggesting that 'gentle' John has gone berserk in battle, just like the Viking warriors who the author so much admired. In a fight to take a Spanish ship, the English, supremely confident that God is indeed on their side and knowing that one Englishman is more than a match for several foreigners, call upon the Spanish to yield, explaining, 'do you not see that you are but fifty strong to our twenty'. The enemy, the author tells us, surrendered, 'some falling on their knees, some leaping overboard'.[22]

Westward Ho!, which revelled in the excitement of battle, was enormously popular with young men and was even distributed to troops in the Crimea. But what the author had done, in effect, was to make war an acceptable subject for the adventure story and introduce the nation's youth to the pleasure culture of war. And Kingsley made another important contribution to juvenile fiction which was to further the development of 'manliness'.

In 1857 he published *Two Years*, a now largely forgotten novel set against the background of the Crimean War. Its importance, however, is that it makes clear many of the author's ideas about war and masculinity. At one point, Kingsley actually claims that war is a 'most necessary human art', and that 'there are noble elements underneath the crust which will come out all the purer from the fire'.[23] War is an experience which enobles and enriches, a rite of passage which tests the sinews of manliness of both the individual and the nation. The heroic nature of the warrior caste and the idea of the just war were also powerfully emphasized in his *Hereward the Wake: Last of the English*, published in 1866. Manliness was enormously important for Kingsley, and for his friend and fellow author Thomas Hughes. Both realized that boys needed to demonstrate their masculinity, and they developed a manly ideal which emphasized physical prowess, tempered by purity, gentleness and concern for others – in other words, the chivalric ideal.[24] Dubbed 'Muscular Christians', both were at pains to differentiate between the muscular Christian and the muscleman; as Hughes explained in his 1857 novel *Tom Brown's Schooldays*:

The only point in common between the two being, that both hold it to be a good thing to have strong and well-exercised bodies . . . Here all likeness ends; for the 'muscleman' seems to have no belief whatever as to the purposes for which his body has been given him, except some hazy idea that it is to go up and down the world with him, belabouring men and captivating women for his benefit or pleasure.

But the Christian, the author tells us, dedicates his body to God and uses it to protect the weak and to advance the righteous cause.[25] Hughes's novel became the great classic of public school life, and Tom the very epitome of what a boy should be: honourable, brave, a born sportsman and never afraid to trade punches with a bully. The book had enormous impact and, as Jeffrey Richards has noted, was read by boys as entertainment and by adults as part of the educational debate.[26] Manliness, particularly as espoused by Hughes, became an important element in the reformed public schools and underpinned the development of the games ethic, which became enormously important in such schools. However, by the last decades of the century, the ideal of manliness had been shorn of much of its moral and religious elements and had became a crude archetype of neo-Spartan virility. It was widely believed that such qualities were best found among the men who had created the empire and who now defended its frontiers. It was the defenders of empire who became the dominant heroes in the adventure stories which began to emerge in the 1870s.

While most adults considered the work of writers like Kingston and Ballantyne to be wholesome and instructive reading, the 1860s also witnessed the emergence of many crudely produced serial papers catering for working-class boys, with titles such as *Black Rollo the Pirate*, *The Dance of Death* or *The Hangman's Plot* and *The Wild Boys of London*. Deprecated as 'penny dreadfuls', they related the sensational adventures of characters who defied authority and revelled in violent behaviour.[27] More acceptable to concerned parents were the magazines published by Edwin Brett from the mid-'60s, like *Boys of England* and *Young Men of Great Britain*. These published articles on self-help, various occupations and British history, but their main programme was exciting fiction written by Captain Mayne Reid, W. H. Stephens and Cecil Stagg. According to Carpenter, by 1871, *Boys of England* was selling 250,000 copies a week.[28] Its most popular character was the anarchic Jack Harkaway, who defied and defeated schoolmasters, cannibals and pirates. Brett's magazines preached crude patriotism and racial superiority. They paid lip-service to conventional morality, but this was never allowed to interfere with a bloody fight or vivid descriptions of sadistic torture of the unfortunate victims of savages and pirates. As James has noted, these characters 'reflected the violence and brutality of an expanding empire'.[29] However, when these stories were set against an imperial background, it was simply an exotic location for adventure and the authors demonstrated little understanding of imperial needs or policies.[30] Crude descriptions of violence and torture played to the latent emotions of adolescent boys and created a fantasy world wherein they could act out their atavistic dreams of masculine prowess. Such fiction proved far more popular than the offerings of the more respectable, and far more expensive, magazines for boys such as Samuel Beeton's *Boy's Own Magazine* (1855) and Tweedie's *Young England* (1862). But in an age where boys had a little money and more leisure they called the tune, and the publisher who wanted to remain in business listened carefully. By the 1870s, there was general concern that such fiction was not only an incitement to delinquency among working-class youth but was being increasingly read by the 'better type of boy'. This anxiety, combined with the realization that increasing literacy would put more boys at risk from this pernicious fiction, led to the emergence of new papers which attempted to combat their dire effects.

In 1879 the Religious Tract Society (RTS) launched the most enduring of these new papers, the *Boy's Own Paper*. While *BOP* was still in the planning stage, its editor, G. A. Hutchinson, continually clashed with RTS directors who wanted yet another pious periodical. Hutchinson, however, insisted that boys wanted exciting fiction as well as articles on sport, science, history and crafts, and it was this combination which appealed to boys, while their parents approved of the moral tone of the publication, and lifted the *BOP* to the highest circulation of any Victorian boys' paper.[31] Although violence, especially in an historical context, was common in the magazine's first decade, there were few stories that dealt with modern wars. Nevertheless, there were many illustrations and stories of warfare in the age of chivalry. 'At Duty's Call', a cover picture by G. H. Edwards, reveals the knight accepting his lady's favour before riding off to war (illus. 14). Recent wars, however, were central in the short-lived but influential *Union Jack*, advertised as 'Tales for British Boys'. Founded in January 1880, by W. H. G. Kingston, the first issue contained his own story, 'Paddy Finn: the Adventures of an Irish Midshipman' and the serial 'Times of Peril, a story of the Indian Mutiny', by his editorial assistant George Alfred Henty. Kingston presumably intended the magazine to reflect his own religious views and belief in emigration, but he was in poor health and it would seem that Henty shaped editorial policy (Kingston retired in May 1880 and died shortly afterwards). Under Henty's control, the paper reflected an aggressive masculinity and war stories became a staple ingredient. The magazine was popular with boys, and its failure in 1883 would seem to have been more a result of Henty's lack of business sense than

No. 440.—Vol. IX.   SATURDAY, JUNE 18, 1887.   Price One Penny.
[ALL RIGHTS RESERVED.]

14 The chivalric knight rides out to war, 1887.

anything else. But the editorship of *Union Jack* helped to familiarize boys with Henty's work and undoubtedly contributed to the success of his third novel, *The Young Buglers: A Tale of the Peninsula War*, published in early 1880.[32] Henty went on to become one of the most successful and influential writers of juvenile fiction of the late nineteenth century. It is worth looking in some detail at his work because, in large measure, he was the seminal figure in creating the model of war fiction for British boys, a model that was slavishly followed by other writers until well into the twentieth century.[33]

Henty inherited much from earlier writers, ideas about manliness and the nation's imperial destiny, for example, but he added to them his own romanticized view of war, developed through his experience as a war correspondent for the *Standard*. His first novels *Out on the Pampas* (1871) and *The Young Franc-Tireurs: and Their Adventures in the Franco–Prussian War* (1872) were largely unsuccessful, but his association with *Union Jack* launched his career, and after 1880 he often managed three novels a year (over 80 were published) as well as stories and serials for the boys' papers. As Robert Huttenback has pointed out, Henty based his fiction on personal experience, on contemporary reports by war correspondents and on popular histories, which he plagiarized shamelessly.[34] Like Balzac, Henty was continually short of money and wrote prolifically in order to solve his financial problems, but he also had another purpose in mind: he 'was determined to 'teach patriotism', to inspire faith in the destiny of the Anglo-Saxon race and to offer 'bright personal examples of morality'.[35] He wanted to show boys how to behave; his biographer and friend George Manville Fenn recalled that he wanted his boys to be bold, 'straightforward and ready to play a young man's part, not to be milksops. He had a horror of a lad who displayed any weak emotion and shrank from shedding blood, or winced at any encounter'.[36] Henty, then, an advocate of imperialism and chivalric manliness, bound these into an idealized portrait of the soldier, the instrument through which the empire would be preserved. Influenced by contemporary historical views, he saw British history as a series of inevitable wars which had created the empire, and believed that future generations must stand ready to wage war to maintain that heritage. In 1885 he expressed these views in the preface to *St George for England: A Tale of Crecy and Poitiers*:

> It is sometimes said that there is no good to be obtained from tales of fighting and bloodshed – that there is no moral to be drawn from such histories. Believe it not. War has its lessons as well as peace. You will learn from tales like this that determination and enthusiasm can accomplish marvels, that true courage is generally accompanied by magnanimity and gentleness, and that if not itself the very highest of virtues, it is the parent of almost all the others, since few of them can be practised without it. The courage of our forefathers has created the greatest empire in the world around a small and in itself insignificant island; if this empire is ever lost, it will be by the cowardice of their descendents.[37]

Unashamedly, Henty took as his subject war and the glory of war. Some 65 of his 80 books deal with wars, and over a third of those with Britain's wars of empire. While he sometimes noted that certain wars were unnecessary, the First Afghan war, for example, was 'reckless' and 'unjust',[38] he viewed most of Britain's conflicts as morally justified. Of the campaign against Tippoo Sahib, he claimed:

> while some of our wars in India are open to the charge that they were undertaken on slight provocation, and were forced on us in order that we might have an excuse for annexation, our struggle against Tippoo Sahib was, on the other hand, marked by long endurance of wrong, and a toleration of abominable cruelties perpetrated upon Englishmen and our native allies.[39]

The Sikh, Mahratta, and most other wars were justified in the same way,[40] as were earlier wars against the French, Spanish and Russians. But in their wars of empire, according to Henty's gospel, the British should not just be seen as conquerors but also as liberators, bringing good government, justice and improvement to native peoples who suffered under tyrants, and once under British rule most native races were quick to see the benefits.

The instrument of liberation, of course, was the British soldier, for whom the author had nothing but praise. In *Through Three Campaigns*, Henty rebukes the nation for ignoring its warrior sons' less spectacular campaigns:

> Our little wars attract far less attention among the people of this country than they deserve. They are frequently carried out in circumstances of the most adverse kind. Our enemies, although ignorant of military discipline, are, as a rule, extremely brave, and are thoroughly capable of using the natural advantages of their country. Our men are called upon to bear enormous fatigue and endure extremes in climate; the fighting is incessant, the peril constant. Nevertheless they show magnificent contempt for danger and difficulty, and fight with valour and determination worthy of the highest praise ... The country has a right to be proud indeed of the prowess of both our own troops and of our native regiments.[41]

Martial prowess and love of fighting had, according to Henty, always been a characteristic of the British race. When Nita, the heroine of *The Soldier's Daughter*, suggests that it is peculiar that men should be so fond of fighting, her companion, Lieutenant Charlie Carter explains:

> It is; I have often wondered over it many a time. All savage races love fighting, and certainly our own people do. If there were a great war,

hundreds and thousands of men would volunteer at once. I am afraid
this instinct brings us very near the savage. I think no other nation
possesses it to anything like the same extent as the British race.[42]

Nita, the daughter of a major on the north-west frontier, is no mean fighter herself and when the fort is attacked by Afridis, she picks up a rifle and shoots back;
she has no 'sense of fear . . . [and] was proud of doing her share of the work. That
she was doing a share she knew, for scarcely one of her shots missed the mark'.[43]

In his early novels, Henty established a formula that he would adhere to
throughout his career.[44] The Henty hero was usually around sixteen years old,
orphaned or has lost his fortune, and who sets out on his travels to make
his mark in an imperial or equally exotic setting. He is tested, fights battles, is
captured, escapes, fights more battles, gains the approval of an imperial warlord
and invariably makes his fortune in the process. Many of his stories make use of
the great figures of the empire around which to construct the novel. Illustration
15, for example, shows the young hero of *With Kitchener in the Soudan* being
presented to the Sirdar. Henty's boy heroes are sometimes from public schools,
sometimes of low birth, but all are manly, resourceful, chivalric and patriotic.
And if Beric the Briton fighting the Romans, or Wulf the Saxon fighting the
Vikings, resemble nineteenth-century public schoolboys, it is not surprising. As
the author noted, he was really writing about manly English boys of his own
time. In *The Lion of St Mark*, set in fourteenth-century Venice, Henty explains
this technique, claiming that while the historical background of the story is
accurate, he has woven into it 'the adventures of an English boy endowed with
a full share of that energy and pluck which . . . have made the British Empire
the greatest the world had ever seen'.[45] It is not possible to deal here with the
author's views on race, but it should be noted that while he had little regard for
other races, those to whom he did award a grudging respect were noted for their
martial qualities. In his hierarchy of race, like Marryatt's, the more violent and
aggressive a people, the more status they deserved.

Henty romanticized war and turned it into an adventure that most boys found
enormously appealing in order to inculcate a commitment to defend the empire.
Through war a young man could show what he was made of and gain fame
and fortune. Being British meant being endowed with an inherent talent for
fighting, so that battle posed little danger for the true Briton. But Henty was not
quite the simple-minded apostle of imperial violence that some writers have
suggested. He had, as Patrick Dunae has pointed out, considerable interest in
the economic dimensions of empire and was 'anxious to promote commerce,
develop local industries, and exploit the natural resources in Britain's imperial

15 A Henty
hero meets the
imperial warlords:
frontispiece to
*With Kitchener to
the Soudan* (1903).

possessions'.[46] Such development was not only essential for Britain, but had positive advantages for indigenous peoples. But the real significance of empire is that it offered the means for the British to prosper, as it does his heroes. Many of them, in fact, do not remain in imperial service but return home with their fortune. For Kingston and Ballantyne, empire provided the opportunity for spiritual development through missionary activity. For Henty it was economic advantage for both conqueror and conquered, and here he simply spoke for the increasingly materialist attitudes of his time. The empire was the source of British power and well-being, and a way in which native people could be imbued with 'Englishness' – qualities which Henty genuinely believed would improve their lives. War was simply the means by which the empire was extended and held secure; it was an experience that was not only enjoyable but necessary as well.

For boys, Henty created an exciting world where battle provided the route to fame and fortune and played to their more primitive emotions and fantasies. But his books were also widely approved by both parents and teachers, who passed them on to their children as presents and prizes because his stories were steeped in the spirit of the age, mirrored many of the enshrined attitudes of late Victorians and powerfully reinforced those beliefs. Certainly his books had an educational content, blending fact and fiction. His usual practice was to place the fictitious hero's adventures against the background of some great episode of British history. But he served a more important purpose, as he successfully redirected the uncontrolled violence of the penny dreadful into approved channels – imperial expansion and a belief in martial prowess, glossed with notions of chivalric behaviour and ideas about the 'sporting' nature of warfare. These were appropriate qualities for boys from the 1880s, for the world of the late Victorians was far less secure than at mid-century. The rapid expansion of the empire after the 1870s, especially in Africa, created even greater demands upon an already stretched British army, while at the same time other European powers were developing imperial ambitions that threatened British interests: German expansion in Africa and the Russian threat to northern India were seen as particularly dangerous to imperial security. The British army's poor performance against the Transvaal Boers at Majuba in February 1881[47] compared unfavourably with German military prowess demonstrated during the Franco–Prussian War. This, combined with increasing economic competition from rapidly-industrializing nations like the USA and Germany, conspired to create a sense of unease for many Britons. Part of the adult approval for Henty and his fellow writers, then, was because they promoted, through the pleasure culture of war, a sense of duty and the martial spirit among British boys upon whom the security of the empire would ultimately depend. However, even though Henty was the seminal figure in selling war to boys, his descriptions of battlefield violence are remarkably muted and unemotional.

During a skirmish in *Through Three Campaigns*, Lisle, the hero of the novel, kills a number of the enemy's leaders, but we are told simply that he 'brought down several of them'. At the Battle of Coomassie, the British, after sweeping the Ashantis with fire from their Maxims, 'clamboured over the stockade, and the enemy, unable to stand the fury of their charge, fled in panic'.[48] Even for the Battle of Omdurman, which contemporaries described as calculated slaughter, Henty's description is particularly detached. The soldiers fired until their rifles were too hot to hold while the Maxims poured bullets into the massed Dervish Army with 'terrible effect'. The ground over which the Dervishes advanced was 'littered with their fallen',[49] but such description gives no indication of the horrors of the battlefield, and even close combat is glossed over. In *Times of Peril*,

Ned, a young Englishman, is attacked by Mutineers: 'the native trooper rushed from the house. As he came out, Ned fired and the native fell forward on his face'. Later, when sepoys break down the gate of the village where British survivors have taken shelter, the British 'fell upon them sword in hand . . . eager to take part in the fray, and the enemy inside the gate were either cut down or driven headlong through it'.[50] Henty's descriptions of battle lack reality, but many of his followers writing for a new generation, dealt with combat in a far more graphic manner and exploited the atavistic nature of their readers.

Henty died in 1902, but the style of juvenile war fiction he had popularized was inherited by a new generation of younger writers who had grown up with his stories, and who began to publish around the turn of the century. Among the most popular were F. S. Brereton, Percy Westerman, Captain Charles Gilson, and George Ely and James L'Estrange, who collaborated as 'Herbert Strang'. 'Captain' Frederick Sadlier Brereton, Henty's cousin and an RAMC doctor who had served in South Africa, began his writing career in 1900. While clearly influenced by Henty, Brereton's descriptions of combat are somewhat more graphic. In his story of the Zulu War, Donald Stewart, a settler's son, is forever shooting Zulus 'between the eyes' or putting bullets in their brains, while at the Battle of Ulundi British fire swept the Zulus away, 'shattered, broken, and bleeding, and the guns, loaded with canister, completed the awful work'.[51] *Tom Graham VC*, by William Johnson, has the hero enlist and take part in the Second Afghan War. At the storming of Peiwar Kotal, the young Tom, protecting his fallen captain, finds himself struggling with a huge Pathan, but 'with a fierce lunge the young borderer drove his bayonet up to the nozzle in the Afghan's chest'. But the native still fights on and only a 'terrific blow' from a rifle butt to his head finishes him.[52] In Percy Westerman's *Building the Empire*, set on the north-west frontier, British soldiers are sometimes 'hacked to pieces', while loyal Gurkhas wreak havoc on the Afridis with their 'razor sharp kukris'. However, none of this is quite as unpleasant as A. J. Chalmers's *Fighting the Matabele* – allegedly based on the author's own experiences in that campaign. Chalmers takes an obvious delight in recalling how, when attacked by a Matabele warrior, 'I caught him by the wrist, wrenched the weapon from his hand, and cracked his crown with it; I shall never forget the sickening thud with which the club descended on his skull' (illus. 16). Meanwhile, Chalmers's companion dispatches the rest of the war party 'more neatly' with his revolver. The author exemplifies the imperialist at his most brutal: at one point threatening to throw native women off a cliff for refusing to reveal where their men are hiding, and later taking great pleasure when an artillery shell bursts among a group of Matabele. Interestingly, Chalmers concludes his book by claiming that there will be more trouble with the Matabele

16 'Cracked his crown with it' – the imperialist at his most brutal. From *Fighting the Matabele* (c. 1898).

if the administration continued to treat them in such a 'mild manner'. The 'iron hand' must not be lifted, he argues, for 'at best, the Matabele, like the Indians in the States, will most likely be a source of periodical trouble and disturbance, and the country ought to be so controlled as to reduce . . . the risk of outrages . . . All outrages should be visited with instant and severe retribution'.[53] The *Liverpool Echo*'s book reviewer curiously suggested that *Fighting the Matabele* described the recent campaign 'with such piquantness' that it would become a great favourite with boys.[54]

Violence, however, was not only a reflection of the imperial realities of the late nineteenth century, since many authors reached back into the national past for their inspiration. Here, unfettered from notions of any 'civilizing' mission, they could allow their imaginations full play. The flavour of such writing was seen in Edgar Pickering's *A Stout English Bowman*, set in the reign of Henry III. The seventeen-year-old hero, Harold Godwith, tricked out of his rightful inheritance, becomes a bowman and sets off to France with the army. He later describes the violent frenzy that overcomes him during his first battle:

> I have been in many a hard-fought battle since that day . . . but never again have such strange feelings been in my heart at the sight of the foe, as I felt when . . . we faced the Frenchmen; nor shall I ever forget the sound of the first flight of our bolts and arrows . . . spreading death . . . amongst our opposers. The French return fire, 'dealing wounds and cruel hurts, slaughtering and maiming us. I saw Thomas the Smith fall . . . and many another bit the dust . . . and I was filled with madness to avenge their fall'.[55]

In Robert Leighton's *The Thirsty Sword*, a story of the Norse invasion of Scotland, Duncan, a friend of the hero Kenric, is slain by the wicked Earl Roderic. But here it is Duncan's lover, Aasta the Fair, who attempts to avenge him. Aasta, wearing armour and fighting as fearlessly as any man, is by Duncan's side when he is killed. Then, 'splashed with her lover's blood she gripped her sword . . . [and] leapt with a wolf-like howl upon Roderic . . . and so pressed him with her blows that he stepped back and back'.

However, she lacks the strength to finish her enemy and it is finally Kenric who avenges Duncan's death.[56] But one of the goriest examples is to be found in *Across the Spanish Main*, by Harry Collingwood. Set in the Elizabethan period, it tells of the adventures of a group of English privateers. In one episode, the Englishmen attack a Spanish pirate ship, *The Pearl*. Several broadsides are fired into the Spaniard, then the English captain leads his men:

> Over the side on to the decks of *The Pearl*, which was by this time a scene of dreadful carnage. Blood was everywhere; her planking was slimy with it that men slipped and fell in it. It ran in little rivulets from the scuppers.

Roger, the central character of the novel, takes on a burly adversary and 'passed his sword through the pirate's body with such force that it penetrated to the hilt'. So violent was the blow that Roger had to plant his foot firmly on his enemy's chest in order to pull free his blade. The English, of course, are victorious, but, the author tells us, 'the carnage was fearful: the dead and dying lay everywhere'.[57]

Many writers produced historical romances, but it was more commonly the little wars of empire and contemporary conflicts that provided their inspiration: the Russo–Japanese War (1904–5) provided the backdrop for Brereton's *A Soldier of Japan* and Herbert Strang's *Kobo, A Soldier of Japan* and *Brown of Moukden*. Westerman dealt with the Italian–Turkish War (1911–1912) in *Captured in Tripoli*, and even the Second Balkan War (1913) featured in Brereton's *The Great Airship*. Many of these novels not only emphasized their hero's manliness, sense of duty and enjoyment of battle, but also argued for the adoption of new weapons, the modernization of the army and even conscription, and frequently warned of the danger from other imperial powers. They reflected the increasing international rivalries of the early twentieth century, and often wrote alarming accounts of the 'great war to come', leaving their readers in little doubt that the day was coming when they would be called upon to play their part (see chapter three).

These same messages were reinforced and even more widely disseminated through the popular boys' papers. As we have seen, 'respectable' papers were introduced from the late 1870s, in an attempt to counteract the deleterious effects of the penny dreadfuls by channelling youthful aggression into acceptable forms. The approved arena for this aggression was the empire – hence the emphasis in the weeklies on exploring, serving and defending the empire, for, as Carpenter has pointed out, the aggression and violence of the penny dreadfuls was 'perfectly acceptable in an imperial context'.[58] The *BOP*, while reluctant to run contemporary war stories, made up for this with a great deal of violent historical fiction, often by Henty. Its rival, *Young England*, published by the Sunday School Union, had no such inhibitions and covered a number of wars both ancient and modern: 'On the Orleans Road', a story of the Franco–Prussian War, 'In Arms for Freedom' (Hereward the Wake) and 'Archers of Old England' (Hundred Years War), as well as articles on 'Boys of the Navy', the 'Heroes of Rorke's Drift' and 'How We Tried to Save Gordon'. Some articles featured quite gruesome descriptions. 'A Bare-Foot Race to Gwelo, or My Terrible Experience of the Matabele Rising', contained the following description by a young English survivor of a Matabele attack on a homestead:

> 'Just as we came out of the store we heard two of the most awful shrieks I ever heard, beginning high up and ending in a sort of gurgling noise, coming from the direction of the hut F— was lying in . . . Outside it two of his Zambesi boys were lying, stabbed all over, and inside the poor fellow was lying on the ground with his eyes punched out, one stab in the throat, and another in the chest. He was almost dead, and was only able to wag his arms up and down feebly.[59]

Retribution against such insurrections was fast and brutal, and in an account of a rising in the Niger Protectorate the same author applauded the summary punishment dealt to the natives.[60]

Chums, first published in 1892 under the editorship of Max Pemberton, was particularly given to imperial violence.[61] The magazine, with its densely printed pages, plentiful illustrations and occasional colour plates proved popular with boys of all social groups and in many cases had a lasting impact on its readers.[62] War, sport and school tales were the staple ingredients of *Chums* fiction, but the paper ran a number of military features, such as 'Fighting for Empire', true stories of action related by officers and men and including battles like Omdurman, Cawnpore and Sebastopol. There were also articles on uniforms, medals and war correspondents, and specially commissioned articles by imperial heroes like Sir Evelyn Wood. War fiction was mainly in the form of tales of young soldiers involved in imperial conflict, and the north-west frontier featured prominently. Equally, war and adventure were also the province of the boys' weeklies published by Alfred Harmsworth (later Lord Northcliffe) from 1893. Starting with *Marvel*, and including *Union Jack*, *Pluck* and *Boy's Friend*, these sold for just one halfpenny and contained vivid illustrations and sixteen pages of stories, competitions and feature articles. The Harmsworth papers, with their emphasis on racial superiority and national destiny, were enormously popular with working-class boys and not only revered the accepted warrior-heroes of the empire but created new ones. In 1896, for example, *Pluck* published 'Dr. Jim of South Africa', a serial based on the adventures of Cecil Rhodes's creature, the appalling Leander Starr Jameson.[63]

Through words and illustrations the boys' papers created powerful myths about the nature of war and the British soldier, and, as Robert MacDonald has suggested, they translated imperial ideology into an accessible code.[64] Physical strength and the use of violence were celebrated as the essential prerequisites of Britons on the path to imperial glory. The true Briton, however, must also be ready to make the ultimate sacrifice. This is made abundantly clear by the repetition of illustrations showing last stands and soldiers freely giving their lives to save their comrades or pave the way for the eventual triumph of the race. The Havelock and Gordon myths are relevant here, with Gordon's story in particularly becoming a popular feature of the weeklies.[65] But while such sacrifice might be called for in exceptional circumstances, most writers and illustrators, trusting implicitly in Social Darwinist theory, had little doubt about the innate martial prowess of the race. In Professor J. F. Hodgetts's *BOP* story of the Anglo-Saxon conquest of Britain, the author relates how King Arthur's noble band was defeated by superior Saxon virility. Writing as a descendant of those Saxon conquerors, the good professor could unashamedly claim, 'we are invaders with no more right to the soil of Britain than we have to that of Spain . . . "English-like" we helped ourselves . . . It is the very nature of the English to claim, take and possess; the Anglo-Saxon is the lord of the earth, not by right but by the sword'.[66] It was a brutal lesson in the realities of imperial aggression that even adolescents could understand. This inherited prowess was such that even a British boy could successfully take on an enemy warrior and win (illus. 17). But the violence of imperial expansion was tempered, firstly, by denying the lethal characteristics of war – the battlefield was most often portrayed as an extension of the playing field complete with 'gentlemens' rules' – and secondly, more importantly, by emphasizing that, for the conquered, improvement was the consequence of defeat: in the wake of the conqueror came Christianity, education and economic improvement under Britannia's benign rule.

These papers undoubtedly provided thrilling entertainment for their readers on a weekly basis, but in the process they instilled powerful ideas about patrotism and duty and the excitement of war, and acted as unofficial recruiting agents. This was made patently obvious in 1912, when the Amalgamated Press *Souvenir Volume* proudly boasted, 'It has been said that the boys' papers of the Amalgamated Press have done more to provide recruits for our Navy and Army and to keep up the esteem of the sister services than anything else'.[67] Their

17 Even an English boy is more than a match for the 'Other'. From *Chums*, 1908.

romantic portrayal of war, reinforced by popular illustrations and tales of martial prowess and heroism, had considerable impact upon the young. The novelist Stuart Cloete, growing up around the turn of the century, clearly described his own introduction to the pleasure culture of war:

> . . . Another picture was Lady Butler's 'Charge of the Light Brigade'. A wonderful picture of British Hussars and Lancers sabring the Russians . . . And . . . the famous 'Thin Red Line' picture – a colourful print of the Battle of the Alma. These all hung in my nursery. Everything was glory to me . . . A child has not seen war. I did know how many of the noble six hundred died or that those fine English chargers had starved in the snows of the Crimean winter. I knew nothing of Florence Nightingale, only glory. 'La Gloire' of the French . . . I heard the clink of their spurs and the clash of steel, of bits and accoutrements. Only glory. I was taught to recite 'The Charge of the Light Brigade' . . . I used to play with my father's sword and he would tell me stories of campaigns. Of Kaffir Wars and rebellions, and colonies, and other older wars when we had fought the French; of how my great-grandfather had been captured by Napoleon . . . of my great-grand-uncle who had fought as a cornet of horse in the Battle of Waterloo when he was fifteen. Only glory.

Cloete later read the novels of Henty and the *Boy's Own Paper*, and recalled with pleasure the satisfaction derived from 'playing war' with his collection of model soldiers.[68] This highlights, perhaps, just how extensive was the pleasure culture of war, since boys not only read about the glory of war but were encouraged to act it out in their games.

Childrens' play mirrors adult behaviour. It is one way in which children make sense of the external world and it may perform preparatory functions for adult life. Undoubtedly boys have always played 'at war', and historians have traced war toys back to the ancient world. Whether this boyhood fascination with war reflects innate male aggression or is simply a social conditioning for the masculine role is by no means certain.[69] What is certain is that, in the later nineteenth century, toy manufacturers took advantage of this interest and began to mass produce a range of war toys, particularly toy soldiers. From the 1850s, realistic, solid metal figures with elaborate hand-painted uniforms were highly coveted by the sons of well-to-do families. While both Winston Churchill and Richard Meinertzhagen later testified to their fascination with model soldiers and war games, ordinary boys made do with gangs – organized as armies – and street games of war with sticks representing swords and guns.[70] However, in 1893, the toymaker William Britain and Sons developed the hollow-cast, lead alloy figure and began to mass-produce models accurately arrayed in uniforms of famous British regiments. The hollow-casting process and mass production meant that costs could be kept down to 1s (5p) a set. Britain's produced fifteen different sets in their first year, but by 1905 had over 50 sets in their catalogue and were selling five million figures a year. Many figures were produced to reflect contemporary events: in 1897 they produced a Jubilee set, and the following year made available the 21st Lancers in celebration of their famous charge at the Battle of Omdurman. During the Boer War, Britains not only produced models of the regiments and irregulars employed in South Africa, but also Boer infantry and cavalry, so that British boys could have the pleasure of 'killing' the enemy themselves.[71] Other manufacturers followed Britain's example and some marketed their models at even lower prices, like Hanks Brothers and Sutton (illus. 18), making them available to almost every boy. As Clifford Hills, the son of an agricultural worker, remembered, 'Nearly always, either in the summer or Christmas, there was a little box of soldiers which we were delighted to have, which we used to play with on the table . . . And we used to arrange 'em between us as battles.'[72]

From 1906, in order to satisfy an ever-increasing market, toymakers were also producing a whole range of war paraphernalia – model forts, artillery pieces, military equipment, uniforms so that boys could dress up as soldiers while playing war, and war games. Britains published *The Great War Game Book* in 1909, full of hints on playing war and photographs showing the 'real thing'. The elaborate coloured cover showed pictures of 'War Lords, Past and Present'

BRITISH-MADE SOLDIERS

Great assortment of Soldiers, **PAINTED AND GILT** from **4d., 6d** and **1s.** per box and upwards to any price. Also **BOY SCOUTS, ZULUS AND INDIANS.**

. Large assortment of .
METAL NOVELTIES.

Wholesale Houses only supplied.

Hanks Bros. & Sutton
37c MILDMAY GROVE, LONDON, N.
Telephone 1507 Dalston.

18 Hanks Brothers' advertisement for toy soldiers, c. 1904.

(including Napoleon and Kaiser Wilhelm II together with British generals Roberts and Kitchener) surrounded by Union Jacks and battle flags. Hanks Brothers followed suit in 1910 with *The Great War Game for Boy Scouts*, which included a board, tents and model figures. The most celebrated work on war gaming, however, was H. G. Wells's *Little Wars*, published in 1913, reflecting a passion the author shared with Robert Louis Stevenson, Jerome K. Jerome and G. K. Chesterton. Wells's intention was to produce a set of rules for gamers, and he used the imaginary 'Battle of Hooks Farm' as his example. No doubt the book sharpened the enthusiasm of many boys and young men for war games, but it also attracted the attention of some army officers, as the author intended, for the appendix offered various suggestions on how 'Kriegspiel' as played by the British Army could be more efficient.[73] What was missed at the time, and by most historians who have since cited it, is the author's real purpose, which is tucked away on the last page:

> You have only to play at Little Wars three or four times to realize just what a blundering thing Great War must be. Great War is at present, I am convinced, not only the most expensive game in the universe, but it is a game out of all proportion. Not only are the masses of men and material and suffering and inconvenience too monstrously big for reason, but the available heads we have for it, are too small. That, I think, is the most pacific realization conceivable, and Little War brings you to it as nothing else but Great War can do.[74]

While little war could be enjoyed as a pleasurable pastime, Wells hoped that it would show just how dreadful real war was, and even the marginal drawings by J. R. Sinclair have a somewhat sinister quality about them (illus. 19). At the time, however, this was ignored and war games became just another element in the pleasure culture of war through which boys could enact their martial fantasies. Such toys and games suggested to youth that war was part of normal everyday life, and helped accustom them to warlike activity. Certainly by 1914, as Grahame Dawson tells us, the National Peace Council saw such toys as helping to generate a militarist spirit among the young, and argued that 'there are grave objections to presenting our boys with regiments of fighting men, batteries of guns and squadrons of Dreadnoughts'. The Council was so concerned that it organized an exhibition of 'peace toys': miniature civilians instead of soldiers and ploughs and tools instead of guns.[75]

The visual image of the battlefield, whether the correspondent's sketch, the elaborate battle painting or the photograph, did little to disabuse the public of romantic and 'cosy' notions of war. The revival of British battle pictures, popularized by Lady Butler during the 1870s, certainly focused more on other ranks than on officers, but did little to portray the realities of combat. Butler herself was reluctant to portray actual violence in her pictures and tended to recreate the aftermath of battle (*The Roll Call*) or the preparations (*The 28th Regiment at Quatre Bras*), and many painters followed her example.[76] Even those few who did show the heat of combat portrayed a somewhat sanitized image little different from the visual material appearing in the boys' papers – many, in fact were reproduced in *Chums* or the *Boy's Own Paper*, especially the studies by Richard Caton-Woodville. Photography, which seemed to promise the perfect means of recording the realities of war, had delivered little, even by 1914. While photographers accompanied many military expeditions through the period, cumbersome equipment and slow film requiring perfect lighting limited what could be portrayed, and the most common result was carefully posed groups which had changed little in style since Fenton's work in the Crimea, as the Boer War photograph in illustration 20 reveals.

British boys were not only encouraged to take a positive attitude to war through leisure activities such as reading and play; they were imbued with martial sentiment through more formal channels. For the sons of the ruling elites, this came primarily through the public school. After mid-century and under the influence of chivalric ideals, notions of manliness and aggressive imperialism, the nature of public schools began to change. The earlier emphasis on Arnoldian intellectual and spiritual values was replaced by a new focus on physical strength, team spirit and patriotism to produce the imperial administrators and warlords

19 Illustrations from
H. G. Wells's *Little Wars* (1913).

20 British soldiers in South Africa: a typically stylized war photograph from *Harmsworth Magazine*, 1901.

the empire needed to maintain itself. As Zara Steiner has noted, 'a positive effort was made to teach upper-class boys that they would be called upon to serve their country and asked to make the final sacrifice. Success in war depended upon patriotism and the military spirit; the cultivation of both was the special responsibility of the public school'.[77] The schools themselves were influenced by the ideas of 'old boys' like Hughes and Kingsley, and in turn fed those ideas back into society through the work of the next generation of old boys – Henty, Newbolt and Kipling. The schools directly influenced very few boys; according to Honey, they probably educated fewer than 20,000 pupils at any one time; about one per cent of boys aged 15–19 in 1901, for example.[78] But not only did they educate the future elites, they also had considerable effect on the minds of many ordinary boys through the enormously popular 'school story' – the type of fiction so perceptively analysed by Jeffrey Richards.[79] Even boys who had never seen a public school were, through their leisure reading, familiar with school life and the ideals they propagated, particularly through papers like *Gem* and *Magnet*. Robert Roberts has testified to the working-class boy's addiction to school stories and concludes: 'The public school ethos, distorted into myth and sold among us weekly in penny numbers, for good or ill, set ideals and standards'.[80] These ideals were also disseminated through the public schools' missions. They provided the model for grammar schools and, in a much diluted form, even for county secondary schools after 1902.

Public schools inculcated the military spirit in a variety of ways, most

effectively through the teachings of masters like Hely Hutchinson Almond
(headmaster of Lorretto 1862–1901) and Edmund Warre (headmaster of Eton
1884–1905). Almond was an ardent disciple of imperial violence and wanted
his boys to be crusaders winning Christian victories against ignorant natives; a
neo-Spartan imperial brotherhood prepared to shed their blood to futher the
pre-ordained destiny of the race. 'The blood of heroes', he announced, 'was the
life of nations'.[81] Such ideas were promoted through the curriculum, with its
focus on classics, which instilled a romantic notion of war and sacrifice and of
the dangers of decadence, and were reinforced by the activities of cadet and rifle
corps.[82] After the invasion scare of 1859, Volunteer Rifle Corps had been formed
at Rugby, Winchester and Eton as well as at less prestigious institutions like
Liverpool College and Rossall School in Lancashire. When the French 'menace'
had passed, these paramilitary school corps remained, and after 1906 were
expanded and established in many other schools as part of Haldane's army reform
package. While some ex-public schoolboys of the period have suggested that
the corps was regarded as a 'bally sweat', in schools like Marlborough it became
'practically a whole school institution'. Nor should it be overlooked that at the
annual OTC camp in late July 1914, over 10,000 boys participated in manoeuvres.[83]
As Geoffrey Best has demonstrated, other powerful links developed between
the schools and the military and these connections became even more obvious
from the 1890s, when more emphasis began to be placed on the individual's future
military responsibility. School audiences were increasingly addressed by speakers
from the Navy League, the National Service League and by senior officers from
the army and navy. However, as Best has explained, it was Lord Roberts who seems
to have been pre-eminently influential in the militarizing of the public school:

> Roberts was touring the public schools from the moment he got back
> from South Africa. Public school records are full of him: 'Lord Roberts
> came to review the corps', 'Lord Roberts came to give the prizes'. 'Earl
> Roberts came to open the Boer War Memorial', and so on. Other military
> grandees were doing the same thing, but Roberts seems to have been
> far and away the chief of them.[84]

General Sir Ian Hamilton had been attached to the Japanese Army during the
Russo–Japanese War and, like many others, had been enormously impressed with
the Japanese spirit of self-sacrifice. Addressing the boys of Glenalmond he
urged them to show the same spirit and to, 'meet death "pro-patri", as a bride-
groom goes to meet his bride'.[85] It is interesting that Hamilton links marriage and
death, and is perhaps an unconscious reflection of the ambiguous school/military
attitude towards women and sex.[86] But public school education, as we have seen,

did more than simply instil patriotism and a sense of duty in their pupils: it also prepared them physically for war through the cult of athleticism.

In the second half of the nineteenth century, athleticism, as J. A. Mangan has pointed out, became almost an ideology. Physical exercise, and team games in particular, were seen as an ideal means of producing physical and moral courage, loyalty, cooperation and the ability to both command and obey.[87] These were desirable qualities, but in the imperialistic and militaristic climate of the later part of the century such characteristics were essential; for the qualities that made a good sportsman – daring, endurance, physical stamina, fairness and sense of duty – were precisely the qualities required for the imperial explorer, administrator and soldier. Accompanying this emphasis on the physical was the emergence of a powerful strand of anti-intellectualism; the empire needed men of character, men of action, not scholars, and this placed even more stress on the physical dimension of school life as preparation for imperial service. Many schools already bore a remarkable similarity to military institutions. A. G. Bradley, writing of his days at Marlborough, recalled, 'might alone was right. Fighting was continuous and fierce . . . The place was not wholly bad. There was a freshness and manliness about it even then, and it is not perhaps surprising that this crude and turbulent period bred a great number of most admirable soldiers'.[88]

The focus on games made this connection even clearer. It has become something of a cliche to link playing field with battlefield, but during the last decades of the century it was common to see games as the ideal training for war. Loyalty to house and school was the same as loyalty to regiment and nation, the 'good sport' was but another dimension of the chivalric ideal and the qualities of the sportsman were the qualities needed by the soldier, and by the end of the century, if not before, the 'terminology of sport had become the vocabulary of war',[89] and in popular culture war had become something of a sporting activity. Newbolt's *Vitai Lampada*, which saw the war in the Sudan as a cricket match between the house team and a rather unruly visitors eleven was not an extreme case; and many officers wrote of battle in exactly the same way. 'Football', said Raymond Gettell of Amhurst, afforded a chance for 'physical combat and satisfied the primitive lust for battle'; 'I've been snipe-shooting, and got five of 'em', said an officer after killing Fuzzie-Wuzzies in the Sudan, while General John Younghusband noted that war was 'more exciting than any of our schoolboy games'. Even at Oxford, Professor Ernest Bennett claimed that 'killing rats with a terrier, rejoicing in a prize-fight, playing a salmon, or potting Dervishes, killing is a big factor in the joy of living'.[90] Learning to kill was part and parcel of a good education, whether it was by riding to hounds or stalking deer. Much of the groundwork in the marksman's

21 Sedburgh School's cadet rifle team, 1913.

skills could be acquired as part of the school rifle team, as at Sedburgh School (illus. 21).

Conceptualizing war as a sporting activity did much to divorce it from its essential brutality and horror. What makes nonsense of the idea of war as sport, of course, is that it can only be a sporting contest when both sides are equally matched and play by the same rules, but in the wars of empire this was clearly not the case. Despite their professed love of 'fair play' and desire to 'play the game', the Victorian officer corps made little concession to the Zulus at Ulundi or the Dervishes at Omdurman, for example, when they countered the enemy's assegais and swords with modern artillery and machine guns. Perhaps Cetewayo and the Khalifa should have appealed against the decision! The public school, then, was a powerful agent of militarist sentiment. But while such establishments were for the select few, even ordinary children were exposed to much the same influences, if on a less lavish scale.

The Education Act of 1870, which created elementary school provision for all children, generated a need for standard reader texts, and these provide a valuable insight into how children were taught about the act of war. Initially, most readers were heavily influenced by utilitarian orthodoxy – self-help, the work ethic and the need for good citizenship. In 1878, however, the Education Department requested inspectors to encourage interest in the empire, and through the 1880s the imperial idea became a major theme in the curriculum.[91] Following the lead of Sir John Seeley, the most influential historian of the period, textbooks came to regard the empire as an historical inevitability, and British history as a sequence of wars that first created the nation and then built the empire, while national heroes were invariably naval or military figures.[92]

Throughout the 1890s, textbooks became increasingly racist and militaristic and justified British violence against the Other; Indians, for example, were cruel and unfit to rule themselves; by the time Lawrence was Viceroy even the natives had come to 'recognise the justice and sound sense of their conquerors', and the Opium Wars were caused because the Chinese were a 'recalcitrant people who refused to accept the benefits of European civilization'.[93] Thus wars of conquest were ultimately for the benefit of the conquered, and had been achieved because God had bestowed upon the British not only a great sense of moral responsibility, but also outstanding martial qualities. Volume Two of *Blackwoods Educational Series* (1883), for instance, had this to say of the victors of Agincourt: 'Never in the history of the world was so great a victory gained by so small a number over so large an army'.[94] Was this perchance one of young Winston Churchill's textbooks at Harrow?

While Britons were outstanding warriors and had won a mighty empire there was no room for complacency, for, as the *King Edward Reader* of 1901 pointed out, while the empire embraces people of every race, colour and religion living in freedom and prospering under the British flag, it was the 'strong arm and brave spirit' of Britons that defended that 'precious gift'.[95] Clearly, the children of the new century must be ready to take on that responsibility. The popular histories of Reverend William Fitchett were even more explicit. *Fights for the Flag* and *Deeds that Won the Empire* focus exclusively on great naval and military events, and chapters are prefaced with heroic verse by Macaulay, Henley and Kipling, while his descriptions, as MacDonald points out, 'are graphic, and seldom shrink from violence'.[96]

These ideas were also a feature of popular histories, not often used as school texts but given by parents or awarded as prizes and rewards. Nevertheless, they were a part of the approved adult world and were intended to inculcate certain attitudes in the child. Probably the most enduring and influential of these was Henrietta Marshall's *Our Island Story*, intended for young readers, which remained in print until after the Second World War. Marshall exemplified the contradictory attitude to war common at the turn of the century. In a chapter on Queen Victoria, the author tells us that war is a 'cruel and terrible thing', yet wars provide the most common topic in her version of Britain's history; it is in fact the organizing principle of the book. Apart from the odd chapter on King John and the Great Charter, and Arkwright and the beginnings of the

industrial system, almost every section focuses on a particular conflict: 'King
Edward – the Hammer of the Scots', 'George II – the Story of how Canada was
Won', and 'Victoria – the Siege of Delhi'. Indeed, Marshall concludes by telling
her young readers that the nation's story is the story of how 'Britons have fought
for freedom, and how step by step they have achieved it'.[97] In the process, of
course, the martial qualities of the British are continually lauded: Richard the
Lion Heart was a 'great soldier and loved to fight'; at Crecy the Black Prince
fought 'bravely and nobly' and even the Charge of the Light Brigade, while
mistaken, was a 'splendid show of bravery'.

   The late Victorian/early Edwardian period also saw the publication of a
considerable number of books for boys which, in an educational guise, presented
war as a romantic and noble adventure. In the introduction to Alfred H. Miles's
collection 52 Stories of the British Army, a military history of Britain for boys,
the editors tells us that the book sets out '52 links in the chain of our military
history which have helped to bind in one solid and powerful confederation
the empire upon which the sun never sets'. But, lest some accuse him of engendering a militaristic sentiment in his readers, he is careful to point out that, 'Happily,
we are able to appreciate the heroism of our soldiers, without endorsing the
policy which has too often given them employment'. Yet he goes on, 'for even
though statesmanship may be misguided and generalship may be unequal there
is always glory at the cannon's mouth . . . It is hoped that this volume will be
found stimulative of the best instincts and noblest aspirations of youth'.[98]
The same author's more ambitious text, The Sweep of the Sword – A Battle Book
for Boys, a handsome illustrated volume, relates the history of the world's wars.
In his introduction, the editor makes the same disclaimer of war: 'this . . . is not
a book in praise of war and contains, the writer hopes, nothing to inflame the
war spirit. It records the struggle of the world for the liberty which it values
more than peace . . .'[99] Yet while he also makes reference to the wastefulness of
war, what follows are such exciting accounts of wars and heroic deeds that they
guaranteed to instil in any boy the belief that war was intensely exciting and
manly, while defending the empire the most important thing they would be
called upon to undertake. Such ideas were preached with almost religious fervour
by teachers fed on Seeley and Kipling, and while ordinary children may have
had little understanding of its complexities, they 'knew the Empire was theirs
and they were going to support it'.[100]

   History was not the only subject used to inculcate boys with the war spirit.
National literature was often plundered for works extolling the glory of battle.
The most successful collection was edited by that most militant of poets, W. E.
Henley, whose enormously successful Lyra Heroica glorified war and warriors

for several generations. The anthology, with poems by Scott, Tennyson, Doyle and others, was designed to 'set forth . . . the beauty and joy of living, the beauty and blessedness of death, the glory of battle and adventure, the nobility of devotion – to a cause, an ideal, a passion, even . . . the dignity of resistance, the sacred quality of patriotism'.[101] Lest there be any doubt as to the author's intent, the richly decorated cover sported Scott's lines:

> Sound, sound the clarion, fill the fife!
> To all the sensual world proclaim
> One crowded hour of glorious life
> Is worth an age without a name.

The *Lyra Heroica* established a trend for collections of battle verse and was followed most notably by Alfred Miles's *The Imperial Reciter* (1900) and Harold Butler's *War Songs of Britain* (1903). Education, however, was not just passive. Schools also offered physical training such as military drill,[102] which inculcated discipline, responsibility and respect for authority as well as providing healthy exercise. These qualities were clearly desirable in the workers of the future, and offered the bonus of providing substantial numbers of potentially disciplined recruits for the military in times of need. By the end of the century such training was not only part of the curriculum, but had been taken out of the schoolroom and turned into a popular leisure activity for boys and young men. The Boys' Brigade, founded in 1883 by William Alexander Smith, provided the model for these paramilitary youth organizations.

Smith was a deeply religious disciplinarian and an enthusiastic officer in the First Lanarkshire Rifle Volunteers. His idea was to use military training in order to control the boys he taught at the Free Church Sunday School. As John Springhall has noted, this 'unique amalgam of militarism and evangelicalism proved so successful with the boys that Smith held meetings to popularise his scheme'.[103] By 1891 the Brigade had over 18,000 members, the majority in Scotland. Cadets wore a military-style uniform and drilled with dummy rifles. Pacifists objected to the militaristic nature of the Brigade, and in 1899 the alternative Boys' Life Brigade was formed. This concerned itself with marching, drill, stretcher drill and life-saving instruction, but despite its pacifistic claims the BLF should still be seen as a less aggressive but nevertheless military form of training.[104] During the 1890s, the Boys' Brigade inspired a number of other youth movements: some with strong religious affiliations – the Anglican Church Lads' Brigade (1891), the Jewish Lads' Brigade (1895) and even the Catholic Lads' Brigade in 1896[105] – and some under the control of the patriotic organizations. The Navy League formed a short-lived Boys' Naval Brigade (which later inspired the Sea Cadets) and the Lads' Drill Association, founded by Lord Meath in 1899. The programme of the latter, intended 'to arouse the British nation to the serious nature of the problem of Imperial Defence', advocated the systematic physical and military training of all British boys and their instruction in the use of the rifle.[106] Given the LDA's aims, it was perhaps inevitable that, when the National Service League was formed in 1902, Meath would incorporate his Association with the League, making it the youth wing of the NSL. In 1910, the Aerial League of the British Empire, formed in 1909 to put pressure on the government to develop military aviation, even created a 'Young Aerial League' for boys interested in the idea of the aeroplane as a weapon of war.[107]

By the early twentieth century, the pleasure culture of war had imbued the youth of Britain with the martial spirit and convinced them that war was natural, honourable and romantic; that on the battlefield, fighting to further the nation's cause, they would achieve their destiny. Writing in later life, William Earl Johns (1893–1968), the creator of the Biggles stories, provides us with the flavour of this turn of the century martial fervour:

> It is difficult for a boy of today to realise the enthusiasm the boys of 1900 had for anything military. Soldiers were gods. Mind you, in those days a soldier in full dress uniform was something to look at. When troops went overseas they did not creep away furtively, for security reasons, in the middle of the night. They marched through cheering crowds in broad daylight, bands playing, colours flying, flowers in their caps. We boys, decorated with as much red, white and blue ribbon as we could afford to buy, marched with them to the railway station and yelled our heads off as the train steamed out . . .[108]

From the 1890s, however, the war young Britons were being prepared for was not simply some vague undefined future struggle. The pleasure culture of war, as we shall see in the next chapter, had already identified the most likely enemy.

3 Preparing for the Great War to Come

Here's-a-sword-for-the Rat, here's-a-sword-for-the-Mole,
here's-a-sword-for-the-Toad, here's-a-sword-for-the-Badger!
Here's-a-pistol-for-the-Rat, here's-a-pistol-for-the-Mole,
here's-a-pistol-for-the-Toad, here's-a-pistol-for-the Badger!
                    Kenneth Grahame, *The Wind in the Willows* (1908)

From the 1890s, the British became increasingly obsessed with the problems of
national and imperial defence. National security had first become a popular
concern in the 1850s, when the French gained a temporary advantage in naval
technology by building steam-powered, iron-clad warships which rendered
much of the Royal Navy obsolete.[1] This supremacy of steam and steel, combined
with the perceived imperial ambitions of another Napoleon – Louis Napoleon –
was sufficient to create widespread fear of invasion. On that occasion the
menace soon passed, but for the remainder of the century further threats ensured
that national defence remained a central issue. The rapid expansion of the empire
in the last quarter of the century, for example, created a major strategic problem
and focused attention in particular on the question of how a small professional
army of around 200,000 men could defend not only the homeland against the
threat of invasion, but an empire of over twelve million square miles and one third
of the world's population against the possibility of insurrection or the ambitions
of imperial rivals. The endless military crises on imperial frontiers throughout
the period were met by a constant shuffling of military resources from one
trouble spot to another,[2] but as Britain could field only a fraction of the force
of its European rivals, pessimists looked with alarm to the day when Britain
might become involved in a Continental war. And with tension increasing
among the European powers, that day might not be far off.

The emergence of the German Empire in 1871, initially welcomed by the British
as a counter to French domination of Continental Europe, soon became a matter
for concern. The decisive success of Prussian arms during the wars of unification
forced the British to reassess their own military capability, and perhaps eased

the path for the much-needed Cardwell military reforms.[3] Certainly, Prussian
military effectiveness provided the illustrated press with the opportunity to fill
their pages with images of the deadly efficient German war machine (illus. 22).
The emergence of Germany was undoubtedly a destabilizing force in European
politics and had considerable implications for Britain. As Disraeli noted at the
time, the Franco–Prussian war was 'a greater political event than the French
Revolution . . . The balance of power has been entirely destroyed, and the country
which suffers most . . . is England'.[4] Concern gradually turned to open antagonism as the British came to believe that German expansion could be gained only
at their expense, and by the beginning of the twentieth century there emerged
a popular and powerful conviction that there 'existed a "German threat" or
"German challenge" that had to be countered'. This view first emerged among
right-wing journalists, but was soon shared by influential figures within the army,
navy, Foreign Office and Cabinet[5] and, sensationalized by the popular press,
permeated much of society. Perhaps more than anything else, it was the German
decision to create a high seas battle fleet in the 1890s which finally convinced most
Britons that Germany was indeed mounting a direct challenge to their naval
supremacy. But in this respect Germany was simply a convenient whipping
boy, for other nations were also developing their naval power, and Britain found

22 The deadly German war machine. From *Illustrated London News, c.* December 1870.

it increasingly difficult to compete. As Paul Kennedy has noted, the Royal Navy could not:

> 'Rule the waves' in the face of the five or six foreign fleets which were building in the 1890s, as it had been able to do at mid-century. As the Admiralty repeatedly pointed out, it could meet the American challenge in the western hemisphere, but only by diverting warships from European waters, just as it could increase the size of the Royal Navy in the Far East, but only by weakening its squadrons in the Mediterranean. It could not be strong everywhere.[6]

Anxiety over defence issues reached a climax during the Anglo–Boer War of 1899–1902, when British military failure combined with the hostility of the other powers to create a deep sense of unease. If the combined military might of Britain and the empire was incapable of subduing a small force of irregulars, how would the nation fare in a 'real' war against a highly trained and well-equipped European army? And given the smouldering resentment of France and Russia towards Britain and the ambitions of Germany, the possibility of such a war could not be ignored.[7]

Equally worrying was the belief that the race was in physical decline, and losing the dynamic 'racial energy' that had carried the nation to pre-eminence. Recruiting statistics during the Boer War appeared to confirm this belief. These fears had been articulated by a minority for some time, but the war brought them to the attention of a wider public and seemed to offer hard evidence in place of the vague, subjective observations of late-nineteenth-century pessimists. The eugenicist Arnold White was among the first to draw attention to the connection between physical deterioration and military failure in South Africa. During the first month of the war, he pointed out that over one-third of the volunteers from industrial cities were physically unfit to serve. He thus doubted the ability of the nation to back up their jingoistic rhetoric.[8] The point was reinforced by General Sir Frederick Maurice three years later, when he claimed that some 60 per cent of volunteers had been unable to meet the physical standard required, even though standards had been lowered at the beginning of the war. Recruits were also found to be smaller and weaker than their European counterparts.[9] The implications were clear: if the physical condition of the nation was not improved, Britain would soon be incapable of defending the empire. And, as Samuel Hynes has noted, physical deterioration quickly became associated with degeneracy and decadence, adding implications of moral decline as well.[10] In the late 1890s, these fears had been temporarily masked by the jubilant celebration of empire in 1897, but with the death of

Queen Victoria in 1901, many faced the prospect of the new century with foreboding. Elinor Glyn, that perceptive commentator on Edwardian England, summed up the prevailing mood when she wrote of Victoria's funeral procession:

> It was impossible not to sense in that stately procession, the passing of an epoch, and a great one; a period in which England had been supreme, and had attained to the height of her material wealth and power. There were many who wondered, doubted perhaps, whether that greatness could continue . . . influenced, perhaps unduly by Gibbon's *Decline and Fall* and by my French upbringing, I felt I was witnessing the funeral procession of England's greatness and glory.[11]

One aspect of this fin de siècle sense of alarm was the developing obsession with national and imperial defence, in particular fear of a surprise invasion of the British Isles by an ambitious rival, or of a future great war in Europe which might well end Britain's role as the premier imperial power. Concern over defence was not restricted to the political-military elite, but became a hotly debated issue among informed citizens and was fanned by a scaremongering press. What amounted to paranoia was manifested in a growing interest in some form of compulsory military service, demands for official investigations into the possibility of invasion, and the formation of pressure groups campaigning for ever greater military expenditure. These anxieties waxed and waned according to the diplomatic situation, and, as Reynolds has pointed out, the country did regain some of its confidence under the Conservative government of 1902–5.[12] But, as we shall see, concern could easily be rekindled by foreign military developments or perceived diplomatic crises. In popular fiction, however, the tale of the great war of the future, the unexpected invasion of the homeland, remained a constant and popular theme.

I. F. Clarke has clearly shown how popular fiction about invasion and future war emerged with Lieutenant-Colonel Sir George Chesney's enormously successful story, 'The Battle of Dorking: Reminiscences of a Volunteer', published in *Blackwood's Edinburgh Magazine* in May 1871. The author's imaginative tale of the conquest of Britain by a superior German army was a plea for military reorganization, especially the need for conscription if the nation was to achieve parity with European armies. Chesney followed an established tradition in which army and navy officers had been 'turning out pamphlets on the problems of national defence ever since the appearance of the steam ship had revolutionized the conduct of war.'[13] What was original about 'Dorking' was the presentation of his argument as fiction – an exciting and realistic narrative that made full use of the author's military expertise. The story, contrasting British weakness and confusion with Prussian 'efficiency', created widespread concern and was even attacked by Gladstone as 'alarmist'. Nevertheless, the story was reprinted in pamphlet form, translated into most European languages, reprinted in the Dominions and even adapted as a music-hall song. It inspired a number of similar works and provoked endless debate in the newspapers, as correspondents praised or damned the author.[14] Chesney's villain was Germany, but given his views on British military weakness and the recent success of the Prussians in their wars of unification, Germany was simply the most effective example for his argument. Over the next two decades, authors would focus equal attention on the French, Russians and even the Chinese as 'the enemy', depending on the ebb and flow of British diplomacy.[15] However, Chesney had, perhaps unwittingly, created the literary stereotype of the ruthlessly efficient, merciless German soldier who would haunt British popular fiction for decades to come. He had also single-handedly created a popular new sub-genre of war fiction – the tale of the great war to come – the type of story that serious authors could employ to make their case for this or that military theory or new weapon, and which the literary hack could exploit to satisfy the public demand for vicarious sensationalism. Curiously, though, many authors, despite their creative attempts to explain the diplomatic breakdown that would lead to the outbreak of war, assumed that the battlefield of the future would follow the conventions and tactics of the Napoleonic era. 'The Great War of 1892', from the illustrated magazine *Black and White*, is typical, imagining the war of the future to be still a matter of infantry squares and cavalry charges (illus. 23). But these stories of future war did more than simply entertain the reader; they reflected public concern and added fuel to the sense of impending catastrophe. The popularity of this type of fiction was such that around the turn of the century it began to emerge as reading matter aimed at the young Briton – the future defender of the nation.

The staple fare of juvenile literature – the school and adventure story or the aggressively militaristic tale of the little wars of empire – remained popular, but from the 1890s these were joined by stories taking as their theme the great war of the future. Like Henty and his fellow creators of the pleasure culture of war, many of these writers believed their role was not simply to create thrilling entertainment but to mould the nation's youth; to prepare young men and boys to play their part in the coming struggle. More than any other single influence, it was perhaps the commercial acumen and paranoia of Alfred Harmsworth (later Lord Northcliffe) which helped establish the theme of future war as a major ingredient in juvenile fiction. As we have seen, Harmsworth wanted his papers to encourage patriotism among the next generation. He almost certainly succeeded, but in the process he visited his own xenophobia and anxiety upon

23 The 'conventional' battlefield of the future, envisaged in 'The Great War of 1892, a Forecast'. From the magazine *Black and White*, 1892.

his impressionable readers. Given his tendency to use his publications for whatever cause he was currently supporting, and his incessant directives to his editors,[16] we can assume that Harmsworth publications very much reflected 'The Chief's' own views, moderated only by the latest circulation figures.

His first future war serial, 'The Poisoned Bullet', had been published in 1894 in the popular family paper *Answers*. At that time, Harmsworth was deeply worried by the developing friendship between France and Russia, neither of whom had little sympathy for Britain. Given Russian ambitions in Afghanistan and north-west India, and French resentment over the British seizure of Egypt, it was widely believed that an alliance between the two would be turned against Britain.[17] The publisher was so concerned that he commissioned the popular novelist William Le Queux to write just such a scenario.[18] While his purpose was to draw public attention to the question of naval defence, the serial was so popular with readers that Harmsworth realized it was possible to combine patriotism and profit by entertaining his audience at the same time as alerting them to potential dangers. Equally gratifying for the publisher was the praise of Lord Roberts, who congratulated him on drawing the public's attention to the threat.[19] The success of this venture encouraged Harmsworth to include such stories in his juvenile papers. Typical of these was Hamilton Edwards's 'Britain in Arms', first serialized in *Pluck* in 1897.

Introduced as 'The story of how Great Britain fought the world in 1899', the editor felt it necessary to explain that this tale of invasion by the French and Russians was:

> No wild dream of the imaginative novelist, this threat of an invasion of our beloved shore. It is solidly discussed in French and Russian – aye, and in German – newspapers . . . The Frenchman and the educated Russian talk of such a thing as coolly as we talk of sending out a punitive expedition to the Soudan or up to the hills of North-West India.[20]

The story suggests that France and Russia, jealous of Britain's empire, attempt to invade the United Kingdom. However, despite some frightening moments, the British sink the invasion fleet, and an expeditionary force under the command of Lord Roberts is sent to France. Having defeated the combined Franco–Russian armies, Roberts ensures the complete humiliation of Britain's enemies. The Fashoda incident and the war scare of the following year amply confirmed Harmsworth's worst fears about the danger posed by the French.[21] Even in 1900, while most public attention was focused on the war in South Africa, the *Boy's Friend* still continued to publish articles such as 'What Will Happen in the Next Great Naval War?', which assumed as a matter of course that the enemy would be France.[22] The Francophobia of the Harmsworth Press continued well into 1903, with a series devoted to the thrilling exploits of 'Captain Strange' – a modern privateer who waged unceasing war against the French in the 'English' Channel. In the last story of the series, Strange foiled a French invasion of Gibraltar and thus prevented the enemy gaining control of the Mediterranean.[23] But the period 1903–4 saw a lessening of the tales of future war against France, for in the light of the Anglo–French agreement of 1904, Harmsworth authors were increasingly encouraged to portray Germany as the real enemy.

Harmsworth's warnings of German intentions were strident and endlessly repeated. In 1907, a Belgian journalist reported him as saying 'we [the British] detest the Germans . . . They make themselves odious to all Europe. I will not allow anything to be printed in my paper which might offend France, but I should not wish anything at all which might be agreeable to Germany to be inserted'.[24] By 1910, an American newspaper article concluded that 'It will be a marvel if relations with Germany are not strained until war becomes inevitable as a direct result of the war scare campaign inaugurated and carried on with the most reckless and maddening ingenuity by the Northcliffe syndicate of newspapers'.[25] Harmsworth did not want a war. In the interests of peace, he even

proposed a Berlin edition of the *Daily Mail* in 1912 so that Germans might get to
understand the English mind – fortunately his plan never materialized![26] But like
many others, including such diverse figures as Admiral 'Jackie' Fisher and Lord
Roberts and the socialists H. M. Hyndman and Robert Blatchford, he was
convinced that the only way to deter German aggression was from a position
of strength.[27] The endless warnings and emphasis on war preparations in his
publications have been read by historians like Caroline Playne as clear evidence
of warmongering, but it would seem that, in reality, they were clumsy and
misguided attempts to avert the war that many believed imminent.[28] Awakening
the nation, and especially the young – the future defenders of the Empire –
to the danger was an essential element in his plan to prepare the country, and this
became policy in his juvenile papers. One of the earliest anti-German stories
which demonstrated this and showed the contribution that even the young
could make was the 1903 serial 'A World at Stake'.

The story tells how the young English inventor, Thorpe Thornhill, develops
a giant airship to be used in war. With the help of the far-sighted Lord Roberts,
Thornhill is able to begin building these 'dreadnoughts of the air' for the military.
Unfortunately, a German spy steals the design and the Kaiser orders a fleet built
to invade Britain. The enemy lands an invading army in Scotland and bombs
Woolwich Arsenal in order to destroy Britain's capacity to wage war. Although
taken by surprise, the British foil the air raid on London while Lord Roberts
marches north to deal with the invasion. The Germans are finally defeated, due
to the ingenuity of the young inventor and the military genius of Lord Roberts.
However, a postscript to the last chapter reveals that, even after peace had been
restored, Germany still bore malicious intent towards the empire, but realizing it
was not powerful enough to defeat Britain, allies itself with Russia. As the author
points out, Germany and her new ally will be sure to strike at Britain again! It
comes as no surprise, then, to find that the next issue of *Boy's Realm* contained the
first chapter of the sequel, 'A Fight for Empire'. Here the Germans and Russians
use what might be called the 'strategy of the indirect approach', as they incite
another mutiny in India in the hope of drawing all British forces to the East. Then,
unopposed, they will swoop on the homeland. The author plays upon the widespread concern of the period that Russia wanted to expand her empire through
Afghanistan and into Northern India. Needless to say, in Wray's story even the
combined military might of the two nations is insufficient to defeat Britain.[29]

From 1906, these tales of the inevitable war against Germany became a
common ingredient in juvenile fiction. Their titles are indicative: 'The Airship
Quest' (1906), 'A World at War' (1908), 'Peril to Come' (1908–9), 'The Invasion
that Failed' (1909) and 'While Britain Slept' (1911). In the last two years of peace

such stories became even more strident: 'Kaiser or King?' 'Legions of the Kaiser', 'When the Lion Awoke' and 'Lion or Eagle?' were just some of the many titles published in the Harmsworth periodicals. Most authors followed a highly predictable formula, although there were some interesting variations. 'Legions of the Kaiser or The Mailed Fist', a serial of 1914, for example, imagines a German invasion of Ireland. Clearly troubled by the threat of civil war in Ireland, the author optimistically suggests that, after Belfast has been reduced to rubble and Dublin besieged by the invaders, both loyalists and nationalists forget their differences and unite with British troops to drive out the 'real' enemy.[30] Virtually all Harmsworth serials were prefaced by the editor, and these introductions leave no doubt as to the purpose of such fiction. The editor's comments introducing 'The War in the Clouds' are typical: 'This is no wild, impossible, and fantastic story . . . "The War in the Clouds" teaches a great national lesson, conveys a grave warning for the happenings chronicled here could easily occur and shatter for all time the hopes of the British Race . . .'[31]

The Harmsworth juveniles were popular with most boys and quickly established a format that competitors had to follow. *Chums* (first published in 1892) is a good example. This quality paper, much given to tales of imperial warfare, had used stories by major writers such as G. A. Henty, Manville Fenn and Gordon Stables. Yet under the onslaught of the Northcliffe papers, by the turn of the century it was almost indistinguishable from its chief rival the *Boy's Friend* in appearance and content.

One of the leading authors of *Chums'* tales of future wars was Captain Frank Shaw. Born in 1880, Shaw later recalled his own introduction to the pleasure culture of war, watching scarlet-clad hussars on parade, hearing Tennyson's 'Charge of the Light Brigade' and Macauley's 'Lays of Ancient Rome' recited, and, of course, enthusiastic reading of Henty and Marrayatt. Looking for adventure, Shaw served as an officer in the Merchant Marine and even found time to become a regular contributor to *Chums*.[32] But his 1908 serial, 'Perils of the Motherland – A Story of the War of 1911' might well have been taken from the pages of the Harmsworth papers. Here the enemy is Russia, for the Tsar has been secretly building a great battle-fleet with which to attack Britain. The central character of the story is Jack Tremont, a midshipman aboard *HMS Cyclops*. While on patrol, *Cyclops* is surprised by a superior Russian force, and although the British fight bravely they take terrific punishment. All the officers and most of the crew are killed, but young Jack rallies a few survivors and under the leadership of the plucky youth they manage to sink one of the enemy warships. At one point during the battle Jack picks up a delayed action Russian shell from near the magazine, and without regard for his own safety hurls it overboard – an act for which he later receives the Victoria Cross. However, it is too late to save the ship. Jack collapses from his wounds, and when he regains consciousness the *Cyclops* has sunk and he is adrift on a grating. But Jack's adventures are far from over. As the author tells us, 'there on a tiny grating, suffering from a dozen wounds, was a lad who was, in the long run, to bring Britain out of the jaws of disaster into the light of crowning victory'.[33] In subsequent chapters we discover how the Russians bombard Whitehaven and Brighton, send an invading army up the River Dee and capture Chester, lay siege to Manchester and fight a great battle outside Leeds. Jack, of course, plays a major part in rallying Britons and defeating the Russians in a number of battles. The whole nation, regardless of class, is united to save the motherland. At one clash in the Midlands, the British army is reinforced by miners from Wolverhampton and chainmakers from Cradley Heath: 'men', the author explains, 'whose lives had never been pleasant, and who looked upon death as a welcome release from the hard conditions under which they lived'[34] (illus. 24). But despite Jack's valiant efforts, the willing sacrifice of the working classes and the combined wisdom of military leaders like Kitchener and Roberts, Britain is defeated. Jack and a handful of men manage to escape, vowing to free the nation from Russian tyranny, which, of course, prepares the way for Shaw's sequel, 'Vengeance of the Motherland', which started in the next issue.

From around 1910, these future war tales even began to emerge in the work of established writers of imperial and historical fiction such as Percy Westerman, Captain F. S. Brereton and Herbert Strang. In 1911, for example, Westerman published *The Metamorphosis of Midshipman Maynbrace*, a story remarkably similar to the opening chapter of 'Perils of the Motherland'. This short piece deals with a war between Britain and the 'Dual Alliance'. The hero of the tale, despite being an admiral's son, is deemed to be a 'bit of a failure'; not interested in sport or having much 'go' about him. However, when his ship is attacked by an enemy cruiser and the officers killed, it is Maynbrace who collects a motley group of survivors and orders one last attack which sinks the raider; an image that foreshadows the exploit of boy seaman Jack Cornwall at the Battle of Jutland in 1916 (illus. 25). Westerman wastes no time on explaining why war has broken out, simply that it came like a 'bolt from the blue'.[35] His purpose, apart from creating an exciting sketch of naval warfare, would seem to be to demonstrate that even a 'duffer' like Maynbrace will rise to the occasion and do his duty when the homeland is in danger.

F. S. Brereton, one of Blackie's most successful authors, wrote two full length novels in the last years of peace, *The Great Aeroplane* (1911) and *The Great Airship* (1913). While neither dealt directly with future war, they did focus on preparations

24 The workers of Cradley Heath defy the Russian invaders. From *Chums*, 1908.

for the coming conflict. In his 1911 title, Brereton tells the story of three young men who help an English inventor save his advanced aeroplane from foreign agents. In return, they are taken on a world cruise by the grateful scientist. After a series of adventures they return home where the machine, 'The Essex Ghost', is hidden away 'until . . . England has need of such a vessel'.[36] Two years later he produced a far more didactic novel, *The Great Airship*. An English engineer,

25 Midshipman
Maynbrace in
action. From
*British Boys
Annual*, 1913.

Andrew Provost, and his young nephew Joe, returning from Hamburg on a
North Sea ferry, witness a Zeppelin practice bombing against a floating target.
Carl Reitberg, a sinister fellow passenger, tells them how useful such machines
will be in the next war, and that only Germany possesses these 'dreadnoughts
of the air'.[37] Concerned at the obvious air superiority of the Germans, Provost
and Joe build a flying machine even more terrifying than Count Zeppelin's
airship. Yet the War Office, bureaucratic and conservative, cannot make up its
mind to buy it for the British Army. While they decide, the two inventors test fly
the machine over Eastern Europe, rescue a British agent from the besieged city
of Adrianople (the novel is set at the time of the Balkan Wars) and foil the plans
of a German spy. Returning to England, they present the airship to the nation.
Implicit in Brereton's novels is the notion that German ambition and jealousy

of British achievement make war inevitable. Thus the British must prepare for the struggle to come. His targets are the politicians who try to ignore the danger and the generals who fail to realize that modern technology has changed the nature of warfare. The same arguments were made far more dramatically in Herbert Strang's novel, *The Air Scout*.

The Air Scout – A Novel of National Defence imagines an attack on Australia by the Chinese. Their invasion fleet is observed by an Australian aircraft, so that the authorities have at least some warning. Nevertheless, the Chinese army lands and establishes itself in a strong position. Only when imperial reinforcements from Britain and India arrive and the Australians create a military air service are the invaders defeated. In the novel's preface, the authors plead for the authorities to rethink imperial defence in the light of new dangers and new technologies and further that:

> The ensuing story will have served its purpose if it succeeds in directing the thoughts of the boys of the present day, who will be called upon to fight our battles to-morrow, to the need for closing-up our ranks, to the benefits of training and cooperation, and to the unity of heart and mind which alone will preserve the goodly heritage our fathers have left us.[38]

This dire warning of what might happen, and the need for some form of compulsory military training for boys implicit in the story, drew a warm endorsement from Lords Curzon and Roberts, the latter noting: 'It is capital reading, and should interest more than boys. Your forecast is so good that I can only hope the future may not bring to Australia such a struggle as the one you so graphically describe'.[39] A year later, the authors were still troubled by the 'yellow peril' and the army's lack of enthusiasm for new technology when they wrote *Air Patrol: A Story of the North-West Frontier*. Here we are faced with a Mongolian invasion of India which the British find difficult to repel. Only the intervention of two young Britons and their aeroplane turns the tide. The author again emphasizes the need to reorganize imperial defence and to take note of the new weapons which technology has made available – in this case the aeroplane. As one Indian Army general claims at the end of the novel, 'what's needed to keep India safe are air patrols . . . we've got the finest navy in the world; for its size . . . the finest army; but we ought to wake up and get the finest air fleet'.[40] Criticism of the Liberal government was also made explicit in the 1912 serial, 'The War in the Clouds'. After a German invasion has been defeated, but with English cities in ruins due to aerial bombing, the British turn their attention to considering how such a disaster could have befallen them. The blame, of course, is firmly laid at the door of the political establishment, which had failed to provide adequate defence: 'what furious indignation there was in Britain against politicians who had failed to arm Britain with an efficient aerial navy'.[41] Nor were such ideas expressed only in fiction. Many of the papers attempted to show just how such an invasion could be mounted. In 1913, *Chums*, for example, demonstrated this with the aid of a party of sailors (illus. 26). Clearly then, in popular reading-matter aimed at boys and young men in the twenty or so years

26 Fear of Germany –
'How Britain might
be invaded'. From
Chums, 1913.

before 1914, a major European war appeared inevitable, and authors portrayed such a conflict as both exciting and romantic to encourage their young readers to play their part when the time came. Shaw's 'Lion's Teeth and Eagle's Claw' makes this abundantly clear, as it ends with a victory parade through London and the comment that:

> George and Roy Carrington were receiving their reward in the acclamations of the throng. Honours would be showered upon them later, but it was enough for them to know they had done their best for England. Boys, it is for you to follow in their path.[42]

Preparation for future war was almost a matter of course, although exactly who Britain would be fighting was not always clear.

Until the Anglo–French Agreement of 1904, France was believed to be the most likely enemy, and even after that date a lingering Francophobia was not uncommon. Russia, that mysterious but tyrannical empire on the frontiers of Europe, was a constant worry for some authors. 'Rule Britannia', a serial of 1905, suggested a war against Russia over the sinking of British fishing boats in the North Sea by the Russian imperial fleet on its way to the Far East. This unprovoked attack was countered by a British expedition to capture St Petersburg. In 'The Death or Glory Boys' of 1909, Lord Roberts leads yet another fictional expedition into France after a Franco–Russian declaration of war.[43] And, as we have seen, Russia was also the aggressor in Shaw's 'Perils of the Motherland'. The 'yellow peril' featured in several serials and novels. In one 1908 story the great war starts when a Japanese airfleet bombs London,[44] while in Strang's novels, *The Air Scout* and *The Air Patrol*, the enemy are the Chinese and Mongolians respectively. In 'Invaded From the Clouds', published in 1914, we even have an attack on Britain by Martians, a story that clearly took its inspiration from H.G. Wells's classic tale *The War of the Worlds*.[45] While French, Russians, Asiatics or even Martians might sometimes be 'the foe', from around 1906 the most common enemy was Germany. Interestingly, Robert Roberts later recalled that in the streets of Salford, the mock-war street game 'English and Romans' had, by 1907–8, substituted Germans for the traditional Roman enemy.[46] In Harmsworth publications, however, even when the Germans weren't actually invading Britain or inciting rebellion in the empire, they were making themselves thoroughly unpleasant in other ways.

Frequently, the most outrageous cheat in sporting stories was German. A 1911 tale by Norman Greaves, 'Flying to Victory', is typical. The hero, a young English competitor in European air races, has his machine sabotaged by a German rival who cannot beat the British lad in a fair contest. The *Boy's Realm* hero, 'Dan the Airman', faces the same Teutonic 'dirty tricks'. And while British sportsmen had to be constantly on guard against 'unsporting' Germans, 'ace' detectives like Sexton Blake and his youthful assistant, Tinker, were continually frustrating German plots and foiling the agents of the Kaiser.[47] Throughout the period, the foreign (usually German) spy made continuous appearances in school, scout and war stories. As Robert Roberts, growing up in Salford during the decade before 1914, later noted:

> Spy stories abounded. Germans who came here to 'work', we were assured, could be spotted by a special button worn in the lapel. Each man had, we believed, sworn to serve Germany as a secret agent. With this, and innumerable myths of the same sort, the seeds of suspicion and hatred were sown . . .[48]

Even the public school stories in *Magnet* and *Gem* were not immune to this spy/invasion mania, for as Turner has noted:

> The warning was sounded even in stories of Greyfriars and St Jim's, of Rookwood and St Frank's. Some Territorials taking cover near St Jim's were mistaken for Germans. One of the schoolboys said: 'It can't be the Germans. We all know they are coming some day, but they have not finished their fleet yet'.[49]

The majority of future war fiction followed a predictable format. A powerful and aggressive enemy, jealous of Britain's position in the world, strikes suddenly at the homeland or some key imperial territory. The British are often taken by surprise, suffer initial defeats but then rally for the life or death struggle. The hero of the tale is usually aged between seventeen and nineteen years old – a young midshipman or a very junior officer, perhaps, or a lad waiting to enter the military. The key factor is that he is to be found wherever the decisive events occur. These fictional heroes often come from military or naval families, or occasionally have fathers who are outstanding engineers or inventors (useful for creating the new super-weapon that will bring defeat to the enemy). Most are accomplished horsemen and athletes, but even a 'duffer' like Midshipman Maynbrace will make good when the homeland is endangered. Even those suffering a disability, like the lame seventeen-year-old Gerald Carrington in 'Lion's Teeth and Eagle's Claws', can show their mettle in these future wars. These plucky lads always know where their duty lies and will do whatever is necessary in the hour of danger, despite wounds and even the threat of imminent death. A young sub-lieutenant in a Frank Shaw serial is typical. Lying propped against a bulkhead of his warship during a hotly fought battle, he is asked by the young hero if he has been hit, 'yes' he replies, 'both legs gone – never mind! Keep fighting – keep fighting'![50] This endurance, skill and courage extended upwards, since British armies were invariably led by outstanding commanders, and here authors attempted to give their fictions credibility by using real military heroes – Redvers Buller, Kitchener or, more commonly, Lord Roberts. Other real-life heroes were sometimes introduced, and British aviation pioneers made frequent appearances. Colonel Cody, for example, builds a giant aircraft, *The Golden Arrow*, to defeat the German invaders in 'The Invasion that Failed', and fellow airmen Claude Grahame-White and Gustav Hamel take on German Zeppelins over London in the 1912 serial, 'War in the Clouds'.[51] Invasion stories always involved raids on, or sieges of, the nation's major cities – a device first employed by the Harmsworth Press to boost provincial readership. The location for the chapter was announced on the cover in bold type: 'MANCHESTER BESIEGED', 'HOW THE RUSSIANS WERE BEATEN OFF AT BIRMINGHAM' or 'THE BATTLE OF BILLERICAY – BALACLAVA WAS NOTHING TO IT'![52] More polemical authors like Herbert Strang and Colin Collins made great play of military inefficiency, the inability of a conservative War Office to consider new weapons and methods of waging war, and liberal politicians who starved the military of funds. This provided authors with the opportunity to speculate on how such weapons might be used in future warfare.

Some stories indulged in the totally fantastic, like the 'green ray' of 'The Flying Armada', which explodes ammunition with which it comes into contact; or the amazingly powerful engines driven by some mysterious substance known only to a British inventor,[53] but most writers exercised their imagination by considering how existing weapons of modern technology would be used. The great set-piece battles between dreadnought battleships were a common ingredient, and reflected the concern that other nations were beginning to challenge Britain's naval supremacy. Curiously, however, while most writers clearly understood that naval technology had changed, they assumed that tactics would remain much the same, and that naval engagements would still be fought in the style of Nelson. Submarines did make the occasional appearance, but few stories saw them as a major factor in future naval warfare. Only Jules Verne's *20,000 Leagues Under the Sea* (1869) and Sir Arthur Conan Doyle's *Danger*, published on the eve of war, suggested how devastating such a weapon could be against an island economy based on maritime trade.[54] But it was the flying machine that really captured the imagination of author and reader alike, and from 1903 they became almost standard equipment for the armies in these fictional wars. Interestingly, Harmsworth's *Daily Mail* was instrumental in creating the so-called 'Zeppelin Panics', which regularly occurred from 1908 onwards and convinced gullible sections of the public that German airships were hovering over British

cities, mapping ports, arsenals and invasion routes, and generally preparing
for the war to come.[55] In fiction, as we have seen, aeroplanes save Australia and
India from Asiatic invaders, while giant airships ferry enemy armies across the
Channel or bombard British cities. The most spectacular of these air war stories
was Colin Collins's serial, 'The War in the Clouds', but such developments were
common in all the papers and many novels. In Collins's serial the German
bombardment of British cities shocks world opinion, as it contravenes the
Hague Peace Convention of 1899 which prohibited the aerial bombardment of
undefended cities. As the author points out, such barbaric behaviour is typical
of the Germans.[56] From the turn of the century, however, young Britons could
not only read about such aerial bombardments, they could see them in moving
pictures on the cinema screen.

The first primitive moving pictures were screened during 1896 in variety halls,
circus tents and booths, but by 1906 purpose-built cinemas or converted theatres
were becoming common. For a few coppers, the audience could see actuality
films and even narrative features. And children were especially attracted to the
moving image. As John Springhall has noted, the 'cinema . . . far outstripped any
previous form of commercial entertainment in its appeal to the young'. Up to
30 per cent of total audiences were aged under seventeen,[57] and war provided
film-makers with an exciting and popular topic. The audience could watch with
awe reconstructions of the Napoleonic Wars (*The Battle of Waterloo*, 1913); the
American Civil War (*The Battle*, 1911) or even the Anglo–Boer War (*The Call to
Arms* or *The Sneaky Boer*, both 1902).[58] The studios were quick to see the audience
potential of future war stories, no doubt influenced by the success of Guy du
Maurier's hit stage play, *An Englishmen's Home*, which opened in January 1909.
The first feature that could be said to be a tale of future war was Charles Urban's
1909 production, *The Airship Destroyer*, directed by Walter Booth. The story is
told in three parts. Part I reveals the anonymous enemy's preparations: a great
airship being loaded with explosives and setting out on a raiding mission.
Meanwhile, in England, a young inventor fails to persuade his sweetheart's father
to allow them to wed. Part II begins with the enemy airship indiscriminately
bombing England. Army aeroplanes take off to intercept the raider, but are easily
destroyed by the giant airship. Part III tells how the young inventor saves
the day by using an electrical torpedo, guided by radio waves, to destroy the
enemy. Having proved his worth, he is now allowed to marry. The film was
well-produced, making use of clever models, and proved remarkably popular,
being re-released several times. Even more spectacular was Booth's 1911 sequel,
The Aerial Anarchists. Made at a time when Anglo–German relations were
apparently improving, Booth was careful not to suggest that the enemy was

German, and makes them international anarchists. Determined to bring about the fall of the British Empire, they use a giant flying-machine to attack London. Trick photography shows the destruction of St Paul's and other city landmarks, and only a sturdy young Briton piloting his own aeroplane can match the enemy and ensure their destruction. The scenes showing the destruction of St Paul's, the symbolic heart of London, must have had considerable impact on the unsophisticated cinema audiences of 1911, adding a new and 'realistic' dimension to the paper wars.[59] The Booth features were followed by a number of similar titles, *The Flying Dispatch* (1912) and *Flight of Death* (1914), for example, all of which dramatically reinforced ideas about future war first expressed in popular literature. Few films took an anti-war stance, one of the rare exceptions being Alfred Machin's *Cursed Be War!* (1913). Despite its plea for the nations of Europe to maintain the peace, the lavish reconstructions of battle and dramatic scenes of the French Military Air Service in action (illus. 27) may well have been read as yet another exciting war adventure by unsophisticated youthful audiences.

In the literature of the period, as one would expect, the more violent and sensational narratives appeared in papers catering to the lower end of the market, particularly those of the Harmsworth empire. But in the last decade of peace even middle- and upper-class papers like *Captain* ('for boys and old boys') carried similar stories aimed at the public school reader, while established and respectable novelists also began to reflect contemporary fears. It is even possible to locate Kenneth Grahame's 1908 classic children's tale, *The Wind in the Willows*, into

27 A scene from the film *Cursed Be War*, 1913.

the future war sub-genre. The climax of the story, after all, is the invasion of Toad Hall by the aggressive and sinister 'Wild Wooders' who, believing Toad is done for, exploit the situation and take over his home. Only by violent action are the normally passive Riverbankers able to dislodge the enemy and return to their idyllic existence 'undisturbed by further risings or invasions'.[60] Such stories both reflected and reinforced contemporary anxieties over national defence, and helped spread the belief among the nation's youth that the 'great war' was imminent and that they would have a major role to play in it. By 1914, boys' papers, novels and films had all played their part and 'awoken youth from sleeping'. As the editor of *Boy's Friend* smugly pointed out in late August 1914:

> For many years war serials have figured strongly in the *Boy's Friend* programme. For many years, through the medium of these serials, we have spoken the words 'be prepared'. For that we have been condemned by many people . . . But now as I sit at my desk, the grim day has come . . .[61]

Britain, however, was not alone in believing that aggressive enemies were waiting to pounce. Other nations suffered from the same anxieties, and for them the 'enemy' was often the aggressive and rapacious British. In 1890, for example, the American Henry Gratton Donnelly published 'The Stricken Nation', a story which imagined a British invasion of the United States, and includes this unflattering description of British ambition:

> Restless activity, and wanton aggression – especially when dealing with weaker powers – have been the controlling factors in British diplomacy for centuries. History presents an unbroken record of arrogant and unjust attacks on the integrity of every nation in the world where a pretext could be found for asserting English domination. This policy had been consistent and continuous, and had succeeded so well in every part of the world as to be thoroughly justified, in the eyes of the British people, by the accomplished results.[62]

And, as I. F. Clarke has demonstrated, much popular fiction published in Germany and France described the British in exactly the same way and carried the same dire warnings: prepare yourselves, the British are coming![63] Many nations, then, felt that the day of reckoning with the British was at hand.

If the pessimists were to be believed, while Britain's youth might be anxious to defend the empire, they were in poor shape for the fight – physically unfit and morally decadent. It was this loss of racial energy which Henry Rider Haggard addressed in his 1910 novel, *Queen Sheba's Ring*, 'an extended allegory on degeneracy and an insistent and contrived prompting to military awareness'.[64] Haggard, author of the immensely popular *King Solomon's Mines* (1885) and other African adventure tales, had long argued that urban living was detrimental to the health of the race, and that this had been clearly demonstrated during the South African war, when urban Britons were seemingly at a considerable disadvantage compared to their rural enemies. By the end of the decade, little had been done to address this problem and Haggard believed it his duty to sound warning bells. The novel tells how an English adventurer stumbles across two lost tribes in North Africa, the Fung, a warlike and aggressive people, and their mortal enemy, the once-great Abati, ruled over by the last descendent of the Queen of Sheba. The Abati are now a weak and degenerate people living on past glories. As the Queen explains, 'In the old days it was otherwise . . . we did not fear the Fung. But now the people will not serve as soldiers. They say it takes them from their trades and the games they love . . . therefore the Abati are doomed'.[65] The Abati, of course, are overrun and enslaved. *Queen Sheba's Ring* resonates with dire warnings of the consequences of the loss of the warlike spirit and military unpreparedness, and is so obviously a portrait of Britain and Germany that even the youngest schoolboy could not fail to learn the lesson.[66] Haggard's intentions were made clear in a 1915 entry in his diary:

> . . . How often have I been vituperated by rose-water critics because I have written of fighting and tried to inculcate certain elementary lessons, such as that it is a man's duty to defend his country and that only those who are prepared for war can protect themselves and such as are dear to them.[67]

While such fictions might help convince young men that a great war loomed upon the horizon, and pointed to the dangers of racial deterioration, other methods were needed to prepare them physically for that coming struggle.

The first organized attempt physically to prepare the youth of the nation for future wars would seem to have grown out of the Rifle Volunteer Movement of 1859. Rifle companies were formed at the universities of Oxford and Cambridge, and by the 1860s, as we have seen, many public schools had followed their example. By the early twentieth century, organized para-military youth movements and the public school Officer Training Corps (OTC) were providing basic physical training to and inculcating a militarist ideology in young Britons. Public schools were deemed to be particularly important in this respect, for here were to be found the leaders, the officers of the future. As Best has shown, a constant stream of generals, admirals and spokesmen for militarist organizations addressed pupils on speech days and other occasions, instilling ideas about duty and patriotism. Lord Roberts, Britain's most popular general, not only toured schools. He endorsed stories and novels of future war fictions, advised authors on how Britain might be invaded, wrote several books on the need to prepare for war, sponsored and opened war memorials (illus. 28) and, in November 1905, became president of the National Service League. He also found time to sponsor the rifle shooting movement for boys – a campaign which gun manufacturers were quick to exploit, as illustration 29 reveals. Roberts had for some time been concerned with the inadequacies of the British military establishment, and believed that only an army of European proportions could safeguard British interests. His views were clearly expressed as early as 1884, when he wrote: 'An Army we must have, if we are to continue as an Imperial Power or even exist as an independent nation; and if this Army cannot be obtained by voluntary means, we must resort to conscription'.[68] Lord Roberts's exhortations to his public school audiences should be seen as an essential part of his campaign to prepare the young for the great war to come. Nor was he a lone voice. In the aftermath of the Boer War, Edmund Warre at Eton advocated compulsory military training for all boys, while R. S. Warren-Bell, the editor of *Captain*, advised all his (public school) readers to learn to shoot. By 1906 he was convinced the 'great war' was imminent and suggested that 'what we need is complete army reform, and the sooner military service is made compulsory the better it will be for everybody'.[69] The ideals and attitudes inculcated through elite schooling filtered downwards through the education system and influenced society at all levels. The patriotic, militaristic elements of private education were clearly important in a period when much of society was concerned about national defence. But, given that compulsory military training was unlikely to ever become official policy, concerned individuals attempted to work through voluntary youth organizations. The most significant, and certainly the most successful, of these was the Boy Scouts, founded by R. S. S. Baden-Powell in 1908.

Baden-Powell first came to public attention during the Boer War as the heroic commander of besieged Mafeking. The hysterical national celebrations which accompanied the relief of the town in May 1900 have been well covered elsewhere.[70] What is important here is that the episode resulted in Baden-Powell becoming an icon in the pantheon of imperial heroes – a role he was happy to play, as Caton-Woodville's engraving of 1900 demonstrates (illus. 30). After the war, Baden-Powell was a national figure, the youngest Major-General in the army but virtually unemployed. It was during this period that he began to consider a scheme based on imperial scouting designed to appeal to boys and intended to improve them morally and physically. Initially, it would seem his plan was to amalgamate scouting activities into the Boys' Brigade programme.[71]

28 Popular war hero Lord Roberts unveiling a memorial to men who fell in the Boer War, Darlington, 1905.

29 Lord Roberts says 'Learn to Shoot': advertisement in *Boy's Friend*, 1908.

30 Baden-Powell, imperial hero, 1900.

However, as is well known, what emerged was a separate organization led by B-P and based on his very popular book *Scouting for Boys*.[72] The movement was phenomenally successful and boasted over 130,000 Scouts by 1912. The Boy Scouts have been subjected to considerable academic scrutiny and, as John Springhall has noted, there are several basic differences in interpretation and emphasis. However, as he suggests, 'it is clear from both internal and external criticism that it was too often identified with insular patriotism, militarism and Tory imperialism'.[73] This certainly appears to be the case if we examine the factors which influenced their creation.

Samuel Hynes has demonstrated how B-P was influenced by the anonymous 1905 pamphlet, *The Decline and Fall of the British Empire* (as were Rider Haggard and many others), which argued that urban living and the growth of luxury and indolence were undermining the ability of the British race to defend itself. This fear of deterioration is clearly expressed in *Scouting for Boys*, when the author tells us, 'recent reports on the deterioration of our race ought to act as a warning to be taken in time before it goes too far'.[74] Combined with these anxieties was fear of a future war which would come like 'a bolt from the blue', as the Royal Navy could easily be taken by surprise and a German army landed on the east coast. With much of the regular army stationed abroad, such an occurrence would be disastrous, as young Britons were physically unprepared to defend the nation.[75] B-P was convinced that the most likely enemy would be Germany. In an address to potential Territorial Army recruits in Newcastle on 2 April 1908, he said Germany was 'the natural enemy of this country' and 'could easily land 120,000 troops on the East Coast within thirty hours'.[76] This may well have been exaggerated to encourage recruiting, but it represented a major concern of many at the time. Baden-Powell's ideas did not remain static and he was prepared to moderate his views, but militarism was a powerful element in the Scout programme. Certainly Scouts were clearly seen as a paramilitary movement by contemporaries.

John Springhall has drawn attention to the considerable number of National Service League officers involved in the Scout movement; and it is significant that *Scouting for Boys* opens by emphasizing that 'Every boy ought to learn to shoot and obey orders, else he is no more good when war breaks out than an old woman'.[77] Chivalry was an equally important factor in scouting, and, as we have seen, chivalry was essentially a romantic but militaristic code of behaviour.[78] St Loe Strachey, editor of the *Spectator*, saw the movement as 'military education', and Birmingham Scouts, told in 1909 that they were 'Peace Scouts', protested they had always understood they were being trained to be of use to the nation in time of war.[79] The *Boy's Own Paper* referred to Scouts as 'little soldiers', and the 1909 *Boy's Herald* serial, 'A World at War', was advertised as 'specially written to appeal to cadets, Brigade boys and Scouts'.[80] A report of the 1911 Scout review by the King in the *Daily Express* reported, 'THE EMPIRE'S HOPE. VAST ARMY OF BOY SCOUTS REVIEWED BY THE KING. The great lack of the mass of our people is discipline. We have nothing to do for us what universal military training does for our neighbours'. The implication is clear – the Boy Scouts will correct this deficiency. The publisher Ward Lock included scouting stories in their *Wonder Book of Soldiers*, and around 1910 the Hanks Toy Company produced *The Great War Game*, advertised as 'war games for Scouts'.[81]

Although the militarist youth organizations recruited poorly among the children of the lower working classes – few in Robert Roberts's working class suburb could afford the fifteen shillings for a Scout uniform[82] – their message of preparation did filter down through society and it is clear that Boy Scouts, like the various cadet forces, were in the mainstream of preparing the nation's youth for military service on the imperial frontiers and for the great war to come. Historians have sometimes suggested that boys, particularly from the working classes, tended to join such organizations simply for the recreational opportunities they offered, and had little real interest in the underlying ideologies.[83] In the final analysis it does not matter why boys joined; the important point is that once enrolled they were exposed to a constant diet of patriotic nationalism and pro-war propaganda. However, as Tim Jeal has argued in regard to Boy Scouts, although *Scouting for Boys* resonates with fear for the future of the British Empire, the 'kindliness and generosity advocated as the basis for good behaviour was not simply included . . . as an expedient facade to conceal the Movement's true purpose'.[84] These characteristics were simply part of the chivalric warrior's code, and B-P was nothing if not a romantic who looked back longingly to a simpler and more adventurous age. The Scouts should be seen, then, as a multi-faceted organization which reflected Edwardian anxiety about

31 British youth stands ready on the eve of the Great War.

physical decline, loss of racial energy and the mounting challenge from European rivals. By 1914, a surprisingly large proportion of the nation's young men had absorbed some form of military training through the cadet forces, para-military youth movements or, from 1908, through the Territorial Force. What they had in common was a determination to play their part when the great challenge came. Illustration 31 shows just such a lad in a pose remarkably similar to the seemingly inumerable portraits so admired by families sending their sons off to war in 1914.

Clearly, then, young Britons exposed to such a constant diet of propaganda could hardly fail to absorb the idea that the nation was poised on the brink of disaster; that a major war was inevitable and that Germany posed the single, most dangerous challenge to the continued well-being of the empire. Such propaganda alone cannot explain why Britain went to war in 1914, but it does go some way to explain why the nation slipped so easily into a major European conflict, and why that war was greeted so enthusiastically by so many young men. As Robert Roberts has explained:

> For nearly half a century before 1914 the newly literate millions were provided with an increasing flow of fiction based on war and the idea of its imminence . . . Popular fiction and mass journalism now combined to condition the minds of the nation's new readers to a degree never possible before the advent of general literacy. In France and Germany, too, writings in the genre were equally successful in stimulating romantic conceptions about the carnage to come. When the final cataclysm did arrive, response to such ideas set the masses cheering wildly through the capitals of Europe. 'Der Tag'! – The Day – was here at last! They could hardly wait.[85]

August 1914 was simply the fulfilment of the expectation of war. It was what the youth of the nation had been prepared for, and as such it was welcomed as an end to uncertainty and the opportunity to take part in the 'great adventure'.

4 Paths of Glory: 1914–18

. . . [W]e are beginning to look forward to the future. The war will end some day, and then, what then? A new army will come back from the fight . . . What a welcome we will give them when they come! How the great hall will be hung with flags, and the homely hearth will be gay for once . . . But not all are coming – some have fallen in the fight, and sad hearts will weep in silence, and lives will seem worthless now they are no more. But it will not all be darkness even to those who mourn, for it is great to die with honour and the service of one's country. And many a home will cherish the memory of its hero, and look forward to a meeting by and by. And Britain will emblazon their names on its roll of honour – this man and that man has died for her.

Reverend W. E. Sellers, *With Our Fighting Men* (1915)

The First World War, as Gerard DeGroot has pointed out, was a 'conflict about empires, capitalism, trade and food, not about democracy, honour, civilization or the defence of trusted friends.'[1] For Britain, the German invasion of Belgium provided a noble excuse, a cause far more satisfying than the sordid business of economics or territory, and most Britons were content to accept Prime Minister Asquith's justification of the war as a moral crusade, in which Britain's role was to play the champion of justice and honour:

I do not believe any nation ever entered into a great controversy – and this is one of the greatest history will ever know – with a clearer conscience and a stronger conviction that it is fighting, not for aggression, not for the maintenance even of its own selfish interest, but that it is fighting in defence of principles the maintenance of which is vital to the civilization of the world.[2]

Such sentiments became common in juvenile literature, and within days of the declaration of war, writers were busy explaining to their youthful readers just why the nation was at war. One of the earliest was Elizabeth O'Neill's *The*

War, 1914: A History and an Explanation for Boys and Girls, published in the autumn of 1914. Her justification for war is worth quoting at length, for it neatly summarizes how most authors at that time dealt with war origins as a chivalric struggle against the forces of evil:

> The war of 1914 was different from other wars in this, that no one but the Germans can say that Germany was in the right. The Allies, as all the world knows, were fighting for justice and right against a country and an emperor who seemed almost mad with pride. The soldiers of the Allies went out to battle not as soldiers have often gone to war, because it is the business to be done, but rather like the knights of old, full of anger against an enemy who was fighting unjustly, and full, too, of a determination to fight their best for justice and right. This is one more reason which has made the Great War of 1914 so wonderful a thing.[3]

For the writers of fiction, F. S. Brereton summed up the overriding cause in his first war novel. It was a war, he claimed, that the Germans had been planning for years, a war that would make them 'masters of the world', and the 'fingers of the mailed fist were already stretched out to snatch in vast possessions'.[4]

In the same way that these writers had believed it their duty to inculcate boys with the martial spirit before 1914, so they now believed it their duty to encourage recruitment for this just war. To their credit, those authors young enough to serve did set an example. Brereton rejoined the Royal Army Medical Corps, Percy Westerman, despite poor vision, wangled his way into the RNAS, as did Frank Shaw, while many others served in some capacity. These authors were not part of the literary establishment recruited by Charles Masterman in 1914 for the war propaganda group at Wellington House,[5] but private individuals who believed in the rightness of the cause – the 'Old Men' who would later be condemned by Wilfred Owen and others for sending the 'Young Men' to their deaths. However, during the first months of the war, few young men needed much encouragement to enlist. As memoirs and biographies clearly reveal, almost everyone wanted to take part in the 'great adventure'. The worst fear among the young was not of being killed or maimed, but that the war would end before they got to the front.

In this context, it is something of a cliche to refer to Rupert Brooke and his enthusiasm for an adventure he believed would rescue him from the dullness of everyday life. But the simple truth is that he really did speak for most of his generation. Robert Graves, for example, was 'outraged' to read about the alleged German atrocities in Belgium, and even though he discounted 'twenty per cent', he enlisted and began training on 11 August.[6] When the autumn term began at

Charterhouse (which Graves had recently left), Huntly Gordon recalled that many of the senior boys were missing; they had 'added something' to their ages in their determination not to 'miss out on the fun'.[7] Julian Grenfall, much given to 'thrashing servants' and with a passion for killing anything that moved, volunteered right away and in October 1914, after his first taste of combat, wrote home, 'it's a great war, whatever. Isn't it luck for me to have been born so as to be just the right age and just in the right place'.[8] This same enthusiasm held for young men from less exalted backgrounds. George Coppard, sixteen years old in August 1914, remembered the newsagents' placards screaming out from every corner, the military bands and martial music and, 'as if drawn by a magnet, I knew I had to enlist right away'. Lying about his age, he enlisted on 27 August.[9] A. Stuart Dolden, a solicitor's clerk in London, was forced by his employers to wait until November before joining up, and was then 'absolutely shattered' to be turned down because his chest measurement was two inches under regulation. Persuading his father to pay for a course of physical training, he was accepted several weeks later.[10] Such accounts could be repeated endlessly, and between August and December 1914 almost two and a half million men volunteered for the new armies.[11]

For those too young or too frail to enlist, reading about the war was probably the next best thing. As Huntly Gordon remembered, 'our curiosity to know what it would be like to be under fire had to be satisfied from the novels of G. A. Henty and Captain F. S. Brereton'.[12] Fiction, together with visual illustrations and popular films, thus played an important role as part of the unofficial propaganda effort to mobilize the nation and prepare boys for future service. Before 1914, authors had found their inspiration in the little wars of empire, now they focused on the fighting in Flanders, the Middle East or in the skies over the Western Front, but they still portrayed war in exactly the same romantic and heroic terms. To show how the Western Front was represented for the youth of the nation, F. S. Brereton, one of Blackie's most successful authors, is a useful example. Despite rejoining the army on the outbreak of war, Brereton still managed to publish some twelve novels between 1915 and 1919 dealing with almost all aspects of the war – Gallipoli, Palestine, the Eastern Front and the Royal Flying Corps (RFC). Among these was a series of four novels which sequentially tell the story of British experience on the Western Front. Their central character is a young English officer, Captain James Fletcher, and it is through his eyes that Brereton recreates the war experience for his young readers.

The first novel, *With French at the Front*, published in early 1915, opens in Berlin on the day war is declared, Fletcher is attached to the British Embassy and has to arrange the evacuation of the staff. This means a hazardous journey to the station through the hostile German crowd that surrounds the building. Jim emerges, carrying his swagger-stick and calmly smoking a cigarette. As he walks through the crowd, the author takes the opportunity to compare this lithe young Briton with the overweight and hysterical Germans: 'Jim had the head and shoulders of our islanders. A small, fair mustache set off a handsome face which was resolute and firm, and had none of the floppy stodginess so often found among the beer-drinking subjects of the Kaiser.'[13] Jim displayed no fear, refused to hurry and never looked over his shoulder, for 'he had nerves of steel'. He successfully arranges the departure of the embassy staff, but at the last moment is separated from his companions. After various adventures behind enemy lines, he eventually manages to return to England and resumes service in the RFC. He carries out a number of observation flights over the front and at one point, serving as a liaison officer, finds himself in the trenches facing a German attack. As the enemy advances, a young English subaltern, already wounded by a shell blast, climbs on to the parapet of the trench:

> 'Boys', he shouted, and at the call the men on either side sat up and cheered him. 'Boys, for the sake of old England, for the sake of the regiment, you'll hold 'em. Fire, boys!'
>
> There was a choking cough, while a shudder ran down his frame. The subaltern collapsed into Jim's kindly arms, and lay white and motionless at the bottom of the trench. He was dead; another victim of the Kaiser's murderous ambition, one more count against the German nation.[14]

But his gallant example is an inspiration, and the Tommies, 'the thin khaki line of heroes, the cool, calm, cheery sons of Empire', fight like demons, beating back the German attack. Using the noble death of the young officer, Brereton then treats us to a lesson in duty and sacrifice. 'It's the price we shall have to pay . . . We'll take on our troubles like men – patiently and with courage – and we will remember'. Here the war is a glorious experience, a romantic adventure. British soldiers are good-humoured, plucky, eager to get into the fight, and happy to give their lives for King and Empire; a sentiment captured perfectly by an illustrator in *Young England*: with his dying breath, the golden youth scrawls a message of encouragement to his comrades (illus. 32). The Germans, by contrast, are dull, robotic and barbarous. *With French at the Front* is typical of the manner in which the war was portrayed in both juvenile and adult literature; justifying and romanticizing the war at a time when the nation was still dependent on voluntary enlistment. Another 1915 novel, Escott Lynne's *In Khaki for the King*, made the propaganda function of such fiction even more obvious. The author opens the novel with a prefatory letter, which ends:

32 A 'Message from the Trenches'. From *Young England*, 1916.

It is up to you boys of today to see that a similar danger never threatens your glorious Empire again. Those of you who have not yet donned khaki, see to it that when you are old enough you train yourselves to defend your homes, your mothers, your sisters, your country, all that you hold dear ... And believe one of those whose proud privilege it has been to wear the King's uniform, that those days you will spend in khaki or blue will be among the fullest and happiest of your lives.[15]

The second novel of the series, *Under French's Command*, published in early 1916, deals with the events of 1915 down to the Battle of Loos, which provides the story's climax. Brereton tells us that the battle started with a 'gigantic' bombardment of the German lines, then 'thousands of warriors leaped from their trenches and made for the Germans'. They 'stormed' across No Man's Land and found the German front line 'unrecognizable, shattered, blasted and filled in with the violence of the explosions . . . As for the men who had been in them, they had ceased to exist'.[16] The 'much-vaunted defences of the Germans . . . were captured'. If the enemy had not had other lines of defence, Brereton tells us, the Allies would have broken through and won the war on the Western Front. According to the author, then, the battle was a success, with the British advancing several miles and taking over 25,000 prisoners.[17] It was 'breathless business' for the khaki heroes! This account, unfortunately, does not accord with the reality. The bombardment failed to destroy the German defences and British casualties were high, over 60,000 dead. It was, wrote Liddell Hart later, a battle which 'failed to improve the general situation in any way and brought nothing but useless slaughter of the infantry.'[18] Yet this was the event which Brereton suggests was the beginning of the end for Germany. Interestingly, the author makes no reference to the British use of poison gas during the battle, a weapon that was entirely inappropriate for his plucky, 'sporting' Britons.

A similarly idealized view of the 1916 offensives is central to the author's *Under Haig in Flanders*. Here Brereton paints a cosy picture of life at the front, where good-hearted Tommies feed on 'frizzling bacon, not to be beaten anywhere, bread that might have graced the table of a Ritz hotel, and jam that would have been the envy of any housewife.'[19] Interestingly, this domestic view of the trenches was featured in a number of official photographs. Before the Battle of the Somme, the guns poured a tornado of bursting steel on the elaborate and often concreted defences devised by the Germans, 'ripping up whole miles of wire entanglements, demolishing trenches, burrowing even to the depths of deep dugouts and annihilating the defenders.'[20] Sturdy British heroes 'tingling with keenness' lob bombs at the Germans as if they were cricket balls and wait for the 'off'. Their advance is cool, orderly, and, although they are unable to hold all their objectives, the battle is largely successful. Brereton tells us that:

> [T]he Battle of the Somme found our soldiers ready and eager for conflict, and thoroughly aware of the fact that it was not ground that they were fighting for, not so much the capture of this village or that, but that they were fighting to break the strength of the German army, to drive in hard blows which should damage his strength and his 'moral'.[21]

There is a curious tension here between the battle-winning acts of individual heroism which were the hallmark of Edwardian juvenile fiction, and Brereton's realization that the Somme was actually the first major battle of attrition – a slogging match of heavy artillery, bombs and machine-gun bullets, where the

British High Command attempted to inflict more casualties on the enemy than its own troops received. Nevertheless, Brereton's young men still do heroic things and, according to the novel, 1 July paved the way for later victories: it was 'a triumph for the Allies and a bitter blow to our ruthless enemy.'[22] In reality, the first day of the Somme was one of the most disastrous days in British military history. The prolonged bombardment failed to destroy the wire entanglements or the German defences and British troops, advancing at walking pace – as they had been ordered to do – were cut down in swathes. There were 21,000 dead and 35,000 wounded on that day alone.[23] Brereton's war was a war of adventure; a romantic escapade that no true Briton would want to miss. But, as Hynes suggests, such fiction performs an important didactic function: it states the British case. So the novels, besides being exciting adventure stories, are 'instant history, explaining how England got where she was . . . and who is to blame.'[24]

Brereton's representation of the Western Front was not exceptional in juvenile fiction. Percy F. Westerman, another prolific writer of juvenile fiction (20 novels published between 1915 and 1919), reconstructs the experience of war in exactly the same manner. His *A Lively Bit of the Front*, published in 1919, opens in 1916 and tells the story of two young New Zealanders. Dick and Malcolm are both seventeen years old and desperate to get into 'the fight'. A letter from Dick's older brother, already serving on the Western Front, tells them, 'We're having a thundering good time with plenty of excitement . . .'[25] This convinces the boys they are missing the 'adventure of a lifetime'. Lying about their age, they enlist in the New Zealand Rifles and arrive on the Western Front in time to take part in the Battle of Messines Ridge. Westerman, writing in 1918, does give us a more realistic description of the battlefield – rats gnaw at the soldiers' puttees and 'The atmosphere reeked . . . traces of poisonous gas, pungent fumes from bursting shells, while the report that a dozen dead huns had been buried on the floor of the trench seemed to find definite confirmation.'[26]

But even these wretched conditions fail to dampen the enthusiasm of the New Zealanders. Just before going into action, both lads admit to being frightened (a major breakthrough, plucky colonials admitting to fear!), but as soon as the action begins those fears are 'thrown to the wind':

> The air was heavy with suffocating smoke; fragments of shells were flying . . . shouts, oaths and curses punctuated the crash of steel and the rattle of musketry, as men in their blind ferocity clutched each other's throats and rolled in mortal combat on the ground.[27]

After the battle, which is, of course, a glorious Allied victory, Dick and Malcolm discuss their experiences, the comrades who have 'copped it' and the immediate future. Although friends have been killed or wounded, the ANZACS have acquitted themselves with honour and Malcolm sums up the dominant attitude of the young warriors: '[I]t'll be worse before the final battle', he tells them, 'but I wouldn't miss it for the world!'

So even in 1918, after four years of battle, Westerman, like Brereton, can still portray the war as a great adventure, a not-to-be missed experience for the young combatants.[28] And we find exactly the same images of the Western Front in the novels of Rowland Walker, Herbert Strang, Alfred Bowes, Robert Leighton and many others, as well as in the short stories and serials published in boys' papers like *Chums*, *Boy's Own Paper* and *Young England*. Clearly, Brereton was not an exception. As one would expect, these novels were persuasive propaganda intended to create attractive heroic stereotypes, role models which would inculcate young Britons with a sense of duty and honour and, if necessary, persuade them to make the ultimate sacrifice. This was equally true of battlefields outside Europe.

The Dardanelles expedition of 1915, for example, resonated with chivalric and heroic overtones; what could be more appropriate for a generation of young men brought up on the deeds of ancient warriors than a crusade against the Turk within sight of the plains of Ilium? 'It's too wonderful', exclaimed Rupert Brooke, when he heard that his battalion was to be part of the Gallipoli landings, and wondered if he would do battle on the same hallowed ground where Achilles and Hector had fought their epic duel.[29] Alas, poor Brooke died of blood-poisoning before the first shots were fired. It was also appropriate that the soldier-poet, General Sir Ian Hamilton, should preside over this modern Greek tragedy. The expedition, brainchild of that romantic, Winston Churchill, was intended to force the Dardanelles, take Constantinople and knock Turkey out of the war. The first landings were made on 25 April 1915, but the Allied advance was held by the Turks and another stalemate ensued. Realizing their objectives could never be achieved, the Allies evacuated the peninsula in January 1916.[30] At the beginning, of course, it was all terribly romantic and exciting, and the first novels and stories about the campaign began to emerge in the summer of 1915, but authors, understandably, had only a vague idea of what it was actually like on the peninsula or how the campaign had ground to a halt.

The Fight for Constantinople, by Percy Westerman, was published just five months after the first landings. Dick Crosthwaite, a young sub-lieutenant aboard the battleship *Hammerer*, is overjoyed at the news that the ship is going on the expedition. 'Glorious news! . . . We're off to the Dardanelles. We'll have the time of our lives', he tells his fellow officers, echoing the sentiments of Rupert Brooke.[31] Dick has various adventures, including bombarding the Turkish defences and a raid on an enemy gun emplacement. He is finally captured, but escapes. The novel was published before the campaign ended, but Westerman finishes on a typically optimistic note. Wounded after a daring escapade and recovering back aboard *Hammerer*, the ship's surgeon tells the Captain, 'He'll be up and fit for duty before we force the Dardanelles, you mark my words. He'll be in at the death when we take Constantinople.'[32] In Herbert Strang's *Frank Forrester: A Story of the Dardanelles*,[33] the hero of the title is the son of a English merchant living in Constantinople. When Turkey declares war, young Frank is arrested as a spy, but escapes. In Egypt, he joins the expeditionary force as an interpreter and takes part in the landings at Anzac. But again we are given very little detail of the campaign.

Only in T. C. Bridges's *On Land and Sea at the Dardanelles* do we gain some idea of conditions on the peninsula. This is a curious work, well-illustrated with official photographs of the campaign, but derivative of earlier novels. Bridges's hero, the young Ken Carrington, enlists in Egypt and becomes a translater. At Anzac, young Carrington is desperate to get at the Turks and performs stout work with the bayonet; one Turk is even 'spitted like a fowl'.[34] There are descriptions of the trench system and lots of special missions and dangerous escapes, and the novel ends on the same optimistic note when Carrington 's captain tells him, 'It will take more than a month to open the Dardanelles. Those who know say it will take three months at least to beat the Turks.'[35] But after the final evacuation of British troops from Gallipoli, the subject lost its attraction for storytellers, and it was an article in *Young England* that completed the story. The author, Guy Waterford, admits that the Allies failure to force the Dardanelles was 'hugely disappointing', but after briefly describing the campaign, concentrates on the magnificent gallantry of the troops and the brilliance of their commanders who achieved such a successful evacuation. His final words:

> So ended the Dardanelles campaign. It closed with a feat of naval and military management which was a veritable miracle. Disaster had been predicted. Even the optimists had feared a heavy toll in men killed and wounded and precious freights sunk. Yet all had been accomplished in orderly and masterly fashion, without the loss of a single man.[36]

But however it was dressed up, the debacle of Gallipoli was still a defeat and best ignored by writers looking for successful tales of British arms. The campaigns in Mesopotamia and Palestine, however, were far more deserving of the phrase 'the Last Crusade', for not only was the Ottoman Empire defeated, but Jerusalem was liberated by a Christian army.

Mesopotamia, at the head of the Persian Gulf, was of considerable strategic importance for the Allies, and following the Turkish declaration of war the

Sixth Indian Division was sent to Abadan to protect oil installations. However, the attempt to advance up the Tigris and capture Baghdad resulted in failure, and the Allied force was besieged at Kut al Amara. Forced to surrender to the Turks in April 1916, the Allies suffered a bitter blow. But the following year, another force under Sir Stanley Maud began a relentless advance up the Tigris and finally captured Baghdad in March 1917. Meanwhile, the British defence of the Suez Canal led to the Arab Revolt, and a guerrilla war against the Turks masterminded by that most romantic hero, T. E. Lawrence, and an advance on Jerusalem by General Sir Edmund Allenby. He entered the Old City on 9 December 1917, the first Christian conqueror of the Holy Land since the Crusades.[37] In September 1918, Turkish military power west of the Jordan was crushed at the Battle of Megiddo (Armageddon) on 21 September 1918, and the Ottoman Empire capitulated at the end of October. The war in the Middle East was largely a war of movement, cavalry patrols, and small engagements in exotic and romantic locations against a non-European enemy. In spite of Gallipoli and Kut, it was above all successful. It was the type of warfare far more familiar to novelists raised in the imperial tradition. Even the cast was much the same – plucky Britons, sturdy colonials (including the glamorous Australian Light Horse), Indian Divisions and a non-European enemy. Little wonder, then, that writers of juvenile fiction found it so fascinating.

The considerable part played by Australian troops was the subject of Joseph Bowes. In a sequence of three novels (*The Young Anzacs*, *The Anzac War Trail* and the *Aussie Crusaders*, 1918–20) the good Reverend provides a romantic and highly partisan account of their heroic deeds. Others titles included Herbert Strang's *Carry On* (1917) and four novels by Brereton.[38] These novels portrayed the campaign against the Ottoman as a war of liberation. In the best British tradition, the empire is fighting not for selfish gain, but to deliver subject peoples from the terrible Turk. This idea is probably best expressed by Brereton in *With Allenby in Palestine*. After the triumphant delivery of Jerusalem by the 'new' crusaders we are told:

> Christendom discovered itself once more, after long weary years, in possession of Jerusalem, the sacred city, while the down-trodden peoples, in Turkey, in Palestine, and in Mesopotamia, breathed freely after years of subjection . . . Christians, Armenians, Arabs, Mohammedans, and Jews greet the arrival of the British with acclamation.[39]

The diverse peoples of the region also provided the opportunity for authors to exercise their views on race. The Turks get off surprisingly lightly; they fight bravely and observe the rules of warfare. Most animosity is reserved for their

German 'masters', and it is clear the consensus view was that 'Johnny Turk' had been led astray by the devious agents of the Kaiser. However, the other races with whom the Allies come into contact are less commendable. Strang has 'villainous Kurds' and 'sly' and 'oily' Arabs, while Bowes provides a number of incidents where straight and manly Aussies are compared with childlike, superstitious and untrustworthy Bedouin: and all heap scorn on the 'Levanters', the mixed-race traders of the area.[40] Nevertheless, writers did need to exercise some caution with racial comment, because in the confused political situation of the Middle East and the Arab Revolt it was not always clear who one's allies were. But if the war in Mesopotamia and Palestine resulted in a decisive victory, it was a victory that had required great effort. This highlighted one of the nation's constant problems – the need to encourage everyone to play their part in the war effort.

Conscription was introduced in Britain in January 1916 for those over eighteen years of age. But boys and younger men could still contribute to victory. The Boy Scouts provided one channel for service through which they could demonstrate their patriotism and serve the cause. Whatever claims Scout leaders later made regarding the peaceful nature of their organization, Baden-Powell's primary intention was to prepare the nation's youth for the future wars of empire. Alongside the helping hand, the good deed and the study of woodcraft, Scouts were trained in many of the skills that would be required in frontier warfare. The emphasis on fun, good fellowship and basic military training proved irresistible to many boys, and by 1914 there were over 150,000 enrolled Boy Scouts and some 12,000 Girl Guides.[41] While the coming of war in August 1914 was a vindication of the anxieties of such men as Baden-Powell (who had made a major contribution to that 'will to war' which was such a powerful force in the last decade of peace), the future of the movement was by no means secure. After 1909, the Secretary of State for War, R. B. Haldane, had mooted the idea of including compulsory cadet training for all boys in his package of military reform. Such a decision would, at worst, mean the end of the Boy Scouts, and at best could only result in Baden-Powell losing control of the movement to the War Office.

As a European war appeared inevitable, the Chief Scout fought a series of rearguard actions, publicly insisting that scouting was actually better training for the military because Scouts were taught to use their initiative rather than the mechanistic skills inculcated through cadet training. In early August 1914, in order to forestall government action, B-P put the Boy Scouts at the service of the government. Thereafter Scouts enthusiastically guarded reservoirs, telephone and telegraph lines and generally kept guard against German spies and saboteurs. Many Scouts acted as messengers for government departments, the Red Cross and the Post Office. On 6 August, the Admiralty asked for 1,000 boys to assist the

Coastguard in watching for an expected German invasion of the east coast, and by the end of the war more than 23,000 Scouts had served in this capacity. Scouts also collected money for establishing 'Scout Huts' run by the boys themselves as recreation centres for men of the British Expeditionary Force. The first of these was opened at the BEF base camp at Etaples, in December 1915. Scouts certainly played their part in the war effort, and as Ascott Hope put it in a 1915 book for juvenile readers, 'At home, we know how the Scouts eagerly came forward to do what they could'.[42] Interestingly, Baden-Powell's 1915 poster, 'Are YOU in this?' (illus. 33), shows Scouts in the middle ground between the home front and fighting front; a link between the worker and the warrior.

However, despite their enthusiastic participation in war work, the movement was never entirely safe during the war. There was always the possibility of the government introducing some form of compulsory military training for boys. It was essential that, if their survival as an independent organization was to be assured, Boy Scouts must be seen to be as patriotic, well-prepared for war and enthusiastic for battle as those boys who had been through some form of cadet training. One highly effective channel for scouting propaganda was the boys' papers. Many of these, like *Chums*, *Boy's Own Paper* and *Young England*, had established regular scouting columns well before 1914, both to proselytize for the movement and to provide scouting tips and news. Now, however, with the independence of the Scouts under threat, propagandists began to focus upon how well Scouts had been prepared for war and on their heroism under fire. The story of Yves Meval, a sixteen-year-old French Scout who had procured an army uniform and rifle and joined the army for the first Argonne campaign was widely reported. Despite wounds in the leg, arm and eye, Meval fought until he collapsed and was awarded the Military Cross for his bravery.[43] Many of these stories were later published by Ascott Hope in his propagandist volume for young readers, *The School of Arms*.

Hope relates several heroic stories of Belgian Scouts during the German invasion of 1914, but his main focus is on British Scouts, such as those who were wounded while serving with the Whitby Coastguard station when it was shelled by a German warship. Special praise was lavished on the three Scouts killed in a similar attack at Hartlepool. Here the author quotes the local Scoutmaster, who claimed the boys 'never flinched from their duty' in helping children and the infirm to safety: 'I felt quite proud of the Scouts, they seemed to think only of duty; heedless of the bursting shells all round them they really behaved like seasoned veterans under fire – quite cool, calm and collected, and anxious to do all they could to help in time of trouble.'[44] Such reports of Scouts under fire provided a common propaganda theme in the boys' papers during the war, but

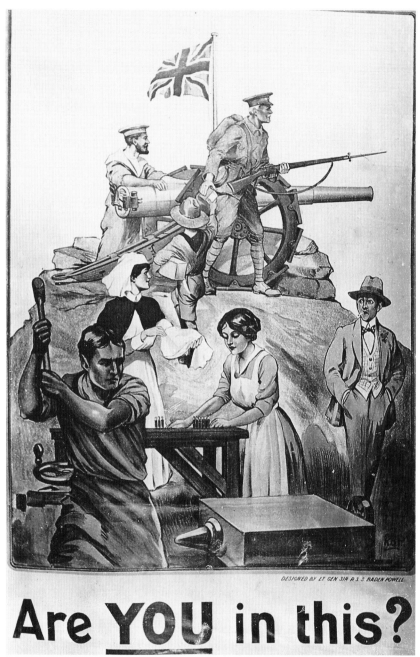

33 'Are YOU in this': a 1915 poster designed by Baden-Powell and emphasizing the role of Scouts.

few scouting enthusiasts went as far as 'Blue Wolf', the Scout correspondent of *Young England*, who, in 1915, suggested the nation should give thanks to God, 'that he had permitted the Boy Scout Movement to be started and to develop for seven years to assist the country, in some measure, at any rate, to be prepared'.[45] But the most impressive scouting adventures were to be found in the popular fiction created by propagandists for the movement.

Popular fiction involving the adventures of Boy Scouts had begun to appear in the boys' papers well before 1914. Most of these stories involved hikes, camps and triumph over natural hazards. Scouts even became involved in the capture of criminals or spies, and Guides sometimes got into the act as well.[46] Now, however, in the midst of war, authors set their tales of Scout adventure in the present conflict and showed how the Scouts were prepared to do their duty, such as William Palmer's 'The Secret Base'. Here a young Scottish Scout discovers a secret U-boat base on the shore of a loch, and is instrumental in the destruction of an enemy submarine.[47] However, the most effective propagandist stories were set on the Western Front, and took their inspiration from the reports of those French and Belgian boys who had already crossed swords with the 'Hun' and demonstrated that Scouts, by virtue of their superior physical and moral training, were capable of playing a major role in the war. Typical of these novels is Rowland Walker's novel, *Oscar Danby, VC: A Tale of the Great European War*, of 1916.

Oscar Danby is the leader of 'Eagle Patrol', a Scout troop camping on the Norfolk coast in early August 1914. When they hear that war has been declared on Germany, John Holland, the Scoutmaster, declares that he will volunteer and would like to take all the boys with him, for they are 'Lion's cubs – strong and resolute both morally and physically.'[48]

Within days of the outbreak of war they encounter a German spy and are instrumental in his capture. As a reward, General Maxwell, the commander of the local division, promises to take them with him when he leaves for France. Getting the boys attached to the division is achieved by simply gaining their parents' consent. At the front, the boys help evacuate Belgian civilians away from the path of the invading Germans. While engaged in this duty, Eagle patrol is attacked by German cavalry, but the Scouts, well-armed and trained, fight off the enemy. Being Scouts, of course, they also take care of those Germans they have wounded. 'Gott in Himmel', exclaims one, 'Have we been fighting Boy Scouts? Donner und blitz! If your Boy Scouts fight like this, what will your army do?'[49] A second attack, however, forces the boys to rejoin the retreating BEF. At the Battle of Mons, the boys work with an ambulance unit, and, while carrying out their mission of mercy, watch a British aircraft land near the front line. The wireless operator has been wounded and the pilot, looking for a German artillery battery, needs someone to help him. Danby, the oldest boy in Eagle patrol, volunteers. Over the front, they are attacked by three German aircraft. And this provides an opportunity for the author to show exactly what Scouts are made of. The British machine is riddled with bullets and the pilot wounded. The aircraft heads for the ground. Danby, of course, takes the attack in his stride, but more shocks are to come:

> 'Danby', called the pilot faintly . . . 'Yes Sir', answered the lad, trying to pull himself together. 'I am blind!' 'Blind?', wailed the youth, realizing the hopelessness of their position. 'Yes, but I can manage to steer, if you give me directions. Guide me to the spot where we started from.'

Oscar, of course, rises to the occasion and with perfect calm, guides the wounded pilot to a relatively safe landing. For this heroic act, the boy is awarded the Victoria Cross.[50] In Walker 's novel, Boy Scouts not only know how to fight, they also know how to die. At the Battle of Ypres, for example, the patrol takes part in a bayonet charge (illus. 34) and Shackleton, one of the boys, is killed. When the others discover his body, they find 'The smile of victory upon his fair, upturned face, which was marred only by a thin streak of blood from a bullet wound in the forehead.' The boys, while mourning their comrade, take comfort from the fact that he died 'like a hero, fighting in a just cause' and has followed the 'great Pathfinder into the unknown'.[51] Unfortunately, the patrol is soon captured. Holland, the Scoutmaster, and one of the boys are shot as spies by the Germans and the others shipped off to a prison camp in Germany. The boys soon escape and, using their scout training, live off the land while eluding their captors. Eventually the four remaining Eagles make their way back to England, where they are welcomed as returning heroes.

Such fiction portrayed Boy Scouts at their most militant. The novels and stories were not only intended to encourage boys to enrol and play their part in the war effort, but, by promoting positive images of Scouts, also to preserve the autonomy of the movement against the possibility of War Office control. Propagandists largely achieved both of these goals. Recruiting remained high throughout the war years and, in 1918, the Boy Scouts organization emerged intact and still firmly under the control of Baden-Powell. Scouts, in both fact and fiction, played their part. But in this struggle for survival even women and girls must also play theirs.

Many girls and young women found the outbreak of war intensely exciting and hoped to play some part in the war effort. But, as Vera Brittain noted in her diary on 6 August, sewing was the 'only work it seems possible for women to do – the making of garments for soldiers'.[52] The offer to serve in some more positive capacity was not appreciated by officialdom. The *Girl's Own Paper* suggested that girls (and their mothers) should 'avoid comic-opera like efforts that involved

34 The Boy Scouts charge the Hun. From *Oscar Danby VC* (1916).

horses, tents or pseudo-military uniforms', and using the war as an excuse to advance the cause of feminism.[53] As Mary Cadogan points out, women were expected to stay at home and send their men to the trenches, and this many women did with a will. The popular adventure story writer, Baroness Orczy, orchestrated the Active Service League to persuade men to enlist, and the Order of the White Feather was formed to present apparently fit men not in uniform with a white feather – the sign of cowardice,[54] while the poet Jessie Pope asked:

> Who's for the trench –
>   Are you my laddie?
> Who'll follow French –
>   Will you, my laddie?

Who's fretting to begin,
Who's going out to win?
And who wants to save his skin –
   Do you, my laddie? [55]

Even posters asked, 'Is your "Best Boy" wearing khaki? If not don't YOU
THINK he should be?' This active campaigning to get men into the armed forces
created considerable bitterness among many young men who, quite unreasonably,
believed they had been forced into uniform by this kind of pressure. This
distorted view of women as unofficial recruiting agents resulted in some
particularly bitter comments by Siegfried Sassoon, Wilfred Owen and Richard
Aldington.[56] This may well have been due to their need to find a scapegoat for
the experience which they, and many others, believed had robbed them of youth,
comrades and the world they had grown up in. Yet from their memoirs it is
clear that the decision to volunteer was more a result of their own romantic
view of war than of any malign female influence. But writing verse, persuading
young men to don khaki or knitting mufflers hardly seemed enough for many
women, and as the realization that the war would not be 'over by Christmas'
sank in, increasing use began to be made of women as nurses, industrial workers
and eventually as auxiliaries in the armed forces.[57] These experiences formed the
basis for some popular fiction intended for girls.

Since the Crimean War, nursing had been an acceptable way in which women
could play some part in the nation's wars, and for those who lacked a nursing
qualification, service with the Voluntary Aid Detachment offered a variety of
domestic jobs in hospitals. Being a VAD was a popular form of participation for
young women during the early years of the war and provided the basis for
Bessie Marchant's novel *A VAD in Salonika*. Here we have sixteen-year-old Joan
Haysome working as a volunteer in Lady Huntly's VAD hospital. Joan was
'patriotic to her fingertips. Indeed, she fairly bristled with patriotism'.[58] When
the unit gets permission to serve on the Salonika Front, Joan's mother surprisingly gives her permission, saying 'I think I shall let her go too. We are compelled
to send our boys into the danger zone, so why should our girls be withheld? We
do not love our daughters better than our sons.'[59] In Salonika, Joan comforts
the wounded (nothing too gruesome, of course), helps capture a spy and finishes
up marrying a gallant young British officer. An illustration from the book shows
the nurse in a pose typical of nursing images of the time (illus. 35). The VAD
were, by and large, educated middle-class girls, but the shortage of male industrial workers created increasing opportunities for young women. While women
performed a variety of roles, the most dangerous was undoubtedly in the

35 Nursing the wounded: *A VAD in Salonika, c.* 1917.

munitions industry. Brenda Girvin's *Munition Mary* and Marchant's *A Girl Munition Worker* both focus on how young women performed a number of unpleasant jobs with skill and tenacity and at the same time coped with the considerable resentment of their male co-workers. In the former, the factory owner is totally opposed to women workers in his factory, and Mary not only has to do her job even more effectively than a man but unmasks saboteurs and spies as well, before the chauvinistic Sir William finally changes his mind about female labour. After 1917, the women's services were created and novels like *A Transport Girl in France* and *Jenny Wren* dealt with the Womens' Auxiliary Army Corps and the Womens' Royal Naval Service respectively.[60] Again the girl heroines of these fictions have to face down male prejudice before proving that they can make a positive contribution to the war effort.

Not everyone took the efforts of women seriously, though, as the appallingly

patronizing collection of rhymes and pictures by Hampden Gordon and Joyce
Dennys reveals. In *Our Girls in Wartime*, Land Girls are dismissed with:

> Lizzie labours on the land.
> What she does I understand,
> Is to make the cattle dizzy
> Running round . . . admiring Lizzie.

This is followed by similar rhymes disparaging virtually every role performed
by women. The authors followed this collection with *Our Hospital ABC* – an
equally patronizing collection of verses.[61] The contribution that women made
was more sensibly summed up by Angela Brazil in *A Patriotic School Girl*, when
the headmistress of Brackenfield College reminds the assembled school that:

> We used to be told that the battle of Waterloo was won on the playing-
> fields of our great public schools. Well, I believe that many future
> struggles are being decided by the life in our girls' schools of today.
> Though we mayn't realize it, we're all playing our part in history, and
> though our names may never go down to posterity, our influence will.
> The watchwords of all patriotic women at present are 'Service and
> Sacrifice'. In the few years that we are here at school let us prepare
> ourselves to be an asset to the nation afterwards.[62]

This is followed by a roll-call of old girls and the part they are playing in the
war: including nurses, teachers, transport girls and, significantly, war widows
who are bringing up their children alone.[63]

Not all girls' fiction was so positive, however, and as Mary Cadogan and Patricia
Craig have pointed out, there was considerable emphasis in many stories that
girls were simply helping out during the present emergency, and that when
the war was won the old status quo would be restored. Tradition was also served
by the many magazine stories for girls which simply used the war as an exciting
background for romance, which invariably ended with the heroine marrying
her plucky Tommy.[64] Recruiting for the womens' services was equally backward-
looking. In early 1918, the War Office produced several films, such as *Sisters in
Arms* and *With the Women's Royal Air Force: Life on a British Aerodrome*. The
former showed little detail of service life, but the latter provided a picture of the
duties performed by airwomen, albeit in a patronizing manner. After an opening
shot of women towing a small airship from a hanger, the film cuts to a scene
of women relaxing in a canteen – 'Mid-Morning Break', the caption tells us. After
another short scene of rigging, comes lunch in the same canteen. Later we see
the women 'Cleaning Aeroplanes', 'Cleaning Engines', carrying out 'Clerical

Duties' and 'Covering Aeroplanes', which appears to consist of sewing new canvas. All these duties involve work little different from familiar domestic chores, and the aim of the film seems to have been to convince potential recruits that the work involved would be familiar, and that in the WRAF they would enjoy companionship and comfortable conditions while helping the war effort.[65] The initiatives taken by girls and young women were both reflected and encouraged in popular culture, but popular culture also emphasized the contribution of those Britons overseas – the sturdy sons of Empire.

As the war dragged on, Britain became more and more dependent on imperial troops, and from 1915 colonials were often centre-stage in war fiction. As Brereton explained:

> This war is no ordinary war, as the least intelligent will admit, and one of the particular points for which it is notorious is the cosmopolitan character of the men who form the magnificent British force which our Empire has thrown into this battle of nations.
>
> In the ranks there are to be found men from every part of the world where the British flag flies, and indeed from many other quarters. They have come from towns and backwoods and prairies of Canada, from the rugged interior of Newfoundland, from the farms and cities of Australia, and from a hundred different places.[66]

The Dardanelles campaign gave authors the opportunity to praise the fighting qualities of the ANZACS. Although the hero of Strang's *Frank Forrester* is English, the author has much to say in favour of the Australians. In one scene a patrol is attacked by a superior Turkish force, but the Aussies, outstanding fighters that they are, stand their ground and calmly return fire, 'calmly, methodically, relentlessly, plying their bayonets upon the few [Turks] who came within their reach.' Even when the enemy is forced to withdraw, the Diggers are anxious to pursue and finish the job, prompting the author to remark, 'The Australian in action has only one glorious failing: like the thorough-bred courser, when his blood is up he is hard to hold'.[67] ANZACS are invariably described as 'bronzed', free and easy with their 'cobbers' and noted for their strength and physique. T. C. Bridges, for example, describes them as 'long-legged athletes from the sheep ranges and cattle runs'.[68] Australians, of course, had their own propagandist in the Reverend Joseph Bowes and, as we have seen, New Zealanders were the heroes in Westerman's *A Lively Bit of the Front*.

'Gallant Canadians' and their exploits at Vimy Ridge and Hill 70 were the subject for Brereton's *Under Haig in Flanders* and a number of articles in *Boy's Own Paper*, *Chums* and the other boys' papers. But praise was not only for white troops, and the Indian Divisions were frequently the subject of stories and articles. *Young England*, for example, ran a series of full-page illustrations of imperial soldiers in action, including sepoys and even the machine-gunners of the West African Field Force (illus. 36, 37). Herbert Strang's novel of the war in East Africa has the English hero defeating the Germans only because of the loyalty and bravery of the native Askaris and Rhodesian Native Police.[69] Equally, in Percy Westerman's *Wilmhurst of the Frontier Force*, victory is also dependent on the King's native troops. However racist these authors might have been before 1914, and however often Indians and Africans featured as the 'Other' in colonial war, it was now imperative that old hostilities be put aside, and to remember that in the present struggle the empire was one family, a group of nations bound together in the great cause: 'Here, there, everywhere along the line in Flanders and in France, the Allies – Belgian, French, Portuguese, and Russians – strike at

36 West Africans in action.
From *Young England*, 1916.

the invader, crush his formidable defences with their overpowering gun-fire, and slay his soldiers.'[70]

In early 1915, Herbert Strang's *A Hero of Liège* focused on two young heroes, the English youth Kenneth Amory and Remi Pariset of the Belgian Air Service, who defy the invader, capture his spies and take part in the heroic defence of the Belgian forts. At the end of the novel, with most of 'little Belgium' in enemy hands, the author suggests that the gallant Belgian army had 'saved France by throwing the German war machine out of gear'. By sacrificing themselves, Belgians had bought time for the Allies, thus ensuring the inevitable German defeat.[71] The Italian war effort was also praised. One article, 'Italy's War in the Mountains', extolled the enthusiasm of Italian troops and the excellence of their equipment.[72] It was comparatively easy for authors to praise Belgians and Italians, as there was a long history of good relations with these nations, but with old enemies like France and Russia antagonism ran deep, and writers like Strang,

Westerman and Brereton had to overcome years of extremely negative portrayal of
these nations. Only a few years before 1914, Brereton, for example, had described
the French in the most unflattering terms as devious, untrustworthy, selfish
and hysterical![73] Equally, in his 1907 novel of the Russo–Japanese War, *A Soldier of
Japan*, Brereton is wholeheartedly on the side of the 'gallant' Japanese, Russians
were usually 'barbaric' and there was considerable criticism of the Tsar's expansionist aims.[74] However, in 1916, Blackie's, his publisher, wanted propagandist
novels that would portray these nations in heroic terms as loyal allies battling
ferociously alongside the British.

Brereton's response was *With Joffre at Verdun*, a story that focused on the
valiant defence of the French fortress, told through the experiences of two young
French soldiers, Jules and Henri. In the novel, the author overcomes his obvious
distaste for the French in truly masterful fashion. Of Henri, he tells us:

> His walk was British, his stride the active, elastic athletic stride of one of
> our young fellows; and the poise of his head, the erectness of his lithe
> figure, a symbol of what one is used to in Britons wherever they are
> met . . . There was nothing exaggerated about his method of raising his
> hat to a lady . . . no gesticulations, no active, nervous movements of
> his hands, and none of that shrugging of the shoulders which, public
> opinion has it, is so eminently characteristic of our Gallic neighbours.[75]

Jules, our other hero, could also be mistaken for a Briton for, 'he too had
the distinguished air, that quiet and unassuming demeanor which stamp[s] the
Englishman throughout the world.'[76] So what is the explanation? How can these
young men be so uncharacteristic of their race? The answer, of course, is that
their fathers, enlightened Frenchmen that they were, fully understood the benefits
of an English public school education and thus sent their sons to a 'fine old
English institution', and on to English universities. There, presumably, under
a regime of cold showers, overcooked beef and organized brutality, all French
foolishness had been eradicated from their characters! Now, with these English
surrogates as his main focus, Brereton can unfold his tale of high adventure
and daring deeds at the defence of Verdun – a battle that was clearly won on the
playing fields of a minor English public school!

Equally, when Brereton writes of the Eastern Front he uses the same device.
His Russian heroes have also benefited from contact with Englishmen or from
an English education.[77] A comparison with other popular and successful wartime authors of juvenile fiction reveals a similar technique in order to make
old enemies acceptable as allies for the present struggle.[78] Although Americans
sometimes appear in later fictions, only one English novel seems to have been

written specifically about their contribution to the war, Brereton's *Under Foch's Command: A Tale of the Americans in France*. But, compared with French or Russians, writing about the Americans presented few problems (after all, they shared the same proud, freedom-loving Anglo-Saxon heritage). After rehearsing the reasons for American intervention (the *Lusitania* incident and German interference with American seaborne trade), the author introduces the heroes of the story, Dan Holman and Jim Carpenter, who, apart from their skill with a six-gun, strongly resemble his young Englishmen – 'lithe, tall, sinewy young fellows' – 'magnificent specimens of American manhood'. After amazing adventures involving spies and U-boats, they arrive on the Western Front in time to take part in the German spring offensive of 1918. After demonstrating how vital a role the American Expeditionary Force has played, Brereton finishes with, 'They are in France as we write. Shoulder to shoulder with their comrades . . . they are opposing the most ruthless enemy that has ever threatened the liberty of mankind'.[79] Thus Pershing's 'Crusaders' had taken their place alongside the other gallant Allies in the Great War for civilization and for democracy.

Chivalry, as Peter Parker has suggested, was one of the most effective means of maintaining enthusiasm. Couching the war in chivalric terms 'gave some sense of higher purpose to the squalor and slaughter'.[80] The Church of England frequently referred to the war as a crusade,[81] and, curiously, one of the most enduring myths of the war concerned the 'Angels of Mons' hovering above the battlefield and rallying the flagging spirit of the BEF during the retreat of 1914. The myth had its origins in a story by Arthur Machen, 'The Bowmen', published in the *Evening News* in September 1914. Here St George and the shades of the bowmen of Agincourt gave their support to the hard-pressed British. Despite the author's later protestations that the story was pure invention, many people believed it to be true, and that the spirit of medieval chivalry was in the fight as well. Curiously, Machen later had correspondence from soldiers who claimed to have seen the vision.[82] The apparent evidence that God was on the side of the Allies was reinforced by new infusions of mystical nonsense at times of need. In the middle years of conflict, for example, Henry Newbolt (now 'Sir' Henry, having been knighted for inspiring public morale with his 1914 poem *The Vigil*),[83] produced several books for boys designed to enthuse them for the present struggle by using chivalric themes. *The Book of the Happy Warrior*, the story of medieval warrior heroes, retold the epic tales of Roland, Richard II and the Black Prince. In the final chapter, 'Chivalry of To-Day', the author linked these warriors of the past with the young men who fought daily with the 'Hun' in France and Flanders, in just another chapter in the endless war between good and evil. Newbolt makes it clear that young men must always be ready to take up their fathers' swords '. . . for so long as there remain in the world wild beasts, savages, maniacs, autocrats and worshippers of Woden, there will always be the possibility [of war]'.[84]

Earlier in the book, Newbolt writes lovingly of public schools, which he suggests are the modern equivalent of the castle school where the 'young squires' learned the chivalric code. It is clear that he believed that the games field was the contemporary version of the tilt-yard, where boys learned the game of life, and honour and war. As we have seen, it was common to link sport and war before 1914, to see warfare as simply the most exciting sport of all, and the metaphor became popular with propagandists during the war years:

> You may find your place in the battle front
> If you'd play the forward game,
> To carry the trench and man the guns
> With dash and deadly aim.
> O, the field is wide and the foe is strong,
> And it's far from wing to wing,
> But we'll carry through, and it's there that you
> May shoot for your flag and King.

So wrote A. Lochhead in 1914, and other writers maintained the fiction.[85] Of course, the squalor of the trenches and the anonymity of death by poison gas, high explosives or the unseen sniper's bullet, did much to undermine the rhetoric of the 'game of war', but in 1916, in company with a number of other propagandists, Newbolt discovered what he believed was the real spirit of chivalry in the war – the airman!

Fighting in the air developed enormous popular appeal during the last years of the war. Here the romance, chivalry and skill of the warrior could be preserved in the face of industrialized mass-killing.[86] According to this myth, heroic young airmen fought their battles according to the knights' code in the clean, clear skies over the Western Front. Air combat seemed to hark back to the days when killing was an art and not techno-industrial murder, as the pilots stalked their prey and closed in for the final duel, in which individual skill made the difference between life and death. As Newbolt wrote in 1916:

> Our airmen are singularly like the knights of the old romances, they go out day after day, singly or in twos and threes, to hold the field against all comers, and to do battle in defence of those who cannot defend themselves. There is something especially chivalrous about these champions of the air; even the Huns, whose military principles are against chivalry, have shown themselves affected by it.[87]

Indeed, with air fighting there was much that was reminiscent of knightly combat. Pilots were carefully selected – young, fit and usually from public schools – and they alone were the cutting edge of the air arm, a fighting elite. Ground crews were the squires who prepared their officers for battle; substitute a Sopwith Pup for a warhorse and the analogy is complete. There were even the champions – the 'aces' – who became popular heroes because of their success in battle. Aces were first identified in France and Germany as a means of creating warrior heroes to inspire the nation, but it was in Germany that the cult of the air fighter really developed. Peter Fritszche has demonstrated how, as part of the propaganda war, successful air fighters were elevated to heroic status and portrayed as the embodiment of the spirit of the nation, and when one young eagle fell another took his place. Thus, when Oswald Boelcke was killed, Max Immelmann took his place, and when he too died there was Manfred von Richthofen, the 'Red Baron' and the most romantic of them all.[88]

The policy of the Royal Flying Corps was not to single out individual airmen, but this did not stop authors creating fictional air heroes in novels like *The Secret Battleplane*, *Burton of the Flying Corps* and *Winning His Wings*.[89] These and many others related the daring exploits of Britain's young fliers in their battles in the sky. However, following the RFC's disastrous showing in the spring of 1917,[90] even the conservative leadership of the Corps realized that a new and more dynamic image was needed. Film was one medium through which the experiences of the airmen could be glamorized, and several official films were made which focused on the heroes of the air. The technical limitations of filming the air war were considerable, but short documentaries like *With the Royal Flying Corps* (1917) and *Tails Up France – The Life of an RAF Officer in France* (1918) played down the dangers and emphasized the boyish high spirits of some fliers.[91] But print provided the most stirring propaganda. In R. Wherry Anderson's popular account of air warfare, for example, the author explained that lion hunting had hitherto been considered the finest sport, but in the author's opinion, 'the finest sport today is to ascend to the upper atmosphere and assist there in the supreme task of defeating the world's tyrants.' Even in the semi-official *Notes on Air Fighting* by Major Rees, it was claimed that British pilots would 'fight for the sport of the affair if for no other reason.'[92] In late 1915, *Chums* printed a letter from the popular writer Frank Shaw, then serving in the balloon section of the RFC. Shaw's purpose was to recruit for the Corps by using the elitist reputation of the RFC and the sporting instincts of his readers. After pointing out how badly they were needed and how the Huns (who were girl and women killers) had to be stopped, he noted that the army's most exciting branch not only offered '. . . honour and glory in this big game', but also that the pay is 'the best to be got'. He ended with,

'Come on lads, be proper sportsmen, now. Come and see me at the Polo Pavilion at Roehampton Golf Club'.[93] In reality, the war in the air was just as brutal, as bloody and as deadly as the war in the trenches,[94] but it was portrayed as almost the last arena for individual knightly combat. The myth of the chivalric air fighter quickly became a major theme in the pleasure culture of war for young men, and proved remarkably enduring.

The education system was also a major channel for inculcating the martial spirit and promoting enthusiasm for the war among the young, even though the war had dramatically disrupted state education. Many children simply used it as an excuse for prolonged absence, but many others were actually involved in some form of war work. As the government admitted in August 1917, over half a million children had been put 'prematurely' to work since 1914.[95] Those that did remain in the classroom were subjected to endless patriotic addresses emphasizing duty and sacrifice, and presented with war books as prizes and rewards. They saluted the flag every morning after prayers, wore copies of their fathers' regimental badges and sang patriotic ditties, like:

> At the cross, at the cross
> Where the Kaiser lost his hoss
> And the eagle on his hat flew away;
> They were eating currant buns
> When they heard the British guns
> And the frightened little beggars ran away.[96]

Boys played at soldiers in copies of their fathers' uniforms, which could be made at home or purchased from toy stores. Gamages, the premier London toy store, offered a splendid selection (illus. 38). After 1916, every London school was

38 Toys and uniforms for boys. From Gamages catalogue, 1917.

39 Boy hero John Cornwall VC:
a patriotic print, *c.* 1916.

adorned with a fine framed reproduction of the painting showing the boy sailor
John Cornwall winning his VC (and losing his life) at the Battle of Jutland – a
patriotic gift from the LCC, and probably the most widely reproduced battle
painting of the entire war (illus. 39). In the public schools, as Peter Parker tells us,
'the war was a constant presence, lurking in classroom and corridor'.[97] Casualty
lists were published in school magazines, black armbands were worn by those
who had lost fathers and brothers, and masters continually praised those
boys who had made the 'great sacrifice' on the field of honour. 'Playing war' was
endemic among boys as they re-enacted the battle stories they read and heard
about from their elders. Robert Roberts recalled the passion for digging trenches
on almost any piece of waste land.[98] Toy manufacturers catered to the huge
interest in modern warfare by producing new toys and variations on old ones;
and girls could be given dolls dressed as British soldiers. A popular board game
of the period was *From the Ranks to Field-Marshall*, where as players moved up
the board they earned promotion, won medals or suffered bouts of enteric fever.

Death was not an option, of course! The toymakers William Britain produced a variety of sets of 'Tommies' and their new equipment – howitzers, lorries, ambulances and other military vehicles – and the Milton Bradley Company marketed a new war game called *At the Front*:

> The box contains soldiers which are to be taken out and fired at, for which deadly purpose there are pistols enough for considerable execution. Each soldier stands until he is shot and then falls like a man and takes no more part in the game. The uniforms are of the latest and most correct styles, representing armies of different countries.[99]

One unintentionally ironic initiative was undertaken by the Lord Roberts Memorial Trust, which established workshops in which soldiers and sailors disabled in the war made toys, including war toys like model soldiers, guns and aeroplanes (illus. 40). The tobacco companies used war pictures for their widely collected cigarette cards, and patriotic postcards were given away as gifts to regular customers in shops and stores. In the summer of 1916, one enterprising clothier and outfitter gave copies of Donald Mackenzie's tribute to the late warlord, *Lord Kitchener: The Story of His Life and Work*, to his more favoured customers.[100]

Throughout the war, most Britons clung desperately to the idea that it was a justified crusade against aggression and tyranny, but by the summer of 1916, and especially after the Battle of the Somme, it was difficult to ignore the enormous casualty lists and the crippled and wounded soldiers to be seen at every railway station. War weariness became widespread, and even the enthusiasm of young men began to wane as the war dragged on into 1917 and 1918 with little sign of victory. However, many of the young men who had marched off so eagerly to war in 1914 found the Western Front had little nobility or romance. Roland Leighton, no doubt partly influenced by his father's books (*The Thirsty Sword*, for example), had gone to war believing it to be an 'ennobling and very beautiful experience', but wrote to his fiancée, Vera Brittain, in September 1915 with a very different perspective:

> Let him who thinks that War is a glorious golden thing, who loves to roll forth stirring words of exhortation, invoking Honour and Praise and Valour and Love of Country . . . look at a little pile of sodden grey rags that cover half a skull and a shin bone and what might have been Its ribs . . . and realise how grand and glorious a thing it is to have distilled all Youth and Joy and Life into a foetid heap of hideous putrescence.[101]

Did he, one wonders, number his father among the guilty?

But much of this reality was carefully concealed from those at home. Under the

BRITISH TOYS

Made by ~ DISABLED SOLDIERS & SAILORS

40 An advertisement for Lord Roberts's Memorial Fund, 1916.

Defence of the Realm Act (1914), strict censorship was invoked, initially to prevent publication of information useful to the enemy. However, as the real nature of the war became evident, it was prudent that this should not be revealed to the public less it sap their will to continue the fight. As Philip Knightley has noted: 'The willingness of newspaper proprietors to accept this control and their cooperation in disseminating propaganda brought them the rewards of social rank and political power.' The correspondents themselves were no less to blame, for they identified with the army and 'protected the high command from criticism, wrote jauntily about life in the trenches [and] kept an inspired silence about the slaughter.'[102] To be fair, most senior commanders in France had little time for reporters and kept them away from the Front.[103] C. E. Montagu, a soldier and later a censor, wrote of how the jaunty tone of correspondents aroused fighting soldiers to a fury. Their dispatches suggested that soldiers enjoyed nothing more than 'going over the top' and that battle was just a 'rough jovial picnic'; a fight never lasted long enough for the men and their only fear was lest that the war should end this side of the Rhine.[104] But such images were common to all forms of popular culture.

War posters, probably the most widely seen form of visual representation of the war, were used for a variety of purposes: to recruit for the armed forces, encourage the involvement of workers on the home front, spread essential information and create negative images of the enemy. Britain was often symbolized by an armour-clad St George slaying the dragon of Prussianism, rescuing Flemish damsels or protecting the 'little nations'. These ideas were reinforced by powerful images of enemy atrocities and the pathetic and helpless victims (usually women and children) of Hun viciousness. British soldiers were clean-limbed, kindly and eager to do their bit. Wounded soldiers were sometimes shown but always with socially acceptable wounds – a bloody bandage around their forehead or an arm in a sling. There was little indication of the horrendous wounds inflicted by high explosive or poison gas. Actual fighting was rarely seen on posters, thus Frank Brangwyn's *War Bonds* (illus. 41) was unusual in showing a British soldier in the act of stabbing an enemy. Although Brangwyn was a respected commercial artist well known for his designs, this particular image was criticized for revealing the brutality of war.[105] Many official war artists were producing similar sanitized images of battle, particularly William Orpen, Muirhead Bone and Augustus John. The work of those who were prepared to show the horrors of the Western Front, C. W. R. Nevison (*The Harvest of Battle* or *Paths of Glory*), Eric Kennington (*Gassed and Wounded*) and John Singer Sargent (*Gassed*), for example, was produced later in the war or even after the Armistice.[106]

The battlefront was widely photographed by official photographers with the

British Expeditionary Force, but their work was heavily censored before being
made available to the press. In 1916, in face of the demand from the public for
more information, the War Office offered for tender the rights to reproduce and
market selected photographic images of the Western Front. The *Daily Mail* won
the contract and issued these images as *The Daily Mail Official War Postcards.*
A number of sets were reproduced and proved enormously popular with the
public. The published images, however, were apparently carefully chosen to
provide a particular view of the war. One set focused on *The King at the Front*,
another on *ANZACS in France.* Others showed artillery in action, with the
inevitable smiling Tommies moving up to the line and German prisoners being
taken. One card showed a chaplain tending British graves (a dozen or so can be
seen) and several show wounded soldiers, but these seem to suggest minimal
casualties and wounds that were far from fatal. In card 142, for example, *Wounded
Waiting for the Field Ambulances*, eleven men lie on stretchers, but most look quite

42 The *Daily Mail Official War Postcards*: '"Tommy" at home in German Dugouts', 1916–17.

comfortable and several are chatting or calmly smoking. Most images suggest that the war really wasn't that bad for the stoical, good-humoured soldiers. For instance, card 20 shows a group of British soldiers tucked up in small dugouts with the caption, '"Tommy" At Home in German Dug-Outs' (illus. 42). It implied not only that the Germans were continually being forced to give up ground, but that Tommy could make himself at home anywhere. The photographs reproduced by the *Mail* were widely reprinted elsewhere, including the *Illustrated London News* and *The War Illustrated* [107] and thus such sanitized images reached a considerable audience. Even cinema, potentially the most powerful and revealing medium for showing the reality of war, produced little for public consumption that could offend even the most tender susceptibilities.

In 1914, film-makers had rushed to exploit war fever and a number of pictures were produced that differed little from the anti-German literature that had emerged in the last years of peace. One of the first, *The Great European War* (1914), was a fictionalized newsreel showing the course of events that had led to the outbreak of war with, of course, the major responsibility falling on Germany. *The German Spy Peril*, *The Outrage*, *Saving The Colours* and *His Country's Bidding* quickly followed, their titles indicative of content. Even by 1918, popular films had progressed little further than George Pearson's filmic version of Bruce Bairnsfather's stageplay, *The Better 'Ole*, based on his famous cartoon characters or the biopic, *Nelson*.[108] The government were hesitant to employ film as a medium of official propaganda despite agitation from the trade press and from film-makers energized both by patriotism and the belief that working for the national cause would help legitimize their industry in official circles. Nevertheless, before the end of 1914, Charles Masterman, head of the Wellington House organization for official propaganda, had recognized that film could play an important role in the propaganda war.[109] Yet negotiations with the service departments and the time needed to produce suitable material meant that the first official film, *Britain Prepared*, was not released until December 1915. Despite running over three hours, it showed little of the realities of the war. But the release of the enormously successful *Battle of the Somme* (August 1916), showed the public, for the first time, something of the conditions at the Front.

Photographed by Geoffrey Malins and J. B. McDowell, the film was produced by the British Topical Committee for War Films under the sponsorship of the War Office. It provides a remarkable record of the preparations, events and consequences of the opening phase of the battle. Using actuality shots and carefully reconstructed sequences, the first third shows the usual columns of smiling troops moving up to the battle line and the bombardment of enemy positions. Even the later battle sequences, however, show little of the fighting, concentrating instead upon the number of prisoners taken and ground gained while minimizing British losses. Nevertheless, as Nicholas Reeves has pointed out, it gave 'contemporary audiences their first authentic images of the horrors of modern war. The pain and trauma of the fighting can be read all too clearly on the faces of the soldiers returning from the line'.[110] As Reeves notes, the two sequences which probably had the greatest impact on contemporary audiences were the scene where British troops go over the top (illus. 43) and the short scene showing the dead. The film was an exceptional source of realism and horrified many who saw it. Nevertheless, it seems to have been overshadowed by more romantic and heroic literary and visual images of the war, and had limited impact, as did the

43 'Over the Top', from the film *Battle of the Somme*, 1916.

later official film *The Battle of the Ancre and the Advance of the Tanks* (1917). Many storytellers and illustrators, then, had no direct access to the fighting front and little understanding of the conditions of trench warfare, and fell back on pre-1914 images of battle for inspiration. But there were some who were better informed about conditions in France.

From their writing, it might well be assumed that Brereton, Rowland Walker, Escott Lynne and Percy Westerman were part of the ill-informed public, but this would be incorrect. Brereton rejoined the army in 1914 and served with the RAMC for two years, before being appointed head of the Committee for the Medical History of the War, and later of the Medical Section for the proposed Imperial War Museum. He had access to privileged medical records and statistics and would have been well acquainted with the realities of modern warfare. One might add that Percy Westerman, despite his poor eyesight, served with the RAF, as did Frank Shaw.[111] Alfred Bowes was an army chaplain in France and Escott Lynne and Charles Gilson served on the Western Front. Robert Leighton's only son, Roland, the most promising boy of his year at Uppingham, was killed on the Western Front in December 1915. His death was followed by that of almost his entire circle of school and university friends.[112] Clearly, then, these writers knew exactly what it meant to serve in the trenches and understood the nature of modern industrial warfare. Yet in their stories we detect no lessening of the romance of war, and only minor changes in the nature of warfare between 1914 and 1919, and in some cases well into the inter-war period. Was this simply a denial of reality, or was it a deliberate distortion for propaganda purposes?

In boys' fiction, the romantic image and heroic spirit of Britons remained constant throughout the last years of war no matter how brutal or deadly it became. In *With the Allies to the Rhine*, Brereton's novel of the end of the war written in 1919, it might be expected that some degree of disillusionment would have tempered the author's view of trench warfare. But no! Even after four years of bloody attrition, Brereton still recreates battle as a glamorous and romantic activity. His soldiers are still eager for battle, still talk about 'ding-dong fights' with the Hun, and still sacrifice themselves without hesitation. The author adds only one sombre note, and that at the end of the novel, when he considers the human cost of the war:

> So ended the Great War, in brilliant fashion for the Allies. Yet consider at what cost, with what misery and suffering and hardship this victory was achieved. More than a million sons of Britain had died for it; two million more had suffered wounds; the young men of this era had almost disappeared – but they had died for their Country.[113]

Westerman, Strang and the others wrote in exactly the same vein. The pleasure culture of war presented it as one long adventurous escapade, a justified conflict that demanded great sacrifice from the warrior sons of empire. That sacrifice had been willingly made, and those who survived would never forget the 'great adventure' – indeed, it was the crowning experience of their lives. The enemy, the barbarous Hun, had been vanquished, his dreams of conquest shattered for ever, and the war weary, but victorious Allies were on the Rhine, ensuring Germany would never again wreak havoc on Europe! The British Empire was not only safe, but greater than ever, and the world would be a better place: it was a glorious victory! There is, in these fictions, a general acknowledgement of the considerable loss of life and the new horrors of technological weaponry – machine guns, aeroplanes, tanks, poison gas and even flame throwers – but in the final analysis their fictions and visual images reveal an essentially romantic and chivalric war fought for high moral purpose; a war that really was the 'great adventure' for its young men, where even the dead were to be envied, as their sacrifice had won them immortal praise. Such sentiments were widespread, and best expressed by the poet H. H. Bliss:

> Would I were with you crowned with victory's bays,
> O Happy Warrior 'midst our English dead.[114]

5 No More War: 1919–39

... as I marched out from Sidi-bel-Abbas and looked back, those five years in the Legion, on a halfpenny a day, seemed to have slipped by all too quickly, so much had happened. But leaving the shores of Algeria to return to England, I felt a big thrill of pride at the thought that I had been a member of the most adventurous of all regiments – the French Foreign Legion.

Roland Wilson, 'My Life in the Legion', *Chums* (1936)

In Britain, the Armistice and subsequent peace treaties were greeted with an immense sense of relief and satisfaction. The nation had fought the most destructive war in history and had triumphed – what greater proof could there be that God continued to smile benevolently upon the British race? Britons belonged to the single most powerful nation in Europe. The Royal Navy still ruled the waves and the Royal Air Force the skies. The Anglo–French agreement, dividing the spoils gained from the Ottomans, added enormous new areas to the empire, which was now greater than ever. The 'Great War for Civilization' had seemingly bound the sons of empire even more closely to the motherland, and not only in the white Dominions had young men willingly given their lives for the imperial ideal, but in the subject colonies as well. Peace had been restored in Europe, and the League of Nations, which promised a new era in international affairs, established. As A. J. P. Taylor has noted, 'Anglo-Saxons envisaged the League as an instrument of conciliation, softening all international antagonisms'.[1] The war had achieved something remarkable after all. In November 1918, Gunner P. J. Campbell believed he had heard the sound of gunfire for the last time, and that 'there would never be another war like this one. The Last War in History! Well, even if I achieved nothing else in life I had done something, I need not feel that my life had been altogether wasted, I had played my part'.[2] There was an equally blind faith that somehow the war would result in a more equitable, more just society; that it would break down the rigid class barriers of Victorian England and bring about a new age in the life of the nation – although not, as Robert Graves and Alan Hodge pointed out, 'a new world, as the politicians promised; [for] the general intention was merely to cleanse the old one'.[3]

Initially, such optimism seemed well-founded, as the country experienced a post-war boom, but hopes for a better future began to collapse when the boom ended in the spring of 1921. The fact that the war had mortally wounded the key industries on which the economy depended was largely disguised by brief periods of temporary recovery, and because the one to two million unemployed were mostly concentrated in the heavy industrialized areas of the north-west, north-east, Scotland and south Wales. In the Home Counties, new industries based around plastics and electricity tended to prosper, and for those in regular employment (mainly in the south) there was a gradual but more or less continuous improvement in the quality of life throughout the period, and much of that improvement affected the young.[4]

After the 1918 Education Act, the school-leaving age was raised to fourteen and many authorities provided scholarships for grammar and county secondary schools. This, together with the marginalization of child labour, meant that childhood lasted longer and most children had more time for leisure activities and at least a few coppers to spend on some form of entertainment. Consequently, the industries catering to their leisure needs expanded, and for the first time more attention was focused on what children actually wanted rather than what their parents thought they should have. New story papers and comics emerged, most importantly the so-called 'Big Five' from the Edinburgh-based publishers D. C. Thomson (see below), and some old favourites disappeared. More significantly, the period also witnessed the beginning of the film industry's awareness of the youth market and the determination by film-makers to cater to adolescent audiences. By the 1930s, even the British Broadcasting Corporation (established in 1922) was featuring a very popular 'Children's Hour'. Yet the written word remained the major channel for popular fiction. Isabel Quigly, growing up through the 1930s, remembered that:

> Books mattered when I was a child. They were central to our lives . . . They influenced our talk and our feelings about the world, they were persuasive, sought for, discussed . . . But I want to stress that I wasn't a peculiarly bookish child: almost everyone I was friendly with, tended to feel the same. Books mattered.[5]

But the new audio-visual media added an extra dimension to the excitement of popular adventure.[6]

It has often been suggested that with the peace treaties came a powerful desire on the part of most people to close the door of memory on the years of conflict.

This now commonplace assumption appears to have first emerged during the 1930s. Writing in 1940, Robert Graves and Alan Hodge noted, almost with surprise, that with the publication of Remarque's *All Quiet on the Western Front* in 1929, 'war books suddenly came back into fashion'; implying that during the first decade of peace no one wanted to be reminded of the war. Such claims have led academics like Samuel Hynes to argue that, for 'most of the Twenties the War was not significantly imagined, in any form'.[7] This myth of the war's aftermath suggests that after 1918, devastated by the scale of loss and suffering, there was little public demand for literary or other cultural reconstructions of the war experience because such reminders were simply too painful. When the war was 'rediscovered' in the later 1920s it was filtered through the memory of bitter and disillusioned veterans who largely portrayed the conflict as a 'horrible mistake, a debacle in which brave young men [the 'golden youth' of Edwardian England] sacrificed themselves in the mud and blood of the Western Front's no man's land'.[8] Once the nation perceived the real nature of the trenches, it was filled with horror and committed itself to pacifism, international disarmament and a policy of peace at any price. As with any myth, there are elements of truth, and although it does represent one contemporary response to the war it was by no means the only one.

For most people, there was a determination to remember and to celebrate the sacrifice of the fallen, as the many war memorials testify, 'They died the death of honour' reads the inscription on a memorial commemorating the fallen who had come from the Harris Orphanage in Preston, Lancashire (illus. 44). A common enough sentiment, but one that firmly placed the sacrifice of these young men in the chivalric tradition: they had died to save King and Empire and for the noble cause of a new and better world. As we have seen, P. J. Campbell, like many others, saw purpose in the war; his comrades had not died in vain and were honoured heroes as the chivalric inscriptions on their memorials indicate. Armistice Day became the great annual Festival of Remembrance, but memorials in every town and village ensured that the fallen were an ever-present memory.[9] Curiously, despite the rhetoric about 'the war to end war', there was often an implication that the next generation might well have to continue the struggle. The memorial at Marlow, Buckinghamshire, was unveiled in 1920 by the Marquis of Lincolnshire. According to the local newspaper, the Marquis 'impressed upon the boys present not to forget . . . the way in which their fathers, brothers and relatives had fought that they might live in peace. If ever they were called upon to do the same, they must do their duty like men'.[10] Even the commonly used phrase, 'before the war', in everyday conversation served as a constant reminder. For the bereaved, there were organized pilgrimages to the Western Front, to view

44 'They Died the Death of Honour':
the Harris Orphanage War Memorial,
Preston, Lancs, *c.* 1922.

the great and sombre war cemeteries and the fields of battle. The Young Mens'
Christian Association undertook the first tours in 1920 and the Red Cross
and British Legion soon followed, while the enterprising travel agent Thomas
Cook began to offer tours of the battlefields on a commercial basis.[11] The more
adventurous could make their own private pilgrimage, using battlefield guides
published by Shell Petroleum or the Michelin Tyre Co. (first published in 1919).
A less expensive alternative was a visit to the Imperial War Museum, opened in
1920 at Crystal Palace in south London. The museum, with its impressive display
of weapons, uniforms, paintings and exciting dioramas proved enormously
popular, but such displays, albeit less impressive, could be seen at numerous
local museums, which, as Omer Bartov has suggested, 'embody the sacralization of
violence' – carefully re-ordered displays of killing machines which have proved
endlessly fascinating for generations of boys and young men.[12] As the memorials
commemorated the fallen heroes and the museums displayed the artefacts of
the war, so the romantic and heroic fictions of battle written for the young
endured long after the peace treaties had been signed; many, in fact, remained

in print for the next two decades, as the publishing and readership history of this fiction demonstrates.

Brereton's war novels remained in print until the Second World War; and were still popular as class and Sunday school prizes for boys and young men. In 1931, the publisher Partridge reissued a whole series of wartime fiction including Westerman's *The Secret Battleplane* (first published in 1916) and *Tanks to the Fore!* (1917), and Rowland Walker's *Oscar Danby VC*, that intensely patriotic tale of willing sacrifice on the Western Front first published in 1916. From 1933 onwards, Oxford University Press reprinted many of Herbert Strang's war stories – *Carry On: A Story of the Fight for Bagdad*, for example, was last republished in 1936. Nor did these volumes sit unwanted on booksellers shelves. They sold well, particularly as prizes and rewards. For example, the London County Council awarded Brereton's *With Allenby in Palestine* (1918) to a secondary schoolboy in 1931, and *Under Haig in Flanders* (1917) was given as a Christmas present in 1933. Aberdeen Education Committee provided Westerman's *The Dispatch Riders* (1915) as a middle school prize in 1934, while Captain Charles Gilson's *U93* was awarded as a Sunday school prize as late as 1942.[13] Throughout the interwar period, then, these novels of the war as the Great Adventure, written during the years of conflict, were still widely read by British youth, and were reinforced by other titles from a new generation of authors.

Between 1928 and 1934, for instance, Seeley Service published John Irving's 'Dick Valliant RN' novels, a series of heroic naval adventures, as well as reissuing T. W. Corbin's 1919 *The Romance of War Invention*, with its wonderfully romantic descriptions of bomber aeroplanes, tanks and heavy artillery. During the 1920s and '30s, the Aldine Library published a number of adventurous tales of the war such as Wingrove Willson's *Stories of the Great War*, E. L. McKeag's *Chums of the Northern Patrol* and Michael Poole's *Macklin of the Loyals*, 'a thrilling story of the Great War for boys and girls of all ages'.[14] These lesser-known authors were joined by others who later achieved considerable popularity, and whose books remained in print for many years, like George E. Rochester. Rochester published his first story, 'The Funk', a tale of the Royal Flying Corps, in the *Boy's Own Paper* in 1925. His war stories continued with a number of flying yarns, and in the 1930s he created the popular 'Grey Shadow' novels recounting the adventures of Britain's most daring wartime spy.[15] Rochester could not be accused of not having first-hand experience of combat, as he had served in the RFC on the Western Front and ended the war a POW. Equally, if the Aldine catalogue is to be believed, writers such as Michael Poole and Ernest L. McKeag were also veterans.

These novels were complemented by the serials and stories published in the popular boys' papers such as *Boy's Own Paper*, *Chums*, *Modern Boy* and

Champion. In the immediate post-1918 period, all the boys' papers were full of war-related material – fiction, articles about heroic episodes and numerous illustrations. However, through the 1920s some change can be detected in the manner in which the war was dealt with in certain papers. By 1930, for example, while the Religious Tract Society's *Boy's Own Paper* had no shortage of blood and guts historical romances, tales of the Great War had been virtually eliminated from its pages. The more secular *Chums*, however, featured war stories and articles throughout the inter-war period. Its 1936–7 annual, for instance carried two stories of flying on the Western Front: 'The Great Spy Capture', in which public school boys apprehend a German spy, and a story where an unpopular schoolboy becomes a hero in the trenches, dying gallantly and earning the respect of his fellows. In addition, there were articles on RFC heroes and accounts of the daring deeds of Lawrence of Arabia; Major Hansen, who won a VC fighting the Turks; and a piece on Rifleman Kulbir Thapa VC, a Gurkha who won his award on the Western Front. Even the 1941 annual carried Peter Tewson's highly appropriate 'Wheels of the Great Retreat', 'a moving picture of the epic battle of Mons'. The *Champion* annual for 1930 not only carried fictional tales of young heroes such as 'The Boy Who Did His Bit' and 'Chums of the Clouds' but also an illustrated article on 'When Britain Was at War', which included an account of trench warfare on the Western Front, complete with pictures of 'cheery Tommies' advancing during the Battle of Arras and descriptions of the 'good-humoured heroes of the trenches'. In all these examples, authors generally accepted that conditions in the trenches had sometimes been 'horrible' and that many soldiers had suffered greatly. Even so, there was never any suggestion that their suffering and sacrifice had been pointless or futile. The war was always portrayed as righteous, justified and, in most cases, heroic, exciting and romantic. These juvenile fictions were mirrored by the adult war stories of 'Sapper' (H. C. McNeile), such as *Sergeant Michael Cassidy, RE* and *No Man's Land*. Originally published during the war when the author was serving in the Royal Engineers, they were reprinted throughout the 1920s. While McNeile acknowledged that the war was not the kind of conflict that had been expected, it was still bravely fought for a noble purpose. And one might equally cite the stories of Ian Hay and the Canadian author Ralph Connor.[16] But heroic images of war were not only transmitted through the printed word.

In post-war Britain, the cinema was the most popular form of mass entertainment for children as well as adults. By 1939, for example, over 4.5 million children attended the cinema at least once a week.[17] Cinema managers initially offered free gifts to their juvenile patrons – raffle tickets or a stick of candy – and special 'childrens' programmes' on Saturday afternoons, but children needed little encouragement, and, as Roberts has noted, they 'begged, laboured and even thieved for the odd copper that would give them two hours of magic, crushed on a bench before the enchanting screen'.[18] Authors of adventure fiction were alarmed by these developments. Charles Gilson, for instance, writing in 1932, believed that cinema and wireless had combined to kill off juvenile romance.[19] He was of course, being unnecessarily pessimistic, as his stories were in demand until well into the 1940s. In many cases cinema and literature complemented each other, with successful fiction being translated into film and popular films suggesting stories and characterizations for the boys' papers. The latter quickly adapted to their readers' interest in cinema, and many papers regularly devoted space to articles on film – particularly *Chums*. In 1920, the long-running *Film Fun* comic appeared, featuring film characters in comic adventures. This was followed by the less successful *Film Picture Stories* in 1934, and by 1938 even popular radio shows were being featured in the comic *Radio Fun*.[20] Throughout the inter-war period, then, cinema was a central leisure activity in children's lives and helped to disseminate heroic images of violence and war. During the 1920s, for example, even heroic images of the Great War were reinforced and carried to a wide audience by a series of elaborate documentary reconstructions produced by British Instructional Films (BIF).

For ten years, beginning in 1922 with *Mons* (remade in 1926 on a more lavish scale), the BIF produced dramatic and exciting reconstructions of incidents from the war.[21] Using actuality footage with reconstructed fictional episodes, the films were intended to provide audiences with a detailed picture of key battles, and were made with the full cooperation of the War Office and Admiralty. Indeed, so closely was BIF connected with the government that Prime Minister Stanley Baldwin was quizzed in the House of Commons on just how far the government was subsidizing these productions. However, as Samuel Hynes has pointed out, the questioner missed the point, which was not who was financing them but whose interpretation of the war they reflected.[22] What BIF actually put on the screen were highly sanitized and heroic images of the war, portraying it as a monument to courage and patriotism. While most critics admired the crisp photography, production values and ability of director Walter Summers (himself a veteran of the Western Front and a participant in many of the battles[23]) in reconstructing the war, some were critical of the messages transmitted.

Mons (1926), was much given to individual heroics; restaging various episodes in which soldiers had won the Victoria Cross, wild bayonet charges which shattered the attacking Germans and the unquestioned willingness of plucky Tommies fight to the last man. Illustration 45 shows such a heroic last stand. The critic 'Bryher' (Winifred Ellerman) suggested it presented the war entirely 'from

45 The Last Stand
of the Tommies.
From the film
Mons, 1926.

a romantic boy-adventure book angle' and criticized it for ignoring the disease and discomfort of the trenches. The whole series, in her view, suffered from a romantic and sentimental approach, and in order to understand war it was essential to 'get away from this nursery formula that to be in uniform is to be a hero; that brutality and waste are not to be condemned provided they are disguised in flags, medals and cheering'.[24] But despite harsh comments from an intellectual elite, other critics claimed the film was 'the most sincere and profoundly moving war picture made in this or any other country'. The series, however, was enormously popular with audiences, and because it was 'educational' was widely seen by the young. The image of war in the BIF documentaries was reinforced by less elaborate films which equally reconstructed the war as romantic and heroic. The Royal Air Force documentary, *The Eyes of the Army* (1922), was made to show inter-service cooperation. While it did employ some combat footage, most sequences appear to be culled from post-war manoeuvres, but what is of interest is the repetitious images of exciting cavalry charges while aeroplanes wheel and dive overhead – very dashing, very romantic! Even *Journey's End* (1930), James Whale's film version of R. C. Sherriff's famous stage play, deals more with the enduring heroism of the soldiers than with anti-war rhetoric.[25] In the later 1930s, feature films such as *Forever England* (1935), in which a young able seaman single-handedly delays the repairs to German battleship off a remote island in the South Atlantic, thus enabling the pursuing Royal Navy units to sink it, focused on the same individual heroism and sacrifice.

Throughout the inter-war years, then, not only was there a determination on the part of many people to remember the war, but to do so in heroic terms. The novels, stories, illustrations and films which reconstructed 1914–18 as the great

adventure remained popular with boys and young men, and in many instances
this fiction was created by men who had direct experience of the war and were
presented to the youth of the nation by parents, schoolteachers and churchmen,
many of whom had themselves served in the war. Yet they consciously made
the decision to pass on to the next generation a basically heroic and justified
construction of the war. This attitude even survived the outpouring of the novels
and memoirs of disillusioned veterans, who by the late 1920s had come to believe
that the war had been a futile massacre of young innocents. The literature of
disillusionment, the poetry of Wilfred Owen and the memoirs of Siegfried
Sassoon, Robert Graves and others, has now become the literature of the Great
War, and the formative influence on the popular perception of 1914–18. But during
the inter-war period it was just one response to the war, and predominantly that
of young intellectuals. There was, then, a major contradiction between this kind
of writing about war and the popular writing that was being provided for the
entertainment of the young. It is this very limited focus on the intellectual
responses to the war, the so-called 'good writing', that has led academics like
Hynes into a somewhat distorted view of how the war was interpreted during
post-war decades. Had they explored genuinely popular culture they would have
found a different picture. Significantly, in her study of the literature of war and
violence, Winifred Whitehead could find only one anti-war story dealing with
the Great War specifically written for children in the 1930s – a German novel
published in 1931, but not translated into English until 1983.[26]

However, the contradiction between the heroic and exciting image of war
portrayed in pre-1914 fiction and in the classroom, and the brutal realities of
modern war, was a lesson learned by many young men who endured the Western
Front. In 1916, the ex-schoolmaster turned soldier, Theodore Cameron Wilson,
wrote to a friend:

> . . . Do teach your dear kids the horror of responsibility which rests on the
> war-monger. I want so much to get at the children about it. We've been
> wrong in the past. We have taught schoolboys 'War' as a romantic subject.
> We've made them learn the story of Waterloo as a sort of exciting story in
> fiction. And everybody has grown up soaked in the poetry of war . . . All
> those picturesque phrases of war writers - such as 'he flung the remains
> of his Guard against the enemy', 'a magnificent charge won the day', are
> dangerous because they show nothing of the individual horror, nothing
> of the fine personalities smashed suddenly into red beastliness . . . [27]

Despite such heartfelt pleas, post-war writers of juvenile fiction made little
attempt to portray war in a less romantic manner, even though pacifists did

attempt to curtail some of the more militaristic activities of young men. In 1927, for example, the Labour Party bitterly opposed the spread of Officers' Training Corps units in grammar schools, and this attack was continued by the popular journalist Beverley Nicholls, who argued that such organizations fostered a militaristic spirit.[28] Changing attitudes were also to be seen in the Boy Scout movement, which began promoting peace and international brotherhood so dramatically that it obscured its own militaristic origins. Nevertheless, Scout membership increased to almost half a million boys by 1931. The Boys' Brigade and other organizations increased their numbers, but the Army Cadet Force declined rapidly, with fewer than 20,000 members by 1939.[29] By the 1930s, there was a widespread pacifist sentiment throughout the country, manifested through support for international disarmament, the Peace Pledge Union (founded in 1935) and substantial support for the National Government's policy of appeasement, which endured until the spring of 1939.[30] Despite this genuine anti-war sentiment among many Britons, much writing about war continued to portray it as an exciting adventure. Clearly, the experience of the Great War had forced many people to reassess their attitude, and this created a tension between those who saw war in general, and the Great War in particular, in more truthful, 'modern' ways as futile, brutal and horrible, and those who continued to see it in traditional terms with the emphasis on necessity, patriotism, glory, heroism and the nobility of sacrifice.[31] Nowhere was this tension more clearly revealed than in the imaginings of war intended for the nation's youth.

As we have seen, adventure narratives written during the war years remained in print throughout the 1930s, but, by the beginning of that decade, anti-war sentiment was starting to appear in the boys' papers, albeit in curious and contradictory ways. A 1929 editorial in the *Boy's Own Paper*, for instance, claimed that the two minutes silence must be retained, as it was essential that the rising generation understood exactly what modern warfare really meant:

> Its wanton waste of men and materials, its appalling destructiveness, its filth and cruelty and beastliness – to use the word in its most literal sense – and its utter futility. Few, if any, of the present generation . . . who have 'passed through the furnace' want, or are likely to want, another war; but, just as soon as the boys of today, the men of tomorrow, slip back into the old error of regarding war as a heroic, chivalrous adventure, so will the danger of war become once more imminent. [32]

Yet in the same issue there was an article on the heroic 'Bowmen of England', pointing out that in the hands of stout English archers the longbow was the most 'potent weapon in the field' in the days before gunpowder, and it included details for constructing such a bow. An article on training RAF pilots was little more than recruiting propaganda, while the serial was George Rochester's 'Despot of the World', in which a heroic British agent, the 'Black Beetle', fought his lonely war against the evil Zandenberg, whose dream was to master the world. The Beetle uses considerable violence against Zandenberg's forces, killing many, shooting down their aeroplanes, as well as lesser violence such as bringing his revolver butt down on their skulls with 'sickening force'.[33] For the *BOP*, there seems to have been a curious distinction between the Great War and other wars of the past or future, which could still be imagined as exciting and romantic, although it seems doubtful if schoolboys saw a difference!

In *Chums*, a far more militaristic paper, the same contradictions were even more obvious. In the article 'To-Day on the Western Front', the editorial claimed:

> November 1932! Fourteen years have rolled away since the last gun barked death on the Western Front. Fourteen long years . . . but Time cannot efface the dread memory of the Great War. The war-scarred battlefields are now but a nightmare of the past, but in their stead stand the gravestones of those who have passed on . . . mute pleas that this thing shall be no more.[34]

But in the same volume are stories of foreign legionnaires at war with marauding Arabs, British soldiers in action against rebellious tribes on the north-west frontier, a story in which British prisoners rise up against their German captors and deal out 'dreadful slaughter', and other tales of the Western Front, Gallipoli and the War in the Air, together with a series on heroes of the Great War, including Lawrence of Arabia. The image of war in these stories is still exciting, romantic and a great adventure in which young men perform heroic deeds and revel in battle. Thus, despite the professed sentiment that 'this thing shall be no more', *Chums* continued to encourage the martial spirit through its rousing battle narratives and recruiting propaganda for the armed forces.[35]

Although we lack sufficient evidence to be certain, it would appear that many boys viewed war with the same ambivalence. Jim Wolveridge, a teenager in the East End of London during the 1930s, recalled that, having heard something of the war experiences of his father and neighbours, and seen the shabby treatment meted out to them after the war, 'I was like the ex-serviceman, I said, "to hell with it, let the upper crust fight their own wars."' At the same time, Wolveridge was deeply involved with the pleasure culture of war, 'bloodthirsty' and with a passion for war films, patronizing in particular the Luxor cinema in Commercial Street, where the manager didn't trouble with certificates but allowed children to see anything. Wolveridge was also addicted to the violent serials in *The Wizard* and other D. C. Thomson papers (see below), and especially fond of *Chums*, when he could find them second-hand in the local markets (at twelve shillings and sixpence these annuals were beyond the means of many working-class boys).[36] The Great War, then, did not kill off the romantic image of war shaped by Henty, Newbolt and Kipling, as Samuel Hynes has claimed, a claim which would seem to be the consequence of academics using only sources from 'high culture'. Isabel Quigly, for instance, remembered that, '[A]t seven I was taken in hand by my father, whose idea of suitable reading for children was G. A. Henty.'[37] But even among those intellectuals who had been too young to fight, the war was regarded with ambivalence, with both 'horror and longing' as Christopher Isherwood put it.[38] For most of the nation's youth, war was still a vital and exciting element of pleasure culture and, as we shall see, became even more violent and bloodthirsty, with heroes employing even more terrible weaponry as authors attempted to upstage the real-life horrors of the Western Front.

Until 1914, the irrationality of battle, the fact that survival was usually a simple matter of luck had been disguised by an emphasis on individual fighting skill and the advantage of belonging to a warlike race. Put more crudely, the more heroic and ferocious the fighter, the better the individual chance of survival. However, the massive use of modern weaponry in the Great War sorely tested this view, for, as Omer Bartov has suggested, the employment of new technological weapons appeared to make the descendants of the chivalric warrior redundant, 'by putting an end to all individual heroism and character, and transforming the battlefield into a factory of death, where victory would be decided by the quality and quantity not of men, but of machines'.[39] Nevertheless, as medieval knighthood had first emerged in the successful combination of man and horse, after 1918 new fighting elites emerged – warriors who had learned to dominate the war machines:

> [T]he new knights of war were the tankmen and pilots, the submarine crews and the highly trained, well-equipped troops of the assault battalions . . . the impersonality of [modern] war consequently appeared to have been done away with; or at least, men could once more be persuaded that war would give them the opportunity to demonstrate personal heroism.[40]

Tankmen, although sometimes appearing in fiction of the 1930s, were to need another war before becoming established as an heroic stereotype. The airman was another matter, for not only was the aviator the master of potentially the most devastating and 'exciting' war machine of all, but an heroic figure who had realized the oldest dream of humankind – conquest of the skies.

Even before 1914, military aviators had begun to see themselves as a military elite, and, as we have seen, during the war years the cult of the air fighter provided useful propaganda to counteract the squalor and anonymity of death in the trenches. This elitist view was well expressed by Cecil Lewis in his elegant memoir, *Sagittarius Rising*: 'Flying alone! Nothing gives such a sense of mastery over mechanism, mastery indeed over space, time, life itself, as this'.[41] Above the front, above the mud and filth of the trenches, Lewis realized just how superior the airman was:

> . . . Invisible men . . . Men! Standing, walking, talking, fighting there beneath me! I saw them for the first time with detachment, dispassion-ately: a strange, pitiable, crawling race, to us who strode the sky. Why, God might take the air and come within a mile of earth and never know there were such things as men. Vain the heroic gesture, puny the great thought! Poor little maggoty men![42]

This elitism became enshrined in Royal Air Force policy after the war, and was a vital weapon of Chief of Air Staff Sir Hugh Trenchard in his battle with the older services to preserve the autonomy of the RAF. Trenchard succeeded partly by selling the air force as a cheap and effective colonial police force – airmen could maintain order on the imperial frontiers at a fraction of the cost of conventional forces – and partly by his extravagant claims that air power had become the decisive weapon of the future, and that the RAF alone could defend the nation through the threat of massive retaliatory air strikes.[43] Thus airmen were not simply the heroes of modern warfare, the ultimate technological warriors, they had become the elite, the guardians of empire and international order. Throughout this period, the elitism of the aviators gained from the RAF's high public profile: record-breaking flights, international air races like the Schneider Cup, and carefully orchestrated annual flying shows at Hendon and elsewhere. The first Hendon pageant, a 'modernist' version of the 'theatre of war', was held in the summer of 1920 and intended to promote the prestige of the air force through such activities as aerobatic displays, mock battles and demon-strations of how the dissidents of the empire could be bombed into submission, as the 1922 'attack on a desert fortress' revealed.[44] Subsequent shows repeated these colonial policing demonstrations, as shown in the *c.* 1934 poster (illus. 46). These events were reinforced by continual developments in civil aviation, the attention-grabbing, record-breaking flights like the first solo trans-Atlantic flight by Charles Lindbergh, the 'American Eagle', in 1927. The airman, then, became the most admired heroic figure of the period and his adventures a central ingredient in war fiction. Throughout the inter-war years, the exploits of the air fighters of 1914 were an enormously popular subject for boys (and many girls)

46 The Hendon RAF air pageant – bombing a native stronghold: poster, *c.* 1934.

and were disseminated through novels, stories, popular illustrations and film.[45]

Much of the pleasure culture of air war was imported from America, particularly feature films. British studios had neither the budgets nor the technical expertise to make convincing and spectacular films of war in the air. The sub-genre really began with William Wellman's 1927 classic *Wings,* the story of two young 'American Eagles' over the Western Front and their struggle with the German ace 'von Kellerman'. This hugely popular film was followed by Howard Hughes's *Hell's Angels* and Howard Hawks's *The Dawn Patrol* (both 1930), and by numerous low-budget derivations which continued to be released until the eve of the Second World War. While these films paid lip-service to the prevailing anti-war sentiment, the constant emphasis on heroic aerial duels and the simple, stoical nobility of the aviators, gave an overriding impression of a romantic and exciting war.[46] Another American import was pulp magazines like *War Aces, Sky Fighters, War Birds* and *G2 Battle Aces* (illus. 47), which began to appear in British newsagents and Woolworths' stores in the late '30s. With their garish coloured covers and tales of hard-fighting and brutal heroes, the pulps had considerable impact on those boys lucky enough to find them.[47] But while *Chums, Champion* and the other story papers extolled the exploits of air fighters week after week, the most influential author of such stories was probably 'Captain' W. E. Johns, the creator of Biggles.

Johns began his prolific literary career by providing popular magazines with illustrations and articles, but in 1932 he wrote 'The White Fokker' – the first Biggles story – for *Popular Flying* and then worked regularly for the appropriately named story paper *Modern Boy.* The Biggles of the early stories, as Denis Butts has pointed out, was no 'stereotyped, tight-lipped hero, but a patriotic, skilful and highly-strung young man, who several times comes close to tears, even hysteria, when comrades are lost'.[48] However, although the author had created a more realistic hero by emphasizing the cruelty of modern war and the potential psychological damage to the warrior, there was never any suggestion that the war had been unjust or futile. Nor could Johns avoid investing his stories with the romantic images of air fighting over the Western Front, which had become commonplace during the war years. The popularity of Johns's fictional hero, which continues to this day,[49] was largely due to the author's ability to continually update his creation for a rapidly changing world. Thus, in the early stories Biggles was a war flier, later a flying knight errant, and by the end of the 1930s a sort of unofficial government agent and even a mercenary prepared to work for foreign governments so long as the cause was right.[50] In many ways Johns was a worthy successor to Henty. When asked by Geoffrey Trease why he wrote, he replied:

47 The pulps: a late-1920s cover illustration from *The Lone Eagle*.

. . . for the entertainment of my reader. That is, I give boys what they
want, not what their elders and betters think they ought to read. I teach
at the same time, under a camouflage. Juveniles are keen to learn, but
the educational aspect must not be too obvious or they will become
suspicious of its intention. I teach a boy to be a man, for without that
essential qualification he will never be anything. I teach sportsmanship
according to the British idea . . . I teach that decent behaviour wins in
the end as a natural order of things. I teach the spirit of team-work,
loyalty to the Crown, the Empire, and to rightful authority.[51]

But he was a 'Henty' who had seen at first hand the horrors of modern war,
having served in the King's Own Royal Regiment at Gallipoli and in Salonika
before transferring to the RFC in 1917. Shot down in 1918, he spent the rest of
the war in a POW camp in Germany.[52] Imbued with middle-class patriotism, an
apostle of imperialism and not afraid to fight for what he believed was a just
cause, Johns had also experienced the realities of the Western Front, and these
experiences shaped his ambivalent attitude to war.

In 1932, Johns became editor of the new magazine *Popular Flying*, and used this
position to express his ideas about war and imperial defence. While he believed
that war was a 'barbaric custom', he could not rid himself of his Edwardian
upbringing and came to believe that peace was best defended from a position
of strength:

If you have a stick in your hand the other fellow thinks twice before
he pulls your nose. If you have a stick and a knife, he thinks harder. If
you have a stick, a knife and a pistol, it is improbable he will pull your
nose . . .[53]

The 'stick' was of course the RAF, the most important weapon in the nation's
arsenal. For the remainder of the decade, Johns's editorials constantly attacked
the government's niggardly defence spending, and in early 1939 his outspoken
anti-government views ensured his dismissal from the magazine.[54] For Johns,
like many others, there was no lack of potential enemies – Bolsheviks, the
Japanese and, after 1933, the Nazis. Nevertheless, it should be noted that Johns's
heroes were much less violent than those of many of his contemporaries.
Biggles, for instance, rarely killed his enemies, relying instead on a swift left-
hook to the jaw. Yet when the situation demanded it, he was prepared to use
the ultimate sanction. Although Johns was the most enduring, he was just one
of a number of authors establishing the sub-genre of air adventure.

We have already encountered George Rochester, but mention should also be made of J. F. C. Westerman (son of Percy Westerman), Captain A. O. Pollard, D. E. Marsh, David Lindsay and Alan Western. Even the long-established Percy Westerman produced a substantial number of air adventures during the period. Dennis Butts has noted that the publisher, John Hamilton, appears to have set out to corner the aviation book market in the early 1930s, issuing not only many novels by Johns, Rochester and others in the 'Ace' series, but memoirs, war novels, instruction manuals and aviation prints as well.[55] Interest in aviation among boys was also promoted by flying displays, magazines and the promotional material published by the Air League (which had begun life in 1909 as the Aerial League of the British Empire). After 1935, the sons of the elite at Oxford and Cambridge could join a University Air Squadron, in which they received flying training. As John James has noted, the primary aim underlying this initiative was not just to recruit pilots, but to imbue future members of the establishment with an understanding of, and sympathy for, the RAF.[56] Boys from less affluent families had to wait until 1940, when the Air Training Corps was established, before getting a taste of RAF life. The popularity of aviation stories was one new development of the inter-war period. Another was the demise of some of the most popular story papers of the Edwardian era and the emergence of new favourites.

The dominance of the story paper market by Harmsworth's Amalgamated Press was finally broken in the 1920s by the Dundee-based publisher D. C. Thomson & Co. with their papers *Adventure* (1921), *Rover* and *The Wizard* (1922), *Skipper* (1930) and *Hotspur* (1933) – the so-called 'Big Five'.[57] These twopenny weeklies sported brightly coloured covers and 28 pages of action and adventure, and by 1938, as one survey of children's reading habits revealed, the Thomson papers were the most popular form of juvenile reading. The average twelve-year-old read between 3.7 and 4.2 titles a month. Some, like Jim Wolveridge, bought one paper and then swapped with friends until he had consumed some 50 'books' per week.[58] Throughout the period, *Rover, The Wizard* and *Hotspur* accounted for between half and two-thirds of all story papers bought by twelve-year-olds, while through the 1930s the weekly circulation for *The Wizard* alone was over 800,000.[59]

Towards the end of that decade, the British story papers were joined by American-style 'comic' books – adventure narratives in picture form usually with some accompanying text. Illustrated comic papers had been available in Britain since the 1890s, when Harmsworth paved the way with *Comic Cuts* and *Illustrated Chips*; these were followed by many others, including the very popular *Puck* and *Rainbow*. However, the emphasis in these comics was on comedy characters, such as the incompetent detective 'Chubblock Homes' and the lazy tramps 'Weary Willie' and 'Tired Tim', but, in Britain, adventure stories in strip form were almost unknown before the Great War. The first successful adventure strip was probably 'Rob the Rover', the young orphan who roamed the world in search of his real identity. 'Rob' began his adventures in *Puck* in 1920 and proved so popular that other young adventurers followed, who, according to Dennis Gifford, 'wandered through a world of wild animals, savage cannibals, mysterious orientals and lost cities'.[60] However, as Carpenter has pointed out, British artists appeared uncomfortable with illustrated stories, and artwork and layout remained unsatisfactory until the 1950s.[61] By the later 1930s, though, American-style comic books began to appear, *WAGS* (printed in the USA) was on sale from January 1937, and offered a mixture of comedy and adventure including the young flying ace 'Tailspin Tommy'. In the same year *OKAY Comics Weekly*, an all-British publication, offered much the same mix. In America, however, all-action books were already available. Beginning with crime and jungle stories and the exploits of ace fliers, they were joined towards the end of the decade by a new heroic stereotype – the superhero. Superman made his first appearance in DC Comics in June 1938, and was soon followed by Batman and The Flash (1939). American superhero comics were on sale in Britain just before the Second World War,[62] and brought a new dimension to juvenile fiction by adding superhuman strength, and sometimes even immortality, to the traditional virtues of the hero stereotype. Meanwhile British papers and comics were developing their own unusual heroes.

The Black Sapper made his first appearance in *Rover* in 1929, a slight figure dressed entirely in black and the inventor of the 'Earth Worm', an underground boring-machine that enables him to function as a human mole. Born of a noble family, the Sapper is an outsider, essentially on the side of right but not above making a profit for himself. *Rover* also created The Flaming Avenger – a vigilante lawman complete with an 'ammonia' gun – and Morgyn the Mighty, a sort of South Seas Tarzan. Marooned on a desert island for thirteen years like some latter-day Crusoe, Morgyn develops super-strength, but still trims his hair and shaves regularly. Eventually escaping from the island, he embarks on various fighting adventures in America and Africa, taking on gangsters, half-breeds and savage tribes. Morgyn rarely kills his opponents but, as Drotner points out, 'the stories centered on fighting for his paramount strength formed the basis of his appeal'.[63] *The Wizard's* most popular adventure hero was Bill Samson, The Wolf of Kabul, a British agent who controls the 'half-mad tribes' of the north-west frontier who continually threaten to overthrow British rule. The Wolf, 'the man who makes peace by starting wars', roams the frontier with Chung, his faithful native servant, whose favourite weapon is a cricket bat – a potent symbol of the force of British civilization!

One noticeable feature of these fictions was the increased level of violence. 'There was more fighting, bleeding and brutality in the pages of the inter-war story papers than ever before'.[64] While the heroes of Henty and the other pre-1914 writers had not shrunk from violence, such acts were usually played out according to an accepted code of behaviour. After 1918, authors commonly employed more direct, no-holds-barred, physical encounters between protagonists – punching, kicking, even biting and gouging their opponents and increasingly relying on physical strength to dominate their enemies. The practitioners of this 'cult of violence', as Orwell put it, asked their readers' not to identify with a young man of about their own age as Edwardian writers had done, but with a

> G-Man, with a Foreign legionary, with some variant of a Tarzan, with an air ace, master spy, an explorer, a pugilist at any rate with some single all-powerful character who dominates everyone around him and whose usual method of solving any problem is a sock on the jaw. [65]

Orwell goes on to suggest that this violence is unconvincing and harmless, and not to be compared with the 'bloodlust of the Yank Mags'. Indeed, Jim Wolveridge, recalling his fondness for Morgyn and the Wolf of Kabul, claimed that '. . . they did me little harm and they did give me a great deal of pleasure'.[66] However, Wolveridge, growing up in a strong socialist-pacifist environment and balancing his reading of these fictions with more sensitive works, would seem to have been exceptional. Yet it may well have been that the continual emphasis on the 'cult of violence' gave many readers a desire to emulate their fictional heroes.

The increasingly violent behaviour of fictional heroes was clearly due to the war, a war far more brutal and violent than could ever have been imagined. In the face of enormous casualties it seemed that only extraordinary men survived. Storytellers thus created super-heroes, since only those who possessed superior strength, intellect or some other quality and who were prepared to adopt any means necessary could survive the vicissitudes of the modern world. Writers were unable to escape the Great War's legacy of brutality, but they also had to compete with an increasing number of exciting and spectacular films which included graphic violence. By the mid-1930s, in films like *The Lives of a Bengal Lancer* (1935), *The Charge of the Light Brigade* (1936), *The Adventures of Robin Hood* (1938) and *Beau Geste* (1939), a youthful audience could watch detailed scenes in which manly heroes dispatched their enemies with lance, sword, bayonet or bullet. Such sequences were reinforced by numerous westerns with a seemingly inexhaustible supply of outlaws or native Americans just waiting to fall to the hero's guns. Such features invariably demonstrated that only through violent action could the girl/town/nation/empire be saved. In many cases the hero himself operated outside 'the law', which was often portrayed as ineffectual or corrupt. This highlights another facet of inter-war fictions, both literary and cinematic:

lack of respect for established authority and the tendency to anarchic behaviour.

Graves and Hodge have suggested that, at the end of the Great War, it was commonly held among veterans that, while the Kaiser's government was malignant, the British government was simply 'criminally stupid'. 'The trend of feeling was towards ... ideal anarchism', the veteran wanted a 'clean sweep ... of all oppressors, cheats, cowards, skrimshankers, reactionaries and liars who had plagued and betrayed him during his service'.[67] But this purging of the establishment was never accomplished. Essentially, those who had led the nation into the war and managed it so badly during the conflict remained in the driving seat. This led to a growing determination throughout the period by veterans that they would 'no longer be "b—d" about by the people in authority'.[68] This disillusionment, this lack of respect for political leaders and other authority figures, became much more widespread with the onset of the Depression, with its emphasis on personal survival, and this explains much of the tendency to anarchic behaviour among the protagonists of popular culture. With typical post-1918 characters such as Sapper's Bulldog Drummond and E. W. Hornung's Raffles, the Gentleman Thief, the Victorian-Edwardian heroic archetype became flawed: Drummond by his sadistic tendencies (he throws one enemy into a vat of acid and deliberately breaks the arm of another) and Raffles because it amuses him to be on the wrong side of the law. Neither respect authority and both deal out their own brand of justice, yet both possess many of the characteristics essential in the traditional action hero – a warrior spirit, gentle birth and a chivalric attitude to women.[69] The popularity of these and similar heroes inevitably created models for the authors of juvenile fiction, and by the late 1920s junior versions of such characters were beginning to make their appearance.

Both Morgyn the Mighty and the Black Sapper operate outside the law, the latter especially so, and both dispense their own brand of justice to evildoers.[70] In the early novels, even the essentially law-abiding Biggles was not above breaking the law when it served a higher purpose, and Johns's characters never allowed red tape to impede their progress. The heroes in the *Chums* serials by Charles Gilson or Frank Shaw have little respect for the 'official mind', and invariably the 'authorities' are proved wrong after the hero has brought the villain to book by his own means. Such characterizations were reinforced by the rediscovery of the outlaw. *Rover*, for example, ran 'The World's Most Famous Outlaws' series which included Ned Kelly, Dick Turpin and Claude Duvall, while the cinema provided Robin Hood, Zorro and a succession of western gunmen who were essentially good 'badmen', who observed their own moral code and imposed their own brand of law and order untroubled by the 'normal' rules of society.

In juvenile fiction, the trend was set by Richmal Compton's *Just William*, the essentially 'decent' boy continually in trouble, and even his gang call themselves The Outlaws. However, the best examples are to be found in the comic papers published by D. C. Thomson, a 'curious mixture of inhibitions and lack of inhibitions'.[71] The Thomson juvenile empire is intensely conservative and authoritarian. Female characters were almost completely absent from their boys' papers, as was even the most innocent reference to sex or religion. Yet they published endless adventure stories involving rebellious characters who continually thwarted the best efforts of parents, teachers and other authority figures, from Desperate Dan and Lord Snooty to anthropomorphic animals like Big Eggo the Ostrich, Korky the Cat and Koko the Pup, whose adventures were centred in conflict with authority,[72] like the comic character portrayed by Will Hay on the cinema screen. These characters were enormously popular with children and remained firm favourites for many years. Nevertheless, they were a clear reflection of growing disillusionment with the accepted order that had so powerfully controlled pre-1914 society.[73] These developments were also reflected in the pleasure culture of war, which continued unabated throughout the period. The Great War remained a source of romantic and exciting adventure, but this was only one conflict among many.

Looking back from 1940 at the *Gem* and *Magnet* story papers, George Orwell suggested that the fictional public school world they portrayed had changed little since the beginning of the century – that whenever they were published it was always 1910:

> The ivy clusters around the old grey stones. The King is on his throne and the pound is worth a pound. Over in Europe the comic foreigners are jabbering and gesticulating, but the grim grey battleships of the British fleet are steaming up the Channel and at the outposts of Empire the monacled Englishmen are the niggers at bay.[74]

This was not only true of public school stories, as there had been equally little change in the mental world of adventure fiction. Indeed, the timelessness of the world of the pleasure culture of war in boys' papers and novels is striking. Even new technologies and concepts of war were simply absorbed into a pre-1914 version of reality. Thus aeroplanes became a more effective means of policing the empire and subduing native tribes. Wars in space became just another arena for tales of exploration, conquest and empire-building, and Britons still exhibited those essential qualities of manliness, patriotism, chivalry and Englishness, albeit with a tad more ruthlessness and brutality towards their enemies than before 1914. For most authors, fighting and war were still most commonly associated with empire; an empire now geographically greater than ever but far more troubled by the rising tide of nationalism. Yet the British Empire Exhibition of 1924, the annual celebrations of Empire Day, the Empire Marketing Board and persuasive schoolroom propaganda still maintained the fiction of the imperial destiny of the Island Race; and the empire remained a popular subject for cigarette cards, postcards, and stamps which filled many a schoolboy's bedroom.[75] War and empire figured prominently on cigarette cards, and sets showing regiments of the empire, badges of RAF squadrons and the latest military aeroplanes were much sought-after (illus. 48). But while there were no more Henty-style wars of conquest, imperial possessions still needed to be defended, and consequently much imperial fiction of the inter-war years focused on policing the frontiers, preventing native uprisings and tribal wars and foiling the machinations of foreign powers. British violence was now directed at maintaining the peace rather than sustaining conquest. And while official rhetoric suggested that the citizens of empire were junior partners rather than 'subject peoples', the firm hand (usually in the guise of an RAF bomber squadron or an armoured car) of the Anglo-Saxon was still required to control their unbridled passions.

48 Military themes were a popular subject for Player's cigarette cards.

In this context, it is interesting to note just how quickly the loyal brothers-in-arms of the war years reverted to 'the enemy' when peace returned. Heroic West Africans, who had stood shoulder to shoulder with Tommy Atkins in the trenches had, by 1919, become 'blubber-lipped' superstitious children, while the fearsome tribesmen of the north-west frontier, who had terrified the Turk, now reverted to an untrustworthy and devious foe stalking British soldiers in the foothills.[76]

India, especially the frontier, provided a popular setting for this new fiction of imperial warfare, and, given that British attention had largely been focused on Europe during the war years, the tribes were more violent and unruly than ever. They had also, apparently, learned a great deal about modern warfare. Walter Bury, who claimed to have served in India, told his *Chums* readers that tribesmen no longer charged with reckless abandon, but sniped at the Tommies from impregnable positions in the mountains and then melted away before they could be engaged. While they could still be worked up into a religious frenzy by 'wild-eyed priests', most warfare was inter-tribal, and yet, 'your tribesman loves nothing better than a fierce encounter with British troops'. But with the 'game' over, peace returns for a while and the tribesmen can be generous hosts and 'quite charming'.[77] The 'wild' nature of the inhabitants of the frontier was further explored in *Chums* in a series of stories written by 'Sheikh Ahmed Abdullah', an Afghan of noble birth and great learning, so we are told. Similar tales were written for the readers of the *Boy's Own Paper* by another noble Indian, 'Sirdar Ikbal Ali Shah', an 'educated' citizen of India who demonstrated 'profound regard for Britain'! Yet, given the growing nationalist sentiment in India and the apparent troublemaking activities by mischievous Bolsheviks, maintaining the King's peace was not easy, and here we see the emergence of the new style of hero. Typical is Robert Harding's 'Sergeant Belbin', an agent constantly in action on the north-west Frontier.

Belbin, we are told, is an ex-soldier of the old school, 'the Tommy Atkins of Kipling'. Middle class, short, stocky and with a massive neck and chest, Belbin has his own ideas about justice. Believing that the authorities are 'too soft' with troublemakers, he favours direct action with fist or bullet. And when he tangles with an enemy it is a brutal affair:

> There are no wrestling rules in the hills. There are no forbidden holds, no fouls of any sort. The fist, teeth, the kicking foot – all is permitted. The game is not to pin the opponents shoulders to the ground, but to twist or wrench or smash him into unconsciousness.[78]

Belbin can also be chivalric on occasions and sometimes turns a blind eye to minor infringements of the law. Indeed, he is not above breaking the law himself when the end justifies the means. The same sentiments were present in the popular Hollywood feature *Lives of a Bengal Lancer* (1935), directed by Henry Hathaway. Here the army is the agent of civilization protecting millions of Indians from the wild frontier tribes. The hero, Alan McGregor (Gary Cooper) has a tendency to disobey orders when it comes to action, but he is a true son of empire (McGregor is supposed to be a Canadian in the film. which explains Cooper's North American accent) who knows exactly where his duty lies. Mohammed Khan, the Afghan leader, raises the frontier tribes for a war against the British, and only the heroic actions of three young officers, led by Mac, prevent the British regiment from massacre. Mac dies gloriously blowing up the rebels' ammunition store and is awarded a posthumous VC.[79] Illustration 49 shows Gary Cooper in typically heroic pose.

Bengal Lancer was one of the most commercially successful films shown in the UK during the 1930s. In Bolton, Leslie Halliwell recalled, 'the whole town turned

49 Gary Cooper strikes a suitably heroic pose in *The Lives of a Bengal Lancer*, 1935.

out to see this oddly-titled Indian adventure'.[80] It also earned considerable praise from the critics. The *Daily Mail*, for example, said it 'paid a remarkable tribute to the wisdom and courage which have marked British government in India. It is a powerful and popular argument for the continuance of that rule'.[81] The film was the first of a series of American adventure movies which paid tribute to the heroes of the empire and included *Charge of the Light Brigade* (1936) and *Gunga Din* (1939). The popularity of these American films was mirrored by those produced by Alexander Korda's London Films, particularly *Sanders of the River* (1935) and *The Four Feathers* (1939).[82] Film adventures reached a huge audience, but predominantly in urban areas, so that the printed word remained an enormously important source for the pleasure culture of war for many, and books and stories offered equally exotic adventures.

The desert had been the exotic setting for that most romantic of all Great War heroes, T. E. Lawrence – 'the Silent Sentinel of the Sand' – and the 'man who won a war on his own', as one boys' paper put it.[83] Lawrence perfectly suited the mood of the times: brilliant, brutal, unconventional and with little patience for the official mind, and the Lawrence legend inspired a number of imitations in juvenile fiction. Percy Westerman's 'The White Arab', for example, related the adventures of Denis Hornby, the nineteen-year-old 'ace' of the British Secret Service, and his quest to discover who was inciting rebellion in the Middle East (Bolsheviks, of course!).[84] The Lawrence influence was also obvious in the 1935 novel *Biggles Flies East*. Set in 1917, Biggles goes undercover in Palestine to foil the plans of the German Lawrence, 'El Shereef'. The villain turns out to be none other than the Prussian aristocrat Erich von Stalhein, destined to be Biggles's enemy through two world wars.[85] Alan Western's *Desert Hawk* was also set in Palestine, this time in the post-war period, when Arab–Jewish rivalry was creating chaos. As the author explains, this antagonism became so bad that the 'League of Nations turned to Britain, "the Policeman of the World", with what they called a Mandate to restore order':

> Once again foreign troops marched through the streets of [Jerusalem] and once again a certain measure of peace was restored. But in trying to hold the balances of justice evenly the British have earned the dislike of both parties, who would rather have favouritism than justice. Both Jew and Arab think that the British are too lenient with the other side, and both are eager to take matters into their hands again and settle it once and for all with a good deal of bloodshed.[86]

Preventing this bloodshed was the job of Captain Benson. Closely modelled on Lawrence, Benson lives in Jerusalem with his family but is frequently away on mysterious trips into the desert disguised as an Arab. His job is to track down and deal with those who would drive Jew and Briton into the sea. On one particularly hazardous mission against foreign agents attempting to stir up a Holy War, Benson is rescued by his seventeen-year-old son, who has just learned to fly. Although on this occasion war is avoided, Western ends on a pessimistic note:

> There is no peace in Palestine. The land is quiet but it is a watchful quietness, with the two ancient antagonists eyeing on another like boxers . . .
>
> The great danger is averted – but for how long? That question can only be answered by the quiet men who go about their business without advertisement, who learn of trouble before it comes and institute steps to stop it, and who often go to a lonely death without even a line in the papers to say how they died. These men serve not only their own country, but the whole world, in the cause of peace . . .
>
> Lawrence of Arabia was a man such as this, but whereas his fame will ring down the centuries, there are many who bring off work of tremendous importance whose names will never be known. The risks are terrifying; the reward is small; but the tradition of service remains an ideal to all who wish the name of England to be coupled with that of Peace.[87]

Thus the violence perpetrated by the British against indigenous peoples was, as always, in the latter's own best interests. What is interesting is the simple acceptance that unceasing warfare is the price Britain must pay to ensure peace throughout the empire and mandated territories: the White Man, particularly the Englishman, must still bear his burden despite the 'war to end war'.

The responsibility for policing the vast inhospitable territories of the Middle East was, as we have seen, one means by which the Royal Air Force preserved its autonomy after the Great War, and this blend of traditional imperial adventure combined with the romance of aviation was enormously appealing. The aeroplane as an agent of imperial control and retribution was a common feature of such stories. In Stuart Campbell's 'Hawk of the Desert', for instance, Flying Officer Teddy Saunders, RAF, deals with air pirates who shoot down and loot air mail carriers over Iraq. The air force also played the colonial policeman in India. In 'The Eagle of Peace' the young RAF pilot stationed on the frontier makes a daring landing to kidnap the 'Red Mullah' and prevent yet another Holy War against the British; as the author notes, 'an eagle swooped in the Himalayas – but this time to bring peace, not destruction'.[88] In reality, the air force rarely relied on such non-violent methods, and destruction from the air was a terrifying weapon to use against unsophisticated natives. As an RAF pilot in a Robert Harding story explains, 'Afghans don't like bombs'![89] The aeroplane was simply the latest technological development by which Europeans overawed and over-powered other races. In the eighteenth and nineteenth centuries it was firearms, in the twentieth, aeroplanes. Compare, for example, the similarity of the images in illustrations 50 and 12. The RAF did display a degree of chivalric behaviour on occasion, for it was common in Iraq to drop leaflets on recalcitrant villagers warning them that an air raid would take place the next day![90] Airmen were, of course, officers, but other ranks could also play a part in the 'new' empire. We have already encountered Sergeant Belbin, but on the River Tigris it is Private Bob Cartwright who is the guardian of empire and who rounds up Arab smugglers and pirates.[91]

If Lawrence of Arabia was a major influence on stories set in the Middle East, the inspiration for African stories was Edgar Wallace's super-human district officer *Sanders of the River* (published in 1909 and filmed by Alexander Korda in 1935). In Percy Westerman's 'The Ju Ju Hand' it is the young district commissioner, Brian Ferrars, who prevents a bloody tribal war by cunning and a little violence. In the same volume of *Chums*, Rex Hardinge published 'White Man's Magic', in which the hero is 'Sandy Carver' of the Gold Coast Regiment. Again we have

50 The flying machine was yet another demonstration of the white man's superiority. From *Modern Boy*, 1936.

a tribal war which is resolved only by the young Briton with the usual mixture of superior intellect and iron hand. Hardinge even has his 'Sandy' emulate the peculiar speech pattern of the Edgar Wallace original: 'I see you man . . . Know you not that I am here with my soldiers, and those who defy me will live this night with ghosts'.[92] The author went even further in later stories and jokingly called his peacemaker 'Sandy Wallace'.[93] As well as maintaining peace in Africa, young Britons were also in action preventing rebellions in China, toppling fiendish warlords and dealing with Malay pirates in the South China Sea. And despite the rhetoric of imperial partnership, the pre-1914 hierarchy of race was still very much in place. Arabs were still devious; the tribes of Northern India were still admired for their bravery but never to be trusted, Africans were childlike savages who could be outwitted by the most simpleminded Anglo-Saxon, but Orientals, and especially the Chinese, were downright evil. In fiction, Chinese villains bore a remarkable likeness to Sax Rohmer's 'Dr Fu Manchu'. They enjoyed torturing their victims and were easy prey for Bolshevik troublemakers.[94] A variation on the imperial adventure theme was supplied by the popular Foreign Legion stories of the 1930s. These usually involved several young Britons looking for adventure or in exile after being falsely accused of some dastardly crime, and were undoubtedly inspired by the popularity of P. C. Wren's *Beau Geste* (1924 and filmed in 1926 and 1939). Typical of this endless war in the desert was Francis Marlowe's series about Sergeant John Lanson of the French Foreign Legion, and 'Sons of the Legion' by an appropriately named Alan Breck (the same name as the hero of *Kidnapped*). Interestingly, Breck's series was set in the Spanish Legion.[95]

Apart from the Legion, the involvement of Britons in foreign wars of the period was rare. E. Malcolm Shard's *Flying for Ethiopia* (1936) was a notable exception. The young hero, Pip Clayton, finds himself flying against the Italians in Ethiopia. Even the Spanish Civil War was largely ignored by authors of juvenile fiction. Percy Westerman's *Under Fire in Spain* and Eric Wood's *Phantom Wings Over Spain* were sympathetic to the nationalist cause,[96] but in 1939, while W. E. Johns was writing *Biggles in Spain*, the climate was more sympathetic to the republicans. However, Biggles and Co. only become involved in the war by accident, and their attitude is summed up by Ginger who:

> . . . realised that he hardly knew what the war in Spain was about. It had never interested him. He had a vague idea that it was a civil war in which certain other countries had taken sides, but since he did not even know the original cause of the quarrel he had no sympathies with either side.[97]

The war in Abyssinia inspired only one reference in the weeklies – a colour plate in the 1936 *Chums* annual showing Italian troops being ambushed by noble

51 Italian soldiers are ambushed during the war in Abyssinia. From *Chums*, 1936.

Abyssinian warriors, an interesting reversal of the racial norm for the boys' paper (illus. 51). Spain was rarely mentioned at all. This was partly due to the peculiarly 'inward-looking' attitude of British society at this time, when it came to the doings of other nations. With Chamberlain, a 'Conservative version of "Little Englandism" prevailed, in which Czechoslovakia, threatened by dictators, was a "a faraway country of which we know little".[98] The traditional inclination of the British was to champion the underdog – the victims of oppression and tyrants – when it came to foreign wars, especially when doing so embarrassed a rival power; but given the pressure from the government not to offend Mussolini or Hitler and to remain strictly neutral over Spain, most editors and authors found it safer to ignore the little wars of the 1930s altogether. There was also, of course, the innate superiority of being English and the inability to believe that the doings of foreigners, however dramatic, had any significance in the scheme of things! Yet there was one European rival who could be attacked with government approval – Soviet Russia. In his analysis of the story papers, Orwell suggested that contemporary history was 'carefully excluded' from their pages, and that Russia, 'when it was mentioned at all', was simply a source of interesting facts or figures'.[99] But Orwell was wrong when it came to Russia. From 1919 onwards, Bolsheviks regularly provided authors with a politically acceptable enemy. As Jim Wolveridge put it, 'poor Russia was a permanent supplier of menaces in those days'.[100]

Tales of a future war against the 'Red Terror' for adult readers began almost immediately the Great War had ended, and were widespread throughout the period. Fear of Communism was founded not on some vague possibility of the Red Army pouring across Europe, but on the belief that agitators would incite revolution among the British working classes. The wave of post-war strikes, the increasing strength of the Labour Party and the growing discontent of some veterans convinced many among the elites that the 'country was on the verge of a Bolshevist uprising'.[101] Juvenile fiction reflected this same fear, and some of the earliest anti-Soviet propaganda was to be found in the imperialistic *Chums*. In 1919, for example, Radcliffe Martin's 'His Bit' told the story of how young Jim Bates prevents a Bolshevik-inspired strike in the aircraft factory in which he works. The magazine continued its anti-Soviet offensive not only in fiction, but in 'factual' articles as well. In the early '30s, under the title 'Red Russia!', a photographic spread showed various scenes of contemporary Russia with suitable captions. Under a picture of Stalin smoking his pipe the caption read, 'This is no pipe of peace that he is smoking'. With a picture of a collective farm, readers were told, 'there is little respect for the wishes of these labourers in Russia's red vineyard'; and explaining a factory scene, 'those who have not worked with a will . . . have paid a big penalty!'[102] Similar propaganda could be found in the other boys' papers, although in the *BOP* it took a more religious slant. Explaining how the 'Reds' were trying to destroy belief in God, an editorial claimed:

> The attitude of a handful of fanatics, drunk with self-importance, who imagine that mere denial can cancel the whole past experience of mankind, would be simply childishly foolish, if it had not such a tragical side . . . Some of the methods which they are adopting to gain their ends are such as cannot be in the 'Boy's Own Paper'. . .
>   . . . common humanity calls us to join our protests to the rest of the civilised world, and to pray that God will turn the hands of the persecutors and lead them to restore freedom of religion . . .[103]

A cynic might suggest that there was a certain irony in the *BOP* condemning the Bolsheviks for enforcing their atheist views with 'rifle and bayonet', when it had supported the same tactics employed by aggressive British missionaries in converting subject peoples to Christianity for the past 200 years! But such propaganda went far beyond pointing out the evils of the Soviet regime.

Fiction of Anglo–Soviet relations took two forms: the undeclared 'cold war' of spying, sabotage and incitement to rebellion among the people of the empire by the agents of the Kremlin, and, more rarely, the all-out shooting war caused by a Bolshevik invasion of the British Isles. As we have seen, many of the stories of peacekeeping within the empire revealed that behind rebellions, holy wars

and general mischief in the Middle East, Africa and Asia lurked the hand of
the Bolshevik. In Sheikh Ahmed Abdullah's story, 'In Red Turkestan', the author
painted a grim picture of life in the Soviet Republic, but, more importantly, relates
how he discovered and helped to destroy a secret bureau established by Moscow
to manufacture and spread anti-British propaganda throughout the region.[104]
Russian agents of course were also active in the motherland, spreading their
poison among discontented workers and generally inciting trouble. It was here
that George Rochester's modern-day outlaw, 'Captain Robin Hood', was at work.
Hood, a daring and patriotic airman, uses unorthodox and sometimes unlawful
methods to deal with spies and saboteurs. Nevertheless, the outlaw has the good
of the empire at heart, for he was much given to pompously lecturing his
Bolshevik captives: 'Do you not realise, you fool', he tells one:

> that the soul of England is the mightiest force for good in the world
> to-day and that she is above all hurt from such as you and those
> whom you serve? Dare to draw that sword . . . and England will draw
> one which will not be sheathed until your invading armies have been
> scattered and your own brought fluttering down to be trampled, for all
> time, into the dust![105]

There is considerable violence in Rochester's serial, committed both by Hood
and by the heavily-bearded Soviets, who enjoy torturing their prisoners with red-
hot pokers. *Fighting the Red Shadow* by 'Vigilant' and Jack Heming's *The Air Spies*
also dealt with the Bolshevik menace to Britain, while J. R. Holden's *Wings of
Revolution* and Rochester's *Scarlet Squadron* dealt with the threat to the empire.[106]

The invasion of Britain by a Bolshevik army was the subject of Frank Shaw's
1922 serial, 'The Red Deluge'. Here Russia and China combine to bring down the
hated British Empire, which had been too generous for its own good. As we
discover, the Russians have accepted loans from Britain 'for the betterment of
Russia', but have used the money to re-arm and prepare for war. Inciting unrest
in India and thus distracting British attention, they destroy the Atlantic Fleet
and fall upon the homeland with terrible fury. The title illustration shows the
teeming hordes of Russia and China marching into battle, their Asiatic and Slavic
faces contorted with hatred for the British (illus. 52). This is no ordinary war,
for, as the author informs us:

> This war – a war of extermination – was not conducted on such lines
> as humanity had previously known. A blood-mad mob of practically
> countless millions of men had been let loose on civilization by the two
> leaders who believed that only by destroying every existing thing could

52 'The Red Deluge': title illustration from an anti-Bolshevik serial, 1922.

the world be made ready for the amazing new edifice of successful Bolshevism that was to stand as a memorial of progress through the coming centuries.[107]

The red deluge is, of course, destroyed by gallant young Britons, in this case Hilary and Clive Bellamy and their scientist father, who invents a 'death ray'. With the menace averted, the brothers and their two friends are rewarded by the King, who creates a new 'knightly honour' for them, 'the Order of Heroes'. The Great War had clearly had little effect on the author, as the serial is virtually identical to the many future war stories Shaw had written before 1914. 'The Red Deluge' provided one of the rare occasions on which the Anglo–Soviet war came to pass, but there were many other tales in which a major war was only just averted.

W. E. Johns's fictional airman, Biggles, began his long struggle against Communism in the 1930s, a battle he was still fighting 30 years later. His first encounter with Bolshevism took place in the curiously titled novel *Biggles and the Black Peril*. Set at some point in the near future, it begins with Biggles and his cousin Algy uncovering a Soviet plot to invade Britain using giant, black-painted flying-boats. In their attempt to discover more details, the two pilots encounter 'Ginger' Hebblethwaite, a sixteen-year-old miner's son who has run away from home to join the RAF. Unable to convince the authorities of the plot, Biggles, Algy and their young protégé track the would-be invaders to their base on the Baltic Coast. Now able to prove their claims, they lure the invaders into a trap, and the enemy machines are destroyed by the RAF. The whole episode is 'hushed up' by the government, and even when the wreckage of the black flying-boats is washed up on the east coast, Biggles tells his companions, 'the Ministry have denied any knowledge of the matter to the Press, as they were bound to without running the risk of starting a war'.[108]

The Black Peril is a curious novel. It contains little of the anti-Bolshevik rhetoric common at the time (and which would become a feature of Johns's later work), nor is there any explanation as to why the Russians want to invade Britain; it certainly does not appear to be part of a masterplan for the domination of Europe. Johns apparently used 'Bolsheviks' as a convenient label for the villains in a basic adventure story influenced by the dominant themes of the period – anti-Bolshevik rhetoric and the widespread fear of aerial attack – and dramatically exploited them in a number of popular titles (see below). To some extent, *The Black Peril* reflected something of Johns's own contradictory attitude to Communism at this time. While he clearly saw the Fascist states of Italy, German and Japan as the greatest danger to world peace, Communism threatened many of his cherished beliefs, especially his belief in the British Empire as an agent of civilization and progress. In the story 'Three Weeks', for example, Biggles and Algy are passing through Karachi when they run into an old friend now working for British intelligence. He tells them that Britain is about to sign an agreement with Persia, and that the top Soviet agent in India, 'Ivan Nikitoff', is out to sabotage it. Biggles asks why the Russian cannot simply be made to 'disappear' for a while, but his friend explains that the authorities are frightened of adverse publicity and diplomatic problems: the 'British Bulldog has lost his teeth', he tells them. However, Biggles and Algy take a hand, and quite illegally ensure that the Russian is stranded in the desert until the agreement is safely signed.[109]

While Johns clearly favoured such direct action when the empire was threatened, his attitude to Russia became ambiguous during the Spanish Civil War. In January 1937, in an editorial in *Popular Flying*, he criticized the Russians for their intervention and likened Bolshevism to a 'mad dog' . . . 'it must bite somebody, even those who have befriended it. There is only one thing to do with a mad dog. Shoot it'.[110] Yet only a few months before he had defended Russian rearmament: 'Russia doesn't want war, but she sees what is coming from the East, so she must get ready'.[111] The East, of course, was a reference to Japan, which he believed was bent on territorial expansion at Russia's expense. But while Johns's attitude to Russia was contradictory, other authors, like Percy Westerman, clearly saw the danger and were consistently anti-Soviet throughout the period.

Westerman wrote a number of anti-Bolshevik stories and several offered interesting variations on the usual themes. 'The Red Pirate' of 1933 opens at the World Disarmament Conference, where the Great Powers have agreed to abolish 'under-sea warfare' for ever. Mishka Kotovsky, dictator of the USSR, is the last to sign (presumably with great difficulty as Westerman has already established that he can neither read nor write!). However, this 'deep-scheming' peasant only pretends to destroy Russian submarines, and in reality orders them to wage all-out war against merchant shipping under a pirate flag – a 'phase of the war between proletarian Russia and the bourgeoisie and capitalists of the rest of the world, especially the English'.[112] Naturally, the scheme is discovered and eventually the red pirates are tracked down and destroyed by the Royal Navy. *The Terror of the Seas* was even more imaginative. This takes place in the near future, when the Bolshevik regime has collapsed. As the author explains, dissension among the Soviet leadership, a disastrous war against Latvia and the discontent of the Russian masses brought about its end and saw a new democratic government established in Moscow. However, Vladimir Klinkov, one of the last 'terrorists' and ex-head of the CHEKA (a man noted for his 'fiendish cruelty') escapes, seizes a submarine and embarks on a career of piracy. In common with many of Westerman's tales, the Royal Navy puts an end to the 'terror'.[113] But, given the tense diplomatic climate from the mid-1930s, it was generally safer to look back at past wars.

The *BOP*, *Chums* and the other weekly papers had frequently turned to the Crusades, the English Civil War and the upheavals of the sixteenth century for safe subject matter through which to explore nationalism, heroism and the romance of war, and this became even more common during the 1930s. Geoffrey Trease, destined to become one of the most enduring authors of juvenile fiction, began his career in 1934 with *Bows Against the Barons*, an interpretation of the Robin Hood legend in which the outlaws are portrayed as revolutionaries who regard all 'masters' as oppressors of the common man. Trease was committed to a left-wing perspective which sought to overturn the conservatism of Henty. Despite its exciting descriptions, *Bows Against the Barons* achieved little success in Britain at the time.[114] Far more successful were C. S. Forester's adventures of Horatio Hornblower, set during the Napoleonic Wars – another period of international crisis and upheaval. The first novel, *The Happy Return*, was published in 1937 and *A Ship of the Line* and *Flying Colours* the following year. In Hornblower, Forester had created a new kind of hero, an enigmatic figure wracked with self-doubt and who continually underestimates his own heroism. Yet Hornblower is still the archetypal chivalric English warrior, modest, humane and patriotic. The novels are a wonderful portrait of naval warfare in the age of sail, and a tribute to the Royal Navy's part in overthrowing the 'Corsican tyrant'. Hornblower enjoyed enormous popularity. Isabel Quigly remembered that she and her friends were 'bowled over' by the stories and discussed them in the minutest detail.[115]

The past was also plundered by film-makers of the period. Alongside those films which justified the Empire (*Sanders of the River*, *Elephant Boy* and *Rhodes of Africa*, for example), ran a cycle of highly popular costume adventures which not only extolled the heroes of the past but contained powerful lessons for the present. Alexander Korda's hugely successful film of Baroness Orczy's *The Scarlet*

Pimpernel (1935) has the noble Englishman, Sir Percy Blakeney (Leslie Howard), standing against the oppression of revolutionary France and demonstrating, once again, that one Englishman is a match for any number of 'demmed Froggies'. More important is the notion of England as a haven of stability and order surrounded by a world in turmoil. The idea of England as a bastion against tyranny was reprised in Korda's *Fire over England* (1937). This retold the story of the Spanish Armada. Produced by Erich Pommer, a refugee from Hitler's Germany, the film, 'set up a strong polarity between England, standing for Freedom, Truth and Justice, and Spain, standing for Tyranny, Fear and Force'.[116] Here, then, is an England standing alone against the forces of darkness. *Fire over England* recalled an age of romance and heroism, but could hardly fail to inspire its audience to stand, once again, against the new tyranny emerging in Europe. England's struggle against Spain, and its climax in the defeat of the Armada, is one of great tableaux of national history constantly resurrected in times of peril, for instance during the Crimean War, when Kingsley used it in *Westward Ho!* The fight against tyranny and injustice was reinforced through a series of very popular Hollywood features loosely based on incidents in the English past. *Captain Blood* (1935), *The Adventures of Robin Hood* (1938) and *The Sea Hawk* (1940) which again retold the Armada story. The pleasure culture of war, then, could safely be located into the past – but it could also be located in the future.

After the Great War, adult literature of future wars as heroic adventure almost disappeared, as 'it proved inconceivable for any writer ever again to dwell on "the pride, pomp and circumstance of glorious war"'.[117] Many authors even turned to imaginative fiction to draw attention to the devastating consequences for civilization of another great war – Shanks's *People of the Ruins* and Wells's *The Shape of Things to Come*, for example. In juvenile fiction, however, while tales of future wars remained popular, dystopian fiction was rare; only Michael Poole's *Emperor of the World* (1923) attempted to describe how a great war in 1934 destroyed civilization. Chemical weapons are used by all the combatants, and only a handful of scientists, led by 'Professor Marckstein', survive in a drug-induced 'hyper-sleep' deep in an underground laboratory. Awakening in 2134, they discover that civilization has disappeared, and human survivors are living in caves and wearing animal skins. Marckstein, by virtue of his technological expertise, makes himself Emperor of the World until he is overthrown by some of the younger scientists, who restore a democratic world order.[118] Curiously, H. G. Wells's later and better known book, *The Shape of Things to Come* (1933), contains a number of similar episodes. Poole, not wishing to offend any one nation, carefully avoided naming the combatants in his story, using vague terms like 'The Quadruple Alliance'. But some authors, mindful of the international antagonisms that had contributed to 1914, fought their imaginary wars against alien life-forms. 'The Raiding Planet' by Brian Cameron has an inter-galactic war fought between the earth and the planet Thor. The story owed a great deal to Wells's *The War of the Worlds*, for the Thoreans use 'fighting machines' similar to those of the Martians in the earlier story, and their base is a 'pit' in the heart of the English countryside.[119] In 1930, *Chums* ran a series of science fiction stories in which the first men land on Venus and witness the terrible war fought between the technically superior inhabitants of the planet – a war even more terrible than the slaughter of the Western Front. John Brunton, the leader of the human expedition, is appalled at the savagery:

> The demoniacal fury of the fighting was appalling – it was like the huge elemental destructiveness of an earthquake rather than the clash of beings fashioned like themselves . . .
>
> 'I was four years in France', said Brunton slowly, 'but I never saw anything approaching this. It makes the Somme seem like child's play'![120]

The war was so horrifying, of course, because of the advanced technological weaponry developed by the Venusians, which easily destroys their modernistic cities (illus. 53). Space wars became increasingly common, no doubt influenced by the immensely popular Saturday cinema serials of Flash Gordon, in which Flash, Dr Zharkov and Dale Arden struggle against the villainous Emperor of Mars, 'Ming the Merciless'.[121] Interestingly, Ming was little more than another manifestation of the evil Oriental.

The potential danger of the 'yellow peril' had been a cause for concern for many authors long before 1914, but anxiety increased after the Great War because of the chaotic state of China and the rise of Japan. These fears were frequently reflected in juvenile fiction, and the stereotypical Oriental owed much to the fictions of Sax Rohmer – sinister, sadistic and with a deep hatred of Europeans, especially the British. As we have seen, the Chinese attempted to destroy the

53 Title illustration from 'A Planet at War', *Chums*, 1932.

empire in Rochester's *Scarlet Squadron* and joined with Soviet Russia in 'Red Deluge' to invade Britain. But the invasion of Manchuria in 1931 clearly signalled the expansionist aims of the militarist Japanese empire, which many Britons saw as a threat to their interests in the Far East. Thereafter, Japan was often the 'enemy' in juvenile war fiction. The Big Five ran a number of invasion serials through the 1930s. In 'Britain Invaded', the attack was led by 'Wu Fang', a brutal Mongolian warlord, supported by the modern technology of the 'Chans' (Japanese).[122] Slightly more realistic about the danger lurking in the East was *Biggles: Air Commodore*. Here Biggles is unofficially sent by British intelligence to the Indian Ocean to investigate the mysterious sinking of a number of British ships carrying armaments to military garrisons in the Far East. He is actually offered a permanent position at high rank in the Service, but replies, '. . . I should be absolutely useless in an official capacity . . . I have my own way of doing things, and they are seldom the official way. If I got tangled up in your red tape I should never get anywhere'.[123] After various adventures, he finds a secret island submarine base which is responsible for the lost ships. The enemy's intention is to starve British garrisons of supplies, and then use the base as a jumping-off point for an impending invasion of India. Finally, after the usual mishaps and daring escapes, Biggles is able to summon help from the RAF and the base is destroyed. But although the enemy is never identified, Johns leaves us in no doubt that it is Japan.

Mindful of the government's attempt to heal the rift with their late enemies, authors rarely used Germany as the enemy until the late 1930s, but even then it never appeared as dangerous as Soviet Russia. A rare exception was Leslie Beresford's 1922 serial, 'War of Revenge', which suggested that the Germans, humiliated by the terms of the Versailles Treaty, set out for revenge in 1962. While they still have a small army and air force (interestingly, the author makes the assumption that the Allied Arms Commission would be effective!), they have developed a number of new weapons, including a radio-controlled aerial torpedo and robotic fighting machines. The British, however, have developed their own advanced weapon – a mysterious ray which dissolves metal. After much bloodshed, Germany is again defeated.[124] The unpredictable Thomson empire, however, ran several serials in the *Rover*, which predicted another Anglo–German War. In 'Britain Attacked' (1936), Commander Silver of the British Secret Service destroys the 'Henkal Robots' – radio-controlled bombing aeroplanes – which would be used to soften Britain before the invasion. Despite his success, the invasion takes place and Britain is devastated by poison gas and other unpleasant weapons before Germany is finally defeated.[125] Two years later, W. E. Johns published *Biggles Goes to War*, an entertaining Ruritanian-style adventure in which the heroes defend the east European state of Maltovia against its more

powerful neighbour, 'Lovitzna'. The latter has signed a secret pact with one of
the Great Powers (Germany) and in return receives aircraft, pilots and other
equipment for its war of conquest.[126] During the last year of peace, cinema became
much more explicit about the dangers of Hitler's Germany, and both Alfred
Hitchcock's *The Lady Vanishes* (1938) and *The Four Just Men* (1939), were set in
unnamed European countries which were obviously Germany. *Q Planes* (1939)
was even more explicit, with its very obviously German agents attempting to
steal a new British invention. Made during the autumn of 1938, while most
Britons basked in the misplaced euphoria of the Munich agreement, the film
took the unfashionable line of criticizing Chamberlain's government for failing
to re-arm earlier. Such fiction was accompanied by a series of official documentaries, including *The Gap* (1937) and *The Warning* (1939), designed to allay fears
about an enemy air attack and prepare the nation for war.[127]

Adult fiction of the period played upon the public belief that the next war
would begin with massive and devastating air raids on cities, and often provided
graphic detail of the effects of such attacks – Nevil Shute's *What Happened to
the Corbetts* or Wells's *Things to Come,* for example. In their juvenile counterparts
the raids were usually foiled at the last moment by heroic young Britons, or
destroyed en route by the RAF. This need to play down the spectre of the bomber
helps to explain the constant appearance in juvenile fiction of British airmen –
probably the most common heroic icon of the period. With young men such
as these, Britons need have no fear of the air raider! The splendidly visual, but
somewhat pompous, film version of Wells's novel was probably one of the most
frightening predictions of future war made during the 1930s. Beginning with
a terrifying air raid on 'Everytown' (London), it clearly demonstrates the author's
belief that modern warfare was so destructive it could lead only to the complete
breakdown of civilization. The young Leslie Halliwell later remembered: 'from
the opening titles we were awed, gripped and frightened'.[128] Significantly, the
first British propaganda film of the Second World War, *The Lion Has Wings*
(previewed on 19 October 1939), dealt not only with the air defence of Britain
but with RAF offensive operations against Germany.[129]

The experience of 1914–18, then, seemingly had little effect on the pleasure
culture of war. In the fictional world of juvenile fiction, young Britons may have
spent much of their energy on preventing wars, but this was only achieved
through a measure of violence – a left hook to the jaw of the agitator or a stick of
bombs on an insurgent village. Paper wars of the 1920s and '30s were brutally
executed and employed a whole range of new and terrifying weaponry, especially
the aeroplane. Yet, in the final analysis, the masculine ideal of the warrior had
changed little since the nineteenth century. The pleasure culture of war still

portrayed war and violence as normal, necessary and justified. Contemporary heroes, perhaps because of disillusionment with the war, now demonstrated a tendency to unorthodox methods, had little respect for authority and little time for 'red tape'; but they were still brave, and still judged their fellows by their ability in a scrap. As Orwell noted, most of the middle and better-off working class:

> are patriotic to the middle of their bones . . . When England is in danger they rally to its defence as a matter of course, but in between times they are not interested. After all England is always in the right and England always wins, so why worry? It is an attitude that has been shaken during the last twenty years, but not so deeply as is sometimes supposed.[130]

There was no rush to the colours in 1939 as there had been in 1914, but there had been a steady stream of young volunteers into the Territorial Army in 1938–9, partly because it was becoming clear that another war was likely, and partly in search of a little excitement to counteract the dullness of everyday life. As Gary Sheffield has explained:

> [M]any young men proved resistant to the trend among the intellectual and social elite of revulsion against the First World War.
>
> . . . [L]ike every other period in history, war and the military life offered glamour and excitement. Many young men who were to fight in the Second World War carried into that War mental images of the Great War quite at odds with the 'disillusioned' view which is popularly supposed to have dominated the British psyche in the 1930s.[131]

That those young men could still view war as exciting and glamorous was due to the heroic and romantic images of war and violence which had been so much a part of juvenile fiction throughout the inter-war period.

6 Fighting the People's War: 1939–45

And so he sailed through sky of blue,
And looking down to get the view.
What should he spot but E-boat crew,
Using our sea to sail in too!

'Of all the cheek!' cried lad. 'Here goes!
I'll pull that Nasti skipper's nose!
I'll make him dance, and hop and skip!
By gum! I think I'll pinch his ship!'

So that's how Ernie got to be,
Admiral of his own Navee . . .

'Our Ernie', *Knock-Out* (September 1942)

Time was when, with many another youth, John had secretly wished
that the war might continue indefinitely. From a selfish point of view
he had regarded life afloat in the R.N.V.R. as far preferable to swotting
in a bank.

Percy F. Westerman, *Operations Successfully Executed* (1945)

The declaration of war against Germany in September 1939 was greeted, not with
the hysterical patriotism of 1914, but in a sombre mood of grim determination
overshadowed by the expectation of an immediate air attack by the Luftwaffe.
'When war was declared, I expected to be dead in a matter of minutes . . .',
Jim Wolveridge remembered, 'and when the siren went a few minutes after the
declaration of war, I was sure of it'.[1] Theatres and cinemas were closed in view
of the expected air raids, BBC schedules were altered to include frequent news
bulletins, and even the fledgling BBC Television was taken off the air. The evacuation of children and mothers from the cities, planned in 1938, took place almost
immediately, and between late June 1939 and the first week of September more

than three and a half million people were moved from areas vulnerable to air attack to places considered safe.[2] Prime Minister Neville Chamberlain formed his war cabinet, reluctantly bringing in Winston Churchill as First Lord of the Admiralty, and the British Expeditionary Force (BEF) under the command of General Lord Gort was dispatched to France, where it 'dug in' and awaited the expected German onslaught.

The immediate task for British propagandists was to justify the war, to demonstrate that German aggression left little alternative but to fight. Secondly, to allay public anxiety about the efficiency of the German war machine. The first presented few problems. Hitler and the Nazis were so evidently wicked, and the attack on Poland so unprovoked, that few Britons had doubts about the essential righteousness of the war. From mid-1940, as the moral crusade turned into a struggle for national survival, any lingering doubts were quickly cast aside. In broadcasts, booklets, newspaper articles and, above all, in films like *Do It Now!*, *The First Days* and *The Lion Has Wings*, the idea that Britain was capable of defending itself against Germany, and especially against an aerial attack, was implanted in the national consciousness.[3] The same message had been expressed in juvenile fiction written in the last days of peace. In Westerman's *Eagles' Talons*, young ex-RAF officer Nigel Heath returns to Britain after his adventures in South America. Unsure of what he should do, he is reminded by an air force friend that, '. . . Great Britain is proceeding with her re-armament plan. We aren't taking any more insane chances as we did when we voluntarily disarmed to danger point. The RAF is training new pilots by the hundreds . . . and . . . inviting former pilots to rejoin'. Nigel, of course, declares that he will rejoin right away, even though he may be in for a 'sticky time'.[4] The implication was that the RAF was now gearing up to defend the nation and strike at the heart of the enemy.

But the predicted air attack on Britain's cities, like the attack on the BEF in France, failed to materialize. In fact, remarkably little seemed to happen between September 1939 and the spring of 1940, and the anxieties of the first days gave way to the complacency of the 'phoney war'. In Richmal Crompton's *William and the ARP* (1939) and *William and the Evacuees* (1940), preparations to withstand air attack and the billeting of working-class children from the city with the Brown family were seen as faintly ridiculous and quite unnecessary activities. In reality, of course, Hitler was making good the losses of the Polish Campaign and considering his next move. The Allies, however, also refused to consider offensive action, either in France, because their strategy was defensive and based on a belief in the impregnability of the Maginot Line, or in Britain, because Chamberlain and the appeasers still cherished hopes that a negotiated settlement with Germany might be possible. Even the much-acclaimed RAF Bomber Command, with its 'hundreds of pilots', was restricted to a few attacks on German shipping and to leaflet raids on German cities. Only Churchill and his circle called for a vigorous prosecution of the war, but few took heed.

There was, however, no phoney war in the pleasure culture of war. W. E. Johns, for example, disappointed by his failure to get back in uniform, turned to lecturing for the Air Defence Corps (the forerunner of the Air Training Corps) and service with the ARP. Yet his main contribution to the war effort was producing propagandist fiction that would encourage the youth of the nation in the struggle against Fascism. According to Jack Cox, a personal friend and a future editor of the *Boy's Own Paper*, 'The Air Ministry woke up to the fact that during the black-out, Biggles became an established boys' hero and was a most valuable recruiting aid for the RAF'.[5] Johns's heroes went immediately into action. Called to the Air Ministry just minutes after the declaration of war, Biggles, Algy and Ginger are commissioned into the air force and sent off to a secret island base in the Baltic, from which 'raids will be launched on military objectives . . . places which could not very well be reached from England or France'.[6] Johns was careful to point out that their targets will be 'military', and not the type of indiscriminate bombing carried out by the Luftwaffe against Polish civilians. Before they are finally forced to abandon the base, the unit has inflicted considerable damage on the enemy. In fiction, there was no lack of daring operations against the Germans. Percy Westerman, for instance, published four novels in 1940: *At Grips with the Swastika*, *The War and Alan Carr*, *In Dangerous Waters* and *When the Allies Swept the Seas* – all offering variations on the theme of a British naval offensive against the enemy. The first propaganda film of the war, Alexander Korda's *The Lion Has Wings*, released shortly after the outbreak of war, carried much the same message.

At the end of August, Korda had apparently promised Winston Churchill a propaganda feature as soon as war was declared. Made with the cooperation of the RAF and several leading directors, *The Lion Has Wings* was completed in less than a month. Using a curious mix of newsreel sequences, extracts from earlier Korda movies and straightforward narrative, the film promotes three basic messages. Firstly, using newsreel material, it points out the differences between democratic, peace-loving Britain and Hitler's aggressive and expansionist Germany. Then, focusing on the RAF in an exciting action sequence, it suggests that Britain has the ability to strike at targets in Germany, and that, through the air defence network, the nation can be defended against a German attack. The sequence of German pilots fleeing from a London defended by barrage balloons is, to say the least, far-fetched! For good measure, the film also uses footage of Queen Elizabeth I's speech to sailors before the attack on the Armada, from the earlier *Fire over*

England. Thus the film reminds its audience that Britain has always defeated tyrants in the end. The finale, spoken by Korda's actress wife, Merle Oberon, explains exactly what the war is about, 'We must keep our land . . . we must keep our freedom. We must fight for what we believe in – truth and beauty and fair play and – kindness'.[7] But in the first few months of the real war there were few exciting episodes to inspire the nation.

One of the few dramatic incidents during the phoney war, but which only indirectly affected British interests, was the Russo–Finnish war of 1939–40, the so-called Winter War. In November 1939, the USSR attacked Finland over a territorial dispute. Despite their overwhelming strength, the Russians were hard-pressed by the determined Finnish army. After the German–Soviet Non-Aggression Pact of August 1939, Russia was clearly believed to be in the Nazi camp. This, combined with the widespread anti-Soviet propaganda of the interwar period, resulted in Britain's wholehearted support for the 'gallant little Finns'. The war provided the background for another early Johns' adventure, *Biggles Sees it Through*. Biggles and his companions are given permission by an accommodating (and clearly anti-Soviet) Air Ministry to accompany a party of volunteers to help the Finns in their struggle 'against Soviet aggression'.[8] While serving with the Finnish Air Force, Biggles and Co. meet a refugee Polish professor who has developed a new alloy which could revolutionize aircraft construction. The professor is being pursued by Nazi agents and, fearing capture, has hidden his research notes in the forest. After a series of adventures, Biggles and his friends manage to retrieve the papers from Soviet-held territory. While Johns demonstrates considerable admiration for the Finns, the novel is not overly anti-Russian. In fact, they play only a minor part in a story as the real villain of the piece is the German intelligence officer Erich von Stalhein, Biggles's old enemy, now serving as a military adviser to the Soviets, but whose real mission is to secure the research papers.[9] Johns's ambiguous attitude to Russia is again evident. While he is clearly on the side of the Finns, he portrays most Russian soldiers as rather simple, good-humoured peasants who have little interest in pursuing the war. They are certainly not driven by ideological motives. When the war ends (March 1940), they are overjoyed, cheering loudly and demonstrating an overwhelming friendliness to their recent enemies. As Biggles's chief, the enigmatic Air-Commodore Raymond, points out, 'Most sensible people would rather cheer than shoot each other.'[10] Unfortunately, Hitler did not share such sentiments.

In spring 1940, the German offensive against Scandinavia began and Denmark and Norway were quickly overrun. The British attempted to relieve pressure on the Norwegians by landing British troops at Namsos and Andalsnes, but their resulting defeat and withdrawal brought about the fall of Chamberlain and the appointment of Winston Churchill as leader of a coalition government. This campaign, however, was but a prelude to the dynamic German attack on Western Europe. Holland and Belgium were taken, the French defeated in six weeks, and the BEF had to be evacuated, less most of their equipment, from Dunkirk and other Channel ports. Britain was now alone, and expecting invasion from a triumphant German Army at any moment. The government's immediate task was to rally the nation and prevent panic and despair. Typical of such moments of crisis were the Prime Minister's rousing speeches broadcast to the nation:

> The Battle of France is over, the Battle of Britain is about to begin. Upon this battle depends the survival of Christian civilization. Hitler knows that he will have to break us in this island or he will lose the war. If we can stand up to him, all Europe may be free and the life of the world may move forward into broad, sunlit uplands; but if we fail, then the whole world will sink into the abyss of a new dark age . . .[11]

War had become not simply a struggle for national survival, but a war for 'civilization', with Britain as the last surviving champion of liberty. It was a cleverly calculated appeal to those qualities that the British believed they embodied – righteousness, honour and the courage to take up the gauntlet on behalf of lesser races – a call used time and time again to persuade the nation to take up the sword. It did encourage a mood of defiance, which was perhaps best reflected in David Low's cartoon of 18 June 1940 (illus. 54). But even belief in the essential rightness of the cause could not allay the public's genuine fear of invasion or aerial attack, particularly among those who, lulled by the complacency of the phoney war, had brought their children back to the cities.

'They're not worried, they're off on a holiday', boomed the confident voice of the Pathé-Gazette newsreel commentator in June 1940, over scenes of the bewildered children of London being re-evacuated. But his confident tone belied the fact that many were indeed worried. While the wealthy and the privileged (Members of Parliament like 'Chips' Channon and Alex Cunningham-Reid, and peers like Lord Radnor, the Earl of March, and Lord Mountbatten) could send their children abroad to safety, to Canada or the USA, the government's official scheme for the evacuation of 'ordinary' children abroad was cancelled after only 2,600 had been sent off, because it was thought to be bad for morale.[12] The majority of the nation's children had to learn to take whatever the enemy threw at them. During the phoney war, however, many children had been disappointed at the lack of action, as the response of one twelve-year-old to a Mass-Observation interviewer (for the independent surveys of everyday life and public needs which began in 1937) makes clear:

54 'Very Well, Alone': David Low's *Evening Standard* cartoon reflected the defiant mood of 1940.

If there was going to be a war there should be a war. Instead of all these high people commanding it and holding them back, why don't they get a party of men together and go and fetch Hitler. People are saying it'll last for a hundred years. Tomfoolery keeping on like that, and what are the air raid wardens to do. I think they aught [sic] to get on and bomb Germany if we've got the armaments like they say.[13]

'Most of the boys would like to have air-raids at once', the Report continues, 'though few girls feel like that'. Presumably girls were less troubled at the prospect of under-employed air raid wardens!

It was to be expected that the disruption caused by evacuation, the expected invasion and the fear of bombing had some adverse effects on the nation's children. In the cities, evacuated schools were often taken over as civil defence depots or auxiliary fire stations, and continued to be used as such even after many children returned home. Norman Longmate suggests that by January 1940, one school in ten was still requisitioned and as many as one-third of all children received no schooling at all.[14] The blitz compounded the problem, destroying school buildings and often leading to the relocation of families in different areas. The campaign to get women to work in industry meant that older children often had to miss school in order to look after younger siblings. Even in 'safe' areas schools were overcrowded, and many resorted to a shift system of half the pupils taught in a morning session and the rest in the afternoons.[15] Most children spent far less time in school than they had before 1939, and it was possible for others to evade the best efforts of overworked teachers and inspectors altogether. The absence of many fathers on active service also meant less parental supervision. As a Sheffield woman later recalled, 'We had more freedom than we would have done had the men been at home'.[16]

Most studies of children in wartime agree that they suffered remarkably little psychological damage from air raids, but there were long-term consequences. Juvenile delinquency (the phrase was increasingly used from the middle of the war) increased and without doubt their education suffered. Angus Calder notes the high incidence of post-war national servicemen who were illiterate or educationally retarded.[17] There was also an increase in violent behaviour, not necessarily directed against others, but of pointlessly destructive acts – a mood brilliantly captured in *Hope and Glory* (1987), John Boorman's semi-autobiographical film about growing up during the blitz, when the leader of a gang of bored young boys says, 'Right! Let's smash things up'. The gang then systematically smashes everything still intact in a bomb-damaged house.

Many children and teenagers found the war exhilarating, 'a terrific and potentially exciting game, played by their fathers', claimed a Mass-Observation reporter.[18] Many did their best to join in the game: collecting shrapnel and other souvenirs, going out in gangs to search for enemy parachutists and imagining themselves performing daring and heroic deeds. Others, however, like Bernard Kops, found that after Dunkirk the war became real, a 'nightmare'. Living in the East End of London during the blitz was even worse:

> I hear sirens. And sirens and sirens. Early in the morning, in the after-noon and in the evening. And we went underground to get away from the sirens and the bombs. Yet they followed me and I heard sirens until the world became a siren. One endless cry of torture . . . night and day was one long nightmare, one long siren, one long wail of dispair. Some people feel a certain nostalgia for those days . . . . Not to me. It was the beginning of an era of utter terror, of fear and horror.[19]

Children wanting to play a part in the war effort could join the Scouts or Guides and collect scrap, help out in hospitals or fill fire buckets.[20] They could also join paramilitary youth organizations such as the Sea Cadets, the Army Cadet Force and, after February 1941, the Air Training Corps, which provided pre-training for the armed forces. Many fifteen- to seventeen-year-olds found their way into the Home Guard. But such activities were relatively tame, and most boys fantasized about doing something really exciting and worthwhile: many wanted to be like 'young George', the evacuee in *Went the Day Well?* (1942), Cavalcanti's imaginative reconstruction of the German invasion of an English village. George, of course, plays a vital role in the eventual defeat of the invaders, risking his life to get word to the authorities that the village has been seized.[21] (illus. 55) Popular fiction provided one channel for these fantasies and for resolving anxieties, and reading became even more popular during the war years, no doubt a consequence of more leisure time and long hours spent in air-raid shelters. But paper shortages ensured that reading matter was often in short supply. The case of the story paper *Modern Boy* is instructive. Extremely popular in the 1930s, the paper closed down in October 1939. However, its ongoing serials were continued in *Gem*. In December 1939 *Gem* was merged with *Triumph*, which, in turn, was incorporated into *Champion* in May 1940.[22] There was also a decline in quality. Story papers, not noted for their paper or print, were forced into smaller print in an attempt to compensate for paper shortages; colour plates almost disappeared from books and black and white illustrations became less numerous. Even the popular *BOP* was eventually reduced to a 5 × 7 inch

55 George the Hero.
From the film *Went
the Day Well?*, 1942.

pocket book. But popular fiction offered a means of inspiring confidence in a final victory. Patriotic adventure novels and the surviving papers were bought, swapped and loaned, and continued to reach an enormous readership, stimulating adventurous and heroic fantasies among their readers and helping to shape attitudes to the war.

Kirsten Drotner has pointed out that, after 1939, war stories for the young developed in two directions: the humorous story, often featuring children as central characters, and the dramatic military adventure, 'where warfare was spiced by elements from traditional adventure stories and westerns'.[23] Humorous stories, often in comic strip form, were a relatively new departure in the pleasure culture of war, and were particularly important in representing war in the dark days of 1939–41. As Drotner has argued, '. . . when the threat of air raids and German invasions became realities, it ceased being possible, apparently, to treat that threat in a manner that was at once probable and pleasing. So the seriousness of battle was turned into a matter of laughter and merriment'.[24] Most comics were printed five weeks in advance, so it was not until early October 1939 that the war featured in the strips.[25] Humorous stories then did their best to allay their readers' fears in two ways: firstly, by reconstructing the enemy, and especially their leaders, as pompous buffoons, and secondly, by demonstrating that any British boy or girl (or even anthropomorphic animal) was capable of outwitting them. Hitler, of course, was the primary target, as in 'Ateful Adolt the Nasti' in the *Jester's* 'Basil and Bert' strip, but all the Nazi leadership was lampooned. The *Dandy*, for example, ran 'Addie and Hermy' (Hitler and Goering) through 1940. The misadventures of the two dumb Germans always ended with them being dumped in a river, covered in paint, punched on the nose or chased by a ferocious dog. *Radio Fun* contributed with 'Lord Haw-Haw – the Broadcasting Humbug from Hamburg', and when Italy came into the war (June 1940), *Beano* chipped in with 'Musso the Wop – He's a Big-A-Da-Flop'. Picturing the enemy in such a fashion placed what were essentially frightening individuals into the standard 'funny foreigner' mould, an image common in British popular culture since the mid-nineteenth century, and every Briton knew how to deal with funny foreigners. Significantly, in a wonderful piece of visual abuse from *Dandy*, Hitler and Goering were shown as the blackface invaders of Bamboo Town, the capital of 'Jungleland'. Given the Nazi view of German racial supremacy, the artist, Chick Gordon, presumably felt this to be the ultimate insult![26]

In the comics, the ridiculous leaders of the Axis Powers and their robotic followers could easily be outwitted by any British lad or lassie with an ounce of gumption. 'Our Ernie' (Mrs Entwhistle's Little Lad), for example, the popular Lancashire character from *Knock-Out*, has himself wrapped and posted to the

BEF in France so that he can personally punch 'Tickler' (Hitler) on the 'conk' for starting the war and forcing up the price of sweets. Ernie eventually comes face to face with the 'Nasty', carries out his promise and for good measure pulls off Tickler's 'silly little moustache'. Using this as a disguise, he walks through the German lines and arrives back in Lancashire in time for tea.[27] Equally, when Lord Snooty and his pals decide to raise money for the war effort, they kidnap Hitler, Goering and other Nazi leaders and use them as targets in fairground games. The money raised is presented to Winston Churchill, while the pals use their pet crocodiles to chase the Nazis back to Germany.[28] Illustration 56 shows Churchill thanking the gang for their efforts in a parody of his speech praising 'the Few'. Facing the likes of Billy Bunter, Desperate Dan or Big Eggo, who continually captured their spies, sunk their U-boats and knocked down their bombers, the Germans really had little chance. These characters all appeared in the illustrated comics intended for younger readers, but story papers for older boys and girls offered another variation on the theme. The *Rover* of 1941 carried 'The Blitz Kids', a gang of young boys and girls who set up a bicycle rescue brigade to save pets, and the occasional adult, from bombed houses and who sometimes captured spies or downed enemy airmen. *Hotspur* had 'School of the Gestapo', where one tutor at a Nazi school for saboteurs is, in reality, a British secret agent. Perhaps the most interesting of these stories was 'The War Time Wonder', also in *Hotspur*. The 'Wonder', Alf Coppins, an unkempt youngster from Rope Street Council School, has an almost magical ability when it comes to breaking

56 Lord Snooty and the Gasworks Gang help Winston. From *Beano*, 1942.

enemy codes. Recruited into the Secret Service, Alf maintains his schoolboy status as cover and is patriotically bound to outwit prying teachers as well as German agents.[29]

The message from such fiction was plain: the Germans were pompous wind-bags easily outwitted by Lancashire lads or the Gasworks Gang, and the frightening reality was diminished. Even the bombing of British cities was less terrifying when Desperate Dan or the Blitz Kids might appear at any moment to lend a hand or effect a rescue. The portrayal of war as comedy was a continuing feature throughout the war, with Pansy Potter and Desperate Dan lending a hand on D-day. But such fiction was not without its critics. C. M. Stern, writing in the *Library Assistant*, the journal for assistant librarians, pointed out that such stories would give children a distorted idea of what the war was really like. It was undesirable that children should be encouraged to believe that, 'A British he-man and his faithful . . . Indian attendant outwit the entire Italian army in the Libyan desert . . . The said Indian is, incidentally, capable of beating the Italians with the aid of a cricket-bat. This is meant to be funny, but it won't help the young reader to appreciate Crete or Norway or Dunkirk'.[30] Some children did come to see the war in much the same way as their comic heroes. One six-year-old boy fantasized about how the Germans might be used to his advantage. 'I would ring Hitler. I'd say bomb that school. Hitler would you be dear to me and bomb my school, please. Then I'd give him 6/– [shillings] for bombing it'.[31]

What is interesting is that the subversive element and lack of respect for author-ity, so much a feature of the 1930s, continued unabated into the era of national solidarity and total war. Churchill, as we have seen, was accorded considerable respect, as were the armed forces, especially General Bernard Montgomery (Monty), but officious ARP wardens, civil servants and other bureaucrats were treated with disdain. Comic and story paper heroes dealt with Nazi leaders and stormtroopers in exactly the same way as they had got the better of teachers, policemen and other authority figures before 1939. *Hotspur*'s 'Blitz Kids' are a useful example. The main theme of the stories is their daring and useful rescue work, but a sub-theme running through the series is the Kids' continual conflict with the authorities who, believing that such work is far too dangerous for the young, try to put an end to their adventurous activities. The Blitz Kids, then, face two enemies – the Luftwaffe and adults! The 1940 Ministry of Health poster encouraging evacuation might well have been drawn with them in mind (illus. 57).

The individual in conflict with authority as well as with the enemy also featured in many of the popular family comedy films of the period. George Formby, Will Hay or the Crazy Gang, provide classic examples of 'muddling through'. Formby,

LEAVE THIS TO US
SONNY — <u>YOU</u> OUGHT
TO BE OUT OF LONDON

MINISTRY OF HEALTH EVACUATION SCHEME

57 'Leave this to us Sonny': an evacuation poster, *c.* 1940.

with his characterization of the irrepressible gormless duffer who makes good, was the top British box-office attraction in the period 1938–43, and extremely popular with the young. In *Let George Do It* (1940), arguably the best of his wartime comedies, the incompetent George finds himself mistaken for a British secret agent and is sent to Norway to track down Nazi agents. After accidentally outwitting the Nazis agents, helping to capture a U-boat and dreaming of punching Hitler on the nose at a Nuremberg rally, George is once again the bewildered hero who has succeeded in spite of himself. *Let George Do It* was due for release just after the fall of Norway, and its topicality had something of a hollow ring about it. Undaunted, Ealing Studios released it with an opening caption explaining that the story '. . . takes place in Norway, before the war spread'.[32] It was enormously well-received and even the *Spectator* noted: '. . . Cast your inhibitions to the winds, and enjoy fully a manifestation of that social equality which in no small measure represents what we are fighting to defend'.[33] Equally well-received was Will Hay's *The Goose Steps Out* (1942). Hay's bumbling schoolmaster character is parachuted into Germany, impersonating an SS officer whose job is to train saboteurs who will later be smuggled into England (an interesting variation of *Hotspur*'s 'School of the Gestapo' serial). Hay, of course, completely undermines their training and causes total chaos before escaping by aeroplane. The same triumphant muddling through was exhibited by the Crazy Gang (as airmen in charge of a barrage balloon in *Gas Bags*, in 1942), and in more sophisticated comedies such as *Pimpernel Smith* (1941). Smith, a seemingly absent-minded don played by quintessential Englishman Leslie Howard, spends his vacations before the war rescuing the victims of Nazi oppression – an interest-ing variation on Howard's portrayal of the *Scarlet Pimpernel* in 1935. Through a combination of pluck and bluff, which plays upon the Nazis own pomposity and stupidity, Smith continually proves that an Englishman can always out-smart a Nazi.[34] Such films obviously raised morale and brought 'a large measure of joy to a good many people in what was for the most part a pretty joyless world'.[35] These stories also helped dissolve fear through laughter; just how efficient could the Nazis be if they were continually defeated by the likes of Formby, Hay or dreamy Oxford dons?

  After 1940, the first task of adventure writers was to explain the failures in Norway and at Dunkirk, and then to demonstrate that Britain was hitting back. In *Fighting for Freedom* (1941), for example, veteran storyteller Percy Westerman dealt with the events of 1940 through the adventures of Sub-Lieutenant John Cloche, RN and Flying Officer Basil Hazletyne, RAF. Westerman likens the British defeats of 1940 to the German spring offensive of 1918, when Haig and the BEF had 'their backs to the wall'. The implication, of course, is that while the nation had suffered a setback in 1918, it had been but the prelude to victory; and would be so again. This idea is reinforced by frequent references to historical precedents such as the Spanish Armada and Napoleon's intended invasion of Britain. Both of Westerman's heroes are present at Dunkirk, a disaster, the author tells us, brought about by the sudden surrender of Belgium, which left the British flank unguarded. 'In consequence it was a defeat for British arms. That there could be no denying, but in defeat they worthily upheld the glorious traditions of Britain when "up against it."'[36] Westerman follows closely the official line on the evacuation, the 'miracle' of Dunkirk, the 'little boats' and the indomitable will of the nation to continue the fight. Protected against invasion by the RN and RAF, the British are undaunted even when the Germans attempt to bomb them into submission. The nation can take it, unlike the Germans, who will 'squeal' when the RAF hits back at their cities. He is careful to point out, however, that while Hitler bombed cities, 'blowing up thousands of civilians, including women and children', the RAF will bomb only military objectives and try to leave civilians out of it.[37]

Having explained the initial British defeat and demonstrated how the Germans wage war, Westerman moves on to show the British on the offensive. John Cloche, aboard a battleship in the Mediterranean, helps chase the Italian fleet back to their base at Taranto, and later takes part in the destruction of the French fleet at Oran. The author's explanation for this unsavoury episode is that, while French sailors would like nothing more than to continue fighting the 'Boche', they could not do so because the Germans would take reprisals against their families in occupied France.[38] Meanwhile, Basil Hazeltyne, flying for the RAF, is taking part in the early stages of the Battle of Britain and demonstrating the inherent superiority of British airmen. The novel ends, like so many of Westerman's stories, with the two young men being decorated for gallantry at Buckingham Palace.

The 'miracle' of Dunkirk had almost immediately been enshrined in the nation's memory – a tangible sign that God was on the side of the British. In 1942, a story by 'Bartimeus', entitled 'The Last Bridge', suggested something of the supernatural quality of this event. The young commander of a destroyer takes his ship close inshore to rescue men from the beaches. The ship takes a direct hit from a German bomb and the commander is severely wounded. However, he refuses to go below and stays on the shattered bridge so that he can steer the damaged ship clear of the wrecks and into the safety of the Channel. His dedication costs him his life, but as his loyal Maltese steward carries his lifeless body below, '[T]he sun rose above a bank of cloud to the eastward, throwing the shadow of the mast and yard athwart the bridge, the shadow of a cross'.[39]

Similarly, in Guy Dempster's *Winged Venturers*, a tale of the fall of Crete in 1941, the author explains the early British failures as due simply to lack of equipment.

While Britain had been trying to prevent war throughout the 1930s, Hitler had been stocking his arsenal; as a young Scots airman explains, '. . . until we have as many planes as he has, and as many tanks and guns and so on, we can do no than just chuck a spanner in the works when he starts of for some place. We can't hold him – yet. But we can impede him and throw his plans all agley'.[40] Once Britons have sufficient armaments they will take the offensive and deal with the Nazis. Dempster's story of the Cretan disaster is told through the adventures of 'Spike' Moreland and Andy McFarlane, both in the RAF. Spike, flying his obsolete Gloster Gladiator biplane against the German invaders day after day, sees his squadron decimated while covering the British evacuation, until he is shot down himself. Refusing to surrender, he joins forces with an RAF gunner, Andy, and a ragtag unit of marines, sailors and airmen in the mountains, and wages guerrilla warfare against the Germans until they can escape from the island.

Dempster's earlier novel, *Fleet Wings* (1940), dealt with Narvik and Dunkirk in much the same terms. These were, however, defeats only in the sense that the British had been forced to retreat, for there was no lack of heroic acts and self-less sacrifice. The morale of nation's young warriors remained high, and they waited only for the chance to hit back at the Nazis. These novels are typical of the manner in which the disasters of 1940–41 were dealt with in juvenile fiction, suggesting that they were simply minor setbacks. The nation would soon begin the offensive and, when it did, the unquenchable patriotism and fighting spirit of young Britons like Spike, Andy and John Cloche would ensure the final victory.

After December 1941 and the series of bloody American defeats in the Pacific, Hollywood adopted the British strategy of turning disaster into the first step in ultimate victory. In a series of exciting filmic battle narratives, widely shown in Britain, the studios demonstrated again and again how the noble sacrifice of American soldiers had gained time for the counter-attack. *Wake Island* (1942) told the story of the doomed Marine garrison on the island and the desperate struggle against a superior Japanese invasion force. After the heroic struggle Wake falls to the enemy, but a final narration tells us, 'This is not the end . . . There are other fighting Americans . . . whose blood and sweat and fury will exact a just and terrible vengeance'. Even more spectacular and heroic was *Bataan* (1943). Set in the last days before the fall of the Philippines, the film tells the story of a ragtag squad of soldiers who act as a rearguard to slow the Japanese advance into the Bataan Peninsula. For every minute, every hour they hold out, more Americans from the main force will be able to escape to Australia and live to fight again. Holding a bridge across a deep gorge, the unit, with no hope of escape, fights desperately to the last man. Finally, alone and almost out of ammunition, the brave sergeant (Robert Taylor) issues his challenge to the enemy: 'Come on, suckers, come and get it'! As he is surrounded the picture fades and an epilogue appears:

> So fought the heroes of Bataan.
> Their sacrifice made possible our victories in the
> Coral and Bismarck Seas, at Midway, on New
> Guinea and Guadalcanal. Their spirit will lead
> us back to Bataan!

Thus their sacrifice bought time for the American war machine to gear up and prepare for the long road to victory.[41]

A characteristic of the Second World War was the blurring between combatants and civilians. This resulted in propagandist attempts to personify the entire population as heroic. By and large, this is how 1940–41 has been enshrined in British memory – the finest hour in a 'people's' war.[42] But the community as hero was too abstract for juvenile entertainment, which wanted heroic individuals to be clearly defined and to provide role models for the young. The most popular of these heroic individuals were, as Omar Bartov has noted, the new warrior elites – airman, tank crews, submariners and commandos. Airmen, as we have seen, had become a popular heroic type before 1939, but the Battle of Britain, fought out in the skies over southern England in the summer of 1940, focused unprecedented attention on 'the Few'. Here was the ultimate theatre of war, clearly visible, but at a distance sufficient to ensure that the full horror of a pilot trapped in a burning aeroplane or smashed by cannon shells did not impact on the public's romantic perception of the war in the air. The battle seemingly fulfilled the criteria of what war should be – heroic, individual and chivalric – and was reported in the press rather like a test match: 'Britain 180 for 34', proclaimed the newspaper placards. Newbolt would surely have approved! Authors responded quickly to the airman's war, for it was, after all, the first British victory over a seemingly invincible enemy. W. E. Johns was one of the first into the fray with his *Spitfire Parade*, published in 1941. Biggles is now commanding 666 squadron, a special operations unit, but one which plays a major part during that 'Spitfire Summer'. For this collection of stories, the author updated many of his First World War tales, but while he was hopelessly out-of-date on technical knowledge and current RAF slang, the book was still enormously popular. Tributes to 'the Few' were common in boys' papers and annuals, not only in story form but equally in bad verse (illus. 58).

The *Champion* had its own flying ace, 'Rockfist' Rogan, so-called because of his boxing prowess. Rogan had first appeared in the paper in the 1930s, as a RFC

To THE FEW'

Stand, Freedom ! Hold thy banner high !
Nor trick nor blow shall lower its proud
        threads,
Whilst yet across the trackless sky
The Island Empire Battle Order spreads.

Slaves ? Not these, who, facing peril, smile
  Fired with the strength that seeks to guard the weak,
To break, not hearts, but Evil's fetters vile,
  Who only Peace in mortal combat seek.

Kneel ? Never ! Look, Tyrants, your own
  Threats they turn upon yourselves. Your arm is
Long ? Know theirs is longer. Lone,
  Six or ten to one they match your armies.

Hark, Thraldom ! Courage spells thy doom,
For here are dauntless men of keener steel
Than thy blunt myrmidons of gloom,
From ends of Earth to fight for Freedom's weal.

Stand, Freedom ! Every land on Earth
  Take heart from them ; fight, as they, if need be ;
Give, not barter, Life's dear worth.
  Kings of the Air ! Masters of Destiny !

J. GORDON ROBINSON

58 'To The Few': a tribute from the *Young Airman's Annual, c.* 1942.

pilot on the Western Front, but in 1939 he was transformed, without explanation, into a Flight-Lieutenant in RAF Fighter Command. In 1945, 'The Flying Fury', another RAF ace, and one of the few stories set in the Pacific theatre, appeared in the shortlived comic book *Four Aces*. But the most imaginative stories were to be found in the D. C. Thomson papers, including 'The Nameless Squadron', a unit of volunteers who took on suicide missions without hesitation. The most heroic airmen were the glamorous fighter pilots, but some attention was also paid to Bomber Command, the only force capable of striking back at the Third Reich until an invasion of Europe could be attempted. The bomber offensive was not simply a means of inflicting damage on the enemy, it was also a necessary propaganda weapon to boost the morale of a nation which needed to know that Britain was hitting back.[43] Perhaps the most effective piece of propaganda in this respect was the widely seen documentary film, *Target for Tonight*.

The film, released in August 1941, was produced by the Crown Film Unit for the Ministry of Information, which was keen to show the public that the RAF was hitting back at the enemy. *Target* was a curious hybrid, scripted as a narrative adventure but using real servicemen and women in situations that were common-place in wartime. In this case, a raid on the important rail junction at 'Freihausen' in the Black Forest region. The film tells the story of the raid from initial planning at the Air Ministry to its execution and return of the bombers. By focusing on just one aircraft, the Wellington 'F for Freddie', the audience become totally involved in the dangerous plight of the crew. The raid is, of course, a great success. Not only does 'F for Freddie' find the difficult target, but accurately puts its bombs directly on the oil storage tanks. The film was widely seen and highly praised for its authenticity and stunning photography. The critic Dilys Powell noted:

> The actors were serving airmen, the dialogue was simple, realistic, ironic in the English manner – but somehow imagination had eradicated a plain story of everyday experience. Here was a new genre in cinema, a fact, a fragment of actual life, which still had the emotional tremor of fiction.[44]

Films using service personnel in fictional but realistic situations were some-times known as 'faction' films, and the success of *Target for Tonight* ensured that others followed. These included *Fires Were Started*, a tribute to the Auxiliary Fire Service, and the splendid *Western Approaches*, highlighting the work of the Merchant Navy. But for most of the public, *Target for Tonight* established that, night after night, the young heroes of Bomber Command were taking the war into the enemy heartland, finding and destroying 'military' targets. Popular fiction reinforced this belief.

One of the most detailed stories dealing with Bomber Command was Percy Westerman's *Combined Operations* (1944). The story focuses on pilot Derek Dundas and the crew of the Halifax bomber 'S for Sylvia'. Like most cultural repre-sentations of bomber crews, the young men of 'S for Sylvia' are a microcosm of society. Dundas is of Scottish ancestry, the co-pilot is Welsh, the radio operator Irish, the engineer a blunt Yorkshireman, while a gunner from New Zealand repre-sents the empire. The bomber crew was often used as a metaphor for a democratic society at war: everyone is a trained specialist, but they operate as a team, with each individual dependent for survival on the specific skills of the others. Westerman's tale is no different. Sent on a daylight bombing raid to Berlin, we see just how cooperation and mutual interdependence ensure the success of the mission and the survival of this particular warrior community. The author's description of the raid owes a great deal to the classic filmic reconstructions of the period, but by 1944 a hard edge of reality had intruded and there is a far more realistic acceptance of the effects of a bomber offensive on the enemy. As we have seen, in 1941 Westerman was at pains to show that the RAF bombed only 'military targets', unlike the Luftwaffe. Now, in 1944, it was impossible to maintain such fiction. At the squadron briefing before the raid, the commander tells the assembled crews:

> '. . . Probably a great many civilians will get hurt, but that cannot be helped from our point of view.

They are all potential war-workers for Nazi Germany, even as our civilian population are for the most part engaged in helping the Allies' war effort. It's not a case of revenge for what the Huns have done to our cities and towns, but rather of retribution. And by hitting the old Hun hard and where it hurts him most we are definitely shortening the war.[45]

'S for Sylvia' successfully returns from the raid, but two of the crew are wounded in an attack by enemy fighters over Berlin (illus. 59), and the plane is badly damaged. Nevertheless, after repairs and healed wounds they are soon back on active duty and feeling 'glorious' when they take off for their next target. Such idealized images of the war in the air created a climate in which every boy wanted to be an airman. The actor/director Bryan Forbes, a young man awaiting call-up in 1943, later wrote, '. . . because of the romance of the Battle of Britain

59 'S for Sylvia' fights off the enemy fighters. From Westerman, *Combined Operations* (1944).

pilots I had set my mind on the RAF . . . We were all mad keen to fly, aped RAF slang and regarded the pilots as Gods'.[46]

Among the other warrior elites of the Second World War were the commandos, the predecessors of today's high-profile Special Air Service (SAS). Commandos, the cutting edge of Combined Operations, were created by the conditions of the war, specifically the period 1940–42 when small hit-and-run raids were all that was possible against Hitler's 'fortress Europe'. Loosely organized into brigades, commandos were highly trained in killing, and their fighting skills and daring exploits had considerable impact on the popular imagination, especially of the young. Fictional adventures about commandos began to appear in 1942. *Hotspur*, for example, ran a series about 'The Black Flash Commandos', an exotic group teamed with resistance fighters in Norway.

Arguably the most interesting stories were the 'Gimlet' novels by W. E. Johns, written in response to a War Office request for a soldier-hero to rank alongside his RAF characters.[47] The result was *King of the Commandos*, published in 1943. Johns's heroes, the 'hard-hitting warriors' of Number 9 Commando, are centred around Captain Lorrimer King, known as Gimlet (his eyes bore right through a man!), and his loyal companions Corporal 'Copper' Collson, an ex-policeman, and 'Trapper' Troublay, a French-Canadian backwoodsman much given to using his skinning knife on the enemy. The novel opens during a raid on occupied northern France, when the commandos encounter sixteen-year-old Nigel Peters. Adopted by the unit and immediately named 'Cub' by the commandos (nick-names were apparently de rigueur in the commandos), Peters has been waging his own war against the Germans in occupied France since June 1940, when he ran away from his public school in order to help bring the Tommies back from Dunkirk. However, to avoid capture, he joined up with young French resisters, known as the 'Grey Fleas of the North', and continued to make life difficult for the 'Boche'. Cub helps the commandos to complete their mission and returns with them to England, where he is unofficially enrolled in the unit.

Gimlet is a vastly different character to the quiet and relatively unassuming Biggles, for Lorrimer King is a member of the landed gentry – the family home is Lorrimer Castle in Devon – and he is often to be found dining at the Ritz or riding to hounds. The family has long-established connections with the army; his father won the Victoria Cross during the First World War and his grandfather was awarded the same honour in South Africa. Gimlet himself is a professional soldier, having joined the Guards after leaving Oxford. However, when things became dull during the phoney war he transferred to the RAF and fought in the Battle of Britain. When a German bullet ended his flying days, he wangled his way into the commandos, took part in the Dieppe raid and eventually became commanding officer of 9 Commando, known ironically as 'King's Kittens' because of the image of a wildcat on their unit badge. Gimlet was probably modelled on the commando leader Lord Lovat.[48] While he is particularly fussy about his uniform – a 'bit of a dandy', Johns tells us – he is ruthless in battle. According to the author:

> His methods are not always as gentlemanly as Biggles. When things get rough he's apt to get tough. Which is why, of course, he was given a bunch of wildcats to command. After all, kid gloves are about as much use to a commando on his job as roller skates would be to a steeple jack.[49]

Despite his military background and social position, Gimlet is no stickler for unnecessary discipline. In many ways, King's Kittens are remarkably informal (as befits an elite where every man is a hand-picked expert fighting a war for democratic ideals). As Gimlet explains to a rather surprised Cub, '. . . [I]n the sort of work we do, when we're on the other side of the Channel – well, badges of rank, social position, rates of pay, and that sort of thing don't matter very much. We're comrades then, and that's all that matters'.[50] The new series was well-received by readers and critics alike: the review in the *Times Educational Supplement* was typical: 'It is to be hoped that there will be many more books about them . . . Everything they do is made to seem plausible, possible and at the same time exciting'.[51] And there were more books! The second adventure in the series, *Gimlet Goes Again*, another adventure set in occupied France, was published in 1944, and the last wartime adventure of King's Kittens came in 1945, when the *BOP* ran the serial 'The Seeds of Trouble', in which Gimlet takes on the Japanese in Indo-China. Although Gimlet was never as popular as Biggles, Johns nevertheless went on to produce another eight Gimlet adventures after 1945. None of these, however, were war stories, but had Gimlet and his companions dealing with international crooks and Communists.

Westerman's young warriors were typical of an older style of hero, one who had been formed by the unquestioning nature of Edwardian patriotism; given their orders, they did their duty without hesitation and according to the rules. But, as we have seen, a new breed had emerged in popular culture after the Great War, heroes who perhaps reflected more accurately the tensions of the nation's youth. These young men were just as patriotic, just as convinced of British superiority, but now they sometimes questioned their orders, employed unorthodox methods, and, if necessary, were prepared to bend or even break the rules in order to gain their objectives. They had little use for red tape or blind obedience to authority. While the traditional Westerman heroes continued to appear in Second World War fiction, there was a marked increase in the new breed. The transition in the nature of the warrior-hero reflected not only a growing lack of respect for those figures of authority who had been largely discredited by the events of the Great War and after, but also the dramatic changes in the nature of warfare itself. The armed forces no longer required blind obedience, but highly trained specialists capable of using initiative and making their own decisions when the situation demanded, as well as a new ruthlessness to counter that of their utterly ruthless enemies.

One of the best representations of the 'new age' warrior was the Michael Powell/Emerich Pressburger film, *The Life and Death of Colonel Blimp* (1943). 'Blimp' – General Clive 'Sugar' Candy, VC (played by Roger Livesey) – is a highly decorated professional soldier who began his career in the days of imperial warfare. Now, in the Second World War, he represents an older style of 'gentlemanly' warfare that died on the Somme. By contrast, the young Lieutenant 'Spud' Wilson, represents the new warfare, efficient and unconventional. He realizes that victory against a ruthless enemy in a total war requires even greater ruthlessness and ingenuity.[52] Individualism was a theme constantly reinforced by propaganda which stressed the democratic objectives of the war – a war being fought to preserve the essential rights and freedoms of the individual. The fact that individual freedom could only be preserved by subordinating the individual's desires to the needs of the community was a contradiction that was not explored. Nevertheless, such a climate produced a number of unconventional and, in some ways, subversive heroes.

Biggles, as we have seen, hated red tape and often adopted his own 'unofficial' methods. However, in *Spitfire Parade* his new squadron is entirely composed of rebels. As Air Commodore Raymond explains just before Biggles takes up his new post:

> In case you feel that you have been given an unusual command, I'd better tell you about it. The fact is, we've started a new stunt, a little register of star turns and officers who do not take kindly to discipline. As you probably know, they've always been a problem – you know the type I mean. The ass on the ground is often the ace in the air. It's no use keeping these fellows on the ground, it only makes matters worse, so we have decided to send them . . . to a special squadron, in the hope that they will at least kill a few Boche before killing themselves in some foolhardy escapade.[53]

And odd they are, such as Lord Bertie Lizzie, the eccentric aristocrat who insists on wearing his monocle while flying and a hunting waistcoat under his uniform jacket; Tex O'Hara, a ruthless ex-policeman from New York, and Tug Carrington, an ex-boxer always looking for a fight. Biggles, of course, shapes them into a tightly knit fighting elite, not through harsh discipline, but by allowing them to indulge their particular skills and teaching them to fight as a team. *Champion*'s Rockfist Rogan was another of these unconventional airmen, possessing amazing energy both for fighting Germans and pursuing his sporting passions, boxing, cricket and hunting. Rogan never actually disobeys orders, but does have a marked tendency to interpret them imaginatively in order to kill the maximum number of Germans.

Working-class warriors also became more commonplace during the conflict, as one would expect in a war sold to the public as a 'people's war'. According to Gimlet, rank didn't count for very much in combat. This was reinforced by the emphasis on the contribution made by the 'other ranks', even in that most elitist service, the RAF; a trend established by the Ministry of Information's widely seen poster about 'the Few', which showed only non-commissioned pilots. This provided a lead that authors were quick to follow. In D. Heming's 'Bill Butler: Sergeant Pilot' the hero, despite his lowly rank, is just as patriotic, just as brave and just as gung-ho as any officer. Bill is determined to get even with a German fighter pilot who makes a habit of machine-gunning British pilots floating helplessly in their parachutes after they have been forced to bail out. This particular German is easily identifiable by the red star painted on the nose of his Messerschmitt 109. In the next dogfight, Bill himself is forced to bale out, but he carries an automatic pistol for just such an emergency. As Red Star comes in for the kill, Bill produces the pistol and fires at the 'grinning face' in the Messerschmitt's cockpit. Whether Bill hits the German pilot or just disables his machine is not explained, but Red Star plunges down and satisfyingly 'crashes in flames'. One might assume that, having performed such a prodigious feat, Bill might need a spot of leave, but no! Once on the ground he wants only to get back to his aerodrome, 'so as to get aloft again before the fun was over for the day'.[54]

Sometimes even the working class was commissioned. In Biggles's 666 Squadron, Tug Carrington has a 'chip on his shoulder' because he feels his comrades look down on his Cockney background. As Air-Commodore Raymond explains, 'I doubt if he should have been given a commission, but it's to late to alter now'. Carrington, of course, eventually justifies his officer status by performing all manner of brave deeds. 'Ferocity' Ferris, the author tells us, 'got his commission on sheer flying ability. There was nothing else he could have got it on, for his family connexions [sic] were obscure, and the back streets of Liverpool wherein he lived, while it may have been all that it should be, was hardly a recommendation'.[55] Johns, of course, had already introduced the working-class

Ginger Hebblethwaite into his Biggles novels in the mid-1930s. In this meritocratic war, the common people could serve their country just as well as their social betters, and might even be promoted to temporary status as 'officers and gentlemen'. They could serve in a variety of ways and, like Alf Coppin, the council schoolboy and code-breaker, could even earn the respect of their public school-educated masters. While British society became classless for the duration, in popular fiction the chief protagonists generally came from the upper or middle classes, with their working-class comrades acting out the subordinate role. But even young working-class males had a far more exciting time than most girls.

Considering the enormous contribution of women to the war effort, they were given remarkably little to do in war fiction. In the humorous comics, a handful of female characters was involved in war activities. Spike-haired Pansy Potter, 'the Strong Man's Daughter', from *Beano*, destroyed German submarines and tanks with the same ease as Desperate Dan, while *Crackers*'s Kitty Clare and her comrades at Coffdrop College formed a cadet unit for 'useful work'. The awful Keyhole Kate, and the equally irritating Meddling Maddie, sometimes created problems for the armed forces, and some comics introduced new characters to reflect wartime experience. *Larks* had 'Peggy the Pride of the Force', an attractive and curvaceous blonde who served in the Auxiliary Fire Service (just at the station, of course). *Comic Cuts* ran 'Big Hearted Martha, the ARP Nut', always doing her best for the war effort. But by and large, comics still regarded war activities as suitable only for boys.[56] Even fiction for older girls was still hidebound by pre-war conventions. Angel Brazil reworked her First World War stories to produce *Five Jolly Schoolgirls* in 1941. But in this tale of an evacuated public school, the pupils seemed remarkably out of step with the mood of the times. The war caused considerable problems for the girls of the 'Chalet School', Elinor Brent-Dyer's popular institution in the Austrian Tyrol. In *The Chalet School in Exile* (1940), set just after the Anschluss, the German boarders turn out to be rampant Nazis and the English girls are forced to flee after standing up for local Jews in the face of Austrian anti-Semitism. Perhaps the most realistic novel to reflect the contribution of girls and young women to the war effort was *Toby of Tibbs Cross*, by Dorita Fairlie Bruce. Toby (short for Tabitha) and her friend Charity Sheringham manage to run a farm, virtually on their own and as well as any man.[57] At the beginning of the war, the *Girl's Own Paper* took a low-key approach to the conflict, suggesting that girls should make every effort to carry on with their everyday routine, concentrating on schoolwork, knitting and so forth. When Dunkirk and the threat of invasion shattered this complacency, the paper announced that, 'We've all been shaken out of our ruts and we have all got to show what we are made of today as never before'.[58] Even with this new determination, what girls and women were allowed to do was limited, and in fiction few young women experienced the sharp end of war. Only W. E. Johns's WAAF officer Joan Worralson, and Dorothy Carter's splendid aviatrice Marise Duncan, went into action.

In 1941, the Air Ministry apparently asked Johns to create a WAAF heroine to boost recruitment, and 'Worrals', as she was known to her friends, was the result.[59] Despite later accusations of sexism, Johns had always been an advocate for equal opportunities in aviation for women, arguing that they could fly as well as the average man. In the mid-1930s, he even suggested that women might fly in combat.[60] In the first story, Worrals is eighteen, a commissioned officer and qualified pilot. Together with her friend Betty Lovell, usually known as 'Frecks', she is attached to 'N' Squadron of the Home Defence Force, ferrying aircraft from aerodromes to factories for repair. In order to create a warrior heroine, Johns embroidered the realities of life in the Women's RAF. WAAFs were not allowed to fly, nor to wear the coveted pilot's wings on their uniforms, even if they were qualified pilots. RAF machines were ferried by women pilots, but they belonged to the Air Transport Auxiliary and not the WAAF, nor did that latter service have a rank of Pilot Officer (although when the story was published in book form, this was changed to the more correct Flight Officer). Nevertheless, Johns had created an enormously interesting character born of wartime conditions.

When the novel opens, Worrals, an experienced pilot, is disgruntled that women are not allowed to fly high performance machines in combat. However, she is no Amazon. Rather, as the author tells us, a slim, attractive girl, studious but with a good sense of humour and an even greater sense of duty.[61] Johns even hints at a romantic attachment, as Worrals is 'keen' on Bill Ashton, a fighter pilot stationed at the same aerodrome. Nevertheless, when it comes to putting the case for equality for women, she is blunt. In *Worrals of the Islands*, one of the later novels, her commanding officer is shocked when she offers her services for a particularly dangerous mission:

'Wars aren't for women,' growled the C.O.
   'If you said they shouldn't be I'd agree with you,' rapped out Worrals. 'Who started the war anyway? Men. Take a look at the world and see what a nice mess men have made of it. No wonder they had to appeal to women to help them out.'
   The C.O. moved uncomfortably. 'I was thinking about certain jobs', he countered.
   'What jobs?' flared Worrals. 'As far as I know there's only one job in this war that hasn't been done by a woman . . . I've never heard of a girl

commanding a battleship – but maybe that's only because there are more spare admirals than ships.'[62]

Worrals, of course, gets the job and succeeds remarkably well.

Throughout the series, which usually involve the two women in dangerous expeditions in occupied Europe or the Far East, both demonstrate that they are as fearless as men and equally competent when it comes to a fight. Nor does Worrals hesitate when dealing with the enemy. In *Worrals of the WAAF*, she has her first experience of killing. Finally given the chance to deliver a high performance fighter aircraft, she spots a German aircraft. Hunting it down, she climbs high above and prepares to dive down for the kill:

> Her face, although she did not know it, was like white marble; her lips a thin straight line; her eyes expressionless. The hand that moved towards the gun control was stone cold . . . Her thumb found the small round button which, when pressed, would spurt a hail of death. 'I've got to do it', she told herself. Then again, 'I've got to do it. This is war' . . .
>
> . . . Almost viciously she jammed down the button. Instantly, little specks of orange flame spurted from the muzzles of her guns . . .

The enemy goes down. Initially, Worrals is shocked by her encounter with the reality of war, but she realizes that she has only done her duty and 'proved herself to be worthy of the uniform she wore'.[63] Although she always feels a certain reluctance to kill as the war goes on it does become easier. By 1945, when she finds herself fighting the Japanese in the Pacific, she comes face to face with a Japanese officer. He does not hesitate to surrender when she levels her pistol, because he sees from her eyes that she is prepared to shoot (illus. 60). Later, in an air fight, she even experiences a 'savage satisfaction' at hitting back at the men who are trying to kill her: 'her entire being had become one irresistible impulse to hit'.[64] The Worrals stories were well-received and apparently fulfilled their recruiting role, for soon after the first story appeared, the WAAFs were over-subscribed. Worrals featured in eleven novels and a number of magazine stories, the last published in 1950. Only one other fictional heroine matched Worrals's combat experience, and that was Dorothy Carter's 'Marise Duncan'.

Marise first appeared in *Mistress of the Air* (1937) as a talented and adventurous airwoman, modelled on Amy Johnson and Amelia Earhart. Her pre-war exploits were related in several novels, including *Star of the Air*, in which the aviatrice is hired by a Hollywood film studio to perform the stunt-flying in a spectacular aviation adventure.[65] However, in her first wartime adventure, *Sword of the Air* (1941), Marise is ferrying RAF machines to France during the phoney war.

60 Worrals the Warrior WAAF, 1945.

Crash-landing in German territory, she becomes involved in sabotage in a
German aircraft factory and outwits the Gestapo before getting back to England.
However, it is *Comrades of the Air*, the second war novel, that is most interesting.
Set in late 1941, Marise is ferrying British aircraft to Russia to help the Soviet
war effort. In the Soviet Union, she is billeted with a women's regiment of the
Red Air Force. Carter was obviously aware of the Soviet Union's policy of allowing
women to fly in combat, and many of the details are authentic.[66] The base
where Marise is stationed is forced to evacuate by a sudden German advance,
and Marise finds herself flying a Red Air Force bomber. Forced down behind
enemy lines, Marise and her Soviet comrades fight their way back to the Russian
lines. Here, having seen the treatment meted out to Russian civilians by the
Wehrmacht, they have no hesitation when it comes to killing Germans. *Comrades
of the Air* is an exciting tale of women in combat. It was one of the few attempts
'to bring home to British readers at least some measure of the achievements of
the Russian women combat pilots'.[67] The last of Marise's wartime adventures has
her ferrying bombers to New Guinea and Australia, killing substantial numbers
of Japanese, and, in the process, working with the US Army Air Force and doing
her bit for the Anglo–American alliance.[68] Girls' fiction of the period, however,

generally fails to reflect fully the wartime contribution of women, in particular their work in factories, in the armed forces and other areas in which they made such a contribution to the final victory.

In the propaganda of 1940–41, much was made of the cliche 'Britain Stands Alone'. Of course, the nation was never really alone. Not only did the empire make an enormous contribution, but there were significant contingents from the armed forces of occupied nations who had managed to fight their way to Britain to continue the struggle. Few of these rated much attention in juvenile adventure fiction. Certainly imperial and Commonwealth troops were not featured to the same extent as they had been during the Great War, and only the odd ANZAC or Canadian was a member of a platoon, commando unit or squadron, to remind the reader of the empire's contribution. Native troops were virtually excluded from the fiction of the period, which portrayed the war as a largely European affair fought exclusively by the white race.

In the summer of 1941, when Hitler invaded Russia and prevented the likely defeat of Britain by pushing it into a Soviet alliance, the nation found itself in a curious partnership. Considering the anti-Soviet propaganda of the inter-war years, popular culture made a remarkably rapid transition from portraying Russia as an enemy to depicting it as heroic ally. Rather surprisingly, even the Prime Minister played up the 'Our Soviet Friends' angle, and Joseph Stalin, a tyrant in the 1930s, became 'good old Uncle Joe' for the British public. Yet despite considerable pro-Soviet propaganda in the newspapers, magazines and cinema,[69] Russia inspired little interest from juvenile fiction. As we have seen, Russian women pilots received some attention in *Comrades of the Air*, but apparently only one other story dealt with the Russian war effort, *Wizard*'s 'Army of the Caverns' (1944). The story, set in Nazi-occupied Odessa, relates the exploits of a Russian partisan unit led by two young Scots, Jim and Stanley Goddard, stranded in Russia by the German invasion, who decide to fight on with their Russian friends. Other European allies made more frequent appearances, particularly the French and Dutch, but again only as background figures – the latter, because they so frequently assisted downed RAF personnel to get home, and the former because France was usually the location for commando raids and resistance stories. An interesting exception was Charles Gilson's 'Jean Loubert: A Story of a Free-French Airmen'. Loubert, serving in the Army of the Air in 1940, is a daring and skilful fighter pilot, but a loner, a 'French Eagle' who likes to hunt on his own. Loubert is stationed in Toulon when the Italians declare war on France, but, as the author tells, the 'macaronies' are no match for the Frenchman. When France falls, Loubert refuses to surrender, flies to England and joins a Free French Squadron attached to the RAF to carry on the fight: 'the Italians – poof! But the Boches, I 'ate them, and I am not nice to know up in the sky, when I 'ate . . .'[70]

Although America was fighting an undeclared war against German U-boats in the Atlantic from the summer of 1941, the Japanese attack on Pearl Harbour officially brought the US into the war. Towards the end of 1942, American service personnel were gradually transferred to Europe. The Eighth Air Force was the spearhead of the American forces in Britain, and was soon joined by increasing numbers of soldiers in preparation for the invasion of Europe. The Americans brought not only their war machines, but vast numbers of comic books.[71] American comics had begun to appear in Britain in the late 1930s, but now they came in bulk, not only through the PX stores on American bases, but also, legend has it, as ballast in transatlantic merchantmen, to be sold on to street traders. These comics offered their own peculiar but fascinating tales of heroes and super-heroes playing their part in the struggle against the Axis powers. Mandrake the Magician, Batman and Dick Tracey, among others, countered spies and sabo-teurs on the home front, while Superman and Captain Marvel wiped out whole enemy divisions in North Africa and the Far East. But there were also comic book heroes created for the moment: The Young Allies, Marine Devil Dogs, Major Victory and Captain Battle and the Fighting Yanks. The most interesting of these were, arguably, Captain America and Blackhawk.[72]

Captain America first appeared in 1941, just before the attack on Pearl Harbour. As Jack Kirby, one of his creators, later explained: 'Captain America was created for a time that needed noble figures . . . We weren't at war yet, but everyone knew it was coming. That's why Captain America was born; America needed a new superpatriot'.[73] The story opened with young Steve Rogers being rejected as unfit for military service. Disappointed, he discusses his problem with the scientist, Professor Reinstein. Reinstein suggests that Steve should be the guinea pig to test his remarkable new serum, developed to create physically superior soldiers (the good professor is presumably playing the Nazis at their own game). The serum transforms Steve from a 97 lb weakling into the formidable Captain America. Reinstein apparently envisioned a legion of super-soldiers capable of keeping the world safe for democracy, but having transformed Steve he is murdered by a Nazi agent, and the secret of the serum dies with him.[74] The Captain, in his red, white and blue costume, puts paid to a host of Axis agents, including his arch-enemy, the evil 'Red Skull', who proved as difficult to kill as Blackhawk. Blackhawk also appeared in the summer of 1941, in *Military Comics*. A Polish aviator whose brother and sister had been killed by the Nazis, Blackhawk is determined to carry on the fight against tyranny. After escaping from Poland, he gathers together a band of like-minded warriors, representatives of most of the Allied nations, including a diminutive Chinese karate expert called 'Chop-Chop'.

Operating from a secret island base, the Blackhawks, as they were collectively known, wage unceasing war against the Nazis.[75]

American comic books were almost exclusively masculine, but there were rare exceptions. One was the Amazon princess, Diana, better known as 'Wonder Woman'. Through an American pilot who has crash-landed on their Pacific island home, a lost race of Amazons learn of the great war being fought against tyranny. The Amazon Queen decides that her daughter Diana should return to the US with the American, and use her magic powers in the cause of freedom. Disguised as a nurse, Diana Prince, she plays a conventional part in the war effort, but as Wonder Woman she also wages a secret war on Axis agents and fifth columnists.[76] Wonder Woman proved enormously popular, and the comic is still running. Other heroines were less successful. 'Pat Patriot' worked in an aircraft factory, but had remarkable talent for detecting saboteurs. Despite being advertised as 'America's Joan of Arc', Pat's adventures ran for less than a year in *Daredevil* comics. 'Miss America', 'Miss Victory' and 'USA – the Spirit of Old Glory' (a blonde in a short blue dress) appear to have lasted only for one or two issues before disappearing into superheroine limbo.[77] It is difficult to assess just how widely American comic books were read in wartime Britain. Some could certainly be purchased from street traders in city markets – the dealers presumably having their own dubious sources of supply – but it would appear that most British boys found them difficult to obtain, and those in circulation were highly prized. Certainly, they offered a more fantastic, but more violent, view of the war than the conventional adventures in British juvenile fiction.

Americans, apart from the handful of volunteers serving with the RAF, such as the New Yorker, Tex O'Hara, in 666 Squadron, were virtually excluded from stories by British writers. Perhaps this reflected something of the peculiarities of the Anglo–American relationship. After 1941, there was widespread relief among Britons that America was finally in the war, but, at the same time, a resentment that the once great British Empire was now incapable of surviving without American assistance. There was also considerable resentment among British servicemen at the well-paid, well-fed and supremely confident Yanks. It was a sore point for many, and one only has to consider the furore over the 1945 Errol Flynn film, *Objective Burma* (which suggested that Americans might have played a major part in recapturing Burma from the Japanese), to gauge the strength of popular anti-American feeling.[78] A notable exception to the lack of American heroes in British fiction was the series of novels by R. S. Bowen, dealing with the adventures of Dave Dawson, an American volunteer in the RAF. These were almost certainly inspired by the exploits of the much publicized American 'Eagle Squadron' in the RAF. The first novel, *Dave Dawson at Dunkirk*, was published in 1942 and followed by Dave's Battle of Britain experiences in *Dave Dawson with the RAF*. The series ran until 1944, when the author transferred his hero to the American Air Corps and duty in the Pacific.[79] Cinema at least attempted to seal the Anglo–American Alliance with a series of films, such as *A Canterbury Tale, The Way to the Stars* and *A Matter of Life and Death.*

While allies were dealt with in a cursory manner, the enemy was usually reduced to basic stereotypes – nameless, one-dimensional figures who could be annihilated without remorse. In British fiction, of course, the 'Huns' had long been portrayed as dangerous and unpleasant since they first appeared in the 1870s, but the deadly efficient soldiers of the 'The Battle of Dorking' had, by 1940, given way to the crop-headed bullies who slavishly followed orders, were noted for their brutality, and much given to using expressions like 'Achtung! Spitfire' or 'Englischer Schweinhund'! The Gestapo and SS were invariably portrayed as the most cruel and merciless of all, but no fictional representation during the war years, however sadistic, ever came close to the reality that was revealed by the liberation of the concentration camps in 1945. Germans were almost always portrayed as a people without history. There was rarely any attempt to explain why they had attacked Poland or what motivated them, other than the vague generalization that Hitler had ordered it. Fiction simply reflected the child's view that Hitler was the arch-fiend. As one twelve-year-old explained:

> Hitler is a dirty rotter. He's the man what started as a painter and wants
> to domineer the world. But he's getting a kick in his pants. He ought to
> be covered with treacle and honey and then let the bees get at him. He
> deserves it because he's been cruel to the world.[80]

Others thought of him a 'beast', a 'rat' or a 'maniac' who enjoyed seeing people tortured. Other targets for abuse among the Nazi hierarchy were Goering and Goebbels, but Ribbentropp and William Joyce – 'Lord Haw Haw', the radio propagandist – were often mentioned. The British war effort in fiction, as well as in reality, was directed mainly against Germany, but the struggle against Japan was occasionally featured by authors, especially after 1943.

The typical portrayal of the Japanese borrowed a great deal from the pre-war image of the 'sinister oriental', a devious, unemotional fanatic with a deep hatred of the white race. The Japanese were invariably shown as undersized, simian in appearance, frequently wearing thick-lensed spectacles and noted for their sadism. Even a National Savings poster (illus. 61) made use of such sterotypical racist images. Typical of the fictional Japanese is Commandant Yashnowada, of an interment camp in Borneo, who made his appearance in a 1943 Biggles story. Yashnowada treats his captives abominably, orders floggings for no reason at all

61 'Beat the Jap':
National Savings
poster, 1945.

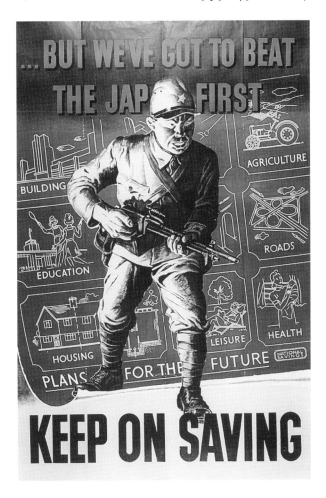

and has those unfortunates who try to escape beaten to death.[81] At the end of the novel, Yashnowada meets a suitable end when he falls into the hands of a party of native headhunters! Of the other Axis partners, only the Italians were painted in sympathic colours. Comic, unmilitary and rarely threatening, Italians were simply a variation on the pre-war 'funny foreigner' stereotype. 'Da-Wow! I am-a da-speechless!' was the favourite expression of *Beano*'s Musso the Wop, but all Italians used such curious language. Even adventure fiction refused to take the Italian armed forces seriously, a notion which apparently found confirmation in press reports of the mass surrender of large parts of the Duce's army during the North African campaign. Italian civilians, of course, had little interest in the war and blamed hostilities on the Germans, who had bullied Mussolini into making war.[82] But, as we shall see, these images of the enemy became permanent fixtures in the pleasure culture of war in the post-war world. Despite the popularity of the war as a subject for fiction and cinema, there was little attempt by authors or feature film-makers to recreate the massed battles of the war for a juvenile audience. These were captured in a series of powerful battle documentaries produced by the Crown Film Unit.

Until late 1942, the German and Japanese armies appeared to be invincible. Then, in North Africa, at Midway and at Stalingrad, the tide began to turn in the Allies' favour. For the British, the turning-point was the Battle of El Alamein in October 1942, and the subsequent advance through North Africa, which destroyed Rommel's Afrika Korps and paved the way for the invasion of Italy. The campaign was celebrated in two outstanding documentaries, *Desert Victory* (1943), covering events from El Alamein to the capture of Tripoli, and the later Anglo–American co-production, *Tunisian Victory*, released the following year and covering the rest of the campaign. *Desert Victory*, however, one of the most celebrated wartime documentaries, is perhaps the supreme example of the battle narrative.[83] The film tells the story of the campaign, focusing on the part played by all the services and the contribution of the home front, using actuality footage assembled by Army Film and Photographic Unit cameramen. The strength of the film lies in its superbly filmed images of battle, from the night barrage which opened Montgomery's offensive, to stirring shots of the rapid advance of the Eighth Army through the harsh Libyan landscape – rich, evocative images that were later copied for a host of post-war feature films, such as *Ice-Cold in Alex* and *Sea of Sand*, as well as American pictures like *The Desert Fox* and *Tobruk*. This is modern warfare at its most effective. Monty's powerful armoured units pursue the retreating enemy, while overhead the Desert Air Force clears the Luftwaffe from the skies, opening the way for the relentless advance of the Desert Rats – the citizen-soldiers of Britain and the empire (illus. 62). With its powerful images,

62 The British advance in North Africa. From the film *Desert Victory*, 1943.

emotive commentary and stirring music, *Desert Victory* is more than a simple record of a successful campaign; it is a wildly romantic tribute to the tenacity of the desert army, the ragged heroes who gave the nation its first real victory.

One consequence of literary and filmic representations of the war was that children, and especially boys, began to re-enact such events in their play activities.

While playing war had always been a popular activity for boys, the Second World War gave such games a new relevance. Even before war was declared, Gamage's catalogue listed a number of toys which reflected the impending crisis. Fifteen shillings (75p) purchased the 'Air Defence Set', comprising two anti-aircraft guns (they actually fired wooden projectiles complete with a flash and smoke) and a battery-operated searchlight. A variety of spring-loaded anti-aircraft guns was available, as were pistols, rifles, a number of different military uniforms and clock-work tanks with 'sparking' guns.[84] At Christmas 1939, the unprecedented demand for war-related toys found many retailers unprepared and a large number of dissatisfied customers. Manufacturers who had reacted quickly to the new situation after September did remarkably well. In January 1940, a Mass-Observation report noted that trench scenes with movable figures were particularly popular, as were board games where model soldiers were moved according to the throw of the dice. One game based on the Maginot Line was especially sought after,[85] but was presumably scrapped after June 1940! Toymakers quickly responded to the interest, and in 1941 the shops were flooded with traditional lead soldiers, model aeroplanes, tanks, guns and uniforms. Among new developments were imitation steel helmets and 'GHQ', a new game from John Waddington, played with infantry, mobile and armoured divisions on a board representing Western Europe. Even the traditional card game, Happy Families, was adapted to the times. Now called War Planes, it featured Spitfires, Hurricanes and Wellington bombers instead of Mr and Mrs Bun.[86] Such toys and games encouraged children to indulge their fantasies about being a part of the conflict, and helped to resolve anxieties. By 1941, however, as factories shifted to war production, toys almost vanished from the shops and children were forced to improvise with whatever was at hand, or to rely on their imagination. When toys began to reappear towards the end of the war, even unmilitary items were marketed with a war connection. Royal Enfield Bicycles, for example, were advertised as 'Made Like A Gun' (illus. 63).

Street and playground games often reflected the contemporary situation, and many commentators noted the predominance of boys running around play-grounds in late 1940 with arms outstretched, alternately roaring and imitating the machine-guns of the RAF's Spitfire fighters. 'We pretend we're English and German', explained one nine-year-old boy, 'and then we have a fight. We play

in our yards, these are aerodromes, and we're the pilots in the planes, and we try
and bomb the aerodromes, and we drop bombs – they're not real ones, but we
pretend they are'.[87] Another topical game was 'Burma Road'. Boys filled their
handkerchiefs with sand and tried to bombard other boys, who pretended to be
lorries travelling up the Burma Road with vital supplies for the nationalist
Chinese armies. One bizarre game described by a Mass-Observation reporter
was 'Concentration Camps'. As one of the players explained:

> We play it outside the church because it has got railings and we pretend
> it's barbed wire. Some of us are the Nazi guards. We've been taken
> prisoner, and they search us for the secret plans, but they don't know that

we've made a lot of different plans; only one of them is real. The rest are only fluff, in case some of our own men turn against us. We try to surround the concentration camp and get our boys away. We slosh the guards and pinch their clothes, and then we get our own men free. We got the idea from the pictures.[88]

Curiously, as Mass-Observation investigators discovered, most children disliked the war, some even hated it; yet playing at war, reading about it or watching it reconstructed on the cinema screen held enormous fascination for them, and even after the restoration of peace in 1945 they did not abandon the pleasure culture of war provided for them by toy manufacturers, publishers and film-makers. Nor, curiously, did they have any reservation about handing on their fascination to their own children in the post-war decades.

Despite the sheer scale of the Second World War, the enormous loss of life and the terrors it unleashed on the world, the pleasure culture of war portrayed it as little different from earlier conflicts. The barbarity of the Eastern Front, of Auschwitz, Dresden, Changi and the Burma Railway, were simply ignored in favour of a representation of conflict that was sanitized, romanticized and reduced to an exciting game in which Tommy and Fritz manfully slugged it out face to face. Perhaps because it was the nation's last great achievement on the world stage before relegation to the second division, 1939–45 has become, for the British people, a never-ending story told and retold to remind themselves of a glorious past, in a far less glorious and depressing present.

7 After the Wars: 1940s – 1990s

There are ... characteristics of the English, well known to their
neighbours, but altogether unmentioned by themselves. Their prop-
ensity for endless aggressive war, for example. The Hundred Years' War
looks quite different from the French side of the Channel. Let those
who think it simply a piece of medieval romanticism ask the Scots –
or the Welsh – about their experiences. It would be inadvisable to
ask the Irish.

... The English are in fact a violent, savage race; passionately
artistic, enormously addicted to pattern, with a faculty beyond all
other people of ignoring their neighbours, their surroundings, or in
the last resort, themselves.

Humphrey Jennings, review of The Character of England

ACHTUNG! SURRENDER
For You Fritz, Ze Euro '96 Championship Is Over.
The *Mirror* declares football war on Germany

Daily Mirror, 24 June 1996

VIOLENCE IS ACCEPTABLE
Cruelty And Hatred For The Alien Should Be Encouraged
PITY IS FOR THE WEAK ...

Dominion Storm over Gift 3
A Todd Porter Game from Eidos Interactive (1998)

In 1945, after the most devastating war in human history, it might well have been
assumed that the pleasure culture of war would disappear, submerged under the
horror of modern warfare, and that war as a source of pleasure and entertainment
would now become impossible. Yet this was not the case. Certainly, since 1945,
British society has in some respects become more pacific; that is to say, never

have there been so many people totally opposed to the practice of war or to representations of violence. Equally, never have so many people been so addicted to the pleasure culture of war in some form or other. It is a curious contradiction that, while there are now more cultural artefacts emphasizing the horror and futility of war than ever before, there are also many more films, stories and video games offering increasingly violent and bloody action scenarios for entertainment, especially for the nation's youth.

In the 60 or so years since the end of the Second World War, parents and public watchdogs have, on several occasions, protested at the level of violence portrayed in American 'horror' comics or in crime and horror stories on film and video, yet such protests have never been aimed at the pleasure culture of war. Parents who took exception to the pernicious violence in the film *Child's Play 3*, which, it was suggested, may have triggered the murder of James Bulger in 1993 by two ten-year-old boys,[1] have seemingly accepted without comment that their children can see the most graphic and explicit violence in war films such as *Starship Troopers* or *Saving Private Ryan*. Clearly, then, even in this age when pacifism appears to be gaining ground, the representation of war still seems to occupy a privileged position in popular culture, suggesting that violence can be entertaining provided it is located in the context of past or future wars. But we should note that the Second World War did, temporarily at least, severely disrupt the idea of war as pleasure, and particularly the idea that the events of 1939–45 could be 'entertaining'.

After 1945, following more than five years of the horror of total war, it was hardly surprising that war weariness was widespread, with most people simply wishing to forget the years of danger and look forward to a more peaceful future. The war as a subject for popular entertainment lost its appeal. This was reinforced as the appalling realities of concentration camps and the atomic bomb became public knowledge. Those living in the immediate shadow of Auschwitz and Hiroshima found it impossible to reconstruct the war as a source of romantic adventure; nor was there any further need for war propaganda. Under these conditions, contemporary war-related fiction disappeared remarkably quickly, and writers of war stories quickly found new employment for their heroes.[2] W. E. Johns published the last Biggles war adventure in 1946. By the following year, his hero had transferred to a new special air police unit at Scotland Yard, where his future battles were part of the endless war against crime.[3] In the comics, war serials that had begun before August 1945 ran their course, and were replaced with more traditional fare. In cinema, the few spectacular battle films of the later 1940s, like *Fighter Squadron* or the John Wayne extravaganza of the Pacific war, *Sands of Iwo Jima*, came from American studios. In Britain, from the end of the war until 1950, only some twenty war-related feature films were produced. None were traditional battle stories, but dealt rather with prisoners of war and European resistance movements, or praised British technical achievements, like *School for Secrets* (1946), which offered a fictionalized account of the development of radar. This is not, of course, to say that war or violent adventure as a generic subject disappeared from popular culture altogether. Pirates, cavaliers, crusaders and cowboys still fought their way across the pages of the story papers or filled the screen with their heroic and violent exploits. But until the 1950s, combat adventures based around the Second World War were difficult to find.

Gradually, however, from the mid-1950s, the Second World War once again became an acceptable subject for adventure films and stories and the dominant event in the pleasure culture of war.[4] The events of 1939–45 were just distant enough for eleven- to twelve-year-olds to have only vague memories of their reality, and even among many of those who had brushed with its dangers memory had begun to fade, leaving only a kind of 'finest hour' nostalgia. At the same time, Britain was experiencing the opening phase in what would become a highly lucrative market for entertainment and leisure among the nation's youth. The baby boom of 1945–9 increased the population by over one million, and ensured a rapidly expanding market among boys and young men from early in the decade. 'Austerity', the economic policy for recovery under Clement Attlee's 1945 Labour Government, had sown the seeds of 1950s affluence, and the rise of a consumer society, arrested by the war, re-emerged, as 'motor-cars, televisions, record-players, bedroom suites and fridges, wondrous toys and sweets for children, pop records for adolescents flooded into the showrooms and supermarkets'.[5] Full employment and larger wage packets meant that most teenagers received at least some pocket money from parents or part-time jobs to spend on leisure activities; and with the invention of the 'teenager' a whole new service economy sprang up to cater to their needs – record companies, coffee bars, jazz clubs, dance halls and, of course, publishers and film-makers, who vied with one another to win a share of the profits. The new 'sophisticated' and affluent young reader or filmgoer wanted something far more exciting, dramatic and realistic than stories about public schools, pirates or cowboys, and, reflecting the nation's renewed interest in the Second World War, this topic gradually became a staple ingredient in entertainment for the nation's youth.

The re-emergence of the Second World War in popular culture began at the end of 1940s, with a number of autobiographies, memoirs and novels written by veterans. Despite the claims of literary critics that the war produced few 'great' novels, many of these war memoirs and fiction enjoyed immense popular success. *From the City, From the Plough* (Alexander Baron, 1948), *The Wooden*

Horse (Eric Williams, 1949), *Ill-Met By Moonlight* (Stanley Moss, 1950), *The Dam Busters* (Paul Brickhill, 1950) and *The Cruel Sea* (Nicholas Monsarrat, 1951) may not have enjoyed much critical acclaim but found great success in the marketplace, as did many other titles.[6] *The Dam Busters*, for instance, has sold more than a million copies and has been continuously in print for over 40 years.[7] Many of these titles were re-issued in junior or 'cadet' editions aimed at younger readers, and both *The Wooden Horse* and *Colditz Story* were republished in abridged form by Windmill Books for use as school readers in the late 1950s; while *The Cruel Sea* is currently on the GCSE English syllabus. Perhaps even more important, the popularity of many of these books ensured that they were quickly adapted for the screen, thus making them available to a far greater audience.

By the 1950s, the British film industry was in the doldrums after the boom years of the war. The rapid growth of television and audience preference for American films, meant that British studios had lost much of the support they had enjoyed during the 1940s. Financial constraints limited film production, while cost-cutting often meant that many British films were technically, and sometimes artistically, inferior to Hollywood productions. Nevertheless, throughout the 1950s and well into the '60s, the rapidly contracting film industry still produced a substantial number of relatively expensive and well-made war films:

> Apart from crime and detection films, ubiquitous in every generation but generally cheaper, low prestige productions, war films were easily the biggest single group of British films made in the early postwar period, larger in number than the more critically-celebrated Ealing comedies . . .[8]

Some 75 feature films about the war were produced between 1950 and 1959, and a further 30 or so in the following decade. Few were well-received by the critical establishment. William Whitebait, writing in the *New Statesman* in 1958, summed up the patronizing but dominant critical attitude to war films: 'They aren't good, most of these films, and they aren't quite bad. They suffice'.[9] What was deliberately overlooked by critics was the enormous popularity these films enjoyed. Under the onslaught of television, cinema audiences were shrinking, but even in 1959 some 14.5 million people went to the cinema every week. That audience was predominantly male and aged between mid-teens and mid-twenties, and what it enjoyed was war films.[10] In 1950, for example, both *Odette* and *The Wooden Horse* were among the top ten British box-office attractions. *The Cruel Sea* topped the list in 1953, *The Dam Busters* in 1955, *Reach For the Sky* in 1956 and *Sink the Bismarck* in 1960.[11] West End premieres were usually attended by the Royals and/or senior officers of the armed forces, while military bands or a guard of honour were often in attendance. Even surburban screenings were accompanied by considerable ballyhoo, with cinema foyers draped with flags and representatives of local military or cadet units present. In 1954, when the *The Dam Busters* was shown at the Penge Odeon (south-east London), the foyer was hung with models of World War Two aircraft, the local Air Training Corps Squadron band played in the foyer between performances, and a representative of the RAF Benevolent Fund addressed the audience from the stage before taking up a collection for the charity. In other local cinemas even more elaborate promotions took place.[12]

There is little need to describe these films in detail. Nearly 50 years after their original release, most are remarkably familiar, even to those born long after the conflict, through frequent television screenings. But what do they tell their audience about the Second World War? What images of the most terrible and destructive war in history do they convey? What first attracts our attention is that these films are largely depoliticized. None deals with the causes of the war, describes the evils of Nazism or explains what Britain was fighting for – an important and recurring element in the films made between 1939–45. In films of the 1950s, it had become a war without beginning or end, and the stories they tell have little more rationale than 'beating the Jerries'. These reconstructions were by and large sanitized affairs; there is no place for Dachau, Dresden or even the horrors of the battlefield. Men die cleanly from a single bullet or bayonet thrust. No-one suffers unspeakable agonies after being mutilated by high explosive. In fact, the absence of brutality or real violence is striking, compared to American combat films of the same period (*To Hell and Back*, or *The Naked and the Dead*, for example).[13] Secondly, there is a distinct lack of emphasis on the national unity of the 'People's War' that was so prominent in wartime films:

> War films of the 1950s do not celebrate the union of classes and regions that was so characteristic of such wartime films as *The Way Ahead* . . . *Millions Like Us* . . . or *Fires Were Started* . . . rather they tend to revert to the stock officers-as-heroes and other-ranks-as-comic figures that were more characteristic of films of the 1930s.[14]

The home front simply does not figure in these films, which focus almost exclusively on the deeds of servicemen or, very occasionally, servicewomen (*Odette*, 1950, *Carve Her Name With Pride*, 1958). If featured at all, women are relegated to minor roles as wives or girlfriends who wait at home, or are sometimes glimpsed in the background in clerical positions in operations rooms or headquarters (*Angels One Five*, 1952, *Sink the Bismarck*, 1960). The blitz provides only a useful location for romantic encounter as the hero takes shelter during a raid (*Appointment in London*, 1952); and the industrial front has disappeared entirely. The only similarity to films made between 1939–45 is the use of black and white photography rather than colour, not only for economic reasons but to add a degree of authenticity, so that actual combat footage can be intercut into the narrative. Overall, the war is reduced to a series of exciting and heroic adventures undertaken by middle-class males – a return to the traditional representation of war in British popular culture – and a specifically British affair that plays down the Commonwealth and Dominion contribution apart from the token Anzac or Canadian, and even pokes fun at naive 'Yanks', betraying not only resentment that the British war effort succeeded largely because of American support, but reflecting a deep anxiety about the increasing Americanization of popular culture after 1945.

The return of essentially middle- and upper-class officer heroes, personified on the screen by actors like John Mills, Jack Hawkins, Trevor Howard or Dirk Bogarde, was yet another way in which the idea of the people's war was undermined. During the later 1940s, the middle classes certainly felt themselves to be under threat from a Labour Government which appeared to be remaking British society. Such anxieties were, of course, groundless, but they were widespread and deeply entrenched at the time and clearly reflected in the perceptive novels of Angela Thirkell, for instance.[15] Thus it might well be argued that the 1950s cycle of war films was part of the counter-attack by essentially middle-class film-makers against the predominance of the common man established by the Second World War. While the films do emphasize the importance of team work and mutual cooperation between officers and men, the centre of attention is invariably the officer, the focus for loyalty and admiration. Whether he plans the operation, leads men into battle or sacrifices himself to save his comrades, it is the officer, obsessed with duty, honour and patriotism, who occupies centre stage, and who differs little from his predecessor, the imperial hero of pre-1914 fiction. In *They Who Dare* (1953), for example, a commando unit raids enemy airfields on Crete in order to cripple Axis air forces before the Battle of El Alamein. Most of the team are appallingly bad-tempered ex-public school boys (officers of course), supported by a few willing and endlessly cheerful professional other ranks. The raid is led by an officer nicknamed 'Boy' (Dirk Bogarde),[16] who is clearly fascinated by playing soldiers. He continually makes patronizing remarks about the Greeks, and, in one scene, tells his men to 'scrag the Jerries'. Boy's enthusiasm to plant 'just one more bomb' at the enemy airfield ruins the group's chance to escape, and most are killed. As the film was directed by Lewis Milestone (the director of the classic anti-war text *All Quiet on the Western Front*), it may have been intended as a demonstration of the stupidity of war; yet what emerges on the screen is a reasonably exciting adventure narrative of brave deeds undertaken by a wildly romantic upper-class hero, who prefers the costume of a Greek bandit to battledress and who finds war hugely enjoyable. Interestingly, as the middle class regained the major role in the 'war story', the image of the enemy was equally transformed so that war could become, once again, an exciting game.

It is noticeable that in these films 'Germans' were not always 'Nazis', but most commonly an honourable (even though a plodding and unimaginative) enemy who generally 'played by the rules'. The occasional appearance of the Nazi fanatic serves only to underline the essential decency of the majority of Germans. In *Ill-Met By Moonlight* (1957), the ex-public school hero (Dirk Bogarde again) spends much of the time helping the German general he has kidnapped surmount the hostile terrain of Rhodes (illus. 64), and between them there develops considerable mutual respect. Curiously, the image of the Japanese was unchanging, and they remained cruel, sadistic and inscrutable – a filmic image that has proved consistent from the early 1950s, in films such as *A Town Like Alice* (1956) to the recent Australian–British co-production about civilian internees, *Paradise Road* (1997). But nowhere is the image of the Germans as softened as in prisoner of war stories.

In 1981, in John Huston's *Escape to Victory*, the war game acted out by captives and captors is openly acknowledged when Michael Caine, playing an ex-professional footballer (and officer by accident) is told by the gung-ho, public school-educated escape committee in his camp to organize the mass escape of the British POW football team. Caine's character is far from enthusiastic, but

64 The upper-class hero: Dirk Bogarde in the film *Ill-Met by Moonlight*, 1956.

is told, 'It's your duty as an officer'. Still reluctant, he is then asked if he is afraid. Angrily he replies, 'Your escaping is just some bloody upper-crust game'. And that is exactly how British cinema has portrayed the POW experience. In *Colditz Story*, *The Wooden Horse*, *Albert RN*, *Very Important Person* or *The Password is Courage*, life behind the wire is transformed into elaborate ritual with well-defined rules which everyone understands and accepts. British officer is captured, the Germans tell him that the camp is escape-proof, whereupon the officer escapes by digging a tunnel, disguising himself as the German commandant or by some other equally ingenious means. While the escape is being plotted, the British irritate the guards as much as possible and the guards retaliate by continuous searches of the prisoners barracks and endless roll-calls, or by resorting to the ultimate sanctions – denial of Red Cross parcels or cancelling the prisoners Christmas pantomime! The whole experience follows a rigid pattern, and everyone involved is generally good-humoured. Escaping appears no more dangerous than creeping out of the dorm after lights out, and even the German guards appear at heart to be decent chaps.

Interestingly, in 1957, in *The One That Got Away*, the story was reversed, with the British paying tribute to the only German to escape from a British POW camp – Luftwaffe officer Franz von Werra. Needless to say, von Werra and his fellow prisoners are played as Englishmen in rather odd uniforms. Only in the American production, *The Great Escape* (1963), are the consequences of escaping taken seriously when a number of escapees are executed by the SS. But even here, the first two-thirds of the film reprise the traditional 'goon-baiting' activities of POWs in British cinema (as the original story was by *Dam Busters* author, Paul Brickhill, we should not, perhaps, be surprised).

Only in the late 1960s did a handful of (usually) low-budget films emerge which attempted to portray the war as a more brutal and bitter experience. But features like *The Long Day's Dying* (1968), *Play Dirty* (1969) and *Overlord* (1975) enjoyed only limited release and were completely overshadowed by war-as-adventure box-office hits such as *Where Eagles Dare* (1969) and *Force Ten From Navarone* (1978). Even the powerful story of the 1944 attack on Arnhem, *A Bridge Too Far* (1977), was more admired for its documentary-style reconstruction and emphasis on British grit than for the criticisms it raised about the planning, conduct and wasted lives of the operation. As cinematic representations of the war gradually faded during the 1970s, television became the main purveyor of the war as visual entertainment. The first coverage of a major national event after the rebirth of the BBC Televison Service in June 1946 was the Victory Parade in London. Since then, the war has remained an important element in television schedules. In the 1950s, this was limited to coverage of Remembrance Day and major anniversaries, or to documentary series such as *The War in the Air* or the American-produced *The War at Sea*, along with hagiographies of war heroes such as Montgomery and Mountbatten. However, by the 1970s, the networks were also producing major fictional dramas like *Colditz* (1972/1974), *Pathfinders* (1975), *Squadron* (1982) and *Tenko* (1981/1982), besides rescreening post-war feature films on a regular basis. From 1989 through 1995, all the networks produced a staggering number of documentaries and dramas celebrating the various 50th anniversaries, besides rescreening a significant number of films under series titles such as 'The British at War'.

The recent 60th anniversary of the beginning of the war has witnessed another bout of war nostalgia and yet another rescreening of 1950s films. While television has attempted to portray the war in much broader terms by including the part played by women, the home front and the problems and strains of life in wartime (*Wish Me Luck*, 1987/8, *A Family At War*, 1970–72 and *We'll Meet Again*, 1981–3), albeit in nostalgic soft-focus, action dramas have tended, like the cinema products from which they were derived, to be biased towards the middle-class officer-hero. Post-war British films thus established the Second World War firmly in the war-as-adventure mould with gutsy, patriotic officers taking the major responsibility for victory; and in so doing they created an image that would be emulated in other forms of popular culture.

In the boys' story papers, Second World War stories had all but disappeared by early 1946. Rockfist Rogan, the RAF's fighting ace, still featured in *Champion*, but by and large the war adventure was absent until the early 1950s, when the popularity of war films convinced publishers that interest in the subject was increasing. In its highly successful early issues, *Lion* (first published in February 1952 by Amalgamated Press), offered its readers a World War Two serial in strip form, 'The Lone Commandos', in which Sergeant Roy Tempest and Private Jack Steel undertake various daredevil operations in occupied Europe. When this came to an end, it was almost immediately followed by 'The Naval Castaways', a tale of RN prisoners of war in the Far East, who, despite their captivity, still manage to sabotage a Japanese secret weapon. Neither of these stories was particularly good or well-drawn, but their importance lies in the fact that they were among the first of a new cycle of Second World War stories that would become a major ingredient of boys' comics, and that they were told through the visual strip format – a relatively new departure, which would become increasingly common.

Lion was intended as an answer to Hulton's enormously successful new comic, *Eagle*, conceived and edited by the Reverend Marcus Morris, a Lancashire vicar, in 1950. Morris intended his paper as an antidote to the excessive violence in American comics. He was concerned by the increasingly popular American horror and crime comics then being imported, but it is significant that in the United States a boom in violent war comics had begun in the early 1950s, with titles such as *Fighting Marines*, 1951, *Star-Spangled War* and *Fighting Air Force*, both 1952, leading the way. *Sergeant Rock*, perhaps the best known American Second World War comic, first published in 1959, was a relative latecomer. Imported war comics attracted curiously little real criticism. Morris, then, was concerned that *Eagle* should not only promote 'decency, courage, fair-play and selflessness', but provide educational material as well as entertainment. The new comic pioneered the narrative adventure in strip form in Britain, with creative use of colour, derived from the American action comics, scrapping lengthy captions and relying instead on bold visual imagery to carry the narrative along. With an initial weekly circulation of around a million, *Eagle* was an immediate success, and not only with boys. Its informative articles and superbly drawn diagrams of aeroplanes, battleships and other machines found favour with parents and the educational press.[17] Despite its Christian values, *Eagle* was an adventure paper providing exciting fiction – most famously the cover strip, 'Dan Dare, Pilot of the Future', and his endless struggle against the alien Treens led by the arch-villain, the Mekon. *Eagle* did not ignore the Second World War, but treated it historically in factual short articles on the Fleet Air Arm, the commandos or in biographies of national heroes like Churchill. However, through its use of these heroes to teach moral lessons, the comic was, as Drotner has pointed out, a rejuvenation of the manly and patriotic ideals of pre-1914 papers such as the *BOP*.[18] Thus *Lion*, in featuring war adventures in visual form, capitalized both on the emerging interest in the Second World War and the new visual style of *Eagle*.

The Thomson papers began to feature war stories around the same time, but used the traditional story format with only a single title illustration. *Rover* offered 'I Flew With Braddock', the exploits of the RAF's most unconventional ace flier (see below), while *Wizard* ran 'The Sitting Duck', set during the ill-fated campaign on Crete. Yet the increasing numbers of young readers through the decade forced publishers to reconsider what they were offering, because children 'demonstrated by their purchases that what they wanted most was all-picture action stories'.[19] At the end of the 1950s, Thomson revamped *Hotspur* as a mainly visual comic, then subjected *Wizard* and *Rover* to the same treatment, and war stories began to figure prominently in their content. The action strip offered its readers exciting visual entertainment with a minimum of explanation or character development, and rushed the reader from one action-packed image to another.

This transition from intellectual enlightenment to emotional intensity reflected the enormous influence of television, which had established visual storytelling as the order of the day for children.[20] A 1976 story from *Battle Picture Weekly*,

'One Man's Fear', the adventures of a British infantryman on D-day, from the boom years of the World War Two action strip, provides a useful example. As the platoon wades ashore, the lieutenant is wounded and falls behind. Sergeant Mulley, who has been distinctly unhappy since leaving England, takes command and throws himself on the enemy with fury. Whatever has been worrying the sergeant, it clearly wasn't fear of combat. In the third frame, we learn that he was at Dunkirk and wants revenge for that humiliation. Frames four to six show the sergeant in action, and in the final frame we learn the cause of Mulley's earlier distress – fear of the sea. The background detail is minimal, but we are shown the impact of shells and bullets through the smoke of battle. Brief bursts of dialogue tell us what we need to know, but it is the visual image that moves the narrative along. The strip provides a substantial amount of information about the war – weaponry, uniforms, attitudes to the enemy and it revels in the excitement of battle and the spirit of the British warrior (illus. 65). A highly successful innova-tion from Amalgamated Press in 1958 was *The War Picture Library*, a pocket-sized, fully illustrated comic with a complete long story in each issue. The stories were almost exclusively confined to World War Two (the first issue was 'The Rats of Tobruk'), and its success provided the model for numerous imitations: *Air Ace Picture Library*, *Combat Picture Library*, *Assault* and, most successful of all, D.C. Thomson's *Commando* (first published in 1961 and still running). The popularity of Second World War stories during the 1970s was also reflected in a number of new, but more traditional-style, comics specializing in tales of combat, including *Warlord* (1974), *Battle* (1975), *Action, Bullet* (both 1976) and *2000 AD* (1977):

> These comics contained an astonishing variety of supplementary material on the apparently inexhaustible subject of war: descriptions of weapons systems, photos and cross-sections of tanks, destroyers and jet fighters; reviews of war films; quizzes on battles; anecdotes about famous soldiers; adverts for war toys; recruitment ads; even accounts of RAF–Luftwaffe reunions.[21]

Although many of these papers did feature earlier wars or even future wars, their main concern was World War Two, which was dealt with from every conceivable angle.

In many respects, comic adventures, like the films that inspired them, recon-structed the same heroic images of the war: a war that was no longer an affair of the whole nation, but of a handful of warriors who exist only to do battle in the jungle, the desert, in the air or on the sea. Women, civilians, the home front, have no place here; the war has lost all meaning and exists only to provide the context in which endless battles take place between the heroes and their enemies.

65 The battle narrative in comics. From *Battle Picture Weekly*, 1976.

Patriotism is intense and the enemy is reduced to a mere cliche – the same stereotypical figures, familiar from pre-1914 fiction, of the bullet-headed German and the sadistic, treacherous oriental. But in one respect they differed markedly from earlier fiction, especially from the post-1950 cycle of films, and that was in the social origins of their heroes.

While 1950s cinema brought the middle-class officer back into the foreground as the natural leader in battle, popular comics still retained a powerful strand of the anti-authoritarianism that had emerged in the 1930s and offered a variety of working-class heroes. 'Ticker' Turner, whose exploits were related in *Victor* during the 1960s was a 'British infantry private during the last war. Ticker did his job well enough, but he was always looking for ways to make his life a bit easier. He was, in fact, the Army's champion wangler'. Ticker's ability as a 'scrounger', however, doesn't interfere with his ability to fight when he has to, as many a German discovered.[22] A more serious character was Bill Saxon, in 'The Sergeant Without Stripes', from the 1970s. Set during the Burma campaign, Bill's platoon is commanded by the aristocratic, petulant and cowardly Lieutenant Flashley. When the men are in danger or the mission looks like failing it is Bill, a born soldier and natural leader, who ensures success, while Flashley makes sure that he personally gets the credit from HQ. But the men are in no doubt who the real leader is and to whom their loyalty is due.[23] During the 1980s, *Warlord* ran the series '"Union Jack" Jackson', a tough British Marine sergeant serving with the American Rangers in Burma. Jackson is an experienced soldier, and in one story his brief is to help the Americans acclimatize to jungle warfare. Naturally, they resent him and this enables the author to work in numerous jibes at the over-confident, over-paid Yanks. By the end of the story, of course, even the American officers have realized that it is Jackson who has ensured the success of the mission: 'We'd never have done it without the Limey'![24] But the archetypal rebellious working-class hero was Matt Braddock, who first flew across the pages of *Rover* in 1952.

Braddock, a Sergeant-Pilot in the RAF, has little time for red tape, armchair warriors or the seemingly endless petty regulations that govern life in the armed forces. His job is to kill Germans, and anything that gets in the way of that is a waste of time. Consequently he is always in trouble and would have been court-martialled had he not been a born pilot and twice winner of the Victoria Cross. His working-class background was established in the seventh series, 'Born to Fly' (1957), in which we learn that he was born in Walsall and apprenticed to an engineering firm. In 1938, convinced that war was inevitable, he decided to learn to fly, but with little education and working-class roots he knows he is unaccept-able to the peacetime RAF. Nevertheless, he pays for his own flying lessons and discovers a natural talent. In one scene, making his way home after a long evening in the public library studying aeronautics, he bumps into a group of upper-class 'loungers' who have 'cut' their class with the RAFVR in order to enjoy themselves. Braddock, who would give anything for their chances, berates them, calling them cheats and the sort of shirkers who make Hitler think he can win. When war comes, Braddock is accepted by the RAF, but only as a non-commissioned pilot, even though he is a better flier than most officers.[25] Braddock's appeal wasn't just as a fighting hero in the most glamorous branch of the armed forces; he represented a tradition of working-class antipathy to authority with which many young readers, resentful of the discipline imposed by school, or looking ahead to a stint of national service, could identify. In fact, the Braddock stories 'could be taken as an attack on the whole officer class ethos' and reflected something of welfare-state Britain's rejection of 'upper-class values, filtered down through middle-class writers for use by working-class boys'.[26] The Braddock stories were enormously popular. They ran until 1973 in *Rover* and were then reprinted in *Victor* and *Warlord*. Braddock even made it into book form, an unusual tribute to his success.[27] Cinema could never really compete here, for even in films where the hero was working-class (*The Password is Courage*, with Dirk Bogarde as escaping POW Sergeant-Major Charlie Coward), the actor's voice, mannerisms and natural authority completely undermine any sense of a lower-class lead. Only rarely did a film like *Private's Progress* (1956) emerge to take a sly swipe at the whole idea of the noble, patriotic, upper-class officer-hero.

The structure of these stories, their characterizations, image and use of language were established in the 1950s, and changed remarkably little over the next half-century. Even the most recent issues of *Commando* look identical to their predecessors, with their square-jawed heroes and conversation larded with wartime slang. Nor has the possibility of European unity had any real effect on how the enemy is portrayed. Even in the late 1990s, the German pilot of a Dornier bomber is still made to exclaim, 'Himmel! An Englander Fighter', and dive away in panic as a Fleet Air Arm ace comes in to the attack.[28] Second World War novels, films and comics put a new vocabulary into the public domain which reflected intense patriotism, is offensively racist and quite unknown among other nations which took part in the war. Such language is still regularly aired at times of international dispute (British interests and the Common Market), crisis (the Falklands War), or on sporting occasions when British teams are matched against Germany (the Euro '96 Cup), by editors and journalists who grew to manhood under the influence of the pleasure culture of World War Two.[29]

These literary and filmic dimensions of the pleasure culture of the Second World War were powerfully reinforced by a new generation of sophisticated toys and games. After 1945, the widespread use of plastics within the toy industry reduced prices and made products available to almost every boy. By the 1960s, 25 pence would buy a whole boxful of German, American or British military figures manufactured by Airfix that could recreate a combat scenario on the dining room table. A few more pennies bought a pre-formed and detailed model of a wide variety of combat aircraft. Other manufacturers offered highly accurate miniature replicas of Second World War tanks, armoured cars, lorries and artillery, along with helmets, handguns and rifles from toymakers like Lone Star, which enabled the young to 'play at war' more realistically. For the less active child, a variety of board-games was available and, for the more mature, complex war games like 'Tank' with which to re-enact the North African campaign or the bloody Battle of Kursk. In the 1960s, on the back of their larger boxes of model soldiers, Britain's offered basic guidance for playing war. Under the heading, 'Let's Fight A Battle – test your skill as a general with this set of basic rules for model warfare', was advice on how to get the most enjoyment from the soldiers, tanks, missiles and 'other military equipment from your toy cupboard'.[30] From America came 'GI Joe', America's 'movable fighting man', a large model that could be dressed in a variety of uniforms or adorned with various pieces of killing hardware.

The enormous popularity of representations of the Second World War in enter-tainment and leisure activities raises interesting contradictions about British attitudes to the war. In 1943, for example, a Mass-Observation survey, 'What Your Child Thinks of the War', reported how 'Frank' and 'John' (both nine) and 'Betty' (twelve) believed the war to be 'terrible' and a 'waste of time'. Frank was particu-larly adamant that war 'means killing people, and thousands called away from their homes, while peace means luxuries and pleasures'. Based upon such evidence, the observer optimistically concluded that, 'These children, when they grow up are surely going to see that war does not happen again. The War is train-ing them what war really means'.[31] Yet some fifteen or twenty years later, Frank, John, Betty and most of their contemporaries had few qualms about letting their own children immerse themselves in the pleasure culture of the Second World War. Equally curious is that the war comic boom reached its peak between 1965 and 1980 – the period in which many young people claimed adherence to 'peace' and 'love', and anti-nuclear, anti-Vietnam War sentiments were widespread.

During this period, then, the young were apparently quite happy listening to the Beatles telling them 'All you need is love', and then reaching for the latest issue of *Warlord* with its equally unambiguous message, 'all you really need is a Thompson sub-machine gun and a grenade'! Such contradictions were possible because cinema and literature had sanitized, romanticized and turned into thrilling adventure the event that their parents had originally found so 'terrible'. The popular image of the war was partial; it recounted only the exciting combats of warriors on distant battlefields and ignored the suffering, persecution and horror inflicted upon millions of hapless civilians. And we should bear in mind that even when the home front and the plight of the non-combatant was explored in popular culture, it was mostly recreated through the rose-tinted lens of nostalgia – as in John Boorman's biographical, but highly-sentimental *Hope and Glory* (1987), a reminiscence of childhood during the London blitz. Curiously, the only real attack on the violence portrayed in boys' comics came in the 1950s and was aimed, not at images of war, but at the horror and crime story in imported American comics. Such was the outcry that these comics were helping to create juvenile delinquents, that they were banned under government legislation.[32] The violence portrayed in war comics when the Second World War was re-fought on a weekly basis was presumably acceptable, because it provided a constant reminder of a great national achievement. The peak years of Second World War story comics, films and novels have now passed, but every anniversary still brings forth its documentaries, its celebratory volumes and the almost mandatory television screenings of 1950s war films. Why have the British found such endless fascination in the war; why has it become almost a national obsession? The answer would seem to be provided by an examination of the British experience after 1945.

As the war ended, the nation was faced with yet another major challenge: an imperial crisis as the peoples of the empire demanded their freedom. India, the Jewel in the Crown of empire, gained independence in 1947, closely followed by Burma, Palestine and Egypt, and these paved the way for other independence movements throughout Asia and Africa. British troops once again found themselves involved in a succession of little wars, in Cyprus, Malaya, Aden and Kenya, for instance, but which, at best, could only delay decolonization.[33] In 1956, desperately unwilling to acknowledge their new position in the second eleven, and facing the loss of empire, the Conservative government under Eden embarked on the foolhardy Suez expedition, to reassert British domination of the eastern Mediterranean and restore national self-confidence in a dramatically changing world. But the days of Pitt, Palmerston and gunboat diplomacy had long since passed, and, instead of triumph, the nation found only humiliation. Interestingly, James Chapman has suggested that a contextual reading of the film *Dunkirk* (1958), set in production soon after Suez, can be seen as a reassertion of national self-esteem following that fiasco:

> For Dunkirk, read Suez: the British Army is pulled out from the beaches after a disastrous intervention in foreign shores. 'Somebody's made a mess of it, but I don't think it's the Army', remarks Bernard Lee's

character towards the end of the film and clearly laying the blame for failure at the politicians' door. As in 1940, so in 1956.[34]

Films about the Second World War can thus have far wider meaning, and can reassert notions of eventual victory even in the darkest hour. But in adventure fiction in a post-colonial world, the traditional image of idealized masculinity, the 'imperial hero', could no longer be sustained. A new and more acceptable image came to the fore – the Second World War hero, the enemy of tyranny and liberator of Europe. The uniform might have changed, but it was predominantly the same old stereotype: the middle- or upper-class, public school-educated officer who looked on war as a game; a sporting adventure. Lest the audience be confused, there were clues as to meaning. In the midst of the war film cycle were rattling imperial epics like *North-West Frontier* (1960), and in the comics, tucked away between the tales of the Desert Rats or the Chindits, were to be found re-tellings of Major Wilson's last stand against the Matabele and references to the 'extraordinary pioneer', Dr Starr Jameson.[35] There were also other factors behind the predominance of the Second World War in popular culture.

For Britain, the price of victory was high. The nation was virtually bankrupt by 1940, and only increasing American aid and the blood-bath endured by the Red Army ensured national survival. For over six years British industry produced only war materials, and the overseas markets that had existed in 1939 disappeared and, even after 1945, were never regained. Staple industries, fatally wounded by the First World War, found it almost impossible to recover from the Second. Faced with fluctuating overseas markets, dependent on foreign loans and facing competition from more rapidly recovering rivals, British commerce was in a parlous state.[36] Even more dramatic was the emergence of the ideologically opposed superpowers, the USSR and the USA, which squeezed most of the European nations into a minor league tied to one or other of the new giants. In 1950, American foreign policy centered on containment of the Communist threat, and this dictated that a stand be taken in South Korea to oppose Communist expansion. Although the Korean war was fought by the United Nations, the major role was played by the United States, which dominated the high command, directed strategy and initiated operations. Britain played its part, but was very much the junior partner – a far cry from 1940–41 when Britain alone had carried the torch of freedom. Korea also seemed to foreshadow a new, more critical phase of the Cold War and put the possibility of another major conflict on the table. Thus, frightened of looking forward to an uncertain future, the nation preferred to look back to past military triumphs, in order to convince itself that Britain was still great. And the war which most epitomized the triumph of national spirit and moral certainty was, of course, the Second World War. In this far less certain age, it would appear that the British people need to continually remind themselves of how, against all the odds, they eventually triumphed in 1945, in order to reassure themselves that national greatness could be regained. The Second World War is the war that the British will not, cannot, allow themselves to forget. Yet while the Second World War has certainly been the single most commonly recurring conflict in the pleasure culture of war, there have been others.

What is particularly noticeable about the conflicts that have been incorporated within the pleasure culture of war is that they were not considered controversial at the time; indeed, they all enjoyed considerable public support. Since 1945, Britain's wars have rarely enjoyed that luxury and have thus been excluded. These were the nation's contentious and inglorious little wars of the last days of empire, including Malaya, Kenya, Cyprus and the undeclared war in Northern Ireland, as well as United Nations conflicts in which Britain played only a minor role, like the Korean War. Curiously, the chilling prospect of a third world war arising out of superpower rivalry, the most terrifying scenario for a major conflict between 1945 and the 1980s – a war in which atomic weapons would almost certainly be deployed and which might well result in the total annihilation of humankind – soon became a source of vicarious entertainment. The frightening realities of atomic warfare had first been brought to public attention through newsreel coverage of the bombing of the Japanese cities of Hiroshima and Nagasaki, in August 1945. The use of atomic weapons was largely justified on grounds that it would force the Japanese to surrender and prevent the enormous casualties that would be incurred in a conventional invasion of the Japanese homeland. Yet even the callous commentary of British Paramount News's first report on Hiroshima could not disguise the full horror of those first images of the devastated city:

> . . . When it's all over, four-and-a-half square miles of Hiroshima was burned and blasted into extinction; the all-shattering devastation in which was born the Atomic Age. In its birthpangs 75,000 people were killed and 70,000 injured. The city's three surviving hospitals were swamped by the myriad sufferers. Their plight glimpsed in these official Japanese pictures . . . The radiation effects were fantastically imprinted on walls and furniture like frozen shadows: a ladder outlined on a building, the design of her dress left on the body of a woman who would die in a few days anyhow – not from her burns or visible wounds, but from radioactivity, the killer that invisibly turns the blood into lifeless water. In atom war, the sins of the father are visited on the children![37]

A more detailed examination of the bombing was John Hersey's best-selling account, *Hiroshima*, which included interviews with survivors. This was followed by official reports and filmic documentaries.[38] Some commentators have suggested that the prospect of such a war was so 'unappetising' that the public preferred to feed their anxieties back into movies [and other fictions] about the Second World War, which was 'over and won',[39] but such a proposition simply cannot be justified, because atomic war quickly become a subject for entertainment, and presumably provided contemporaries with that same frisson of danger that Edwardians had experienced through the invasion story.

For many writers, 'nuclear war meant the Apocalypse – for others it underwrote a utopian future',[40] and here, perhaps, lies the fascination of such stories, for 'the End' was often the 'Beginning' for the handful of survivors who were able to create a new and better society out of the ashes. The best known of this fiction is probably Pat Frank's *Alas, Babylon* (first published in 1959 and reprinted over 30 times by 1975). Here, a small, isolated Florida town survives the war and its inhabitants are able to create a new community in which many of the ills of contemporary society are eliminated – racism, inequality, drop-outs, drugs and junk food. The survivors invoke the cherished memory of the pioneering spirit and mark a return to the communitarian values on which the nation had been built.[41] Such ideas had already been mooted in British juvenile fiction, most notably in John Wyndham's novel *The Chrysalids*, set several generations after a nuclear war in a community dominated by bigoted fundamentalist elders. The elders, believing that man is created in God's image, are constantly on guard against mutation, which, of course, must be destroyed in order to preserve the purity of God's creation. However, some children in the community develop telepathic powers and other minor mutations. In danger of their lives, they make contact by chance with a community in New Zealand, which has survived and is far more tolerant, regarding their talents as a gift. The novels ends with those children who have survived the witch hunting of the Elders setting out to help create a better, more tolerant world; as one of the 'Sealanders' explains, 'We are able to think together and understand one another . . . we are beginning to understand how to assemble and apply the composite team-mind to a problem – and where may that not take us one day'?[42]

In *Z for Zachariah*, Patrick O'Brien tells the story of survival through the diary of sixteen-year-old Anne, who, isolated in the rural valley that has protected her from fallout, believes herself to be alone. A scientist, John Loomis, stumbles into the valley and tells her of his travels through the contaminated regions (Loomis has survived with the aid of an anti-radiation suit) looking for other survivors. Loomis's paranoia forces Anne to leave the valley, yet the novel ends on an optimistic note as Anne, convinced that there must be other more rational survivors, sets out to find them.[43] Interestingly, O'Brien's novel was adapted as school reader for younger children in the early 1980s and is still commonly used in schools.

Despite their grim subject matter, these novels seek to find at least something positive in the doomsday scenario and are markedly different from what has become known as 'survivalist literature' – fiction where the breakdown of civilization has resulted in the emergence of a Darwinian world in which only the strong survive. Such stories contain endless slaughter, rape and pillage as savage survivors revert to tribal groups and wage endless war on one another. Perhaps the best known, and least violent, of such tales are the Mad Max movies. Max, a member of the highway police before the Apocalypse, roams the Australian outback, endlessly pitting himself against psychopathic bikers, crazed warlords and those who would enslave any weaker than themselves.[44] Thus, even the terrifying prospect of a nuclear holocaust could be subsumed into the pleasure culture of war, and transformed into exciting adventure. But this fiction focused on the consequences; it explained little about the cause of this 'last' war – that became the subject for other storytellers.

Most fiction relies on one of two major explanation: the madman or the computer malfunction. Examples of the 'madman' triggering the war include *Dr Stangelove* (1963) and *The Bedford Incident* (1965). In the latter, it is the rabidly anti-Communist naval captain who, pursuing a Soviet spy submarine in the Arctic, exceeds his orders to simply drive it off and instead sinks it, with tragic consequences. In Stanley Kubrick's better-known black comedy, it is the unstable USAF general who, believing the Russians are somehow draining his body fluids, orders his bomber wing to attack the Soviet Union.[45] But it was not always Americans who were to blame. In George O'Smith's 1963 novel, *Doomsday Wing*, a deranged Russian general seeks a permanent solution to Cold War tensions.

The 'accident', most often some form of computer malfunction, was an equally popular mechanism to explain how the war began. *Fail Safe* (1964), based on the novel by Eugene Burdick and Harvey Wheeler, suggests a simple component failure on board the lead bomber of a patrolling Strategic Air Command[46] patrol that apparently orders the planes to bomb their prearranged target – Moscow. Once triggered, they cannot be recalled, and even though SAC cooperates with the Russians to shoot down the bombers, one gets through. Only the decision by the American President to destroy New York in a 'quid pro quo' bombing averts nuclear war.[47] Perhaps the most ingenious explanation, however, was in *War Games* (1983), when teenage computer wizard David Lightman (played by Matthew Broderick), hacks into the US National Defence computer, believing that

'Thermonuclear War' is just another game. Lightman's gaming ability takes the world to the brink of extinction before the crisis is resolved – a wry comment on the dangers inherent in 'war-gaming'.[48] The regularity with which madmen unleashed the forces of destruction, or computers malfunctioned and triggered the Apocalypse, would seem to reveal considerable public anxiety about the quality of military and political leadership in the mid-twentieth century, and a general widespread fear of losing control to the machine as society became increasingly computerized.

The USAF, concerned to demonstrate that the bomb was in safe hands, promoted their nuclear strike force through a series of Hollywood movies, using actors such as James Stewart, who had served in World War Two and was sympathetic to the air force. The loose trilogy, *Strategic Air Command* (1955), *Bombers B52* (1957) and *A Gathering of Eagles* (1962), was concerned to show the professionalism of the men who held the nation's safety in their hands, and in the process demonstrated the superiority of American weaponry. Illustration 66 shows the sleek but menacing lines of the B36 bomber in *Strategic Air Command*.

66 The B36 killing machine. From the film *Strategic Air Command*, 1955.

But the real object of Stewart's desire is the new jet B47, 'the most beautiful thing I've ever seen in my life', he says, when he sees the machine for the first time.[49] This type of fiction was produced almost exclusively in the United States, but such was the American domination of popular culture at this time that it was as widely known in Britain as in its country of origin. British film-makers and writers rarely ventured into this arena – understandably, perhaps, for while the British had their own 'independent' nuclear capability, the defence of the 'Free World' through deterrence was largely an American concern.

The Korean War, the first head-to-head clash of the Cold War, was, in popular culture at least, almost exclusively an American affair. It was celebrated in battle films like *The Steel Helmet* (1951) and *The Bridges at Toko-Ri* (1954), and through comic books such as *US Fighting Men*, *Fighting Marines* and *Attack – Our Fighting Forces in Action*. Despite British units serving in Korea, film-makers, writers and comics at home almost ignored the war. Only one British film was made about the conflict, the low-budget *A Hill in Korea* (1956). Yet the climate of the times was constantly evoked in numerous spy stories in literature and film. Biggles and his fellow freedom fighter, the ex-commando Gimlet, regularly carried out clandestine operations behind the Iron Curtain to rescue friends or scientists imprisoned by Communists, or to smash spy rings operating in Britain.[50] Dick Barton, radio's phenomenally successful and long-running secret agent series of the 1940s, provided exciting listening for its young audience as the hero escaped from one desperate situation after another, and thwarted the plans of heavily accented mid-European villains intent on the destruction of Britain. The radio scripts provided the basis for three films made between 1948 and 1950, *Dick Barton – Special Agent*, *Dick Barton Strikes Back* and *Dick Barton at Bay*, in which Barton defeats the sinister foreign agent 'Volkoff'. The notion of the enemy within working to bring about the collapse of democratic society was reinforced by a series of more adult, but equally low-budget, films such as *High Treason*, *Highly Dangerous* or *The Master Spy*. More sophisticated in its approach was *Ring of Spies* (1963), based on the activities of the Portland spy ring. While spy fiction lost some of its popularity after the 1960s, the Cold War, in one form or another, continued to provide an exciting background for war fiction until well into the 1980s. One aspect was the revival of invasion stories, particularly in boys' comics. One of the most interesting was *Wizard*'s 'The Yellow Sword', in which a warlike Asian race, the Kushanti, conquer America and Europe. The story centres on the English village of Hopebridge, where the schoolmaster becomes a focus for resistance while the underground army prepares to strike back at the invader.[51] The illustration for chapter two shows the Kushantis attempting to 're-write' the history of the British Empire by removing any record of national warrior heroes

67 The Kushanti conquerors rewrite English history, 1955.

(illus. 67). Such fiction, while obviously reflecting the mood of the times, rarely attempted to explain the causes of the Cold War or why reasonable and intelligent British men and women worked for a foreign power with such enthusiasm. When such an attempt was made, it was invariably banal. As W. E. Johns explained in *Gimlet Bores In*:

> 'Listen', said Gimlet distinctly, 'These men are Bolsheviks. How can they look anything but sour-faced when their minds are warped by envy – hatred of anyone better off than themselves? They go through life scheming how they can get by force, or by talking, what other people get by working. That's how it is here. They boss the country. Now you know why it is as you see it. No country can thrive under a parcel of tyrants'.[52]

Like earlier conflicts, the main focus of the pleasure culture of war was exciting action; it had little to say about why such action was necessary. Britain's wars of de-colonization, which were sometimes inspired by the greater events of the Cold War, were, as we have seen, too contentious for popular culture and were largely ignored by it. But the Falklands War provides an interesting case study of how a conflict, initially enjoying considerable support as a justified military action, and containing all the elements for entertainment purposes, is not automatically subsumed into the pleasure culture of war.

In the spring of 1982, General Leopoldo Galtieri, leader of Argentina's military junta, ordered the invasion of the Falkland Islands – known to Argentinians as the Malvinas – in order to settle the long-running dispute with Britain over sovereignty. The invasion force took the British garrison and raised the Argentinian flag over Port Stanley. In the House of Commons the following day, Margaret Thatcher, the 'Iron Lady', as the Russians had mockingly dubbed her, responded to the first invasion of British territory since the Second World War by promising to get the islands back, and stated that a military task force was even then being assembled.[53] What began as a deeply embarrassing incident for the Prime Minister was soon turned to her advantage, as it was realized that here was the perfect opportunity to wipe away the humiliation of Suez, restore national confidence, boost the flagging popularity of the Conservative Government and re-establish Thatcher's's own reputation as a dynamic, purposeful political leader in the 'Churchillian' mould: 'We have ceased to be a nation in retreat', she later claimed.[54] Despite ongoing diplomatic negotiations to settle the crisis peacefully, Thatcher was, as President Reagan noted, 'set on a skirmish' – clearly a peaceful resolution would not have the same dramatic effect as a short victorious little war.[55]

Like most modern wars, the Falklands conflict was a 'spectator sport – just another element in a consumer culture'.[56] The public expected entertainment, an exciting spectacle, an apparently just war, fought far away, and in which the hard-nosed professional British army would make mincemeat of the raggle-taggle conscripts of a banana republic. The racial and xenophobic aspects of the war were immediately obvious from the stereotypical images of the enemy in most cartoons, and in the abusive language used by much of the tabloid press. But the media, looking forward to an unlimited supply of exciting and dramatic war stories for the amusement of their readers, were to be disappointed. The government, well aware of the problems that unlimited press access to the war zone had created for the Americans in Vietnam, had already decided that their war would be subject to rigid censorship. This, together with the lack of satellite communications and the difficulties of sending copy across 8,000 miles, ensured that news was rigidly controlled or subject to considerable delay. Thus the unpleasant face of war could be played down, enabling it to be portrayed, initially at least, in traditional and heroic terms:

> In news stories of the sailing and subsequent trials of the Task Force, the British nation was represented as strong, freedom-loving and prepared (as in the 1940s) to go to war in defence of democratic principles . . . it appealed to different components of [the] nation in different ways, among the most significant of these being gender . . . The 'feminine' narrative stance concentrated on the tearful goodbyes of girlfriends, wives and mothers; on their hopes, anxieties and grief; on their sense of the terrible vulnerability of those they waited for, and pride in their suffering and loss. The 'masculine' version, by contrast, found the military technologies and strategies of the war fascinating, the prospect of battle exciting, and British soldiers, sailors and airmen heroic.[57]

Incited by the tabloids, the departure of Task Force South was an occasion for demonstrations of patriotic sentiment. News cameras lovingly recorded every detail: the flag-bedecked warships, the latest military hardware displayed on their decks, the waving Union Jacks, the cheering crowds, weeping wives and a military band playing Rod Stewart's hit single, 'I am Sailing'. It was a scene rich in historical symbolism; a replay of Drake sailing out to meet the Armada or the Normandy invasion fleet heading for occupied Europe. It was the perfect image of Britons doing what they had so often done before – going to war. The recapture of South Georgia was hailed as a cause for celebration; a 'triumph', according to the Prime Minister, but the fact that two reconnaissance helicopters had crashed during the operation, and that the SAS/SBS had come close to disaster through faulty leadership, was simply ignored. The absence, or delayed screening, of images from the Task Force enabled the war to be presented as a replay of World War Two. Television reports, limited to voice transmission alone, developed the technique of screening traditional style images created by studio artists to accompany the reports – pictures remarkably similar to the work of illustrators from earlier wars and employing their traditional romantic portrayal of combat. Nor were the correspondents' reports markedly different. Robert Fox, reporting for the BBC on the Paras digging in on 23 May, pointed to their good humour and ability to make the best of any situation: 'The Paras have makeshift shelters in the hills. The ground is so soggy here, the trenches fill with water if they're dug too deep. I visited one position . . . manned by a team operating blowpipes – hand-held missiles. "You're the first bloke we've seen for two days, Mate, have a wet"'.[58] A few days later he covered the liberation of Goose Green:

> The surrender came after a 14-hour battle the previous day. It began before dawn – a full battalion assault on an enemy twice as numerous as expected, almost 1500 in all and very well dug in . . . Time and again we were pinned down by fire from morters and anti-aircraft guns . . . We were told that the commanding officer, Lt-Col. H. Jones, always known as 'H', had been shot by machine-gunners as he led an attack against machine-gun nests which had held up the battalion for over an hour. A generous, extrovert man, he died in the manner in which he led his battalion, in peace and war . . . The victory was entirely his. 'It was his plan that worked', said the Second-in-Command . . . 'He was the best, the very best'.[59]

Thus the outnumbered British, led by the hero, stormed the enemy and took Goose Green; it was just another El Alamein or Normandy beachhead after all.

In the immediate aftermath of the war, there were the usual celebratory mementos – a Falklands Task Force commemorative medal, BBC and ITN videos of their (delayed) film reports, a Vera Lynn recording, 'I Love This Land', and an exhibition of the work of Official War Artist, Linda Kitson. Kitson, like many another war artist, had closely identified with the military, but had deliberately refrained from representations of the 'guts and glory' approach and focused instead on the domestic and familiar – the rough, tough, fighting man having his hair cut in the Rudolf Steiner Salon aboard the SS Canberra on the voyage out, for example. An approach that much of the press and public (expecting a more traditional and heroic portrayal), found 'uninformative' and 'uninspired'. But the heroic was not ignored: the large-scale painting, The Canberra's Return to Southampton, by David Cobb, showed the tumultuous welcome given to the Task Force, or Peter Archer's Sergeant Ian McKay VC storming an enemy position on Mount Longdon. In the popular culture of war, there was some attempt to celebrate the war as a justified triumph. The battle series Strike Force Falklands, by Adam Hardy, comprised six novels published between 1983 and 1985, and attempted to do for the Falklands what Frederick E. Smith or Alexander Fullerton had done for the Second World War.[60] The series followed the adventures of a Strike Force landed on the Islands to create 'merry hell' and pave the way for the main invasion. The author makes clear that this is an elite unit – physically fit experts who are resolute and 'bloody-minded'. The enemy are 'stupid Argies' who 'tried to steal what wasn't theirs', while their leaders are 'latter-day fascist dictators'. Thus the novels simply reprise the gung-ho rhetoric of Thatcher's government. Equally, Jack Higgins Exocet (1983) left little doubt about his political views. Here the Russians plan to assist the Argentinians to acquire more Exocet missiles, a plot defeated by British intelligence. Higgins artificially attempts to locate the war into the Cold War as justification. More informative are Walter Winwood's Rainbow Soldiers (1985) and Alexander Fullerton's Special Deliverance (1987). While both portray both sides of the conflict, the novels cannot avoid heroic depictions of British soldiers, not because of their fighting skills, but simply because of their discipline, endurance and loyalty to the army and above all to their comrades. Despite these attempts to represent the Falklands War as a continuation of World War Two, the cultural legacy of the war has been predominantly oppositional – just another unpleasant chapter of the Thatcher years.

Criticism of the government's bellicose attitude had emerged even before the Task Force sailed, and even mild questioning of Cabinet policy was greeted with hysteria by the government and the patriotic press. On 10 May, after the sinking of the Argentine battleship Belgrano by a British submarine and the loss of HMS Sheffield, the BBC's Panorama programme examined the breakdown of diplomacy and questioned the government's apparent commitment to solving the problem by force. The following day, the BBC was virtually accused of treason by some Tories, and the programme was re-named 'Traitorama' by the *Daily Express*. While public support for the war remained high, as the casualties mounted some critics became increasingly bitter. *Private Eye*, for example, consistently portrayed the conflict as a monument to Thatcher's cynical use of the crisis to boost her own popularity (illus. 68). Such criticism was reinforced as the real images of the war (often not screened until three or four weeks after the event) began to appear in newspapers or on the television screen, displacing the sanitized and heroic artists' representations: the Argentine air attacks on the supply ships *Sir Galahad* and *Sir Tristram* (filmed on 8 June, but not shown until 24 June), for instance. Voice reports tended to be upbeat and focus on the heroism of the rescuers, but when the pictures were shown they told another story, of burning ships, and badly wounded or traumatized men, the shock of combat still in their eyes. Reporting

68 Margaret Thatcher and the Falklands. From *Private Eye*, 1982.

from the Falklands was strangely at odds with reports of the Israeli invasion of Lebanon and the siege of Beirut, which overshadowed the end of the Falklands campaign. Here, virtually 'instant' images from the war zone spared the viewer little of the carnage – but, after all, this was only one lot of foreigners killing other foreigners![61]

The traditional heroic images of Peter Archer and David Cobb were countered by Michael Sandle's powerful bronze, *Caput Mortuum: A Commentary*, in which the shrouded and gagged corpse bore mute witness to the war, or Graham Ashton's *Lifeboat, Ha!*, a testament to wasted lives. Jock MacFadyen's representation of the Task Force's return, *With Singing Hearts . . . Throaty Roarings*, contrasts darkly with David Cobb's. In the style of George Grosz, MacFadyen reveals a dockside scene dominated by the distorted brutish faces of unthinking nationalism. Cynicism was also the central element in Raymond Briggs' picture book, *The Tin-Pot Foreign General and the Old Iron Woman* (1985); while in his novel for younger readers, *Falklands Summer* (1987), John Bramfield explored the manner in which war fever could still be aroused through the experiences of 16-year-old Matthew. Matthew is already a devotee of the pleasure culture of war and is fascinated by World War Two. During the Falklands war he becomes obsessed with this latest conflict, re-enacting its events with his friends and desperately longing to be 'one of the heroes sailing to the South Atlantic'. He rejoices when the *Belgrano* is sunk and when the Argies surrender, but regrets that there will be no more war reports. Carried away by romantic images of war, he even visits the local army recruiting office to find out how to enlist. Only a near-tragic accident while 'playing war' shows him the folly of trying to act out his make-war fantasies.[62] Equally, in Jan Needle's *A Game of Soldiers* (1985), the realities of the war are explored through the experiences of three young Falklanders, especially Michael, who believes that war is glamorous stuff. Only when he comes face to face with a dying sixteen-year-old Argentinian soldier does he realize that there is little romance in battle. By 1986, when Andre Deutsch published Eduardo Quiroga's *On Foreign Ground*, the political climate was such that this Argentinian novel enjoyed considerable praise. The story deals with Enrique, a young conscript whose experiences of brutality and terror stretch back to the Perón regime and the mysterious disappearance of his elder brother. Yet the war he has been forced into is even more horrifying than he could have imagined. His fear ends only with his death at the hands of the British, as he and his friends try to defend Port Stanley – a testament to the folly of war.

Such fiction was reinforced in *When the Fighting is Over* (1988), by John and Robert Lawrence. At 16, looking for adventure and imbued with ideals of manliness and the romance of war, Robert joined the Scots Guards. At 22, he was

involved in the Battle for Tumbledown Mountain and suffered a head wound that
left him paralyzed on one side and incontinent. But, he notes, initially he retained
his idealism and envied his comrades still fighting. Later, his cold reception at
home, in particular being 'kept out of sight' during the victory celebrations,
followed by a struggle to get a disability pension, forced him to reconsider:

> I had, and still have, this white-hot pride. The kind of pride that the
> Army trains young soldiers to build up. The kind of pride that enables
> them to go off to war and fight and kill for what they are taught to believe
> in ... What I didn't realise, until, like so many others, I came back
> crippled after doing my bit for my country, was the extent to which we
> had been conned. Conned into believing in a set of priorities and
> principles that the rest of the world and British society in general no
> longer gave two hoots about. We had been 'their boys' fighting in the
> Falklands, and when the fighting was over, nobody wanted to know.[63]

His words, echoing those of of Roland Leighton and that earlier generation of
victims of the 'fiction' of war, have a depressingly familiar ring. The same cynicism
is evident in films about the Falklands – *Tumbledown*, Charles Wood's 1988
production based upon the Robert Lawrence story, and Martin Stellman's *For
Queen and Country* (1989), in which Denzil Washington plays the Black Falklands
veteran Reuben James. James returns to London and then falls victim to the
1981 British Nationality Act, which deprives him of his citizenship. Forced into
a London ghetto, he becomes a target for racist police and is finally killed in a
riot on a London housing estate. *For Queen and Country* is an intensely bitter
and angry film suggesting that loyalty and honour are empty phrases, trotted out
when the occasion demands and quickly forgotten.

In the aftermath of the war, many academics expressed dismay that the nation
could be so effectively mobilized in support of an 'unnecessary' war – a shocking
return to an imperial past.[64] But, unlike those manifestly unjust little wars of
the nineteenth century, a predominantly jingoistic mood was maintained during
the South Atlantic conflict by carefully selecting what the public was allowed to
see, it could not be sustained in the longer term. Blind, unquestioning patriotism
can no longer be relied on. The Falklands War has not become a part of the
pleasure culture of war, because a national consensus never really existed. The
issues at stake were too clouded and the nation too cynical. And much the same
might be said of the Gulf War of 1991.

The Gulf War was perhaps the most televised war in history. Almost every
action was recorded on camera and beamed around the world by satellite.[65] By
demonizing Saddam Hussein and building on the rape of 'poor little Kuwait'

(echoes of the rallying cry of 1914, 'poor little Belgium'), the coalition was able to create a wide consensus of support for the war. For America, it was essentially a 'good' war, just, easily won and effective in erasing the shadow of Vietnam. But for Britain, the sale of weapons to Iraq, the slaughter of the retreating enemy, the continued survival of Saddam, and Gulf War syndrome ensured it became contentious. Film-makers and writers have not found it inspiring, and its only real consequence for the pleasure culture of war has been as the final factor in the elevation of the SAS (Special Air Service) to premier position among British military elites. The SAS first became a subject for media attention during the Iranian Embassy siege in London in May 1980, an event which unhappily inspired the film *Who Dares Wins*, released appropriately in 1982. This truly awful compendium of guts, glory and xenophobia was perfectly in tune with Thatcher's Britain. As *Sight and Sound* noted, it was 'cinematically antiquated and with hawkish politics poking unappealing through a thin cloak cloak of fiction'.[66]

During the Gulf War, the SAS were the first British troops in contact with the enemy. Subsequently, there have been several accounts of their actions by veterans and a host of pulp fiction based on imaginary incidents.[67] Appealing to presumably much the same hawkish market is Sega's war game, *Desert Strike: Return to the Gulf*. It is loosely based on the conflict, with direct political references removed, but General Kilbaba sends his fanatical armies into a neighbouring emirate and the player's mission is to destroy them. There is nothing here about cause or effect; simply unlimited opportunities to 'zap' the enemy. Interestingly, the game relies heavily on the graphic simulations employed by BBC and ITN during the reporting of the war.[68] As Jeffrey Walsh has noted, the live pictures of Tomahawk missiles hurtling down the streets of Baghdad seeking their targets, often seemed like 'an amusement-arcade contest where blips substituted for human deaths'.[69] The only novel specifically aimed at young readers is Robert Westall's *Gulf* (1992), a bitter attack on television news's coverage of the war as if it were a daily soap opera.[70] These case studies of the Falklands and the Gulf might be taken as evidence that the British are at last losing their taste for entertainment based on war and violence, but this is not so. Producers of war entertainment will rarely risk alienating potential customers by focusing on contentious issues: controversy is simply bad business. Instead, the industry has found it safer to choose subjects from the politically neutral distant future or from the distant past; subjects which are so obviously fantasy that they risk little criticism.

The future war in space has had a long history, and was first popularized around the turn of the century by H. G. Wells. By the 1930s, such fiction was relatively common in the boys' papers. However, in the 1950s, when man appeared to be on the edge of inter-planetary travel, such fiction took on a new lease of life. *Eagle*'s Dan Dare and *The Lion*'s Captain Condor paved the way for enormously popular space sagas like *Star Wars*. Woven around a storyline that closely resembled the events of the Second World War, the *Star Wars* quartet makes considerable use of the icons of war entertainment: the freedom fighters' struggle against the tyrannical dark empire, heroic fighter pilots and chivalric Jedi Knights. Its phenomenal success led to a whole range of toys and games intended to help the young re-enact the great conflict, and inspired other space war epics. Among the more recent have been *Independence Day* (1996), a brilliant retelling of Wells's *War of the Worlds*, and *Starship Troopers* (1997), Paul Verhoven's ultra-violent spectacle in which the Earth Federation fights for survival in the 'Great Bug War'. Based on Robert Heinlein's Cold War novel of the same name, the film exploits virtually every cliche from the war film genre, even down to a parody documentary within the film based on Frank Capra's 1940s series, 'Why We Fight'. Using the latest special effects, Verhoven has created incredibly violent battle sequences, which reveal just how frail the human body is, even a body wearing the latest space armour. Originally released as a '15', the film was reclassified as an '18' for its video release, yet it is difficult to find any child who has not seen it. *Starship Troopers* is equally interesting for its neo-fascist rhetoric suggesting that, in the Federation's new order, only veterans can have full citizenship; the right to vote must be earned on the battlefield. Yet even in this hi-tech future war, the clean-cut heroes and heroines are identical to those who fought in earlier wars, and share the same sense of honour and duty and demonstrate the same camaraderie (illus. 69). In the same mould is the television series, *Above and Beyond*, which follows the exploits of a company of Space Marines in their unending war to prevent the alien 'Chigs' conquering the galaxy. These films are just part of war in the space sub-genre, which includes novels, comics and video games that encourage the young to interact in the latest alien invasion. A 'safe' alternative to the war of the future is the war set in the past, preferably in some distant age before history began.

The model for this sub-genre was J. R. R. Tolkien's masterpiece, *Lord of the Rings* (1954–5), a saga of the Third Age of Middle Earth, which saw the epic struggle between the Fellowship of the Ring and the Dark Lord of Mordor. Tolkein's work was undoubtedly the major influence on what have become known as 'Sword and Sorcery' adventures: films such as *Hawk the Slayer* (1980), *Conan the Barbarian* (1981) and *The Beastmaster* (1982), or the novels of the prolific Michael Moorcock and others. This fiction, set in an age of chaos, invariably suggests that order can only be restored (and maintained) by the sword of a champion who has superhuman power. Characterization and narrative are minimal, and the hero's quest is simply a device for an almost endless

69 Warrior of the future.
From the film *Starship
Troopers*, 1997.

sequence of spectacular battles in which he demonstrates his martial prowess.

Nevertheless, the Sword and Sorcery cycle is extremely popular, and is manifested not only in films, novels and comics, but equally through war games and
interactive video. Today, the most popular of these are supplied by Games
Workshop, which markets its tabletop war fantasies under the 'Warhammer' trade
name. 'Warhammer' deals in a Tolkienish world and offers players beautifully
modelled figures, including 'Chaos Warriors', 'Reiksgaard Knights' and 'Wood Elf
Glade Riders', complete with fantastical war machines, scenery and gaming
equipment. Their other major game is 'Warhammer 40,000' – 'The nightmare
future of the 41st Millennium [when] the galaxy-spanning imperium of man
is beset on all sides by ravening aliens'; a curious blend of orcs, dwarves, dragons,
space marines and hi-tech weaponry.[71] However, unlike sword and sorcery
fictions, it is not just the battle that gives 'Warhammer' and similar games their
appeal, because a player must painstakingly paint the elaborate figures and
prepare the battlefield and equipment before even firing the first shot. The game

is played according to established rules, not unlike Wells's 'Little Wars', and the company offers a monthly magazine, *White Dwarf*, which deals with all aspects of gaming and modelling. In representations of past wars, it is perhaps worth noting the tendency to draw on the less distant past for subject matter. One might make reference to recent films such as *Braveheart* or *Last of the Mohicans*, whose battle scenes contain images of violence which are terrifyingly realistic. While not war films in the traditional sense, the fighting skills of their heroes are, nevertheless, deeply rooted in the warrior tradition.

An interesting and significant development since 1945 has been the manner in which women have been drawn into war entertainment as warriors. Traditionally, women played little part in the war story except as victims to be protected from the 'Other'. Henty's soldier's daughter, 'Wonder Woman', or Johns's 'Worrals' were the exceptions. However, from the late 1970s such women have become increasingly common. In part, this is a development that began with the Home Front films of the Second World War, such as *Millions Like Us* and *The Gentle Sex*. These and others demonstrated that in a total war women played a significant part, if only in the factory or as logistical support for the armed forces. By the 1950s, *Odette* and *Carve Her Name With Pride* showed the active role of women in the resistance movement in occupied Europe – stories that could not be told before. Yet in films such as *Alien* (1979), it is the woman who has become the warrior. *Alien* was so successful it spawned three sequels, each focusing on First Officer Ripley (Sigourney Weaver) and her battle with the deadly alien life-form. Both *Starship Troopers* and *Above and Beyond* feature women space marines, who are just as deadly as their male colleagues and in some ways better soldiers. But the fighting heroine has not only appeared in science fiction. Changes in the law which allowed women to train as soldiers and pilots in both Britain and America have been reflected in popular culture. In *Iron Eagles II*, women were among the hand-picked team of ace fighter pilots, while in *Courage Under Fire* (1997), Meg Ryan played a helicopter pilot during the Gulf War who sacrificed herself to save her male comrades. The most recent example, however, was *G.I. Jane* (illus. 70), in which Demi Moore plays an American naval officer who persuades her superiors that she should have the chance to undertake the gruelling training programme for the elite fighting unit, the SEALS. Overcoming physical hardship, harassment and sabotage from her superiors, who want her to fail, she not only completes the course, but takes part in a successful fire-fight as well. The point is not just that she is as tough as her male comrades, but that she demonstrates the 'right stuff', the mental machismo that eventually enables her to take her place in a male-dominated fighting elite. With the acceptance of women into almost all branches of the armed forces, it would

70 A 1996 poster for *G.I. Jane*.

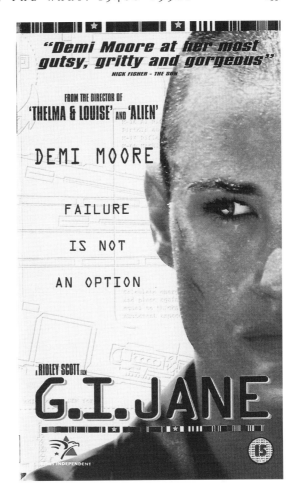

be surprising if the female warrior does not become a recurring theme in the war story.[72]

While the pleasure culture of war is alive and well, it has not been without its opponents. Nevertheless, anti-war novels and films are commonplace today. It is almost de rigueur to label spectacularly violent stories as 'anti-war', and to assure the consumer that the product has been created to demonstrate the 'horrors of war'. But, as Omer Bartov has rightly noted, the 'paradox of anti-war films is that the closer they come to "actual battle" and its (for many often exciting) horrors, the less effective they are in evoking anti-war sentiments'.[73] Steven Spielberg's *Saving Private Ryan* (1998) is a good example. Undoubtedly, the director's intention was to reveal the waste and futility of war, yet battle is reconstructed in such a 'realistic' manner, and the leading characters are so sympathetic and heroic, we might almost be persuaded that the experience of war draws out the real

nobility of man. Bartov suggests that fiction which distances the reader from
battle by focusing on the experience of 'non-battle' casualties, especially children,
is the most effective anti-war propaganda. This is exactly what some authors
have attempted.

Perhaps the most powerful anti-war texts are those dealing with nuclear war, for
here everyone is a casualty, even future generations. In Eleanor Coerr's moving
novel, *Sadako and the Thousand Paper Cranes*, Sadako is two years old when the
bomb falls. Apparently uninjured, she lives a normal life until her eleventh year,
when she develops leukaemia. Believing an old Japanese legend that if a sick
person folds a thousand paper cranes the gods will make them well, she begins
her mammoth task. Making the tiny cranes sustains her in her fight for life, but
with only 600 finished, she loses the battle. Her classmates complete the task and
the cranes are buried with the little girl.[74] Toshi Maruki's *Hiroshima Story* and
Christobel Mattingley's *The Miracle Tree* tell similar stories for young readers and
bring the suffering of the innocent to the fore.[75] As the possibility of nuclear war
between the superpowers became more likely through the 1950s, adult fiction
which predicted the likely consequences of such a war became commonplace.
One of the most interesting was the 1951 film, *The Day the Earth Stood Still*. Klaatu,
a representative of the other inhabitants of the galaxy, visits Earth to warn
humankind that, as they are on the brink of space travel, their aggression can no
longer be tolerated. The point is forcefully made when Klaatu offers a gift to the
American President, and is promptly wounded by a nervous guard. Having failed
to secure a meeting with the Earth leaders, the visitor leaves after a final warning:

> Your civilization has not progressed beyond violence and destruction . . .
> At the first sign of violence, your earth will be reduced to a burned-out
> cinder. Your choice – join us in peace or face obliteration. The decision
> rests with you.[76]

Other fiction chose to show the 'end' in explicit detail. Typical of these was
Nevil Shute's bleak novel, *On the Beach*. Set in Australia after nuclear war has
devastated the northern hemisphere, the survivors wait for the cloud of deadly
fallout encircling the globe to reach them. How the war began, or who was to
blame, are not explained, but this is of little consequence, for what matters is that
in such a war there are no winners – the whole human race loses.[77] Many writers
followed Shute's example in showing nuclear war as the end of humankind,
notably Raymond Briggs in his curious bestselling picture book, *When the Wind
Blows* – 'for 'readers of all ages'. James Bloggs and his wife are a very ordinary and
not very bright couple living in retirement. Jim, with absolute faith in the government and pleasant memories of 'muddling through' in 1939, follows the advice

of civil defence leaflets and builds an indoor shelter as the international situation worsens. In order to calm his anxious wife, James explains how the war will develop: how, when 'innumerate Russian hordes will sweep across Europe', the Americans will send in their long-range bombers and parachute in the Marines, and the Russians will surrender to the 'big generals' like Ike and Monty. But when the attack comes, it is beyond anything they could imagine. They are unhurt in the blast and wait patiently for the mobile canteens, soup kitchens, teams of doctors and nurses, and relays of helicopters bringing aid, that will never come. There is no help; only a painful and prolonged death from radiation poisoning. What makes the book so frightening is James's unshaken faith in 'the powers that be' to make everything better, and his conviction that a nuclear war will be simply a replay of World War Two – not as it was, but as it appears in popular myth.[78] Some texts have even reached back to challenge the sacred cow of the Second World War, not to suggest that it was unjustified, but simply to strip away the gloss of romantic nostalgia that is embedded in the subject, for example, Jill Paton Walsh's *Fireweed* (1969) and Susan Cooper's *Dawn of Fear* (1972).[79] Significantly, the highly praised 1999 television adaptation of Michelle Magorian's novel, *Goodnight, Mr Tom*, returned its mass audience to the cosy 'finest hour' image.[80] Now that the nation has entered the 21st century, nostalgic, romanticized and, above all, sanitized images of war, and of the Second World War in particular, are still a powerful and popular theme in British popular culture.

It is not difficult to understand why the pleasure culture of war developed as a form of mass entertainment in the mid-nineteenth century. The empire was expanding rapidly as Britain imposed its rule on the inhabitants of Africa and the East, and these far-flung outposts of empire needed to be pacified and their frontiers secured. At the same time, increasing tensions among the European powers meant that Britain lived in a constant state of alarm. The youth of the nation had to be inculcated with the martial spirit, and be prepared to take their place in the line of battle to defend, and extend, the frontiers of empire. The pleasure culture of war, then, was one means by which the young could be imbued with the right values and attitudes to ensure national survival.

In popular culture, war was reconstructed in a highly sanitized form; an exciting adventure in which men demonstrated their patriotism and defined their masculinity. War, it was often argued, brought out the best in men – a sense of duty, honour, and loyalty to cause and comrade. Success in war was not only proof of true masculinity, but an attribute of a dynamic and expanding nation. The memory of past victories was enshrined in the nation's story, and its warrior-heroes were venerated as role models to inspire future generations to follow the

same path, thus ensuring continued national vigour. To reveal the true horrors
of battle, to strip the war story of its facade of glamour and chivalric conduct,
would ensure that no-one would willingly submit himself to the brutality of the
battlefield.

In the aftermath of the Great War, some of the young men who had survived
the slaughterhouse of the Western Front began to question what they had been
taught about the romance and excitement of war. Yet so deeply-ingrained were
these ideas about war and patriotism, that the war story managed to survive
this holocaust; and during the inter-war period, while public attitudes to the
Great War itself were ambiguous, attitudes to war in general remained largely
unchanged. Surprisingly, the pleasure culture of war survived even a second and
more devastating world war. But the saturation bombing of cities, the Final
Solution, atomic warfare and increasing political cynicism have taken their toll.
Post-1945 wars have not been absorbed into the nation's war story in the same
way, and writers, film-makers and illustrators are increasingly focusing on the
truth about war. Yet today, despite the protestations of many adults that war
is terrible, wasteful and barbaric (especially in the aftermath of a really bloody
little war), those same adults pass on to their children entertainments that
trivialize the act of war – whether such wars are located in the distant past or
far into the future – and the image of the warrior is still the most powerful heroic
icon for boys and young men.

From the testimony of those who created the pleasure culture of war, and those
who grew to manhood under its influence, we must concede that, during the age
of empire, it was intended to serve the purpose of preparing the nation's youth to
fight for Crown and Empire. Judging from the widespread enthusiasm for war
in 1914, it succeeded in its purpose remarkably well. But what purpose does the
war story now serve? Is it simply exciting entertainment? Has the pleasure culture
of war lost its potential to arouse patriotism and a martial spirit? Here we are
in the uncharted waters of speculation and opinion.

In 1950, the *Report of the Departmental Committee on Children and The Cinema*
suggested that, with the effects of exposure to images of violence:

> we are . . . on uncertain ground, moving among subtle and profound
> human factors where measurement and interpretation are difficult
> and where specific research has, so far, made little headway. There is a
> good deal of prejudice and strong feeling, both favourable and hostile
> to the cinema . . .[81]

Our understanding of the connections between media images of violence and
violent behaviour in individuals has progressed little since then. Despite limited

investigations by psychologists and claims by film censors and others,[82] there is no real evidence that images of violence trigger aggressive and violent behaviour; equally there is no real evidence that they are harmless. Claims that war-based entertainment does have dangerous consequences are usually countered by suggestions that fictional violence performs a useful social function. In 1948, for example, Geoffrey Trease quoted educators James Hemming and A. S. Neill to the effect that 'children's literature should contain a certain amount of violence as a safety-valve for aggression'.[83] This argument has now been reduced to a standard response, neatly encapsulated in a recent television documentary: 'We all want to kill someone sometime. So in watching killing we transfer our hostility, our aggression, our latent violence. Films act as a substitute to relieve tensions and hostility.'[84] This unresolved debate has nearly always centred on images of violence in crime/horror stories and films, or occasionally on the western, and only rarely on the war story, which, by its nature is seldom considered in the same way.

The Victorians and Edwardians clearly believed that exposure to the pleasure culture of war helped to foster an aggressive imperial race full of vim, vigour and the martial spirit. Today it would seem that all suggestion of this dubious purpose has been expunged. Apart from its obvious profitability, even the producers of such material are unclear about its consequences. Martin Kenright, chairman of DID Interactive Computer Games, claimed in a recent discussion about his enormously popular war game. 'Wargasm':

> Some people may argue it condones war. I really don't know, the jury is out. I don't have an opinion on whether our products in particular have that effect. But historically there was no such thing as computer games or similar entertainments and we've fought wars for ever. I think we're intelligent beings and we should be wising up to realise that this is entertainment. This is not real.[85]

No doubt it could be argued that the generation of 1914 knew that the war stories and heroic images of battle they had grown up with were 'not real' either, but those same images still helped to create the mind-set that sent those young men to the Western Front looking for the 'great adventure'.

What does seem reasonable, however, is that the trivialization of war as entertainment does help to foster a society which accepts conflict as normal behaviour. Martin Bell MP, a former BBC war correspondent, has pointed to the dangers:

> The long-term consequences of prettifying war are extremely dangerous. We live in a civilianized society where few people have any real experience of warfare at all . . . No-one in government knows what war is really

like . . . so they can commit the nation to war without knowledge of what they are committing the nation to . . . War is still not portrayed realistically, not even news reporting. Producers believe war is 'good news' but they are careful not to show anything too horrible which might cause the viewer to switch off. Consequently reporting sanitizes warfare and makes it an acceptable option for settling differences.[86]

John Heeley's investigation into the effects of war comics during the bellicose Thatcher years suggests other consequences. Heeley argued that boys' comics like *Warlord* and *2000 AD* met the needs of certain social groups which reflected the patriotic, authoritarian, 'dog eat dog' mentality of the British people and promoted a particular definition of violence that sees it as normal, natural and inevitable.[87] War comics, and the filmic style of violence they have inspired, have also contributed to negative stereotypes of foreigners who are easily subdued by the warlike English. Even three years after the end of the Falklands War, xenophobia and nationalism continued to influence the lager louts of English football. Journalist Ed Vuillamy wrote of the English supporters at the Heysell Stadium disaster in 1985:

> Their drunken, blood-thirsty and racist English 'honour' [demanded] that the terraces be cleared of 'spiks' and the Union Jack flown unchallenged. I saw one English fan with a T-shirt: 'Keep the Falklands British' as though he and his mates were the Task Force . . . Indeed, there was little to differentiate the drunken hysteria in the bars of Brussels and one night in a packed pub in Tufnell Park in 1982, when gleeful patriots celebrated the sinking of the 'Belgrano' in a wash of beer.[88]

Clearly, then, the bellicose images of the war had had some effect on some people. A recent study based on the letters, diaries and memoirs of twentieth-century soldiers argues that while most disliked the idea of war, many found that they came to derive pleasure from the act of killing – 'a certain amount of the pleasure that men took in killing came from the way they fantasised themselves as heroic warriors just like those in combat books and comics, games and films'.[89] There does seem to be evidence to suggest that the pleasure culture of war continues to help create unquestioning, xenophobic nationalism, a tendency to accept war as a legitimate process for settling differences, and fantasies about perceived ideal masculine behaviour.

Interestingly, the last decades of twentieth century have witnessed a dramatic transformation in the British experience of war, which may have considerable significance for its future representation. Britain's recent wars have been too morally ambiguous to be absorbed into the pleasure culture, and involvement in another major conflict is unlikely. 'The worst of war is behind us', concluded the *Daily Telegraph* defence correspondent John Keegan in a recent public lecture. Public tolerance of state violence in advanced societies has diminished, as war is now simply too dangerous to contemplate.[90] Nevertheless, if the last decade is any indication, there will be no lack of little wars in which British troops, alongside other United Nations contingents, will participate as peacekeepers or ensure that humanitarian aid reaches the victims of conflict. This raises interesting possibilities for future representations of the soldier. In Peter Kosminsky's recent television film, *Warriors*, the director explored the inner tensions that arise in soldiers who, trained in a culture of aggression, suddenly find themselves acting as peacekeepers in Bosnia. This role is far removed from the traditional duties of the warrior, but still requires courage and tenacity, albeit of a different kind; not the heroism of the battlefield, but a self-control and discipline that will enable them to control their natural tendency to resort to violence, and the fortitude to enable them to achieve their purpose in extremely difficult circumstances.

Will the representation of the soldier of peace ever be able to exert the same fascination for young men as the traditional image of the warrior? Only time will tell. One thing is clear: as long as popular culture continues to represent the brutality of war as a legitimate exciting adventure, and the warrior as the masculine ideal, so will humankind resort to violence as a means of settling differences.

References

Introduction

1 The *Sun*, 25 March 1999; the *Daily Star*, 25 March 1999.
2 Anne Summers, 'Militarism in Britain Before the Great War', *History Workshop Journal*, 2 (Autumn 1976), pp. 104–23
3 Graham Dawson, *Soldier Heroes: British Adventure, Empire and the Imagining of Masculinity* (London, 1994).
4 Mark Girouard, *The Return to Camelot: Chivalry and the English Gentleman* (London, 1981).
5 Cecil Eby, *The Road to Armageddon: The Martial Spirit in English Popular Literature, 1870–1914* (Durham, NC, 1988), p. 3.
6 George Orwell, 'Boys' Weeklies', *Collected Essays, Journalism and Letters* (Harmondsworth, 1970), p. 528.

1 Discovering the Pleasures of War

1 'Civilianism' was the phrase coined by Vagts as the opposite of 'militarism' – the dominance of the military in politics. See Alfred Vagts, *A History of Militarism*, (London, 1959), p. 17. Sociologists such as C. B. Otley, using this narrow definition of militarism, have claimed that Britain has been 'singularly free of militarism'. See C. B. Otley, 'Militarism and the Social Affiliations of the British Army Elite', in J. Van Doorn, *Armed Forces and Society* (The Hague, 1968), p. 84.
2 Linda Colley, *Britons: Forging the Nation, 1707–1837* (London, 1992), p. 5.
3 John Wolffe, 'Evangelicalism in Mid-Nineteenth Century England', in Raphael Samuel, ed., *Patriotism: The Making and Unmaking of British National Identity*, vol. 1 (London, 1989), p. 189.
4 Harold Perkin, *The Origins of Modern English Society, 1780–1880* (London, 1969), p. 281.
5 Wolffe, 'Evangelicalism', p. 197.
6 *Ibid.*, pp. 192, 194.
7 See for example, John Greene, *Vicissitudes of a Soldier's Life* (Louth, 1827) or William Surtees, *Twenty Five Years in the Rifle Brigade* (Edinburgh, 1833).
8 Wolffe, 'Evangelicalism', p. 197.

9   Colley, *Britons*, p. 60.

10 *Ibid.*, p. 109.

11 See Martin Green, *Dreams of Adventure, Deeds of Empire* (London, 1980) and Patrick Brantlinger, *Rule of Darkness: British Literature and Imperialism, 1830–1914*, (Ithaca, 1988).

12 See Scott Hughes Myerly, *British Military Spectacle* (Cambridge, MA, 1996), pp. 30–33.

13 Colley, *Britons*, pp. 192–3, on which the following discussion is based.

14 *Ibid.*, pp. 191–2.

15 *Ibid.*, p. 198.

16 *Ibid.*, p. 181. For an interesting discussion of the social attractions of military rank in the work of Jane Austen, see Donald F. Bittner, 'Jane Austen and Her Officers: a Portrayal of the Army in English Literature', *Journal of the Society for Army Historical Research*, LXXII (1994), pp. 76–91.

17 *Ibid.*, p. 3; and Gillian Russell, *Theatres of War: Performance, Politics and Society, 1793–1815* (Oxford, 1995).

18 Geoffrey Best, *War and Society in Revolutionary Europe, 1770–1870*, (Leicester, 1982), p. 199.

19 Edward M. Spiers, *The Army and Society, 1815–1914* (London, 1980), p. 73; see also B. H. Liddell Hart, ed., *The Letters of Private Wheeler, 1809–1828* (Bath, 1951); Greene, *Vicissitudes of a Soldier's Life*, and Surtees, *Twenty-Five Years*.

20 J. W. M. Hichberger, *Images of the Army: The Military in British Art, 1815–1914* (Manchester, 1988), p. 13.

21 On the so-called 'Jack Tar' dramas, see J. S. Bratton and R. A. Cave *et al.*, *Acts of Supremacy: The British Empire and the Stage, 1790–1930* (Manchester, 1991), p. 43.

22 On war weariness see Colley, *Britons*, pp. 338–9.

23 P. J. Cain and A. G. Hopkins, *British Imperialism: Innovation and Expansion, 1688–1914* (London, 1993), p. 103.

24 *Ibid.*, p. 100.

25 Bernard Porter, *The Lion's Share: A Short History of British Imperialism 1850–1983* (London, 1984), p. 11.

26 For a short account of the conflict see Byron Farwell, *Queen Victoria's Little Wars* (New York, 1972), pp. 12–22; David French, *The British Way in Warfare, 1688–2000* (London, 1990), pp. 126–8.

27 *Illustrated London News*, 18 February 1843.

28 Farwell, *Queen Victoria's Little Wars*, p. 27.

29 C. J. Bartlett, *Defence and Diplomacy, Britain and the Great Powers, 1815–1914* (Manchester, 1993), pp. 67–8. It should be noted, however, that Palmerston did become more cautious and more committed to negotiation and conciliation, especially after the American Civil War. The establishment of the British Army, which had reached its lowest strength in 1825 (87,993 men), had expanded to over 116,000 men by 1846 and increased annually thereafter to keep pace with its extended imperial role.

30 French, *British Way in Warfare*, p. 121.

31 Interestingly, the British use of war as an extension of diplomatic policy existed long before Clausewitz's famous treatise was published in English. See Michael Howard, *Clausewitz* (Oxford, 1983).

32 On Cobden's views on war, see Daniel Pick, *War Machine: The Rationalisation of Slaughter in the Modern Age* (London, 1993), pp. 19–27. For the later 'enemies of war' see Caroline Moorehead, *Troublesome People* (London, 1987).

33 Girouard, *The Return to Camelot*, p. 16.

34 *Ibid.*, p. 33.

35 Kenholm Digby, *The Broad Stone of Honour* (London, 1823), pp. 2–3.

36 Green, *Dreams of Adventure*, p. 98.

37 Perkin, *Origins of Modern English Society*, p. 274.

38 Not everyone subscribed to the value of the chivalric code. Matthew Arnold, for example, called it the 'spirit of evil' because it fostered a sense of honour rather than a sense of duty. Arnold did, however, testify to the seductive power of the idea. See Green, *Dreams of Adventure*, p. 65.

39 Digby, *Broad Stone of Honour*, p. 487.

40 *Ibid.*, p. 492.

41 Jeffrey Richards, 'Popular Imperialism and the Image of the Army in Juvenile Literature' in John M. Mackenzie, ed., *Popular Imperialism and the Military 1850–1950* (Manchester, 1992), p. 87.

42 See Graham Dawson, *Soldier Heroes: British Adventure, Empire and the Imagining of Masculinity* (London, 1994), chap. nine, pp. 233–58.

43 Myerly, *British Military Spectacle*, pp. 8–9.

44 Douglas Jerrold, *The Shilling Magazine* (1845), p. 151.

45 Patrick Brantlinger, *Rule of Darkness*, pp. 73–6.

46 *Ibid.*, p. 75.

47 Charles Dickens, *The Life and Adventures of Nicholas Nickleby* (1839; Odhams Popular Edn, n.d.), p. 189.

48 Brantlinger, *Rule of Darkness*, p. 49.

49 *Ibid.*, p. 64.

50 Sir Francis Doyle, 'The Red Thread of Honour' (*c.* 1848) and republished several times, most notably in Doyle, *The Return of the Guards and Other Poems* (London, 1866), pp. 90–94 and W. E. Henley, ed., *Lyra Heroica: A Book of Verse for Boys*, (London, 1892), pp. 242–5. Poems in praise of the military by more well-known poets might also be cited: Lord Byron's *The March to Waterloo* or Charles Wolfe's *The Burial of Sir John Moore*, for example.

51 Sir Francis Doyle, 'A Private of the Buffs', in *Return of the Guards*, pp. 95–6.

52 Sir Henry Yule, 'The Birkenhead', *Edinburgh Courant*, 1852.

53 *Illustrated London News*, 22 July 1843.

54 David Mayer, 'The World on Fire . . . Pyrodramas at Belle Vue Gardens, Manchester, *c.* 1850–1950' in Mackenzie, *Popular Imperialism and the Military*, pp. 179–97.

55 See Myerly, *British Military Spectacle*, pp. 135–65.

56 Thomas Makepeace Thackeray, *Vanity Fair, A Novel Without a Hero* (1848; Modern Library edn, London, 1979), p. 330.

57 For a detailed analysis of the interaction of army and society at this time, see Spiers, *Army and Society*, chap. 3, pp. 72–96.

58 See for example, Eric Hopkins, *A Social History of the English Working Classes, 1815–1914* (London, 1979), p. 45.

59 H. O. Arnold-Foster, in Alan Ramsey Skelley, *The Victorian Army at Home* (London, 1977), p. 15.

60 Carolyn Steedman, *The Radical Soldier's Tale* (London, 1988), p. 39. The 1840s were a particularly rich decade for soldiers' memoirs and autobiographies. For a comprehensive listing, see William Matthews, *British Autobiographies* (Berkeley, CA, 1955).

61 'J. M'. 'Fragments From the Portfolio of a Field Officer' (1831), in Myerly, *British Military Spectacle*, p. 151.

62 See Colonel S. D. Cleave, 'Army Scripture Readers Society and the Soldier's Friend Society', *Quarterly Journal of the Royal Army Chaplains Department*, 11 (1923).

63 Olive Anderson, 'The Growth of Christian Militarism in Mid-Victorian Britain', *English Historical Review*, 86: 338 (1971), p. 40.

64 Philip Knightley, *The First Casualty* (London, 1978), p. 4.

65 For a brief discussion of the topic, see Philip Taylor, *Munitions of the Mind: War Propaganda from the Ancient World to the Nuclear Age* (Wellingborough, 1990), pp. 149–53. See also Lucy Brown, *Victorian News and Newspapers* (Oxford, 1985).

66 Knightley, *The First Casualty*, p. 4. For the origins of war reporting, see Joseph J. Matthews, *Reporting the Wars* (Minneapolis, 1957).

67 Anderson, 'Growth of Christian Militarism', p. 46.

68 Catherine Marsh, *Memorials of Captain Hedley Vicars, Ninety-Seventh Regiment*, (London, 1856), p. xi.

69 *Ibid.*, p. 285.

70 Marsh, *Memorials*, p. 292.

71 Anderson, 'Growth of Christian Militarism', p. 46.

72 Mayer, 'The World on Fire', p. 187. For a more detailed account, see J. S. Bratton, 'Theatre of War: The Crimean War on the London Stage, 1854–1855', in David Bradby, Louise James and Bernard Sharratt, eds, *Performance and Politics in Popular Drama, 1800–1976* (Cambridge, 1980).

73 War artists in the Crimea are examined in Peter Johnson, *Front Line Artists* (London, 1978).

74 Spiers, *Army and Society*, pp. 116–17.

75 Bartlett, *Defence and Diplomacy*, p. 126.

76 Anderson, 'Growth of Christian Militarism', p. 49.

77 Dawson, *Soldier Heroes*, p. 86.

78 *Ibid.*, p. 87.

79 Brian Stanley, 'Christian Responses to the Indian Mutiny of 1857', *Studies in Church History*, 20 (1983), pp. 277–8.

80 Anderson, 'Growth of Christian Militarism', p. 51.

81 John Clark Marshman, *Memoirs of General Sir Henry Havelock* (London, 1860), p. 296–7.

82 Dawson, *Soldier Heroes*, p. 93. For an alternative view of British military skill, see V. G. Kiernan, *European Empires from Conquest to Collapse, 1815–1960* (Leicester, 1982), pp. 48–50.

83 Dawson, *Soldier Heroes*, p. 104.

84 *Ibid.*, p. 99.

85 The titles of the 1858 biographies, sermons and pamphlets are indicative of the intent of the authors: J. P. Grant, *The Christian Soldier: Memories of Major-General Havelock*, Rev. W. Owen, *The Good Soldier: A Memoir of Major-General Sir Henry Havelock*, W. H. Aylen, *The Soldier and the Saint, or Two Heroes in One*, and E. P. Hood, *Havelock: The Broad Stone of Honour*, which firmly placed the hero into the chivalric tradition.

86 *Baptist Magazine*, 50 (1858), p. 323.

87 On the Gordon cult see Douglas H. Johnson, 'The Death of Gordon: A Victorian Myth', *Journal of Imperial and Commonwealth History*, 10 (1982), pp. 285–310; see also John M. Mackenzie, 'Heroic Myths of Empire', in Mackenzie, ed., *Popular Imperialism and the Military*.

88 Mackenzie, 'Heroic Myths of Empire', p. 116.

89 Even after the Second World War the Mutiny continued to fascinate popular novelists. See for example, John Masters, *Nightrunners of Bengal* (1951); William Clive, *Dando on Delhi Ridge* (1971) and *Blood of an Englishman* (1977); and J. G. Farrell, *The Siege of Krishnapur* (1973).

90 Brantlinger, *Rule of Darkness*, pp. 208–9.

91 On contemporary fiction of the Mutiny, see Brantlinger, *Rule of Darkness*, chap. 7, pp. 199–224.

92 See Mayer, 'The World on Fire', and Brantlinger, *Rule of Darkness*, pp. 205–6.

93 Hichberger, *Images of the Army*, pp. 61–5.

94 An interesting example is George Atkinson's, *The Campaign in India* (1859). The author had served with the Bengal Engineers throughout the Mutiny and made a number of sketches that were later used to illustrate his account of the event.

95 Michael Howard, 'Empire, Race and War in pre-1914 Britain', in Hugh Lloyd, Valerie Pearl and Blair Warden, eds, *History and Imagination: Essays in Honour of H. R. Trevor-Roper* (London, 1981), p. 349.

96 Dawson, *Soldier Heroes*, p. 1; John Ruskin, 'War', in *The Crown of Wild Olive and the Cestus of Aglaia* (London, 1908), p. 79.

97 J. A. Mangan and James Walvin, eds, *Manliness and Morality: Middle-Class Masculinity in Britain and America, 1800–1940* (Manchester, 1987), p. 1.

98 On the Volunteer movement, see Hugh Cunningham, *The Volunteer Force* (London, 1975), Ian F. W. Beckett, *Riflemen Form: A Study of the Rifle Volunteer Movement, 1859–1908* (Aldershot, 1980).

99 Harold Perkin, *The Origins of Modern English Society, 1780–1880* (London, 1969), p. 280.

100 Bernard Semmell, *Imperialism and Social Reform* (London, 1960), p. 30.

101 Karl Pearson, *National Life* (1905), in Semmell, *Imperialism and Social Reform*, p. 41.

102 Cecil D. Eby, *The Road to Armageddon: The Martial Spirit in English Popular Literature, 1870–1914* (London, 1987), p. 2.

103 Michael Adams, *The Great Adventure: Male Desire and the Coming of World War I*, (Bloomington, IN, 1990), p. 51.

104 Myerly, *British Military Spectacle*, p. 154–8.

105 Harold F. Wyatt, 'God's Test by War', *The Nineteenth Century*, LXIX (1911), p. 599; W. J. Reader, *At Duty's Call* (Manchester, 1988), pp. 25–7. On attitudes to war at the end of the century, see John Gooch, 'Attitudes to War in Late Victorian and Edwardian England', in Brian Bond and Ian Roy, eds, *War and Society* (London, 1975), pp. 88-102; and Zara Steiner, 'Views on War', *Moirae*, 5 (1980), pp. 14–32.

106 Rudyard Kipling, *The Light That Failed* (1898; Harmondsworth, 1992), p. 48. Kipling notes elsewhere that the outcome of the war in the Sudan was largely immaterial as far as the public were concerned. What matters is that 'England at breakfast should be amused and thrilled and interested, whether Gordon lived or died, or half the British army went to pieces in the sands.' (See p. 19.)

107 On war correspondents see Knightley, *The First Casualty*; Matthews, 'Reporting the Wars', and Roger Stearn, 'War Correspondents and Colonial War, *c.* 1870–1900' in Mackenzie, *Popular Imperialism and the Military*, pp. 139–78; on war artists, see Johnson, *Front Line Artists* and Pat Hodgson, *The War Illustrators* (London, 1977).

108 Anne Summers, 'Militarism in Britain Before the Great War', *History Workshop Journal*, 2 (Autumn 1976), p. 108.

2 The Little Wars of Empire

1 On the development of literacy and popular literature, see Louis James, *Print and the People, 1819–1851* (London, 1976) and Richard D. Altick, *The English Common Reader: A Social History of the Mass Reading Public, 1800–1900* (Chicago, 1957).

2 James, *Print and the People*, p. 38.

3 Altick, *English Common Reader*, p. 299.

4 Linda Colley, *Britons: Forging the Nation, 1707–1837* (London, 1992), pp. 239–40.

5 For the development of juvenile literature and the adventure story, see F. J. Harvey Darton, *Children's Books in England* (3rd edn, Cambridge, 1982); J. S. Bratton, *The Impact of Victorian Children's Fiction* (London, 1981); Jeffrey Richards, ed., *Imperialism and Juvenile Literature* (Manchester, 1989); Denis Butts, ed., *Stories and Society: Children's Literature in its Social Context* (London, 1992); Joseph Bristow, *Empire Boys: Adventures in a Man's World* (London, 1991).

6 Richards, *Imperialism and Juvenile Literature*, p. 3.

7 Bratton, *Impact*, p. 102.

8 Richards, *Imperialism and Juvenile Literature*, p. 3.

9   Patrick A. Dunae, 'New Grub Street for Boys', in Richards, ed., *Imperialism and Juvenile Literature*, pp. 14–15; on 'boy labour' see John Springhall, *Youth, Popular Culture and Moral Panics* (London, 1999), pp. 46–7.

10 Butts, *Stories and Society*, p. xiii.

11 *Mark Seaworth* (1852), in Bratton, *Impact*, p. 122.

12 On Kingston, see Bratton, *Impact*, pp. 115–33.

13 Stuart Hannabuss, 'Ballantyne's Message of Empire', in Richards, ed., *Imperialism and Juvenile Literature*, p. 55.

14 R. M. Ballantyne, *The Young Fur Traders* (London, 1852), p. 351.

15 Hannabuss, 'Ballantyne's Message of Empire', p. 69.

16 *In the Track of the Troops: A Tale of Modern War*, in *ibid.*, p. 68.

17 For Captain Mayne Reid, see Eric Quayle, *The Collector's Book of Boys' Stories* (London, 1973), pp. 77–81.

18 Mark Girouard, *The Return to Camelot: Chivalry and the English Gentleman* (London, 1981), pp. 130–44, on which the following comments are based.

19 *Ibid.*, p. 141.

20 See Robert MacDonald, *The Language of Empire: Myths and Metaphors of Popular Imperialism, 1880–1918* (Manchester, 1994), p. 69.

21 Charles Kingsley, *Westward Ho!* (London, 1855), pp. 310–11.

22 *Ibid.*, p. 305.

23 *Two Years*, in Girouard, *Return to Camelot*, p. 141. Kingsley's comments here are remarkably close to the later Social Darwinist ideas of Karl Pearson. See chap. one.

24 On 'Manliness' see J. A. Mangan and James Walvin, eds, *Manliness and Morality: Middle-Class Masculinity in Britain and America, 1800–1940* (Manchester, 1987), and M. Roper and J. Tosh, eds, *Manful Assertions: Masculinities in Britain Since 1800* (London, 1991).

25 Hughes, *Tom Brown's Schooldays*, in Jeffrey Richards, *Happiest Days: The Public Schools in English Fiction* (Manchester, 1988), p. 33.

26 *Ibid.*, p. 59–60.

27 On penny dreadfuls see E. S. Turner, *Boys Will Be Boys* (London, 1948); Kirsten Drotner, *English Children and Their Magazines, 1751–1945* (New Haven, 1988); Kevin Carpenter, *Penny Dreadfuls and Comics* (London, 1983); Louis James, 'Tom Brown's Imperialist Sons', *Victorian Studies*, 17 (1973), pp. 89–99; Patrick Dunae, 'Penny Dreadfuls: Late Nineteenth-Century Boys' Literature and Crime', *Victorian Studies*, 22 (1979), pp. 133–50; Patrick Dunae, 'Boy's Literature and the Idea of Empire, 1870– 1914', *Victorian Studies*, 23 (1980), pp. 105–21; and Springhall, *Youth, Popular Culture and Moral Panics*, pp. 38–97.

28 Carpenter, *Penny Dreadfuls and Comics*, p. 12.

29 James, 'Tom Brown's Imperialist Sons', p. 99; for graphic descriptions of violence, see Drotner, *English Children and Their Magazines*, pp. 98–111.

30 Dunae, 'Boy's Literature and the Idea of Empire', p. 107.

31 Carpenter, *Penny Dreadfuls and Comics*, p. 42.

32 Quayle, *Collector's Book of Boys' Stories*, p. 32. The literature on Henty is extensive; see in particular Guy Arnold, *Held Fast for England: G. A. Henty, Imperialist Boys' Writer* (London, 1980); Dunae, 'Boys' Literature and the Idea of Empire', pp. 105–21; Robert A. Huttenback, 'G. A. Henty and the Vision of Empire', *Encounter*, 35 (1970), pp. 46–53; Mark Naidis, 'G. A. Henty's Idea of India', *Victorian Studies*, 8 (1964), pp. 49–58; and Jeffrey Richards, 'With Henty to Africa', in Richards, *Imperialism and Juvenile Literature*, pp. 72–106.

33 Henty's chief rivals, George Manville Fenn and Dr Gordon Stables, were also advocates of patriotic manliness and imperial expansion, but wrote few novels with a war setting until the 1890s. On Stables, see Dunae, 'Boys' Literature and the Idea of Empire'.

34 Huttenback, 'Henty and the Vision of Empire', pp. 46–7.

35 *Ibid.*, p. 47.

36 Richards, 'With Henty to Africa', pp. 75–6.

37 Richards, 'Popular Imperialism and the Image of the Army', p. 89.

38 See *To Heerat and Cabul* (London, 1902). Henty was also critical of the East India Company directors, who he saw as waging war for their own selfish gain; see *In Times of Peril* (London, 1881).

39 *The Tiger of Mysore* (London, 1896), p. 5. Interestingly, Bernard Cornwall's long-running and popular series of adventure novels about the nineteenth-century soldier, Richard Sharpe, has the valiant rifleman gaining Wellington's attention and winning his first promotion at the siege of Seringapatam, Tippoo's capital. See Bernard Cornwall, *Sharpe's Tiger* (London, 1997).

40 See Richards, 'Popular Imperialism and the Image of the Army', pp. 94–5.

41 *Through Three Campaigns* (London, 1904), pp. 5–6

42 *A Soldier's Daughter* (London, 1906), p. 24.

43 *Ibid.*, p. 35.

44 The following section is based largely on Richards, 'Popular Imperialism and the Image of the Army' and Arnold, *Held Fast for England*.

45 Arnold, *Held Fast for England*, p. 67.

46 Dunae, 'Boys' Literature and the Idea of Empire', p. 110.

47 See Bernard Porter, *The Lion's Share: A Short History of British Imperialism 1850–1983* (London, 1984), pp. 96–7.

48 *Through Three Campaigns*, pp. 217, 301–2.

49 *With Kitchener in the Soudan*, pp. 230, 229–33.

50 *In Times of Peril*, pp. 48, 132.

51 Captain F. S. Brereton, *With Shield and Assegai* (London, 1900), pp. 118, 304.

52 William Johnston, *Tom Graham VC* (London, 1906), p. 217.

53 A. J. Chalmers, *Fighting the Matabele* (London, 1898), pp. 200, 210, 211, 286.

54 Blackie & Sons Ltd catalogue, *c.* 1900.

55 Edgar Pickering, *A Stout English Bowman* (London, n.d. but *c.* 1912), p. 141.

56 Robert Leighton, *The Thirsty Sword* (London, 1900), p. 301.

57 Harry Collingwood, *Across the Spanish Main* (London, 1907), pp. 229–32.

58 Carpenter, *Penny Dreadfuls and Comics*, p. 43. On later boys' papers, see also Turner, *Boys Will Be Boys* and Drotner, *English Children and Their Magazines*.

59 *Young England*, XIX, (1898), p. 18.

60 *Ibid.*, p. 184–7.

61 On *Chums* see Richards, 'Popular Imperialism and the Image of the Army', pp. 101–6.

62 Oral testimony collected by the author.

63 See John Springhall, 'Healthy Papers for Manly Boys; Imperialism and Race in the Harmsworth's Halfpenny Boys' Papers of the 1890s and 1900s', in Richards, *Imperialism and Juvenile Literature*, pp. 118–23.

64 Robert MacDonald, 'Signs from the Imperial Quarter: Illustrations from *Chums*, 1892–1914', *Children's Literature*, 16 (1988), pp. 31–55.

65 Douglas H. Johnson, 'The Death of Gordon: A Victorian Myth', *Journal of Imperial and Commonwealth History*, 10 (1982), pp. 285–310.

66 MacDonald, 'Signs from the Imperial Quarter', pp. 35–36.

67 Turner, *Boys Will Be Boys*, pp. 115–16.

68 Stuart Cloete, *A Victorian Son: an Autobiography* (London, 1972), pp. 17–18. See also Huntley Gordon, *The Unreturning Army* (London, 1967), pp. 1–2, for the author's account of his boyhood game, 'Britons and Boers'.

69 Antonia Fraser, *A History of Toys* (London, 1966); Graham Dawson, *Soldier Heroes: British Adventure, Empire and the Imagining of Masculinity* (London, 1994), pp. 238–40.

70 Dawson, *Soldier Heroes*, p. 235; Robert Roberts, *A Ragged Schooling* (Manchester, 1976), pp. 155–9.

71 James Opie, *The Great Book of Britains* (London, 1993).

72 Thea Thompson, ed., *Edwardian Childhoods* (London, 1981), p. 53.

73 T. H. E. Travers, 'Future Warfare: H.G. Wells and British Military Theory, 1895–1916', in Brian Bond and Ian Roy, *War and Society* (London, 1975), p. 79.

74 H. G. Wells, *Little Wars* (London, 1913), p. 100.

75 Dawson, *Soldier Heroes*, pp. 235–6.

76 See Paul Usherwood and Jenny Spencer-Smith, *Lady Butler – Battle Artist, 1846–1933* (London, 1987); Paul Usherwood, 'Officer Material', in John M. Mackenzie, ed., *Popular Imperialism and the Military 1850–1950* (Manchester, 1992, pp. 162–78.

77 Zara Steiner, 'Views on War', *Moirae*, 5 (1980), p. 20. On public schools, see David Newsome, *Godliness and God Learning* (London, 1961); J. R. de S. Honey, *Tom Brown's Universe* (Millington, 1977); Jonathan Gathorne-Hardy, *The Public School Phenomenon* (Harmondsworth, 1979).

78 W. J. Reader, *At Duty's Call* (Manchester, 1988), p. 84.

79 See Jeffrey Richards, *Happiest Days*.

80 Robert Roberts, *The Classic Slum* (Manchester, 1971), p. 161; Frederick Willis, *101 Jubilee Road* (London, 1948), pp. 108–12.

81 See J. A. Mangan, *The Games Ethic and Imperialism* (London, 1986), pp. 24–8.

82 Steiner, 'Views on War', p. 21.

83 'The OTC at Marlborough College', *The Captain*, XXXI (1914), pp. 985–8. See also

Peter Parker, *The Old Lie: The Great War and the Public School Ethos* (London, 1987), pp. 62–7.

84 Geoffrey Best, 'Militarism in the Victorian Public School', in B. Simon and I. Bradley, *The Victorian Public School* (Dublin, 1979), p. 137. I am indebted to the work of Professor Best, on which the following discussion is based.

85 *Ibid.*, p. 148.

86 See Adams, *The Great Adventure*, pp. 9–12.

87 J. A. Mangan, 'Athleticism: A Case Study of the Evolution of an Educational Ideology', in Simon and Bradley, *The Victorian Public School*, p. 147; see also Mangan, *The Games Ethic and Imperialism.*

88 Reader, *At Duty's Call*, p. 91.

89 Steiner, 'Views on War', p. 21.

90 Michael Adams, *The Great Adventure: Male Desire and the Coming of World War I*, (Bloomington, IN, 1990), pp. 42–4.

91 MacDonald, *The Language of Empire*, pp. 62–4.

92 While Seeley was no great advocate of modern war and was sometimes critical of the manner in which 'Greater Britain' had been created, there is nevertheless a contradictory note in his work, as there is also an acceptance that war has been the necessary means for such expansion and for achieving those 'philanthropic desires to put an end to enormous evils'. See *The Expansion of England* (London, 1883) pp. 134, 304. See also Peter Burroughs, 'John Robert Seeley and British Imperial History', *Journal of Imperial and Commonwealth History*, VI (1972), pp. 191–211 and Mackenzie, *Popular Imperialism and the Military*, p. 2.

93 Valerie E. Chancellor, *History for their Masters: Opinion in the English History Textbook, 1800–1914* (Bath, 1970), pp. 122–3, 135. See also MacDonald, *The Language of Empire*, pp. 62–9, and John Mackenzie, *Propaganda and Empire* (Manchester, 1984), pp. 173–97.

94 Chancellor, *History for their Masters*, p. 132.

95 *Ibid.*, pp. 127–8.

96 MacDonald, *The Language of Empire*, pp. 64–5.

97 H. E. Marshall, *Our Island Story: A History of England for Boys and Girls* (London, 1905), p. 10.

98 Alfred H. Miles, ed., *Fifty-Two Stories of the British Army* (London, 1897), pp. 6–7.

99 Alfred H. Miles, *The Sweep of the Sword: A Battle Book for Boys* (London, 1910), p. v. Similar sentiments are to be found in Alfred H. Miles, *The Imperial Reciter* (London, 1900), pp. 5–6, and Harold E. Butler, *War Songs of Britain* (London, 1903), p. 6.

100 Roberts, *The Classic Slum*, p. 142–4.

101 W. E. Henley, *Lyra Heroica: A Book of Verse for Boys* (London, 1892), p. vii.

102 See Alan Penn, *Targeting Schools: Drill, Materialism and Imperialism* (London, 1999).

103 John Springhall, 'The Boy Scouts, Class and Militarism in Relation to British Youth Movements', *International Review of Social History*, 16: 2 (1971), p. 129; see also John Springhall, *Youth, Empire and Society: British Youth Movements, 1883–1940* (London, 1977).

104 Springhall, 'The Boy Scouts', p. 130.

105 See Springhall, *Youth, Empire and Society*, and Richard A. Voeltz, 'A Good Jew and a Good Englishman: The Jewish Lads' Brigade, 1894–1922', *Journal of Contemporary History*, 23, (1988), pp. 119–27.

106 See John Springhall, 'Lord Meath, Youth and Empire', *Journal of Contemporary History*, 4 (1970), pp. 97–111.

107 Michael Paris, *Winged Warfare: The Literature and Theory of Aerial Warfare in Britain, 1859–1917* (Manchester, 1992), p. 91.

108 Peter Berrisford Ellis and Piers Williams, *By Jove, Biggles! The Life of Captain W. E. Johns* (London, 1981), p. 11.

3 Preparing for the Great War to Come

1 Paul Kennedy, *The Rise and Fall of British Naval Mastery* (London, 1976), pp. 171–3. The public concern at the possibility of a French invasion in the 1850s resulted in the creation of the Rifle Volunteer Movement, a largely middle-class response to the perceived danger. See M. J. Salvoulis, *Riflemen Form: The War Scare of 1859–60 in England* (London, 1982).

2 See Edward M. Spiers, *The Army and Society, 1815–1914* (London, 1980).

3 On the Cardwell reforms, see *ibid.*, pp. 2–28.

4 David Reynolds, *Britannia Overruled: British Policy and World Power in the Twentieth Century* (London, 1991), p. 20. The developing enmity between Britain and Germany has been analyzed in Paul Kennedy, *The Rise of the Anglo–German Antagonism: 1860–1914* (London, 1980).

5 See *ibid.*, pp. 251–88.

6 Paul Kennedy, *The Rise and Fall of the Great Powers: Economic Change and Military Conflict from 1500–2000* (London, 1988), p. 293.

7 For a detailed account of the Anglo–Boer War (1899–1902) see Thomas Pakenham, *The Boer War* (London, 1979).

8 Arnold White, 'The Cult of Infirmity', in Richard Soloway, 'Counting the Degenerates: The Statistics of Race Deterioration in Edwardian England', *Journal of Contemporary History*, 17: 1 (January, 1982), p. 140.

9 'Miles' (General Sir Frederick Maurice), 'Where to Get Men', *Contemporary Review* (January 1902), pp. 78–86.

10 Samuel Hynes, *The Edwardian Turn of Mind* (London, 1968), pp. 23–4.

11 Hynes, *The Edwardian Turn of Mind*, p. 17.

12 Reynolds, *Britannia Overruled*, p. 66.

13 I. F. Clarke, *Voices Prophesying War: Future Wars, 1763–3749* (Oxford, 2nd edn, 1992), p. 29.

14 Clarke, *Voices Prophesying War*, pp. 33–8. The story has been reprinted in I. F. Clarke, ed., *The Tale of the Next Great War, 1871–1914* (Liverpool, 1995), pp. 27–73.

15 For a comprehensive list of future war fiction, see I. F. Clarke, *The Tale of the*

Future (London, 3rd edn, 1978). Joseph S. Meisel, 'The Germans Are Coming! British Fiction of a German Invasion, 1871–1913', *War, Literature, and the Arts*, 2: 2 (Fall 1990), pp. 41–77, surveys some of the better-known examples of the fiction of the Anglo–German war to come. An excellent collection of British and German stories is reprinted in I. F. Clarke, ed., *The Great War with Germany, 1890–1914*, (Liverpool, 1997).

16 See Reginald Pound and Geoffrey Harmsworth, *Northcliffe* (London, 1959), *passim*.

17 Bernard Porter, *The Lion's Share: A Short History of British Imperialism 1850–1983*, p. 125. The Franco–Russian Alliance was not made public until 1895. See also James Joll, *Europe since 1870* (London, 3rd edn 1983), pp. 94–5.

18 The story was clearly inspired by 'The Great War of 1892', by Admiral Philip Colomb and others, *Black and White* (January–June 1892). See also I. F. Clarke, *Voices Prophesying War*, pp. 62–3.

19 Pound and Harmsworth, *Northcliffe*, pp. 151–2.

20 *Pluck*, 96, 1897 (later reprinted in *Boy's Friend*).

21 The Fashoda Incident of 1898 occurred when a French expedition, attempting to lay claim to eastern Sudan, was forced to withdraw by a superior British force. See Porter, *The Lion's Share*, pp. 163–5.

22 See E. S. Turner, *Boys Will Be Boys* (London, 1948), pp. 173–5.

23 A number of Captain Strange stories appeared in *Boy's Herald* during 1903.

24 Caroline Playne, *The Pre-War Mind In Britain* (London, 1928), p. 117.

25 Turner, *Boys Will Be Boys*, p. 175.

26 See Pound and Harmsworth, *Northcliffe*, pp. 425, 443–5.

27 In 1909 Blatchford was commissioned by the *Daily Mail* to write a series of articles on the German danger. The first article opened with, 'I write these articles because I believe that Germany is deliberately preparing to destroy the British Empire . . .' The series was reprinted as a pamphlet, *Germany and England*, the same year.

28 See Playne, *Pre-War Mind in Britain*, chap. two.

29 Reginald Wray, 'A World At Stake', *Boy's Realm*, 1903. The sequel, 'A Fight for Empire', appeared in the Autumn/Winter issue, 1903–4.

30 John Tregellis, 'Legions of the Kaiser or The Mailed Fist', *Boy's Friend*, June–September 1914.

31 Editor's preface to Colin Collins, 'War in the Clouds', *Dreadnought*, 26, 23 November 1912.

32 Captain Frank H. Shaw, *Seas of Memory* (London, 1958). See also the comments of Jeffrey Richards in 'Popular Imperialism and the Image of the Army in Juvenile Literature' in John M. Mackenzie, ed., *Popular Imperialism and the Military 1850–1950* (Manchester, 1992), pp. 80–81, 104–6.

33 Captain Frank Shaw, 'Perils of the Motherland', *Chums*, 1908.

34 *Ibid.*

35 Percy F. Westerman, 'The Metamorphosis of Midshipman Maynbrace', *The British Boy's Annual* (1911), pp. 213–19.

36 Captain F. S. Brereton, *The Great Aeroplane* (London, 1911), p. 396.

37 Captain F. S. Brereton, *The Great Airship* (London, 1913), p. 19.

38 Herbert Strang, *The Air Scout* (London, 1913), p. viii.

39 Henry Frowde, Hodder & Stoughton catalogue, *c.* 1912.

40 Herbert Strang, *The Air Patrol* (London, 1914), p. 431.

41 Colin Collins, 'War in the Clouds', *Dreadnought*, 1 February 1913.

42 Frank Shaw, 'Lion's Teeth and Eagle's Claw', *Chums* (1914), p. 598.

43 'Rule Britannia', *Boy's Friend*, 1905. 'Death or Glory Boys', in Turner, *Boys Will Be Boys*, p. 176. The incident which sparks the war in 'Rule Britannia' was based on the so-called Dogger incident of 1905, when the Russian Baltic Fleet on its way to the Pacific fired on British trawlers, having mistaken them for Japanese torpedo boats.

44 The serial was Andrew Gray's 'A World at War', *Boy's Herald*, 1908.

45 Max Rover, 'Invaded from the Clouds', *Boy's Friend*, 1914.

46 Robert Roberts, *A Ragged Schooling* (Manchester, 1976), p. 156.

47 Norman Greaves, 'Flying to Victory', *Boy's Herald*, 1911; Sidney Drew, 'Dan the Airman', *Boy's Realm*, 1912. For Sexton Blake's adventures, see for example, 'Tinker's Boyhood', *Boy's Friend*, 1913. However, it should be pointed out that Sexton Blake was sometimes employed by the Kaiser.

48 Robert Roberts, *The Classic Slum* (Manchester, 1971), p. 181.

49 Turner, *Boys Will be Boys*, p. 177. For an examination of spy fever in Britain during the period, see David French, 'Spy Fever in Britain, 1900–1915', *Historical Journal*, 21 (1978).

50 Shaw, 'Lion's Teeth and Eagle's Claw', p. 242.

51 Ambrose Earle, 'The Invasion that Failed'; *Boy's Herald* (1909); Colin Collins, 'War in the Clouds'.

52 Examples from Shaw's 'Perils of the Motherland'.

53 John Tregellis, 'The Flying Armada or War Scouts of the Air', *Boy's Friend* (1913–1914).

54 See for example, 'The Skipper and the Submarine'. Sir Arthur Conan Doyle's 'Danger' was first published in *Strand* magazine in July 1914. The story has recently been republished in Clarke, *The Tale of the Next Great War, 1871–1914*, pp. 293–320.

55 On Harmsworth's air propaganda see Alfred Gollin, *The Impact of Air Power on the British People and their Government, 1909–1914* (London, 1989) and Michael Paris, *Winged Warfare: The Theory and Literature of Aerial Warfare in Britain, 1859–1917* (Manchester, 1992).

56 Collins, 'War in the Clouds'.

57 John Springhall, *Youth, Popular Culture and Moral Panics* (London, 1999), p. 99; Rachael Low, *The History of the British Film*, vol. 1 (London, 1998).

58 Ivan Butler, *The War Film* (London, 1974), pp. 13–16.

59 On early films of aerial warfare, see Michael Paris, *From the Wright Brothers to 'Top Gun': Aviation, Nationalism and Popular Cinema* (Manchester, 1995).

60 Kenneth Grahame, *The Wind in the Willows* (London, 1971), p. 261.

61 *Boy's Friend*, 690 (29 August 1914).

62 Hugh Gratton Donnelly, 'The Stricken Nation' (1890), reprinted in Clarke, *The Tale of the Next Great War*, pp. 166–7.

63 See Clarke, *The Great War with Germany*.

64 Wendy Katz, *Rider Haggard and the Fiction of Empire* (Cambridge, 1987), p. 45.

65 H. Rider Haggard, *Queen Sheba's Ring* (London, 1910), p. 108.

66 For an extended discussion of the novel, see Katz, *Rider Haggard*, pp. 45–50.

67 Haggard's diary entry for 16 January 1915, in Katz, *Rider Haggard*, p. 28. Interestingly, Henty had made the same argument, using the example of Carthage as a decadent empire which fell to the more vigorous Romans. See G. A. Henty, *The Young Carthaginian* (London, 1896).

68 Henry Birchenough, 'Our Last Effort for a Volunteer Army', *Nineteenth Century* (April 1901), p. 547. See also Lord Roberts, *The Nation in Arms* (London, 1907). While the conscription lobby included a number of well-known individuals, many others worked behind the scenes, not wishing to be publicly associated with the National Service League. These included General Sir Henry Wilson and Lord Esher. An example of the latter's involvement, and his conviction that a great war was inevitable, is to be found in his letter to Lord Roberts of 28 August 1907 (Roberts Papers, National Army Museum).

69 *Captain* (1906), in Dunae, 'Boys' Literature and the Idea of Empire', p. 118.

70 See Tim Jeal, *Baden-Powell*, (London, 1989), pp. 302–4.

71 John Springhall, 'The Boy Scouts, Class and Militarism in Relation to British Youth Movements', *International Review of Social History*, 16: 2 (1971), pp. 131–2.

72 R. S. S. Baden-Powell, *Scouting for Boys* (London, 1908). B-P's classic was first published in six fortnightly parts in early 1908.

73 Springhall, 'The Boy Scouts', p. 156. For an alternative analysis, see Alan Warren, 'Citizens of the Empire: Baden-Powell, Scouts and Guides and an Imperial Idea, 1900– 1940', in John Mackenzie, ed., *Imperialism and Popular Culture* (Manchester, 1986), pp. 232–56.

74 Hynes, *Edwardian Turn of Mind*, pp. 24–6; Baden-Powell, *Scouting for Boys*, pp. 335–6.

75 Tim Jeal, *Baden-Powell*, p. 359.

76 *Ibid.*, p. 399.

77 Springhall, 'The Boy Scouts', p. 135; Baden-Powell, *Scouting for Boys*, p. 3. See also Martin Dedman, 'Baden-Powell, Militarism, and the "Invisible Contributors" to the Boy Scout Scheme, 1904–1920', *Twentieth Century British History*, 4: 3 (1993), pp. 201–23.

78 On the chivalric element in the Boy Scout movement, see Mark Girouard, *The Return to Camelot: Chivalry and the English Gentleman* (London, 1981), pp. 249–58.

79 Hynes, *Edwardian Turn of Mind*, p. 29.

80 The serial was 'The World at War', *Boy's Herald* (1909), p. 538.

81 W. J. Reader, *At Duty's Call* (Manchester, 1988), p. 78.

82 Roberts, *The Classic Slum*, p. 161, n. 4.

83 A similar argument has been used by Hugh Cunningham regarding Volunteer Riflemen in the late nineteenth century. See Hugh Cunningham, *The Volunteer Force*, pp. 153–4

84 Jeal, *Baden-Powell*, p. 409.

85 Roberts, *The Classic Slum*, pp. 179–80.

4 Paths of Glory: 1914–18

1 Gerard J. DeGroot, *Blighty: British Society in the Era of the Great War* (London, 1996), p. 7.
2 *Hansard*, 6 August 1914.
3 Elizabeth O'Neill, *The War, 1914: A History and an Explanation for Boys and Girls*, (London, 1914), p. 1; Sir James Yoxall, *Why Britain Went to War*, in Christopher Martin, *English Life in the First World War*, (London, 1974), p. 97. Interestingly, O'Neill's interpretation of the cause of the war changed very little over the next 40 years – see Elizabeth and Mary O'Neill, *A Nursery History of England*, (London, n. d. but *c.* 1954).
4 F. S. Brereton, *With French at the Front* (London, 1915), p. 2.
5 On the Wellington House group, see Cate Haste, *Keep the Home Fires Burning: Propaganda in the First World War* (London, 1977); Peter Buitenhuis, *The Great War of Words: Literature as Propaganda, 1914–1918 and After* (London, 1989); Samuel Hynes, *A War Imagined: The First World War and English Culture* (London, 1990).
6 Robert Graves, *Goodbye to All That* (1929; London, 1977), pp. 60, 62.
7 Huntley Gordon, *The Unreturning Army* (London, 1967), p. 10.
8 See Michael Adams, *The Great Adventure: Male Desire and the Coming of World War I*, (Bloomington, IN, 1990), pp. 99–100.
9 George Coppard, *With a Machine Gun to Cambrai* (London, 1969), p. 1.
10 A. Stuart Dolden, *Cannon Fodder: An Infantryman's Life on the Western Front* (Poole, 1980), p. 11.
11 On the volunteers of 1914, see Ian F. W. Beckett and Keith Simpson, *A Nation In Arms: A Social Study of the British Army in the First World War* (Manchester, 1985); Peter Simkins, *Kitchener's Army: The Raising of the New Armies, 1914–1916* (Manchester, 1988).
12 Gordon, *Unreturning Army*, p. 11.
13 Brereton, *With French at the Front*, pp. 10–11.
14 *Ibid.*, p. 145.
15 Escott Lynn, *In Khaki for the King* (London, 1915), preface.
16 F. S. Brereton, *Under French's Command* (London, 1916), p. 330.
17 *Ibid.*, p. 332.
18 Basil Liddell Hart, *History of the First World War* (London, 1970), p. 203.
19 F. S. Brereton, *Under Haig in Flanders* (London, 1917), p. 58
20 *Ibid.*, p. 81.
21 *Ibid.*, p. 182.
22 *Ibid.*, p. 184.
23 On the Battle of the Somme, see Martin Middlebrook, *The First Day on the Somme*, (London, 1971); Lyn Macdonald, *Somme* (London, 1983) and J. M. Bourne, *Britain and the Great War, 1914–1918* (London, 1989), pp. 59–67.
24 Hynes, *A War Imagined*, pp. 44–5.
25 Percy F. Westerman, *A Lively Bit of the Front* (London, 1919), p. 13.

26 *Ibid.*, p. 122.

27 *Ibid.*, p. 147.

28 See Barry Johnson, 'In the Trenches with Brereton and Westerman', *Gunfire*, 18 (n. d.), pp. 14–19.

29 Peter Parker, *The Old Lie: The Great War and the Public School Ethos* (London, 1987), pp. 217–18.

30 The standard works on the Gallipoli campaign are Alan Moorehead, *Gallipoli*, (London, 1956); Robert Rhodes James, *Gallipoli* (London, 1964); and Peter Liddle, ed., *Men of Gallipoli* (London, 1976). Interesting more than revealing is Sir Ian Hamilton's *Gallipoli Diary, 1915*, two vols (London, 1920).

31 Percy F. Westerman, *The Fight for Constantinople* (London, 1915), p. 18.

32 *Ibid.*, p. 256.

33 Herbert Strang, *Frank Forrester: A Story of the Dardanelles* (London, 1915).

34 T. C. Bridges, *On Land and Sea at the Dardanelles* (London, n. d. but *c.* 1915), pp. 31–2.

35 *Ibid.*, p. 198.

36 Guy Waterford, 'Last Days at Gallipoli', *Young England* (1916), p. 235.

37 See Bourne, *Britain and the Great War*, pp. 92–7.

38 Brereton's other novels of the war in the Middle East are: *At Grips with the Turk* (London, n. d. *c.* 1915); *The Armoured Car Scouts* (London, 1916); *With Allenby in Palestine* (London, 1919); and *On the Road to Baghdad* (London, 1920).

39 Brereton, *With Allenby in Palestine*, p. 286.

40 See 'A Good Word for the Turkish Soldier', *Young England*, 37 (1915–16), pp. 155-6; for negative racial stereotypes, see Strang, *Frank Forrester*; Bowes, *The Aussie Crusaders*; and Brereton, *With Allenby in Palestine*.

41 John Springhall, *Youth, Popular Culture and Moral Panics* (London, 1999), p. 138–9.

42 Ascott R. Hope, *The School of Arms: Boy Soldiers and Sailors* (London, n. d. but *c.* 1915), p. 328.

43 *Young England* (1915–16), p. 38.

44 Hope, *School of Arms*, pp. 330–31.

45 *Young England* (1915–16), p. 78.

46 See for example, Brenda Girvin, *The Girl Scout* (London, n. d. *c.* 1913).

47 William T. Palmer, 'The Secret Base: The Story of a Scout and a Submarine', *Young England* (1915–16), pp. 296–8.

48 Rowland Walker, *Oscar Danby, VC: A Tale of the Great European War* (London, 1916).

49 *Ibid.*, p. 120.

50 *Ibid.*, pp. 178–9.

51 *Ibid.*, pp. 195–6.

52 Allan Bishop, ed., *Vera Brittain's War Diary, 1913–1917* (London, 1981), p. 89.

53 Mary Cadogan and Patricia Craig, *Women and Children First: The Fiction of Two World Wars* (London, 1978), p. 59.

54 Haste, *Keep the Home Fires Burning*, pp. 56–7.

55 Jesse Pope, 'The Call', reprinted in Catherine Reilly, ed., *Scars Upon My Heart: Women's Poetry and Verse of the First World War* (London, 1981), p. 88.

56 This view is best expressed in Richard Aldington's novel, *The Death of a Hero* (London, 1929) and in the poetry of Siegfried Sassoon, especially *Blighters* and *Glory of Women*. See also E. A. Mackintosh, *Recruiting*, and the comments of Michael Adams in *The Great Adventure*, pp. 128–30.

57 An excellent survey of women's war work is to be found in Gail Braybon and Penny Summerfield, *Out of the Cage: Women's Experiences in Two World Wars* (London, 1987).

58 Bessie Marchant, *A VAD in Salonika* (London, 1916), p. 53.

59 *Ibid.*, p. 88.

60 Bessie Marchant, *A Transport Girl in France* (London, 1918); Brenda Girvin, *Jenny Wren* (London, 1920).

61 Hampden Gordon and Joyce Dennys, *Our Girls in Wartime* (London, n. d.), p. 7. See also the same authors, *Our Hospital ABC* (London, n. d.).

62 Angela Brazil, *A Patriotic Schoolgirl* (London, 1918), p. 135.

63 *Ibid.*, pp. 136–7.

64 See Cadogan and Craig, *Women and Children First*, pp. 59–70.

65 *Women's Royal Air Force: Life on a British Aerodrome* is available on the Imperial War Museum videotape, *War Women of Britain: Women at War, 1914–1918* (1991).

66 Brereton, *Under Haig in Flanders*, p. 181.

67 Strang, *Frank Forrester*, pp. 220–21.

68 Bridges, *On Land and Sea at the Dardanelles*, p. 30.

69 Herbert Strang, *Tom Willoughby's Scouts* (London, 1919).

70 Brereton, *Under Haig in Flanders*, p. 264.

71 Herbert Strang, *A Hero of Liège* (London, 1915), pp. 246–7.

72 'Italy's War in the Mountains', *Young England* (1915–16), pp. 251–2.

73 F. S. Brereton, *Foes of the Red Cockade* (London, 1904).

74 F. S. Brereton, *A Soldier of Japan* (London, 1907).

75 F. S. Brereton, *With Joffre at Verdun* (London, 1917), pp. 9–10.

76 *Ibid.*, p. 11.

77 See *The Armoured Car Scouts: A Tale of the Campaign in Caucasus* (London, n. d.).

78 See Captain Charles Gilson, *In Arms for Russia* (London, 1917) and F. S. Brereton, *With Our Russian Allies* (London, 1917).

79 F. S. Brereton, *Under Foch's Command* (London, 1918), p. 287.

80 Parker, *The Old Lie*, pp. 226–7.

81 See Albert Marrin, *The Last Crusade: The Church of England and the First World War* (Durham, NC, 1985).

82 Arthur Machen, *The Bowmen and Other Legends of the War* (London, 1915), pp. 38–43.

83 'The Vigil' was published in *The Times* on 5 August 1914, the morning after the ultimatum to Germany expired. The poem opens with:

> England! where the sacred flame
> Burns before the inmost shrine,
> Where the lips that love thy name
> Consecrate their hopes and thine,

Where the banners of thy dead
Weave their shadows overhead,
Watch beside thine arms tonight,
Pray that God defend the Right.

Newbolt claimed to have written the lines sixteen years earlier in 'Mystical anticipa-
tion of the moment'. See Hynes, *A War Imagined*, p. 25. The poem is reprinted in
Henry Newbolt, *Collected Poems, 1897–1907* (London, c. 1908), pp. 134–46.

84 Henry Newbolt, *The Book of the Happy Warrior* (London, 1917), p. 283.

85 Colin Veitch, "'Play Up! Play Up!, And Win the War!" Football, the Nation and the
First World War, 1914–1918', *Journal of Contemporary History*, 20, (1985), p. 372.

86 See Omer Bartov, *Murder in Our Midst: The Holocaust, Industrial Killing, and
Representation* (Oxford, 1996).

87 Henry Newbolt, *Tales of the Great War* (London, 1916), pp. 248–9.

88 Peter Fritzsche, *A Nation of Fliers: German Aviation and the Popular Imagination*
(Cambridge, MA, 1992)

89 Among the more interesting air war novels are Percy F. Westerman, *Billy Barcroft,
RNAS*, (London, 1917) and *The Secret Battleplane* (London, 1916); Herbert Strang,
The Secret Seaplane (London, 1915) and *Burton of the Flying Corps* (London, 1916);
Rowland Walker, *Deville Keen, Mystery Airman* (London, 1917); W. A. Henry, *The Red
Kite* (London, 1915); Claude Grahame-White and Harry Harper, *The Invisible War
Plane* (London, 1915).

90 The disastrous losses of the Royal Flying Corps in the spring of 1917 are examined in
Alan Morris, *Bloody April* (London, 1967), and Peter Liddle, *The Airman's War*,
(Poole, 1987), pp. 55–69.

91 The official air war films are *The Eyes of the Army* (1916); *With the Royal Flying Corps*
(1917); *Tails Up France* (1917); *Life of an Airship Squadron* (1918); *The Air Force: 'Per
Ardua Ad Astra'* (1918). All these films are held in the film archive of the Imperial War
Museum. See also Michael Paris, *From the Wright Brothers to 'Top Gun': Aviation,
Nationalism and Popular Cinema* (Manchester, 1995), pp. 24–33.

92 R. Wherry-Anderson, *The Romance of Air Fighting* (London, 1917) p. 24; Major Rees,
Fighting in the Air (London, 1916), p. 8; see also Mrs M. Hewlett, *Our Fighting Men*
(London, 1917).

93 Captain Frank Shaw, 'Join the Royal Flying Corps', *Chums* (1915), p. 346.

94 On the realities of air warfare on the Western Front, see Dennis Winter, *The First of
Few: Fighter Pilots of the First World War* (London, 1982).

95 DeGroot, *Blighty*, pp. 220–21

96 Martin, *English Life in the First World War*, pp. 97–8; Michael Powell, later one of
Britain's most celebrated film directors, also recalled being 'soldier-mad' during the
war years, and his mother making him a uniform that he wore on every possible
occasion. See Michael Powell, *A Life in Movies: An Autobiography* (London, 1986),
pp. 56–7.

97 Parker, *The Old Lie*, p. 259.

98 Robert Roberts, *A Ragged Schooling* (Manchester, 1976), pp. 157–8.

99   Antonia Fraser, *A History of Toys* (London, 1966), p. 184.

100 Copy in the author's collection.

101 Bishop, *Vera Brittain's War Diary*, pp. 114, 272.

102 Philip Knightley, *The First Casualty* (London, 1978), pp. 80–81. See also Philip Gibbs, *Adventures in Journalism* (London, 1923) and *The Realities of War* (London, 1938); Martin Farrar, *The War Correspondents: The Western Front, 1914–1918* (Stroud, 1997).

103 Knightley, *The First Casualty* p. 96.

104 C. E. Montague, *Disenchantment* (London, 1922), pp. 97–8.

105 See Joseph Darracott and Belinda Loftus, *First World War Posters* (London, 1972), p. 17.

106 See Nigel Viney, *Images of Wartime: British Art and Artists of World War I* (London, 1991).

107 The full series has been reproduced in *Gunfire*, 42 (1998).

108 See Ivan Butler, *The War Film* (London, 1974), pp. 17–28.

109 Nicholas Reeves, 'Official British Film Propaganda' in Michael Paris, *The First World War and Popular Cinema* (Edinburgh, 1999), pp. 27–54; Nicholas Reeves, 'Cinema, Spectatorship and Propagada: The Battle of the Somme (1916) and its Contemporary Audience', *Historical Journal of Film, Radio and Television*, 17: 1 (1997), pp. 5–28; and Roger Smither, 'A Wonderful Idea of the Fighting: The Question of Fakes in The Battle of the Somme', *Historical Journal of Film, Radio and Television*, 13: 2 (1993), pp. 149–69. For an analysis of the film and its impact on audiences, see S. D. Badsey, 'The Battle of the Somme: British War Propaganda', *Historical Journal of Film, Radio and Television*, 3: 2 (1983), pp. 99–115; and Nicholas Reeves, *Official British Propaganda During The First World War* (Beckenham, 1986). An excellent videotape of the film is available from the Imperial War Museum.

110 Reeves, 'Official British Film Propaganda', p. 38.

111 Hynes, *A War Imagined*, p. 44; Johnson, 'In the Trenches with Brereton and Westerman', pp. 14–19.

112 Bishop, *Vera Brittain's War Diary, passim.*

113 F. S. Brereton, *With the Allies to the Rhine* (London, 1919), p. 283.

114 Adams, *The Great Adventure*, p. 112.

5 No More War: 1919–39

1   A. J. P. Taylor, *English History, 1914–1945* (Oxford, 1965), p. 133.

2   P. J. Campbell, *The Ebb and Flow of Battle* (Oxford, 1979), p. 166.

3   Robert Graves and Alan Hodge, *The Long Weekend* (London, 1940), pp. 15–16.

4   The most recent social history of Britain in the interwar period is Peter Dewey, *War and Progress: Britain, 1914–1945* (London, 1997). Still useful is Charles Loch Mowat's magisterial *Britain Between the Wars, 1918–1940* (London, 1955), and Noreen Branson and Margot Heinemann, *Britain in the Nineteen-Thirties* (London, 1973).

5   Isabel Quigly, 'A Catholic Reader of the Thirties', *Signal*, 70 (January 1993), p. 5.

6   See Kirsten Drotner, *English Children and Their Magazines, 1751–1945* (New Haven, 1988), pp. 184–5, 192–5.

7   Graves and Hodge, *The Long Weekend*, pp. 26, 216; see also Samuel Hynes, *A War Imagined: The First World War and English Culture* (London, 1990), p. 424.

8   Lloyd Clark, '"Civilians Entrenched": The British Home Front and Attitudes to the First World War, 1914–1918' in Ian Stewart and Susan Carruthers, eds, *War, Culture and the Media*, (Trowbridge, 1996), p. 38. See also Robert Wohl, *The Generation of 1914* (London, 1980), pp. 85–121.

9   The meaning and significance of war memorials is explored in Alan Borg, *War Memorials from Antiquity to the Present* (London, 1991); Catherine Moriarty, 'Christian Iconography and First World War Memorials', *Imperial War Museum Review*, 6 (1991), pp. 63–75; Jay Winter, *Sites of Memory, Sites of Mourning* (Cambridge, 1995), pp. 78–116; Joanna Bourke, *Dismembering the Male: Men's Bodies, Britain and the Great War*, (London, 1996), pp. 227–9.

10 Catherine Moriarty, 'Private Grief and Public Remembrance: British First World War Memorials', in Martin Evans and Ken Lunn, eds, *War and Memory in the Twentieth Century* (Oxford, 1997), p. 128.

11 Gerard J. DeGroot, *Blighty: British Society in the Era of the Great War* (London, 1996), p. 286.

12 Omer Bartov, *Murder in Our Midst: The Holocaust, Industrial Killing, and Representation* (Oxford, 1996), pp. 154–5.

13 Details from books in the author's collection.

14 Aldine Library Catalogue, *c.* 1934.

15 See Bill Bradford, 'George Ernest Rochester, 1898–1966', *Biggles and Co.*, 29 (Winter 1996), pp. 33–5.

16 See Hynes, *A War Imagined*, pp. 47–9; Ian Hay, *The First Hundred Thousand* (London, 1915 and subsequent edns); and Ralph Connor, *The Sky Pilot of No Man's Land* (London, 1921).

17 Drotner, *English Children and the Magazines*, p. 184; Jeffrey Richards, 'Cinemagoing in Worktown: Regional Film Audiences in 1930s Britain', *Historical Journal of Film, Radio and Television*, 14: 2 (1994), pp. 147–66. On the history of children's cinema, see Terry Staples, *All Pals Together: The Story of Children's Cinema* (Edinburgh, 1997).

18 Robert Roberts, *The Classic Slum* (Manchester, 1971), p. 175.

19 Charles Gilson, *Chances and Mischances: An Autobiography* (London, 1932), p. 26.

20 See Dennis Gifford, *The International Book of Comics* (London, 1984), pp. 62–4.

21 The films were *Mons* (1922); *The Battle of Jutland* and *Armageddon* (1923); *Zeebrugge* (1924); *Ypres* (1925); *Mons* (1926); *The Battle of the Coronel and Falklands* (1927); *The Somme* (1927); *Q Ships* (1928) and *Blockade* (1932), a re-edited version of *Q Ships* with soundtrack added.

22 Hynes, *A War Imagined*, pp. 443–4.

23 See 'The Man Who Made Mons', *Picturegoer* 13: 73 (January 1927), p. 31.

24 Hynes, *A War Imagined*, pp. 446–7.

25 See Michael Paris, 'Enduring Heroes: British Feature Films and the First World War',

in Paris, *The First World War and Popular Cinema* (Edinburgh, 1999), pp. 51–73.

26 Winifred Whitehead, *Old Lies Revisited: Young Readers and the Literature of War and Violence* (London, 1991), pp. 49–51. The novel was *Der Schadell des Negerhauptlings Makua* by Rudolf Frank (Potsdam, 1931), published in English as *No Hero for the Kaiser* (London, 1986). In her recent PhD thesis, Rosa Maria Bracco has also argued that the Fussell/Hynes analysis of post-war literature ignores popular fiction that continued to stress meaningfulness, courage and worthwhile self-sacrifice. See Daniel Pick, *War Machine: The Rationalisation of Slaughter in the Modern Age* (London, 1993), p. 201, n. 41.

27 T. P. Cameron Wilson to Mrs Orpen, 3 May 1916, in John Laffin, *Letters from the Front, 1914–1918* (London, 1973), p. 8.

28 Graves and Hodge, *The Long Weekend*, pp. 215, 269.

29 Figures from John Springhall, *Youth, Empire and Society: British Youth Movements, 1883–1940* (London, 1977), pp. 138–9, 78–9. On the Scouts as an agency for international peace, see *Boy's Own Paper*, 52 (1929–30), p. 101.

30 Graves and Hodge, *The Long Weekend*, pp. 320–30; Taylor, *English History*, pp. 361–2, 379–80.

31 On modern versus traditional explanations of the war, see Winter, *Sites of Memory, Sites of Mourning*, pp. 1–11.

32 *Boy's Own Paper*, 52 (1929–30), p. 101.

33 *Ibid.*, p. 73.

34 *Chums* (1933–4), p. 243.

35 See for example, *Chums* (1936–7), pp. 94, 225, 243.

36 Jim Wolveridge, *Ain't It Grand (This Was Stepney)*, (London, 1976), pp. 15, 19–20, 27, 32.

37 Quigly, 'A Catholic Reader of the Thirties', p. 7.

38 Samuel Hynes, *The Auden Generation: Literature and Politics in England in the 1930s* (London, 1976), p. 22. For attitudes of young intellectuals to the war see pp. 19–21.

39 Bartov, *Murder in Our Midst*, p. 21.

40 *Ibid.*, p. 26.

41 Cecil Lewis, *Sagittarius Rising* (London, 1936), p. 134.

42 *Ibid.*, pp. 54–5.

43 The RAFs battle for survival and the development of imperial policing are dealt with in David E. Omissi, *Air Power and Colonial Control, The Royal Air Force, 1919–1939*, (Manchester, 1990). On the doctrine of air power as a deterrent to war, see Richard Overy, 'Air Power and the Origins of Deterrence Theory Before 1939', *Journal of Strategic Studies*, 15: 1 (March 1992), pp. 73–101.

44 See David E. Omissi, 'The Hendon Air Pageant 1920–1937' in John M. Mackenzie, ed., *Popular Imperialism and the Military 1850–1950* (Manchester, 1992), pp. 198–220.

45 Air stories for girls are covered in Kirsten Drotner, 'Schoolgirls, Madcaps, and Air Aces: English Girls and Their Magazine Reading Between the Wars', *Feminist Studies*, 9: 1 (Spring 1983), pp. 33–52.

46 Aviation films are dealt with in Michael Paris, *From the Wright Brothers to 'Top Gun':*

Aviation, Nationalism and Popular Cinema (Manchester, 1995). On anti-war films, see the interesting comments by Bartov, *Murder in Our Midst*, pp. 8, 157–61.

47 See Bill Bradford, 'Pulped to Death', *Biggles Flies Again*, 2 (Winter 1997), pp. 20–22. See also Dominick Pisano, Thomas Dietz, Joanne Gernstein and Karl Schneide eds, *Legend, Memory and the Great War in the Air* (Washington, 1992).

48 Dennis Butts, 'Imperialists of the Air – Flying Stories 1900–1950', in Jeffrey Richards, ed., *Imperialism and Juvenile Literature* (Manchester, 1989), p. 131.

49 Red Fox have reissued a number of Biggles titles including the Great War stories, *The Camels Are Coming, Biggles in France, The Rescue Flight* and *Biggles Flies East*.

50 Biggles's adventures as a war flier are dealt with in the above titles. As knight-errant, see, for example, *Biggles Flies North*. In *The Black Peril* and *Biggles – Air Commodore* he acts as an unofficial agent of the government, and in *Biggles Goes to War* he acts as a mercenary for a small European state threatened by a more powerful neighbour.

51 Geoffrey Trease, *Tales Out of School* (London, 1948), pp. 94–5.

52 See Peter Berrisford Ellis and Piers Williams, *By Jove, Biggles! The Life of Captain W. E. Johns* (London, 1981).

53 Editorial, *Popular Flying. Ibid.*, p. 147.

54 See Ellis and Williams, *By Jove, Biggles!*, pp. 170–71.

55 Butts, 'Imperialists of the Air', p. 133.

56 John James, *The Paladins* (London, 1990), p. 211.

57 *Marvel* and *Boy's Friend* were dropped in 1922; *Pluck* in 1924 and *Boy's Realm* in 1924. On D. C. Thomson, see Kevin Carpenter, *Penny Dreadfuls and Comics* (London, 1983), pp. 63–4; Drotner, *English Children and Their Magazines*, pp. 187–91.

58 Wolveridge, *Ain't It Grand*, p. 29.

59 Drotner, *English Children and Their Magazines*, pp. 189–90; circulation figures from Carpenter, *Penny Dreadfuls and Comics*, p. 65.

60 Gifford, *International Book of Comics*, p. 66.

61 Carpenter, *Penny Dreadfuls and Comics*, p. 89.

62 Gifford, *International Book of Comics*, p. 7; see also Ron Goulart, *Over 50 Years of American Comic Books* (Lincolnwood, IL, 1991). The most detailed analysis of the emergence of 'Superheroes' is William H. Young, 'The Serious Funnies: Adventure Comics During the Depression, 1929–1938', *Journal of Popular Culture*, 3:3 (1969), pp. 404–27. See also William Savage, *Comic Books and America* (Oklahoma City, 1990).

63 Drotner, *English Children and Their Magazines*, p. 228.

64 Kelly Boyd, 'Knowing Your Place: The Tensions of Manliness in Boys' Story Papers, 1918–1939', in Michael Roper and John Tosh, eds, *Manful Assertions: Masculinities in Britain since 1800* (London, 1991), p. 146.

65 George Orwell, 'Boys' Weeklies', *Collected Essays, Journalism and Letters*, (Harmondsworth, 1970), p. 193.

66 Wolveridge, *Ain't It Grand*, p. 31.

67 Graves and Hodge, *The Long Weekend*, p. 15.

68 *Ibid.*, p. 16.

69 For a useful discussion of the topic see Jeffrey Richards, *Visions of Yesterday* (London, 1973), pp. 28–43.

70 Drotner, *English Children and Their Magazines*, pp. 228–30.

71 E. S. Turner, *Boys Will Be Boys* (London, 1948), p. 223.

72 See Paul Harris, ed., *The D. C. Thomson Bumper Fun Book* (Edinburgh, 1977).

73 Their popularity owes much to the fact that they brought to the fore the essential rebelliousness of working-class children which had previously been played down in popular culture. As Stephen Humphries has argued, 'larking about' was a product of the clash between independent working-class traditions and the attempt to control and discipline these through a popular culture dominated by the middle class. See Stephen Humphries, *Hooligans or Rebels? An Oral History of Working-Class Childhood and Youth, 1889–1939* (Oxford, 1981), pp. 121–49.

74 Orwell, 'Boys' Weeklies', pp. 189–90.

75 See John Mackenzie, *Propaganda and Empire* (Manchester, 1984); and Stephen Constantine, '"Bringing the Empire Alive": The Empire Marketing Board and Imperial Propaganda', pp. 192–231; John M. Mackenzie, '"In touch with the Infinite": The BBC and the Empire, 1923–1953', pp. 165–91; both in John Mackenzie, ed., *Imperialism and Popular Culture* (Manchester, 1986).

76 See for example, J. K. Carrington, 'Ju Ju and Justice', *Chums* (1929–30), pp. 426–8.

77 Walter Bury, 'Outlaws of the Hills', *Chums* (1936–7), pp. 197–8.

78 Robert Harding, 'Belbin of the Police', *Chums* (1932–3), p. 455.

79 Jeffrey Richards, *Visions of Yesterday* (London, 1973), p. 123.

80 Leslie Halliwell, *Seats in All Parts: Half a Lifetime at the Movies* (London, 1985), p. 21.

81 Jeffrey Richards, *The Age of the Dream Palace: Cinema and Society in Britain, 1930–1939* (London, 1984), p. 139.

82 See Richards, *Visions of Yesterday*, and George MacDonald Fraser, *The Hollywood History of the World* (London, 1988), pp. 137–65.

83 'Lawrence of Arabia', *Chums* (1936–7), pp. 105–6.

84 The serial ran through 1932 in *Chums*.

85 W. E. Johns, *Biggles Flies East* (London, 1935). Biggles and von Stalhein crossed swords on many occasions until they were finally reconciled in *Biggles Buries a Hatchet* (1958). In many of the later novels they work together to fight Communists.

86 Alan Western, *Desert Hawk* (London, 1937), p. 13.

87 *Ibid.*, pp. 287–8.

88 Stuart Campbell, 'Hawks of the Desert'; Cecil Gordon, 'The Eagle of Peace'; both in *Thrilling Air Stories* (London, 1939), n. p.

89 Robert Harding, 'The Amateur Agent', *Chums* (1932–3), p. 140.

90 See Omissi, *Air Power and Colonial Control*, p. 154.

91 Robert Harding, 'The River Patrol', *Chums* (1930–31), pp. 277–80.

92 Rex Hardinge, 'White Man's Magic', Chums (1933–4), p. 207.

93 Rex Hardinge, 'Nkubwa the Terrible', Chums (1933–4).

94 See for example Nigel Lee, 'The Adventures of Midshipman Ratters', *Thrilling Air Stories*, n. p., or the Percy Westerman serial, 'The Gate of Kwei-Nan', *Chums* (1933–4).

Charles Gilson seems to have specialized in stories of the wicked Oriental for both *BOP* and *Chums*.

95 See *Chums* (1932–3).

96 Percy F. Westerman, *Under Fire in Spain* (London, 1937). Eric Wood, *Phantom Wings Over Spain* (London, 1938).

97 W. E. Johns, *Biggles in Spain* (London, 1940), p. 83.

98 Raphael Samuel, ed., *Patriotism: The Making and Unmaking of British National Identity*, 1 (London, 1989), p. xxii.

99 Orwell, 'Boys' Weeklies', p. 196.

100 Wolveridge, *Ain't It Grand*, p. 30.

101 I. F. Clarke, *Voices Prophesying War: Future Wars, 1763–3749* (Oxford, 2nd edn, 1992), p. 142.

102 *Chums* (1933–4), p. 726. The same volume carried a picture article (p. 743), 'Contrasts in Revolution', which showed illustrations of the Reichstag fire, '. . . believed to be the work of communists', and another of the war in Spain, 'Nothing is sacred when the red flag of revolution is hoisted', and compares these frightening images with a picture of a rural English village and the caption, 'Nothing disturbs the calm of the British countryside'.

103 Editorial, *Boy's Own Paper*, 52 (1929), p. 536.

104 Sheikh Ahmed Abdullah, 'In Red Turkestan', *Chums* (1932–3).

105 George Rochester, 'Captain Robin Hood – Skywayman', *Chums* (1932–3), p. 712.

106 'Vigilant', *Fighting the Red Shadow* (London, n. d. but *c.* 1934); Jack Heming, *The Air Spies* (London, 1936); J. Railton Holden, *Wings of Revolution* (London, 1934). See also Butts, 'Imperialists of the Air', pp. 139–41.

107 Captain Frank Shaw, 'The Red Deluge', *Chums* (1922), p. 78.

108 W. E. Johns, *Biggles and the Black Peril* (London, 1935), p. 181. The story was originally serialized in *Modern Boy* during 1932, under the more appropriate title of 'Winged Menace'.

109 W. E. Johns, 'Three Weeks', *Popular Flying* (April 1934).

110 *Popular Flying* (January 1937).

111 *Ibid.* (May 1936).

112 Percy Westerman, 'The Red Pirate', *Chums* (1933–4), p. 25.

113 Percy Westerman, *The Terror of the Seas* (London, 1927).

114 I am indebted to Brian Shelmerdine for this information.

115 Quigly, 'A Catholic Reader of the Thirties', p. 9.

116 Richards, *Age of the Dream Palace*, p. 287.

117 Clarke, *Voices Prophesying War*, p. 136.

118 Michael Poole, 'Emperor of the World', *Boy's Magazine* (1925); see Turner, *Boys Will Be Boys*, pp. 185–6.

119 Brian Cameron, 'The Raiding Planet', *Boy's Magazine* (1924); see Turner, *Boys Will Be Boys*, pp. 186–90.

120 John Sylvester, 'Planet At War', *Chums* (1930–31), p. 65.

121 The Flash Gordon serials were *Flash Gordon* (1936), *Flash Gordon's Trip to Mars*

(1938) and *Flash Gordon Conquers the Universe* (1940).

122 Drotner, *English Children and Their Magazines*, p. 231.

123 W. E. Johns, *Biggles – Air Commodore* (London, 1937), p. 22.

124 The serial ran in *Champion* during 1922. See Turner, *Boys Will Be Boys*, pp. 182–4.

125 See Drotner, *English Children and Their Magazines*, p. 231.

126 W. E. Johns, *Biggles Goes to War* (London, 1938).

127 See K. R. M. Short, *Screening the Propaganda of British Air Power* (Trowbridge, 1997). Fear of aerial attack was undoubtedly a major influence on the government's policy of appeasement. See Uri Bialer, *The Shadow of the Bomber: The Fear of Air Attack and British Politics, 1932–1939* (London, 1980).

128 Halliwell, *Seats in All Parts*, p. 128.

129 See Short, *Screening the Propaganda of Air Power*.

130 Orwell, 'Boys' Weeklies', p. 189.

131 Gary Sheffield, 'The Shadow of the Somme: The Influence of the First World War on British Soldiers' Perceptions and Behaviour in the Second World War', in Paul Addison and Angus Calder, *Time to Kill: The Soldier's Experience of War in the West, 1939–1945* (London, 1997), p. 31. See also Hew Strachan, 'The Soldier's Experience in Two World Wars: Some Historiographical Comparisons', in the same volume, pp. 369–70.

6 Fighting the People's War: 1939–45

1 Jim Wolveridge, *Ain't It Grand (This Was Stepney)*, (London, 1976), p. 70.

2 Angus Calder, *The People's War: Britain, 1939–1945* (London, 1969), p. 35.

3 See Michael Balfour, *Propaganda in War* (London, 1979), and K. R. M. Short, *Screening the Propaganda of British Air Power* (Trowbridge, 1997). The most recent study of wartime film propaganda is James Chapman, *The British at War: Cinema, State and Propaganda, 1939–1945*, (London, 1998).

4 Percy F. Westerman, *Eagles' Talons* (London, 1940), p. 317.

5 Peter Berrisford Ellis and Piers Williams, *By Jove, Biggles! The Life of Captain W. E. Johns* (London, 1981), pp. 177–8.

6 W. E. Johns, *Biggles in the Baltic* (London, 1940), p. 13. The story was first published in serial form in the magazine *War Thriller* from 9 March 1940 and in book form later that year.

7 Short, *Screening the Propaganda of British Air Power*.

8 W. E. Johns, *Biggles Sees it Through* (London, 1941), p. 8.

9 One of the curiosities of the Winter War was that Germany, despite having a non-aggression pact with Russia, was also aiding the Finns in their struggle against the Soviets.

10 W. E. Johns, *Biggles Sees it Through*, p. 184.

11 Winston Churchill gave the speech to the House of Commons on the 18 June 1940. A revised version was broadcast the following day. The extract here is from the

broadcast version. See Angus Calder, *The Myth of the Blitz* (London, 1991), pp. 29–30.

12 See Clive Ponting, *1940: Myth and Reality* (London, 1990), pp. 147–9. See also Ruth Inglis, *The Children's War: Evacuation, 1939–1945* (London, 1989), and Ben Wicks, *No Time to Wave Goodbye* (London, 1988).

13 Mass-Observation File, 87 (30 April 1940), p. 2.

14 Norman Longmate, *How We Lived Then: A History of Daily Life During the Second World War* (London, 1971), p. 191.

15 *Ibid.*, p. 191. The evacuation experience became the focus for a number of children's books. Among the more interesting early titles were Kitty Barnes's *Visitors from London* (London, 1940) and Malcolm Saville's *Mystery at Witchend* (London, 1942). In P. L.Travers's *I Go By Sea, I Go By Land* (London, 1941), the central characters are evacuated to the United States.

16 Longmate, *How We Lived Then*, p. 200.

17 Calder, *The People's War*, p. 225.

18 Mass-Observation File 87, p. 3.

19 Bernard Kops, *The World is a Wedding* (London, 1963) pp. 61, 68.

20 Longmate, *How We Lived Then*, pp. 201–5.

21 See Anthony Aldgate and Jeffrey Richards, *Britain Can Take It: British Cinema in the Second World War* (Edinburgh, 1994), pp. 115–37.

22 Details from Ellis and Williams, *By Jove Biggles!*, pp. 180–81.

23 Kirsten Drotner, *English Children and Their Magazines, 1751–1945* (New Haven, 1988), p. 232.

24 *Ibid.*, p. 234; see also Dennis Gifford, *Comics at War* (London, 1988).

25 See Colin Morgan, 'The Day War Broke Out', *Story Paper Collector's Digest* (June, 1998), p. 618.

26 'Bamboo Town', *Dandy* (September–October 1940).

27 *Knock-Out* (4 June 1940).

28 *Beano* (August 1942).

29 See Drotner, *English Children and Their Magazines*, pp. 232–3.

30 C. M. Stern, 'Bloods', *The Library Assistant*, 34 (1941), pp. 161–2.

31 Mass-Observation File 87, p. 1.

32 Aldgate and Richards, *Britain Can Take It*, p. 86.

33 *Ibid.*, p. 87.

34 Aldgate and Richards, *Britain Can Take It*, pp. 44–75.

35 *Ibid.*, p. 93.

36 Percy F. Westerman, *Fighting For Freedom* (London, 1941), p. 135. *Chums* (1941). equally appealed to the lessons of the past in its story, 'Wheels of the Great Retreat', by Peter Tewson, a tale of the retreat of the British Expeditionary Force after the Battle of Mons in 1914.

37 Westerman, *Fighting for Freedom*, pp. 131, 138.

38 *Ibid.*, pp. 168–9.

39 'The Last Bridge', *The Young Airman's Annual* (London, *c.* 1942), p. 20.

40 Guy Dempster, *Winged Venturers* (London, 1942), pp. 19–20.

41 On American war films see Thomas Docherty, *Projections of War: Hollywood, American Culture and World War II* (New York, 1993). Jeanine Basinger, *The World War II Combat Movie: Anatomy of a Genre* (New York, 1986).

42 Calder, *The Myth of the Blitz*, pp. 16–19.

43 See Richard Overy, *Why the Allies Won* (London, 1995), p. 108.

44 Dilys Powell, *Films Since 1939* (London, 1947), p. 17.

45 Percy F. Westerman, *Combined Operations* (London, 1944), pp. 18–19.

46 Bryan Forbes, *Notes For a Life* (London, 1974), p. 76.

47 Ellis and Williams, *By Jove, Biggles!*, p. 190.

48 I am grateful to Jeffrey Richards for pointing this out.

49 Publicity material, see Ellis and Williams, *By Jove, Biggles!*, p. 191.

50 W. E. Johns, *King of the Commandos* (London, 1943), p. 39.

51 Ellis and Williams, *By Jove, Biggles!*, p. 191.

52 Anthony Aldgate and Jeffrey Richards, *The Best of British: Cinema and Society from 1930 to the Present*, new edn (London, 1999), pp. 79–93. See also Chapman, *The British at War*, pp. 192–4.

53 N. E. Johns, *Spitfire Parade* (London, 1941), p. 13.

54 D. Heming, 'Bill Butler – Sergeant Pilot', *Young Airman's Annual*, p. 114.

55 Johns, *Spitfire Parade*, pp. 13, 18.

56 On comic strip girls see Gifford, *Comics at War*, pp. 112–17.

57 Dorita Fairlie Bruce, *Toby of Tibbs Cross* (London, 1943). On girls' fiction see Mary Cadogan and Patricia Craig, *Women and Children First: The Fiction of Two World Wars* (London, 1978), pp. 212–37.

58 *Girl's Own Paper* (October 1940), in Mary Cadogan, *Women With Wings* (London, 1992), p. 160.

59 Ellis and Williams, *By Jove, Biggles!*, p. 187.

60 See his editorial in *Popular Flying* (June 1934).

61 W. E. Johns, *Worrals of the WAAF* (London, 1941), p. 11.

62 W. E. Johns, *Worrals of the Islands* (London, 1945), pp. 19–20.

63 Johns, *Worrals of the WAAF*, pp. 29–30.

64 Johns, *Worrals of the Islands*, p. 169.

65 See Cadogan, *Women With Wings*, pp. 130–35.

66 See Bruce Myles, *The Night Witches* (London, 1981); and Reina Pennington, 'Offensive Women: Women in Combat in the Red Army', in Paul Addison and Angus Calder, eds, *Time to Kill: The Soldier's Experience of War in the West, 1939–1945* (London, 1997).

67 Cadogan, *Women with Wings*, p. 195.

68 Dorothy Carter, *Maisie Flies South* (London, 1944).

69 For examples of pro-Soviet propaganda see the feature films *Demi-Paradise* (1943) and *Tawny Pipit* (1944). The latter, although a celebration of 'Englishness', has one scene where a renowned Soviet woman sniper visits the village to consolidate Anglo–Soviet relations.

70 Charles Gilson, 'Jean Loubert: The Story of a Free-French Airman', *Young Airman's Annual*, p. 76.

71 On the GI 'invasion' of Britain see Julia Gardiner, *Over Here: The GIs in Wartime Britain* (London, 1992).

72 For a useful survey of American war comics see Ron Goulart, *Over 50 Years of American Comic Books* (Lincolnwood, IL, 1991). British comics are dealt with in Gifford, *Comics at War*.

73 Goulart, *Over 50 Years of American Comic Books*, p. 117.

74 *Ibid.*, p. 129.

75 Ron Goulart, *Encyclopedia of American Comic Books* (New York, 1990), p. 36.

76 Goulart, *Over 50 Years of American Comic Books*, p. 114. See also William Savage, *Comic Books and America, 1945–1954* (Oklahoma, 1990).

77 Goulart, *Over 50 Years of American Comic Books*, pp. 129–30.

78 See Ian Jarvie, 'The Burma Campaign on Film: "Objective Burma" (1945), "The Stillwell Road" (1945) and "Burma Victory" (1945)', *Historical Journal of Film, Radio and Television*, 8:1 (1988), pp. 55–73.

79 The Dave Dawson novels were *Dave Dawson at Dunkirk, Dave Dawson with the RAF* (both 1942); *Dave Dawson, Flight Lieutenant, Dave Dawson in Libya, Dave Dawson on Convoy Patrol* (all 1943); *Dave Dawson With the Air Corps* and *Dave Dawson with the Pacific Fleet* (both 1944).

80 Mass-Observation File 1910 (20 May 1943), p. 2.

81 W. E. Johns, *Biggles in Borneo* (London, 1943), p. 49. Biggles also fought the Japanese in two other novels, *Biggles In the Orient* (London, 1945) and *Biggles Delivers the Goods* (London, 1946).

82 See for example, Westerman, *Combined Operations, passim.*

83 On desert victory and Tunisian victory, see Anthony Aldgate, 'Creative Tensions: Desert Victory, The Army Film Unit and Anglo–American Rivalry, 1943–5' in Philip Taylor, ed., *Britain and the Cinema in the Second World War* (London, 1988), pp. 144–67; and Michael Paris, 'Filming the People's War', in Alan Burton and Tim O'Sullivan, eds, *The Family Way: The Boulting Brothers and British Film Culture* (Trowbridge, forthcoming).

84 Gamages Catalogue, 1938, p. 6.

85 Mass-Observation File 17 (January 1940).

86 Longmate, *How We Lived Then*, p. 187. See also pp. 188–90.

87 Mass-Observation File 1910, p. 4.

88 *Ibid.*

7 After the Wars: 1940s–1990s

1 John Springhall, *Youth, Popular Culture and Moral Panics* (London, 1999), p. 1.

2 Brian Edwards, 'The Popularisation of War in Comic Strips, 1958–1988', *History Workshop Journal*, 42 (1996), p. 182.

3 Biggles's last war adventure was *Biggles Delivers the Goods* (London, 1946). The first air police novel was *Sergeant Bigglesworth CID* (London, 1947).

4 Edwards, 'The Popularisation of War', p. 183.

5 Paul Addison, *Now the War is Over: A Social History of Britain, 1945–1951* (London, 1995), p. 54.

6 On the fiction of this war, see Holger Klein, *The Second World War in Fiction* (London, 1984) and Michael Paris, *The Novels of World War Two* (London, 1989).

7 John Ramsden, 'Refocusing "The People's War": British War Films of the 1950s', *Journal of Contemporary History*, 33: 1 (1998), p. 39.

8 *Ibid.*, p. 45. See also Nicholas Pronay, 'The British Post-Bellum Cinema: A Survey of the Films Relating to World War II Made in Britain Between 1945 and 1960', *Historical Journal of Film, Radio and Television*, 8: 1 (1988), pp. 39–54; James Chapman, 'Our Finest Hour Revisited: The Second World War in British Feature Films Since 1945', *Journal of Popular British Cinema*, 1 (1998), pp. 63–75.

9 Chapman, 'Our Finest Hour Revisited', p. 65.

10 Philip Corrigan, 'Film Entertainment as Ideology and Pleasure: Towards a History of Audiences', in James Curran and Vincent Porter, *British Cinema History* (London, 1983), p. 33.

11 Chapman, 'Our Finest Hour Revisited', p. 67.

12 Oral testimony collected by the author; Ramsden, 'Refocusing the People's War', p. 53.

13 On American war films see Jeanine Basinger, *The World War II Combat Movie: Anatomy of a Genre* (New York, 1986).

14 Ramsden, 'Refocusing the People's War', p. 56.

15 See particularly Angela Thirkell, *Peace Breaks Out*, *Private Enterprise* and *Love Among the Ruins* (London, 1945, 1947, 1948).

16 During the 1950s, Bogarde dominated the British box-office and starred in a number of popular war adventures. Yet his casting as the archetypal warrior hero reveals something of the sham of the pleasure culture of war, for besides his own sexual ambiguity, the actor despised such roles and longed to make more substantial films. See Andy Medhurst, 'Dirk Bogarde', in Charles Barr, ed., *All Our Yesterdays: 90 Years of British Cinema* (London, 1986), pp. 346–54, and Dirk Bogarde, *Snakes and Ladders* (London, 1978), *passim.*

17 Kevin Carpenter, *Penny Dreadfuls and Comics* (London, 1983), pp. 93–4.

18 Kirsten Drotner, *English Children and Their Magazines, 1751–1945* (New Haven, 1988, p. 243.

19 Edwards, 'The Popularisation of War', p. 183.

20 Drotner, *English Children and Their Magazines*, p. 245.

21 Carpenter, *Penny Dreadfuls and Comics*, p. 117.

22 'Ticker Turner', *The Victor*, 44 (23 December 1961).

23 'Sergeant Without Stripes', *Battle Picture Weekly Annual* (London, 1980), pp. 16–19.

24 'Union Jack Jackson', *Warlord Book for Boys* (London, 1981), p. 72.

25 See Colin Morgan, 'Braddock: Master of the Air', *Golden Fun*, 13 (Spring, 1983), pp. 1–12; Des O'Leary, 'Matt Braddock: The Working-Class Biggles', *Biggles Flies Again*, 4 (January 1999), pp. 21–5.

26 Owen Dudley Edwards, 'Boy's Comics' in Paul Harris, ed., *The D. C. Thomson Bumper Fun Book* (Edinburgh, 1977), p. 78.

27 The Braddock novels were *The Bombs Go Down* and *Braddock and the Flying Tigers* (both 1959).

28 'Carrier Ace', *Commando*, 3141 (1998).

29 Edwards, 'The Popularisation of War', p. 183.

30 James Opie, *The Great Book of Britains* (London, 1993), p. 511.

31 Mass-Observation File 1910, (1943), pp. 1–2.

32 Springhall, *Youth, Popular Culture and Moral Panics*, pp. 121–46.

33 David Reynolds, *Britannia Overruled: British Policy and World Power in the Twentieth Century* (London, 1991), pp. 185–92.

34 Chapman, 'Our Finest Hour Revisited', p. 71.

35 *The Okay Adventure Annual* (London, n.d. but *c.* 1954).

36 Interestingly, Corelli Barnett has suggested that it was largely the inefficiencies of wartime economic performance and the subsequent creation of the welfare state, a package the nation could ill-afford, that were responsible for national decline. See *The Collapse of British Power* (London, 1972) and *The Audit of War* (London, 1986).

37 British Paramount News, (August 1945); see also Erick Barnouw, 'The Hiroshima-Nagasaki Footage: A Report', *Historical Journal of Film, Radio and Television*, 2 (March 1982), pp. 91–100.

38 John Hersey, *Hiroshima* (London, 1946). Hersey's Hiroshima report first appeared in the *New Yorker* earlier that year.

39 Raymond Durgnat, *A Mirror for England* (London, 1970), p. 83

40 Jeffrey L. Porter, 'Narrating the End: Fables of Survival in the Nuclear Age', *Journal of American Culture*, 16: 4 (Winter 1993), p. 41.

41 *Ibid.*, p. 41–4.

42 John Wyndham, *The Chrysalids* (London, 1955), p. 196.

43 See Winifred Whitehead, *Old Lies Revisited: Young Readers and the Literature of War and Violence* (London, 1991), pp. 174–5.

44 See I. F. Clarke, *Voices Prophesying War: Future Wars, 1763–3749* (Oxford, 2nd edn, 1992), pp. 204–7.

45 See David Seed, *American Science Fiction and the Cold War: Literature and Film* (Edinburgh, 1999), pp. 145–56.

46 Strategic Air Command was the nuclear attack force which was maintained in a state of constant readiness to retaliate to a Soviet attack. Its ability to make a split-second retaliatory blow was highly publicized as a warning to the USSR.

47 See Frank Cunningham, *Fail Safe* (Trowbridge, 1999)

48 Seed, *American Science-Fiction*, pp. 119–31.

49 Michael Paris, *From the Wright Brothers to 'Top Gun': Aviation, Nationalism and Popular Cinema* (Manchester, 1995), pp. 184–7.

50 See for example, W. E. Johns, *Biggles Follows On: A Story of the Cold War in Europe and Asia* (London, 1952) or *Biggles Looks Back* (London, 1963).

51 'The Yellow Sword', *Wizard* (1955–6). See also 'Britain Invaded', *Adventure* (1952) and 'Secret Weapon W1', *Wizard* (1956). I am grateful to Colin Morgan for providing me with copies of these stories.

52 W. E. Johns, *Gimlet Bores In*, in Ellis and Williams, *By Jove, Biggles!*, pp. 219–20.

53 Paul Eddy, Magnus Linklater and Peter Gillman, *The Falklands War* (London, 1982), pp. 97–102. See also Max Hastings, *Battle for the Falklands* (London, 1982).

54 Reynolds, *Britannia Overruled*, p. 261.

55 Eddy, *The Falklands War*, p. 243.

56 Martin Shaw, 'Past Wars and Present Conflicts: From the Second World War to the Gulf', in Martin Evans and Ken Lunn, *War and Memory in the Twentieth Century* (Oxford, 1997), p. 191.

57 Graham Dawson, *Soldier Heroes: British Adventure, Empire and the Imagining of Masculinity* (London, 1994), p. 2.

58 Brian Hanrahan and Robert Fox, *I Counted Them All Out and I Counted Them All Back*, (London, 1982), p. 40.

59 *Ibid.*, pp. 44–5.

60 Nigel Leigh, 'A Limited Engagement: Falklands Fictions and the English Novel', in James Aulich, ed., *Framing the Falklands: Nationhood, Culture and Identity* (Milton Keynes, 1992), p. 119, to which the following section is indebted.

61 See for example the excellent 'Reporting the Falklands', Flashback Television for Channel 4 (first transmitted 1983).

62 Whitehead, *Old Lies Revisited*, pp. 224–7.

63 *Ibid.*, p. 231.

64 Dawson, *Soldier Heroes*, p. 2; Geoff Hurd, 'Introduction', in Hurd, *National Fictions: World War Two in British Films and Television* (London, 1984), p. iv.

65 Philip M. Taylor, *War and the Media: Propaganda and Persuasion in the Gulf War* (Manchester, 1992); and David E. Morrison, *Television and the Gulf War* (London, 1992).

66 Leslie Halliwell, *Halliwell's Film Guide*, 6th edn (1988), p. 1138.

67 Andy McNab, *Bravo Two Zero* (London, 1993) and Chris Ryan, *The One That Got Away* (London, 1995) both deal with the same ill-fated mission and have been both televised. They are available on videotape.

68 Jonathan Bignell, 'The Meanings of War-Toys and Games', in Ian Stewart and Susan Carruthers, eds, *War, Culture and the Media*, (Trowbridge, 1996), pp. 177–8.

69 Jeffrey Walsh, 'Remembering Desert Storm: Popular Culture and the Gulf War', in Evans and Lunn, *War and Memory*, p. 205.

70 Robert Westall, *Gulf* (London, 1992), p. 83.

71 Warhammer Catalogue, 1999.

72 Mention might also be made of women gunfighters (*The Quick and the Dead*, *Bad Girls*); Sword and Sorcery heroines (*Red Sonja*, and the current television series *Xena: Warrior Princess*) and highly-trained government assassins (*Nikita*, *Assassin*).

73 Omer Bartov, *Murder in Our Midst: The Holocaust, Industrial Killing, and Representation* (Oxford, 1996), p. 157.

74 Eleanor Coerr, *Sadako and the Thousand Paper Cranes* (London, 1981); see also Whitehead, *Old Lies Revisited*, pp. 129–30.

75 Maruki Toshi, *The Hiroshima Story* (London, 1983), Christobel Mattingley, *The Miracle Tree* (London, 1985).

76 Peter Biskind, *Seeing is Believing* (New York, 1983), pp. 145–59.

77 Nevil Shute, *On the Beach* (London, 1957, released in 1959).

78 Raymond Briggs, *When the Wind Blows* (London, 1982). An animated film version was released in 1986.

79 Jill Paton Walsh, *Fireweed* (London, 1969); Susan Cooper, *The Dawn of Fear* (1972) (London, 1974). See also Whitehead, *Old Lies Revisited*, pp. 92–4.

80 Michelle Magorian, *Goodnight Mr Tom* (London, 1983). The television adaptation was first screened in 1999.

81 *Report of the Departmental Committee on Children and the Cinema*, cmd 7945, May 1950, p. 45.

82 See for example H. J. Eysenck and D. K. B. Nias, *Sex, Violence and the Media* (London, 1978). Recently the outgoing chief film censor, James Ferman, claimed that excessively violent films have generated a 'violence is cool' attitude among young cinema-goers, for whom violence has little meaning. Curiously, Ferman drew a distinction between films such as *Mortal Kombat II*, which exploits violence, and *Saving Private Ryan*, which explores it. One wonders if young filmgoers can see this distinction?

83 Geoffrey Trease, *Tales Out of School* (London, 1948), p. 102–4.

84 *Twentieth Century Sins*, Granada Television, 10 October 1999.

85 Martin Kenright interviewed in *ibid.*

86 Martin Bell interviewed in *ibid.*

87 John Heeley, 'Boys' Comics: Violence Rules', *Sunday Times*, 27 February 1983.

88 James Aulich, 'Wildlife in the South Atlantic: Graphic Satire, Patriotism and the Fourth Estate', in Aulich, *Framing the Falklands*, p. 91. See also pp. 92–5.

89 Joanna Bourke, 'When Johnny Got His Gun . . . He Loved Killing', *Times Higher Education Supplement*, 16 October 1998. See also Bourke, *An Intimate History of Killing: Face to Face Killing in Twentieth Century Warfare* (London, 1999).

90 John Keegan, 'War', BBC Reith Lectures, 1998.

Acknowledgements

It would have been impossible to have written this book without reference to the painstaking research of so many colleagues in the historical profession who have, so to speak, prepared the way for the present study. While my debt to them has been acknowledged in the references, this hardly does justice to the pleasure and enlightenment that their work has so often provided. In particular, I wish to thank Dave Russell and Wendy Webster for their comments on various sections of the manuscript, and Colin Morgan, that unrivalled expert on the D. C. Thomson papers, for kindly supplying me with a number of stories.

Photographic Acknowledgements

The author and publisher wish to express their thanks to the following sources of illustrative material and/or permission to reproduce it. Items from the author's own collection have not been credited separately.

Battle Picture Weekly: pp. 3, 233; *Black and White*: p. 88; *Boy's Friend*: p. 104 (bottom); *Boy's Own Paper*: pp. 59, 220; *The British Boys Annual*: p. 94; *Captain*: p. 78; *Chums*: pp. 70, 93, 96, 175, 178, 182, 261; First Independent Pictures: p. 255; *Harmsworth Magazine*: p. 75; *Illustrated London News*: pp. 22, 35, 40, 84; Imperial War Museum, London: pp. 122, 141; *London Evening Standard*: p. 191; *Modern Boy*: p. 173; The National Army Museum: pp. 37, 106; *Private Eye*: p. 248; Public Records Office, London: pp. 197 (PRO INF 13/171/2), 217 (PRO NSC 5/139); Royal Air Force Museum, London: p. 159; D. C. Thomson: pp. 195, 244; Touchstone Pictures, Tristar Pictures: p. 253; *Young Airman's Annual*: p. 202; *Young England*: pp. 114, 130, 131.

Index

Page numbers in *italics* denote illustrations.